AF478296

THAT DAY

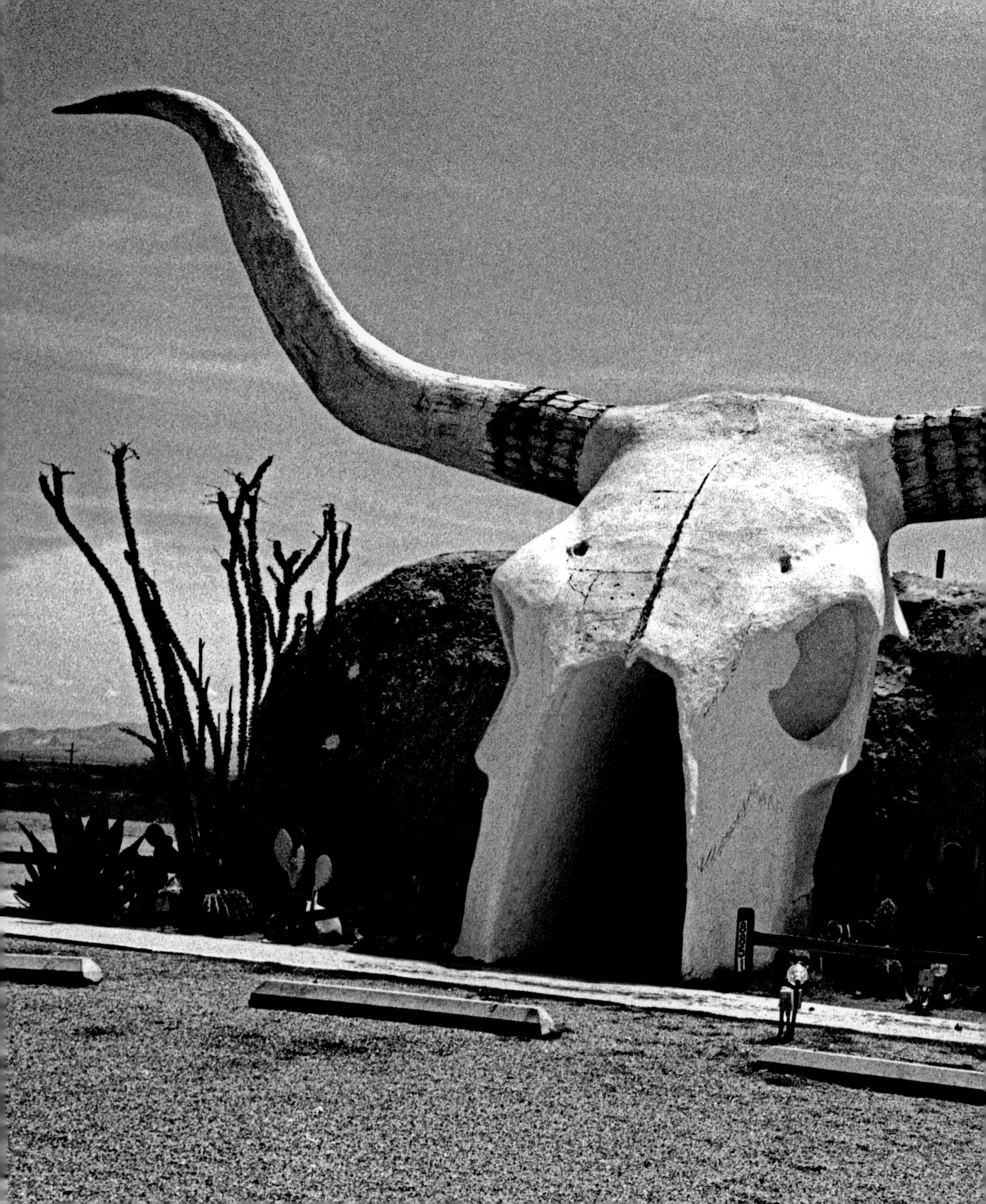

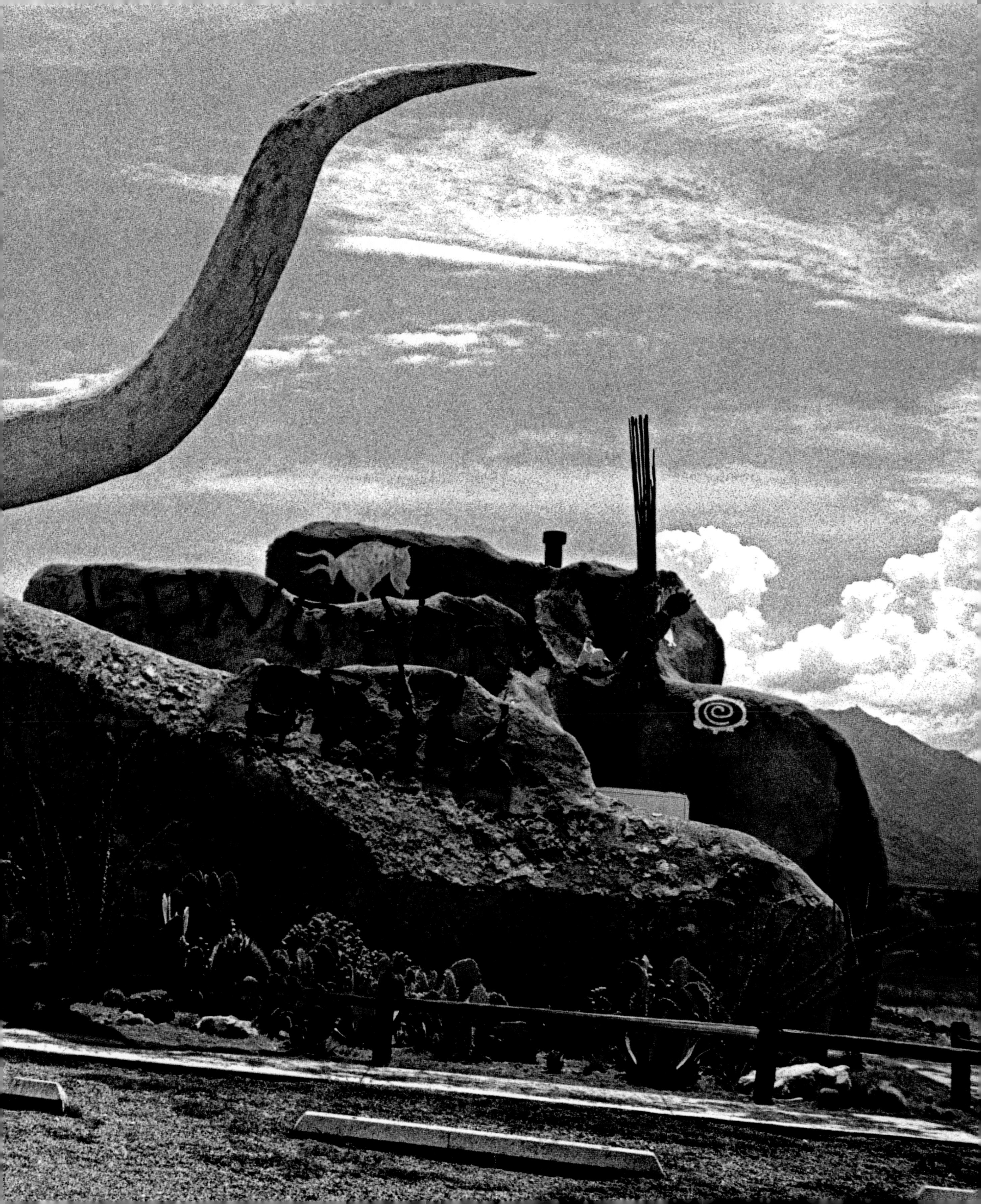

THAT DAY

Pictures in the American West

LAURA WILSON

With an essay by John Rohrbach

The William P. Clements Center for Southwest Studies at Southern Methodist University, Dallas
in association with Yale University Press, New Haven and London

This book is made possible by the William P. Clements Center for Southwest Studies at Southern Methodist University in Dallas, Texas, which would like to acknowledge the following individuals and entities for their very generous support of *That Day*:

Anonymous
Jon and Lou Bauman
George and Vickie Bayoud
Peter Beck
Susan Aspinall Block
The John and Dorothy Castle Advised Fund at the Dallas Foundation
The Rita Crocker Clements Foundation
Roy C. Coffee, Jr.
Jackie McElhaney
Thaddeus Edgar (Ted) and Nancy P. Paup
The Perkins-Prothro Foundation
Caren Prothro
Joe and Linda Staley
The Law Office of Joe H. Staley, Jr., P. C.
The Summerlee Foundation
Jim A. Watson

This book is for my son

Luke Cunningham Wilson

Contents

Foreword

Andrew R. Graybill
Director
William P. Clements Center for Southwest Studies
Southern Methodist University

This project began with a conversation at Laura Wilson's Dallas house on a surprisingly chilly evening in October 2011. I had arrived in Texas that summer to assume the directorship of Southern Methodist University's William P. Clements Center for Southwest Studies, a research institute dedicated to the study of Texas, the Southwest, and the greater U.S.–Mexico border region. Laura and her husband, Bob, hosted a reception welcoming me to Dallas, and that evening I showed up a bit before the party began and ambled about, admiring the many photographs that fill their house, thinking I recognized several of them from Laura's books.

Other images caught my eye that evening, but one in particular intrigued me. In the dining room was an enormous, framed portrait of a young blonde woman in a lavish ball gown, attended by a pair of Mexican assistants. I asked Laura about the photograph, and she explained that it was part of a series she had taken in Laredo, Texas, in 1994 at a debutante ball held annually around the time of George Washington's birthday. Having grown up in South Texas, I was vaguely familiar with the event, which dates to 1898, when locals of this dusty border town dreamed up the affair as a means of symbolizing binational (and biracial) cooperation along the Rio Grande. For me, the photograph instantly called to mind *Las Meninas*, the famous 1656 painting by the Spanish artist Diego Velázquez depicting Margaret Theresa, the young daughter of King Philip IV of Spain, surrounded at court by her attendants.

As I came to understand, Laura's photo of the debutante was emblematic of her larger body of work, showing us a West that is unfamiliar and riddled with paradoxes. For instance, if the Colonial Ball was intended to symbolize the relative racial accommodation governing Laredo, what should we make of the juxtaposition between the blonde girl at the center of the image and her two Mexican assistants? Furthermore, how does the viewer square the elegance of the affair—characterized by the debutantes' gowns, which can cost as much as thirty thousand dollars—with the mundane surroundings, including transport to the main event in the back of a tractor-trailer (the only kind of vehicle large enough to accommodate the women in their eighty- to hundred-pound dresses)? Likewise, how should we make sense of the Hutterites of Montana—the subject of another of Laura's books—who, like their "spiritual cousins" the Amish and the Mennonites, have forsworn the trappings and conveniences of the modern world (including photography), only to find themselves increasingly ensnared by them?

That fall evening, Laura and I began discussing a possible collaboration for a new book of her photographs and writings to be produced with the Clements Center's support. This struck me as an ideal vehicle for furthering the center's mission to promote understanding of the Lone Star State and the Southwest, but this time reaching a public audience as well as an academic one. Rather than choosing a single, discrete subject (such as an iconic West Texas cattle ranch or six-man football teams from the Great Plains—the themes of two of her previous books), Laura opted to cast a much wider net, encompassing the entire sweep of her four-decade career and mixing depictions conjuring the romantic West of the past with those suggestive of its unsettling present and future.

That Day is an arresting series of visual narratives about the late twentieth- and early twenty-first-century West, capturing the region's sharp incongruities, conditions that make the region fascinating but also deeply confounding. It is a seemingly empty landscape that is the most urbanized part of the country; a place of enormous racial diversity but also stark segregation, marked by an archipelago of Indian reservations; a playground for the rich and the famous, as well as a collector of the dispossessed and the utterly anonymous; and a region of unyielding religious piety undercut by irreverence and vulgarity. Or, to paraphrase the writer Wallace Stegner, it is America, but only more so.

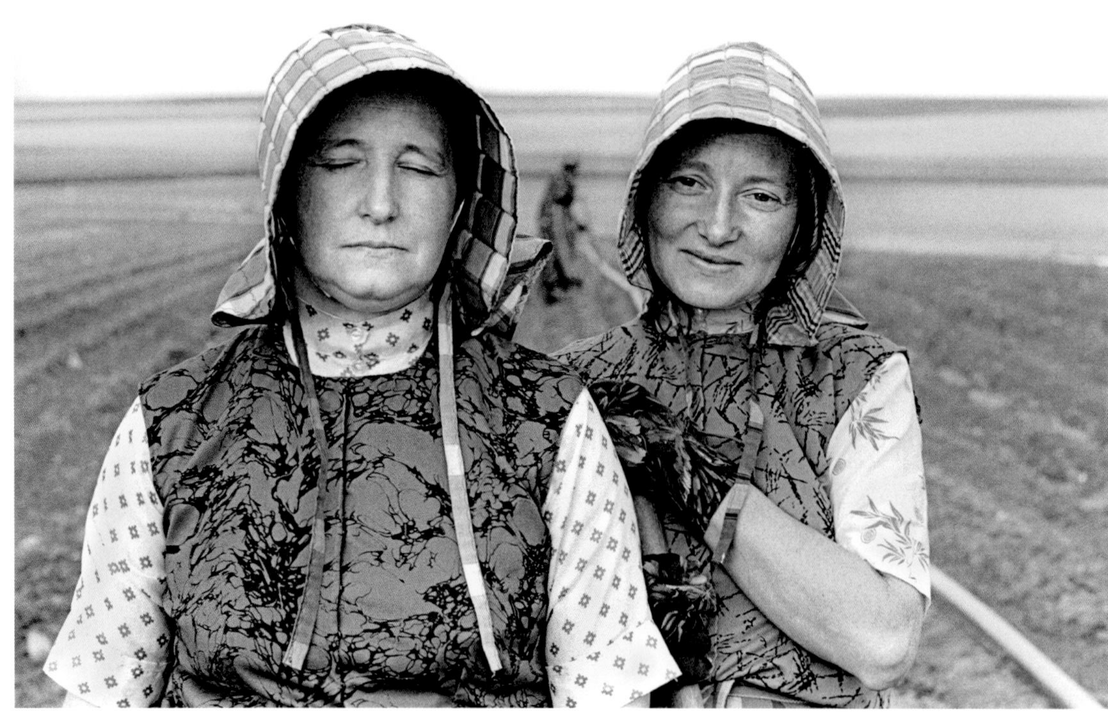

Figure 1. Laura Wilson, *Hutterite Women Gardeners,* Riverview Colony, Chester, Montana, June 22, 1994.

Reflecting the Moment

John Rohrbach
Senior Curator of Photographs
Amon Carter Museum of American Art

Two women wearing similarly patterned, traditional dresses and sunbonnets stand in a freshly plowed field, posing close to the camera. A third woman is positioned in the distance directly between them, but her out-of-focus body elicits only a quick acknowledgment, a reference to their work and to the deep open space that surrounds them (fig. 1). Against this expanse of rolling farmland, the two women's faces draw us in with their expression, fatigue, and separation. The woman on the left stands upright, her eyes closed, accepting the camera but not fully offering herself to it. Her friend stares directly into the lens with a half smile that suggests her slight wariness but ultimate acceptance of it. The portrait beautifully conveys the convergence of individuality, community, and otherness that marks Laura Wilson's photography.

Wilson understands the American West as a blend of history and tradition melded into a scattering of distinct, close-knit communities. It is a place where people live outside the suburban mainstream, in a world framed by federal oversight but shaped by local customs. It is a hard-bitten, competitive land where success is often crossed by compromise and failure. If it reveals itself in equal measure through a glorious view toward Shiprock, New Mexico, and the sight of a tree filled with dead coyotes, it also is a place that delivers itself through the lives of its inhabitants, and especially their faces. Here, the modernity of cars and cell phones is less important than the region's ranching heritage. The heyday of the open range may have been a short-lived, nineteenth-century phenomenon, but the cowboy archetype has a strong grasp on Wilson, even if it appears in the persona of a Hollywood stuntman performing a trick with a falling horse. Many ranch operations may now be large corporate entities, but one would never know it from her pictures. She does not embrace the New Topographics preoccupation with the fast-expanding national infrastructure. Rather, she holds on to the older ideal of heroic individualism that was defined first by dime novels and Buffalo Bill's Wild West extravaganzas, and refined by a stable of films and early television shows. Her figures may now take the form of a wealthy Mexican-American ranch owner, a female rodeo performer, or an artist, but they are still muscular, self-reliant, and courageous.

It is not difficult to find where Wilson gets her views. She has lived in Texas for the last fifty years, a state that proudly proclaims its trinity of oil, ranching, and independence. "Don't mess with Texas" is more than just a tagline designed to stop littering. It is a proclamation of self-righteous assurance about the right to do what Texans want—as Texas goes, the nation goes, or at least the West goes, save for the left coast, which will fall into the ocean someday anyway. Good riddance, many Texans will say. Yet Wilson also is a transplanted New Englander who has not let go of her appreciation for her small-town roots.

Wilson got her start in photography in 1979 when Richard Avedon left his New York City studio to take up the charge of photographing the West. Hired to set up Avedon's itineraries, she quickly made herself indispensable. Each time the group would reach a prospective locale, she would find "interesting" faces—ones that showed the wear of living—and then coax these often hesitant subjects into posing for her boss's bulky eight-by-ten-inch view camera. Over the six years it took for Avedon's project to come together as the now-classic exhibition and book *In the American West,* Wilson saw a lot of the rural West, and by watching Avedon interact with his sitters, and by practicing her own photographic documentation of him at work, she established the terms for her own art.

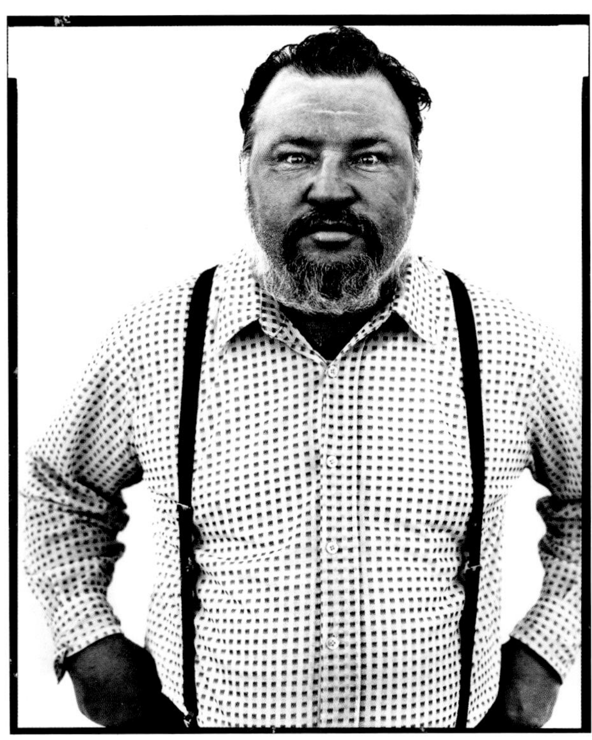

Figure 2. Richard Avedon, *Eli Walter, Jr., chicken man, Hutterite Colony, Stanford, Montana, July 23, 1983,* 1983.

Avedon's version of the West turned out to look nothing like what his Texas sponsors imagined. His carnies, homeless folk, roustabouts, and truckers were not the upstanding successes that those who paid for the project expected or wanted to see. His goal, instead, was to herald the humanity ignored by those who live comfortably. Over the course of working for Avedon, Wilson embraced this same passion for revealing the human condition, but she broadened this vision and brought to it her own particular eye. Even before completing her work for Avedon, she began documenting the operations of a pioneering West Texas ranch led by Watt Matthews and celebrating the lives of Montana's Hutterites. While Avedon always set his subjects against his signature white backdrop, isolating them from their surroundings to better attend to their clothes, their physical mannerisms, and the lines etching their faces (fig. 2), she chose to embed her subjects in the world in order to highlight her recognition that going it alone rarely works in the vast, often unforgiving landscape of the West. Whereas Avedon's portraits are in many ways pictures of himself, Wilson's photographs present communities beyond herself.

In a country that proclaims "In God We Trust" on every dollar and "Liberty" on every quarter, the Hutterites chose to retreat to the harsh northern prairies to escape persecution for their conservative, pacifist ways. Wilson's photographs most often present them outdoors to evoke their connection with the land and their isolation. Place, though, is less her subject than the deep commitment they feel to each other. She documents the men in groups attending to the chores of the farm and the women harvesting, cooking, and child-rearing as a team. As a mother herself, she pays a most loving attention to their children, capturing them engrossed in their chores, in moments of quiet, and in flashes of self-amusement. In the

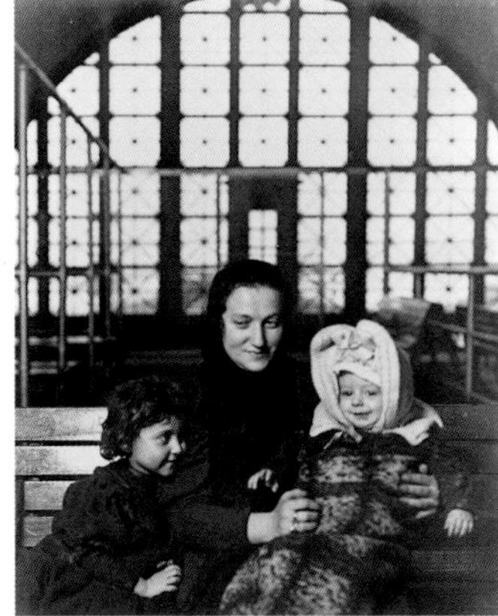

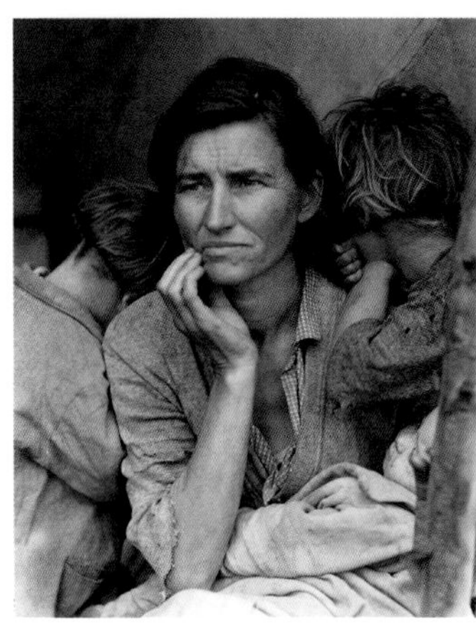

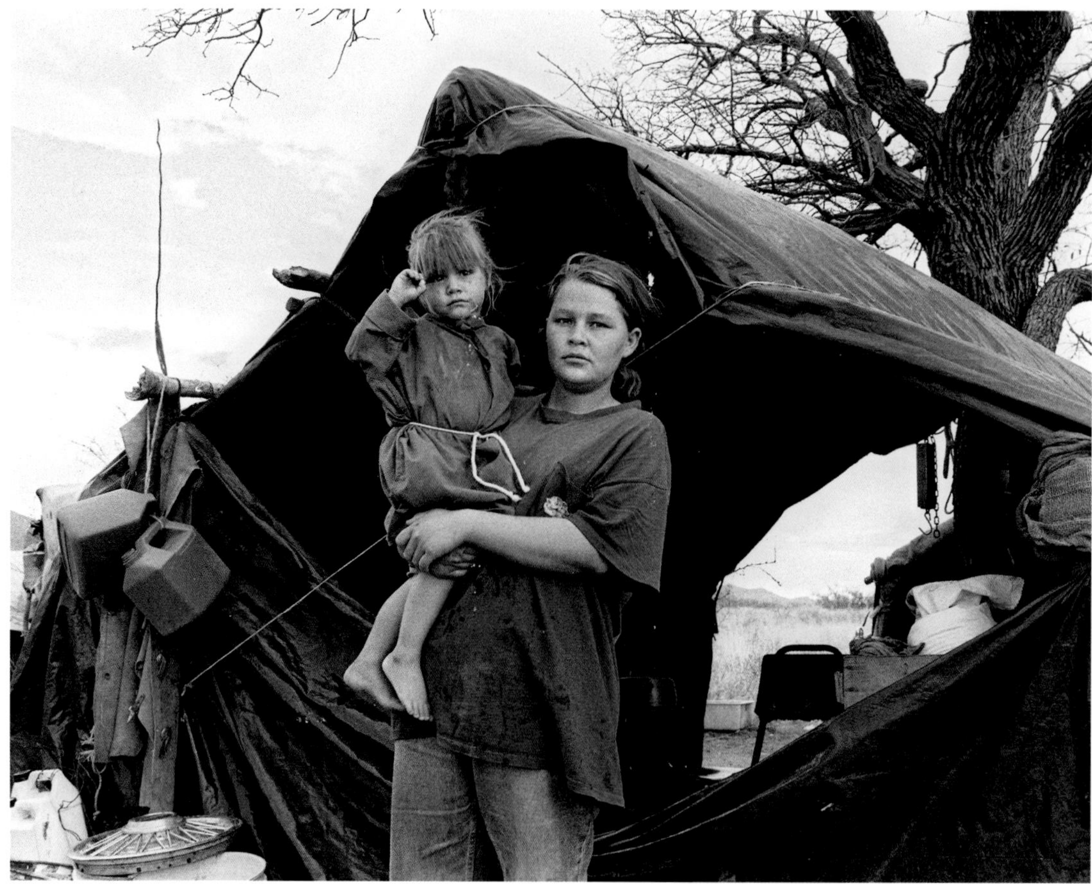

Figure 3. Lewis Hine, *A Russian Family Group at Ellis Island,* 1905.
Figure 4. Dorothea Lange, *Migrant Mother, Nipoma, California, March 1936,* 1936.
Figure 5. Laura Wilson, *Young Woman with Child,* border camp, Arizona–Sonora border, June 30, 2000.

health and well-being of these youth, she recognizes the community's long-standing success. The Hutterite project eloquently reflects Wilson's empathy for her subjects. It evidences her realization that the West's expansive spaciousness allows a wide range of cultures and opinions to coexist. In this region, activities that would be out of place or even outlawed in mainstream society are sustained, and new traditions created: for example, six-man football teams in towns too small and remote to allow the fielding of a standard eleven-man side.

Photography has a long tradition of drawing attention to people living on the edges of mainstream society. In the 1870s, the Scotsman John Thompson paired up with Adolphe Smith to document the lives of London's street people. The Danish reformer Jacob Riis used a camera in the late 1880s to document the wretched living conditions across the slums of New York City; and shortly after the turn of the twentieth century, Lewis Hine began photographing people arriving at Ellis Island, adding a human face to acerbic debates over immigration (fig. 3). Wilson's many photographs along the U.S.–Mexico border remind us of how we continue to cope with the complexities of America's expansive ideal of being a beacon of liberty and freedom, openly welcoming immigrants from across the world. She introduces us to the cat-and-mouse game between undocumented people and border officials, showing us a husky Texas Ranger stationed along the Rio Grande in Webb County whose self-assurance, bulging stomach,

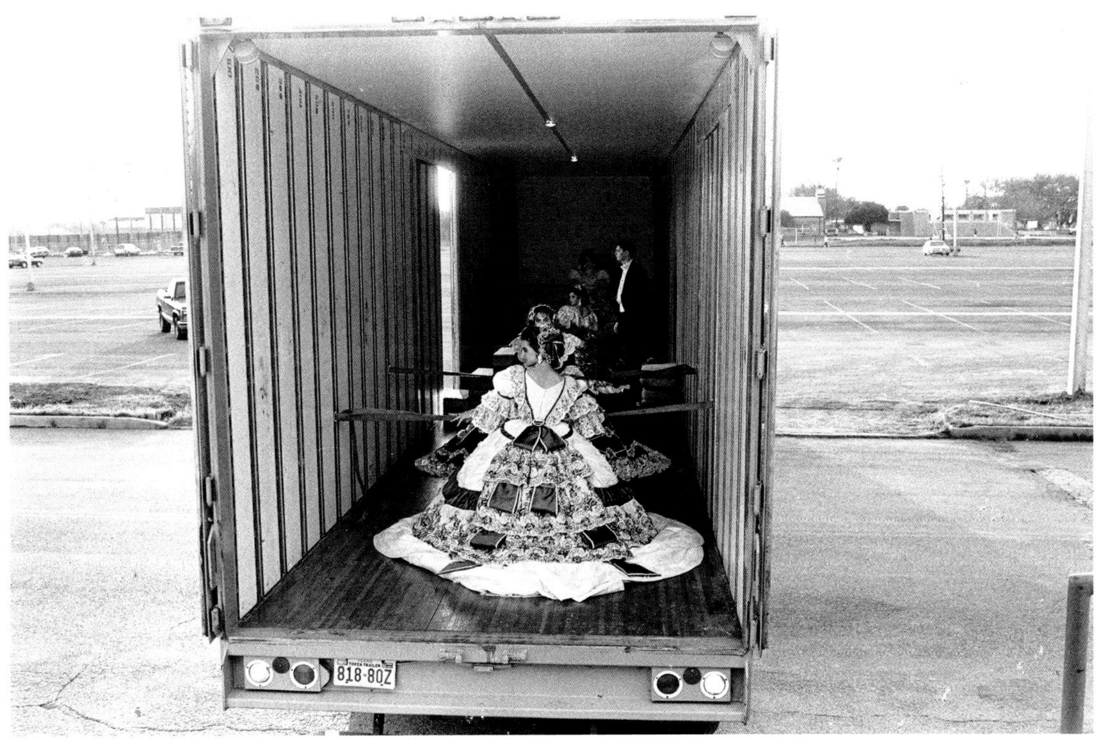

Figure 6. Laura Wilson, *Debutantes Arriving at Ball,* Laredo, Texas, February 19, 1993.

clean white shirt, cowboy hat, and tie resemble the demeanor and garb of one of the Huntsville prison guards photographed by Danny Lyons in the late 1960s, or any number of hard-nosed sheriff characters from television and movies. Her photographs of a truck being searched for drugs by a dog and of captured men being led out of the Texas brush mirror those we see repeatedly in the news. However, she takes the tale beyond the chase and into the tent camps to show us a group of itinerant laborers, and a young woman and child whose hard-luck condition cannot help but evoke Dorothea Lange's 1936 masterpiece, *Migrant Mother* (figs. 4–5). Yet empathy alone is too easy. She counters such heartfelt scenes with glimpses into the cultures of cockfighting and dogfighting that are very much alive today in some border communities.

Back and forth we are pulled. If pain, poverty, and violence fill parts of the West, so does the sweetness of young girls dressed for their first communion. Depicting the elaborate preparations for the annual debutante ball in Laredo, Texas, Wilson introduces a culture in which young women on the cusp of adulthood take on the persona of colonial dames. Months of sewing and fittings by expert Latina seamstresses give rise to elaborate cage dresses so styled with layers of fabric, beads, lace, and ribbons that they can weigh as much as eighty pounds. The dresses are so large, in fact, that the young women have to travel to the dance standing in the rear cargo boxes of moving vans (fig. 6). The whole affair is a fascinating feat of borderland patriotic assertion that takes place each year as part of a citywide celebration of George Washington's birthday.

Even today, many people insist on subscribing to the image of the American Indian warrior in perfect balance with nature. Wilson, instead, shares her encounters with the poverty and alcoholism that so often infuses Native American communities. But

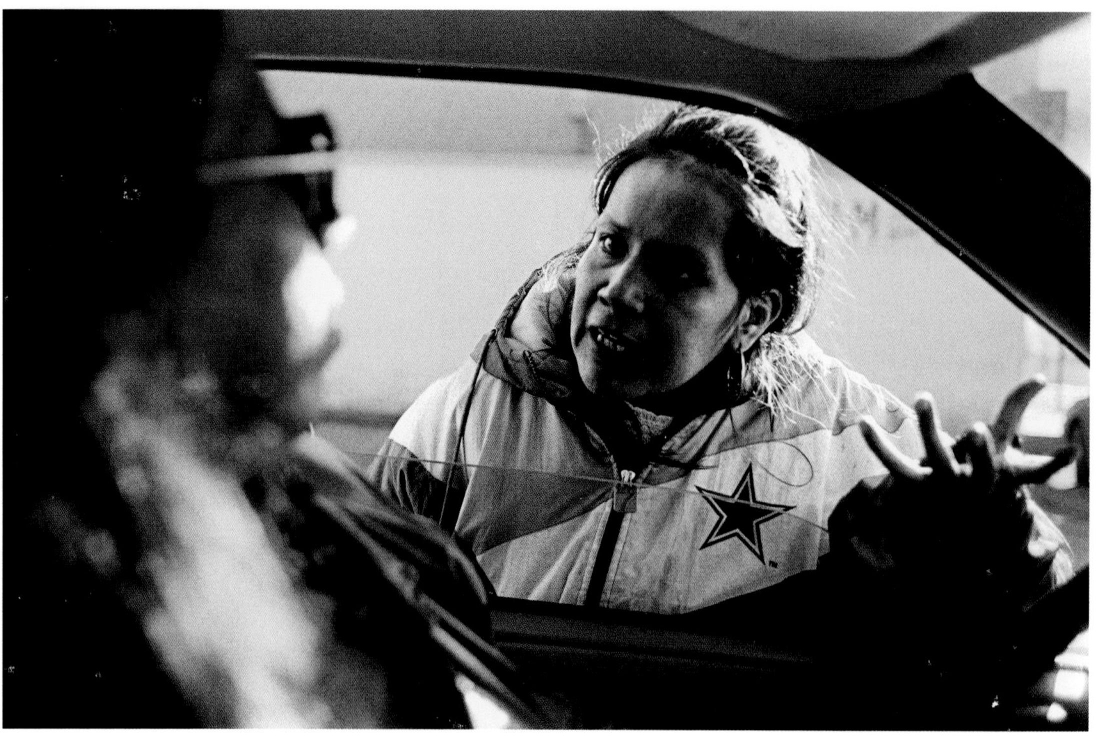

Figure 7. Laura Wilson, *Oglala Sioux Woman Pleading with Tribal Leader,* Whiteclay, Nebraska, December 13, 1996.

beware reading stereotypes into Wilson's images: the woman she portrays in the Dallas Cowboys coat is not a drunk panhandling for another dollar to buy more beer, but rather a wife pleading with outstretched hand to the tribal leader for a job for her husband (fig. 7). Again, the face is what carries the picture. The woman's determined expression and desperate eyes stay with you. Likewise, images of a deserted hacienda and a sidewalk filled with a troop of stuffed armadillos come from Mexico, but they would fit just as well in the United States. The border is arbitrary, except in the eyes of the American and Mexican governments. In this peculiar world, insider and outsider are two sides of the same coin. Though Wilson presents Eduardo Longoria with his two dogs at his ranch in Mexico, outside Nuevo Laredo, she could have photographed him just as easily in his other home in Laredo, Texas.

Wilson clearly envies the independence of her subjects, their self-assurance, and their hard intensity, for it is these characteristics that she locates in the artists, musicians, and writers whom she photographs for London's *Sunday Times*, the *New Yorker*, and other magazines. Her portraits of Jimmie Dale Gilmore, Donald Judd, and Sam Shepard show wary men. Jim Harrison looks as if he has not slept in weeks, though he could be simply projecting the haunting exhaustion that comes from extended, focused work. All offer weathered faces to the camera's unforgiving eye.

What is it then that Wilson gives us? Her vision is not photojournalistic in the traditional sense of seeking to sum up a situation with a single image and a two-sentence caption. She does not chase after the decisive moment in which all is resolved within the frame, nor are her photographs the pleas of a concerned documentarian, seeking to right the wrongs of humanity. Instead, Wilson offers up chance encounters, fragments that caution against judgment. We step quickly

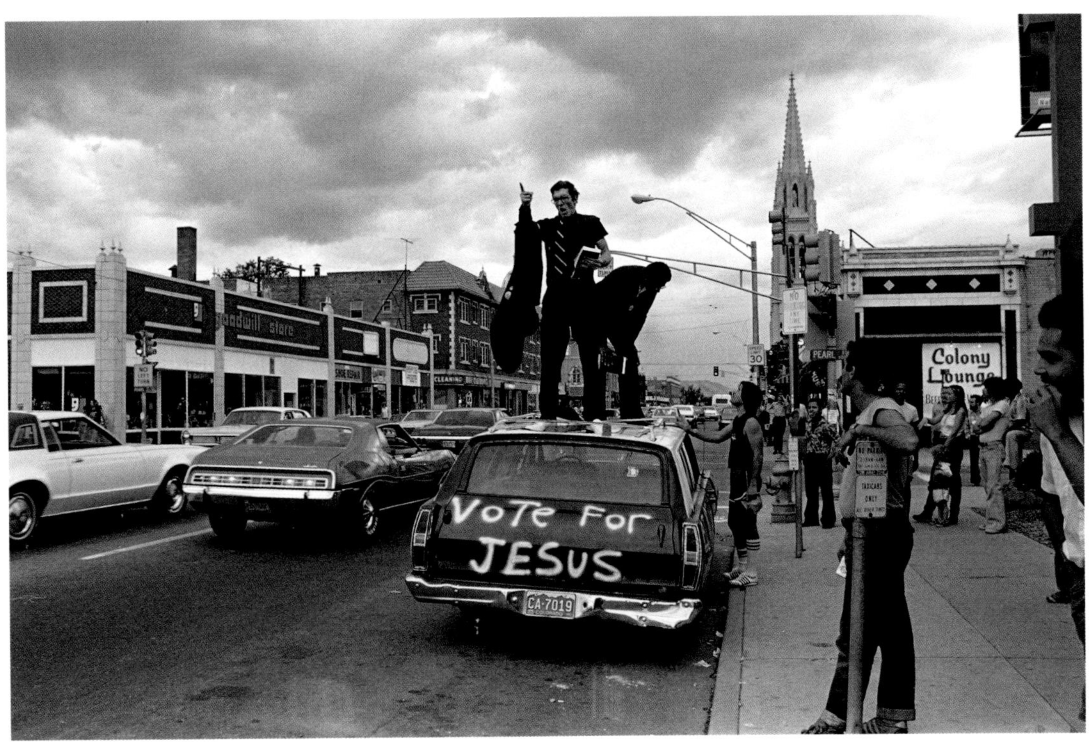

Figure 8. Laura Wilson, *Evangelical Preacher,* Denver, Colorado, August 19, 1980.

in and out of lives and cultures, for her object is not to explain but to reflect the immediacy of the moment: "This day I met . . . That day I ran into . . ." Her vision is in the vein of Robert Frank and his photographic excursion across the United States in 1955 and 1956, summed up in his classic book *The Americans.* Wilson is not an outsider like Frank, though. She does not grab the quick shot and move on. This is *her* West. Where Frank found alienation, exhaustion, and sadness, she is just as likely to zero in on proud strivings, as in the trick riders performing at the Fort Worth Stock Show and Rodeo and showing off their muscular bodies in a dressing room.

Wilson infuses her fragmentary encounters with humanism in a way that is reminiscent of the work of Paul Strand, even if her vision more openly incorporates a range of emotions—from exultation and laughter to anger and confrontation. If we pull back in horror from her image of two men positioning their wiry pit bulls for a fight, then she has achieved her goal, which is not to judge but to acknowledge. If we uncomfortably sympathize with the exhausted man and his two daughters posing at the unglazed window of their unpainted, plywood *colonia* home, then she has succeeded in making us account for the poverty-stricken living conditions along the southern border of the United States.

What are we to make of this culture in which Christian Glory Riders are clad in white to perform at small-town events, a fundamentalist preacher can declare the power of God from the roof of his station wagon (fig. 8), and outfitter-hunters and old-school trading-post operators share the world with Ed Ruscha? Rather than present the proverbial melting pot, Wilson asks us to recognize a West that, if not always a land of patriotic, wholesome community, is at least a place where, against a backdrop of aridity and expansive space, diverse lives coexist.

Y-6 Ranch

JEFF DAVIS COUNTY, TEXAS
JUNE 3–5, 1992

It is as much Mexico as it is Texas. It's *The Wonderful Country* of Tom Lea, the "cruelly civilized" land of Cormac McCarthy. It's arid desert, and it's not going to change anytime soon. In other parts of Texas, ranchers say that oil and a pump jack make a fine cross with a Hereford. But here in Jeff Davis County, where there is no oil, ranching is a hard way to make a living. The margin of profit on cattle is so slim that the Means family can barely hold on to land that they've worked for three generations to put together. Yet the land has a grip on them. They come from men and women who felt that land was the only measure of wealth. Alf Means's great-uncle was the famous Texas Ranger James B. Gillett. Born in 1856, eleven years after Texas was granted statehood, Gillett wrote late in his life, "Oh, how I wish I had the power to describe that wonderful country as I saw it then."

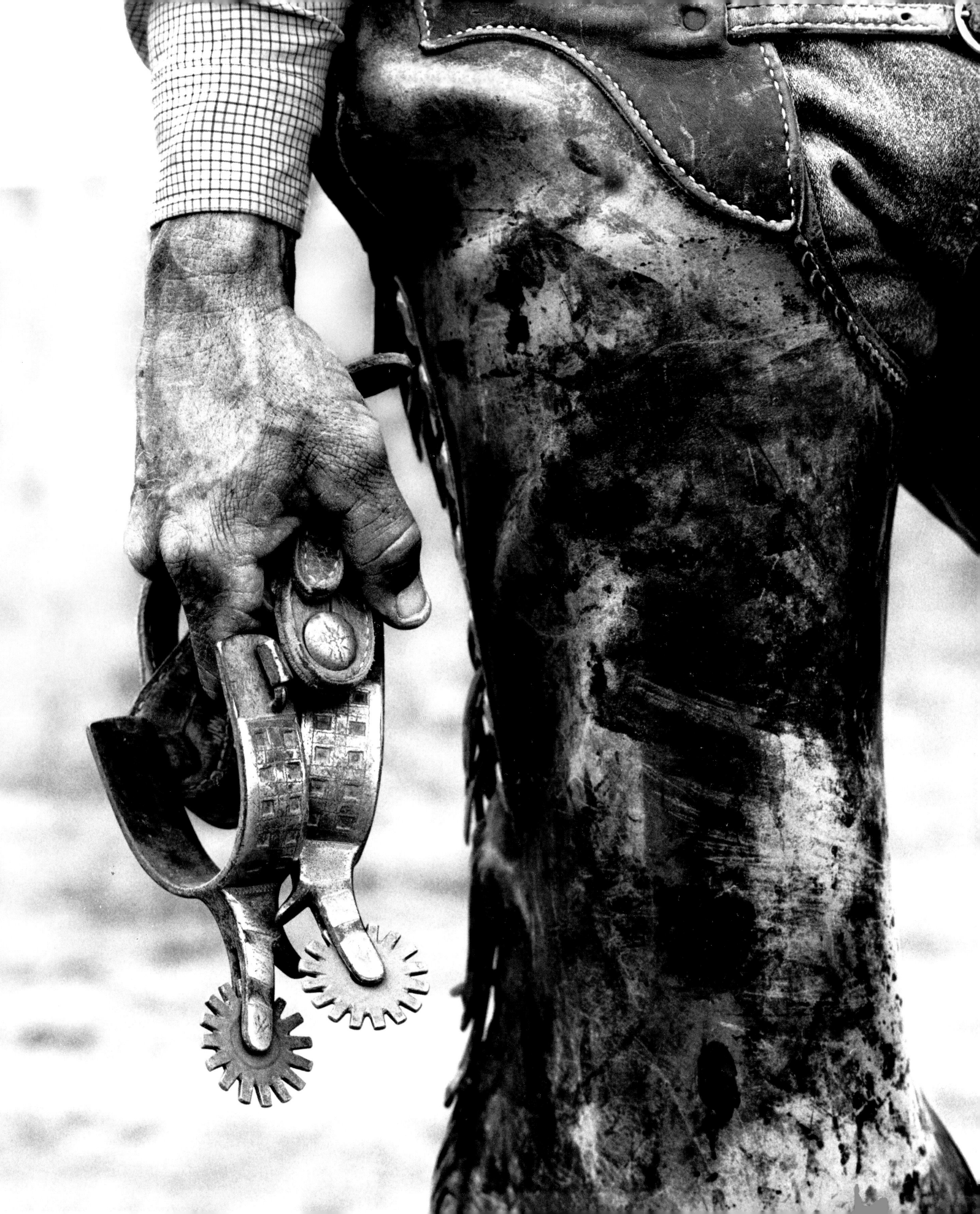

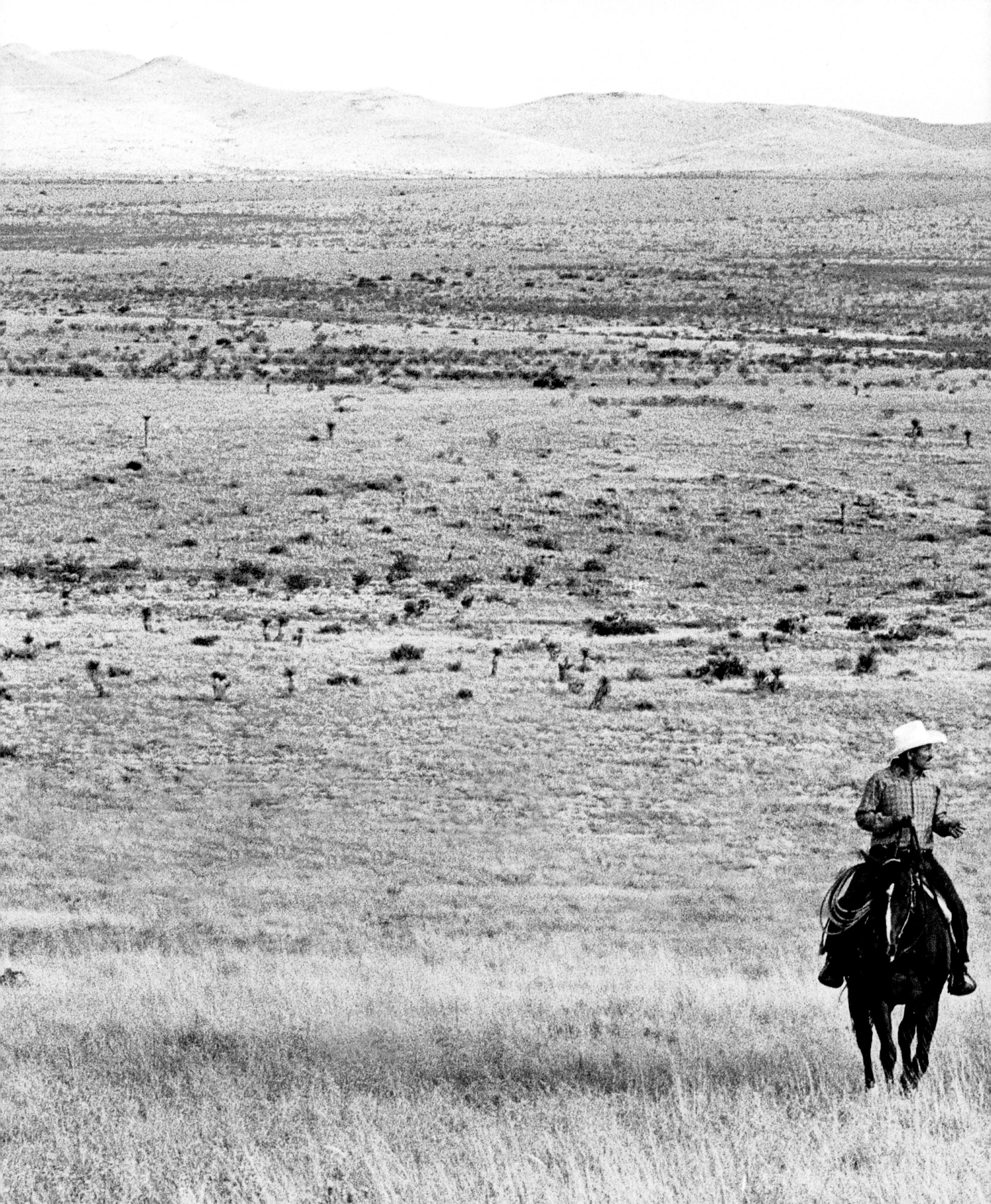

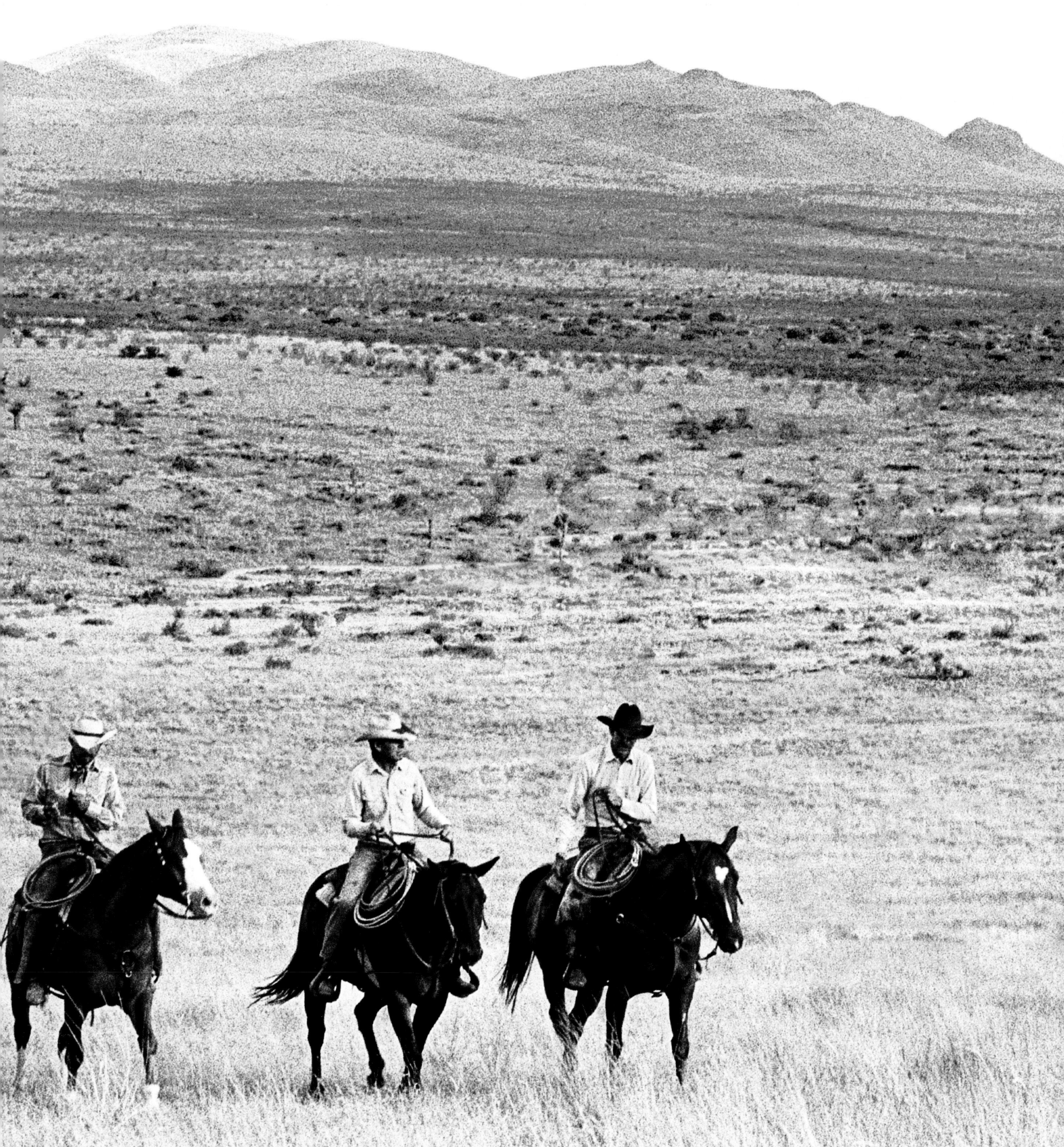

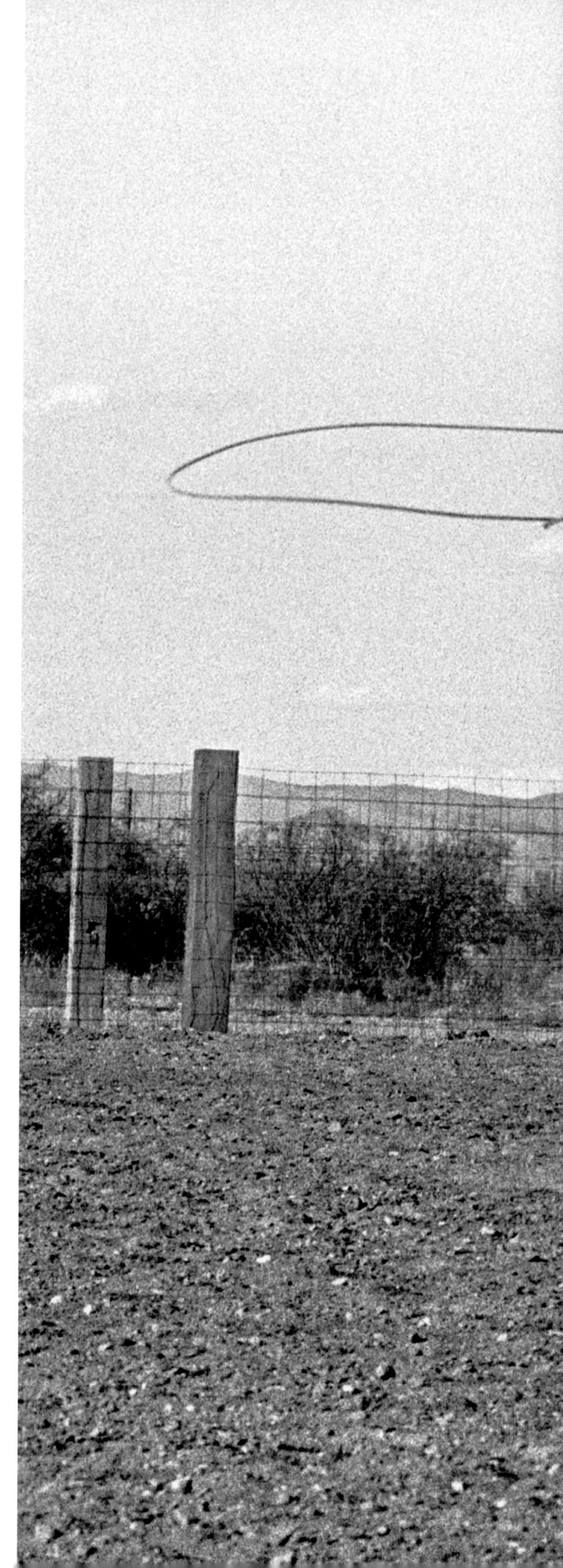

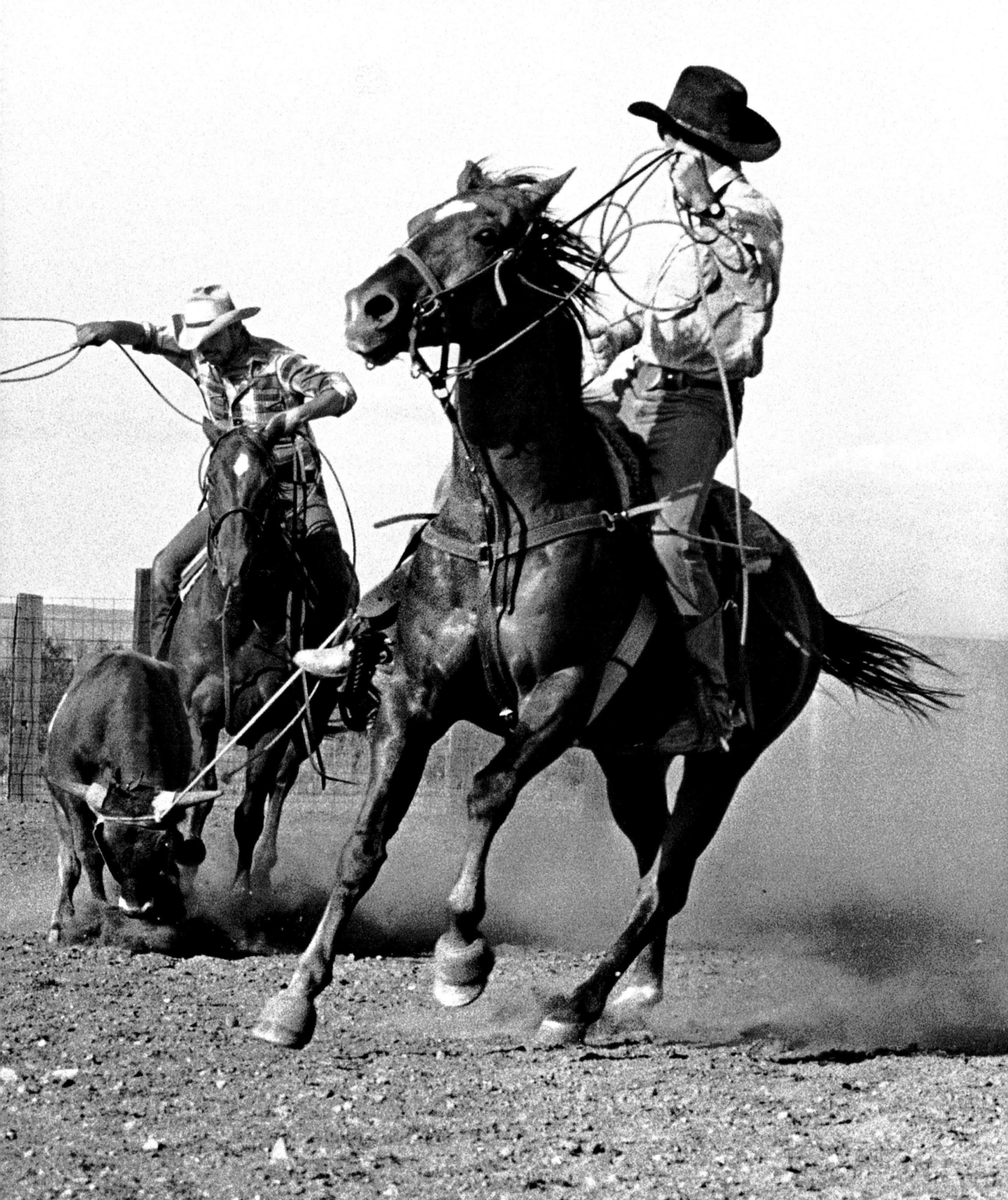

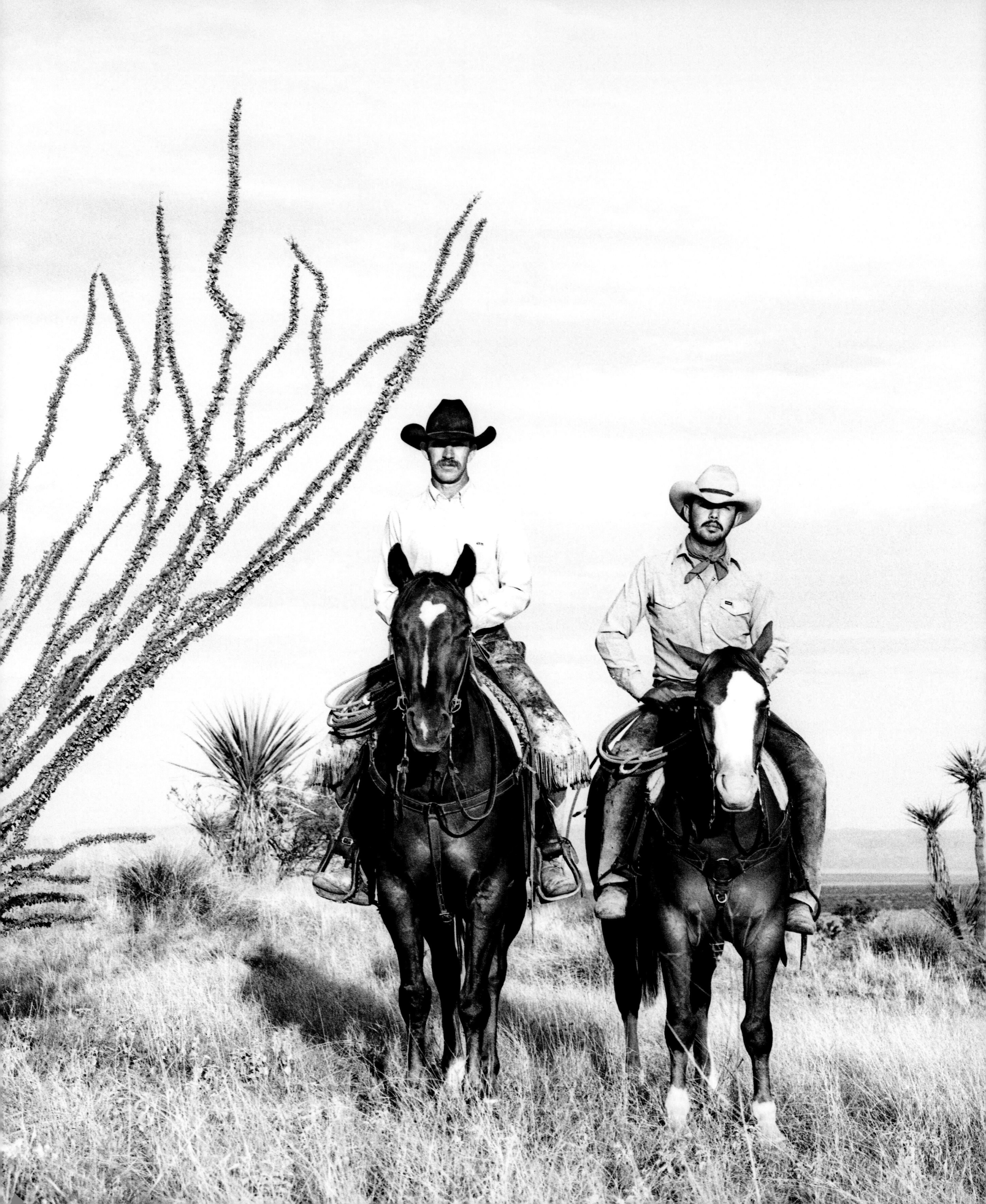

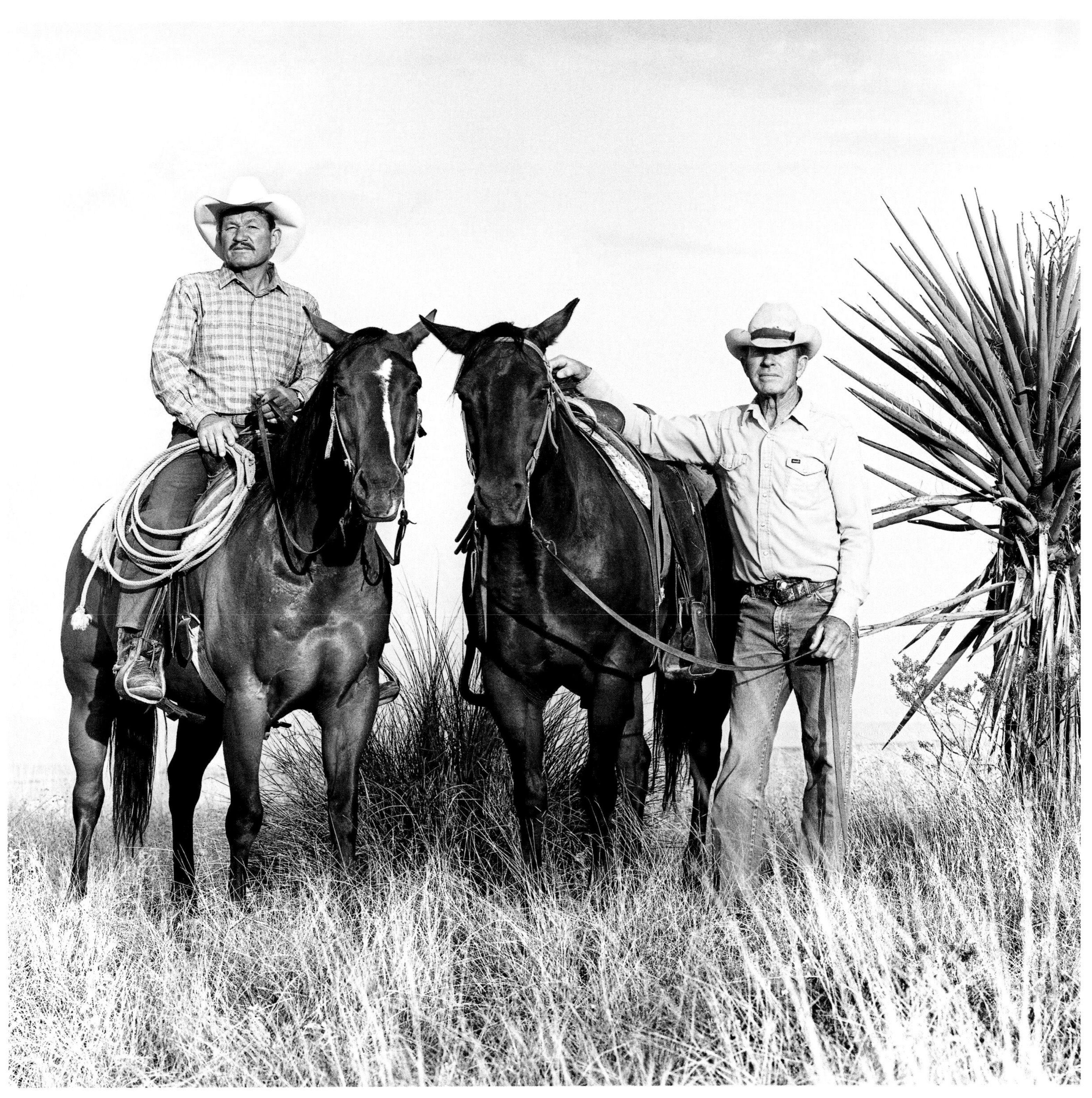

I photographed the Means men apart from the women, the father and son each with a *vaquero*, or cowboy. The men spoke Spanish mixed with English among themselves. They were out on the land all day, working cattle, providing supplementary feed, tending water pumps—whatever it took to squeeze some value out of sixty thousand acres.

I photographed the women with their husbands, but the stronger portrait seemed to me to be the one of the women and girls together, separate from the men. On the Y-6, the women led more traditional lives within a domestic setting. They tended to their families and kept their households running, and on the Y-6 that's a big job—it is, after all, a hundred-and-twenty-mile round trip to the closest grocery store in Alpine. To ward off the isolation in their lives, there was a necessary closeness among the generations.

Debby Means Armerding spoke about ranch women: "I'm saddened that, often, we are quick to assume that the traditional role of a woman does not require intelligence, resourcefulness, and a lot of strength. Ranch life is almost always depicted through the eyes of the men, but the role of the ranch wife is essential. She must have patience with distances and time, two elements fundamental to running a household on a ranch so far from any urban areas. For us, it was a hundred and sixty miles one way to a shopping mall and our orthodontist appointments in El Paso. And when the men couldn't stop working to make a two-hour-plus trip for oil for the generators or washers for a pump, it was my mother who did it. She had to have enough food stocked up to make three complete meals a day for a family doing hard physical labor as well as for any guests who might stop by. Just the cleaning and the laundry, or the windblown dust and tracked-in dirt, make life for a ranch woman hard. It takes perseverance and sacrifice. Yet we children felt an intangible security in the home my mother created. We all felt it."

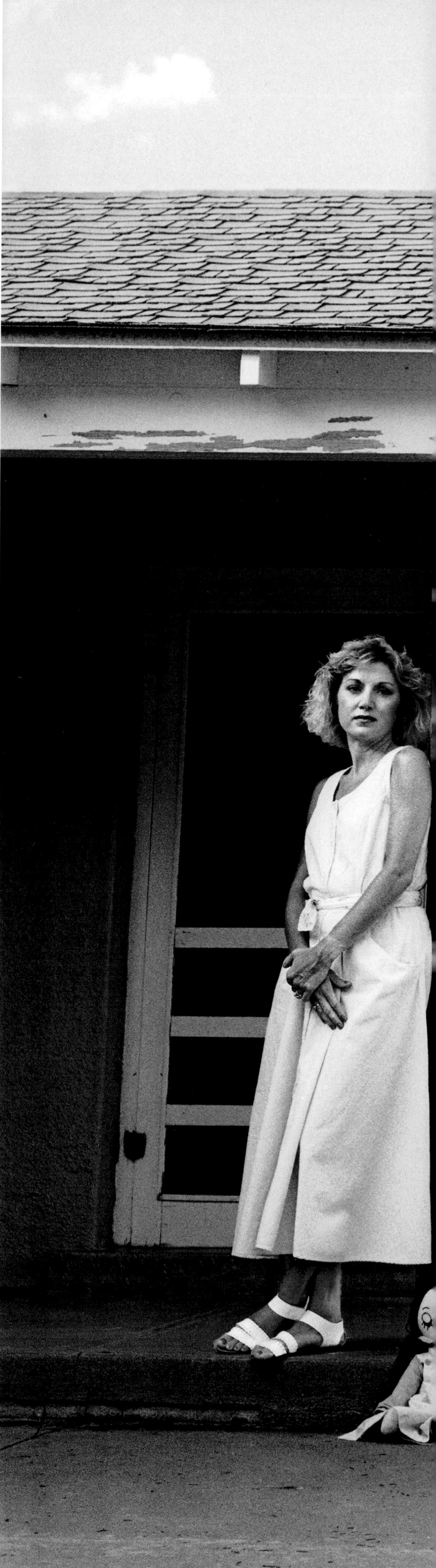

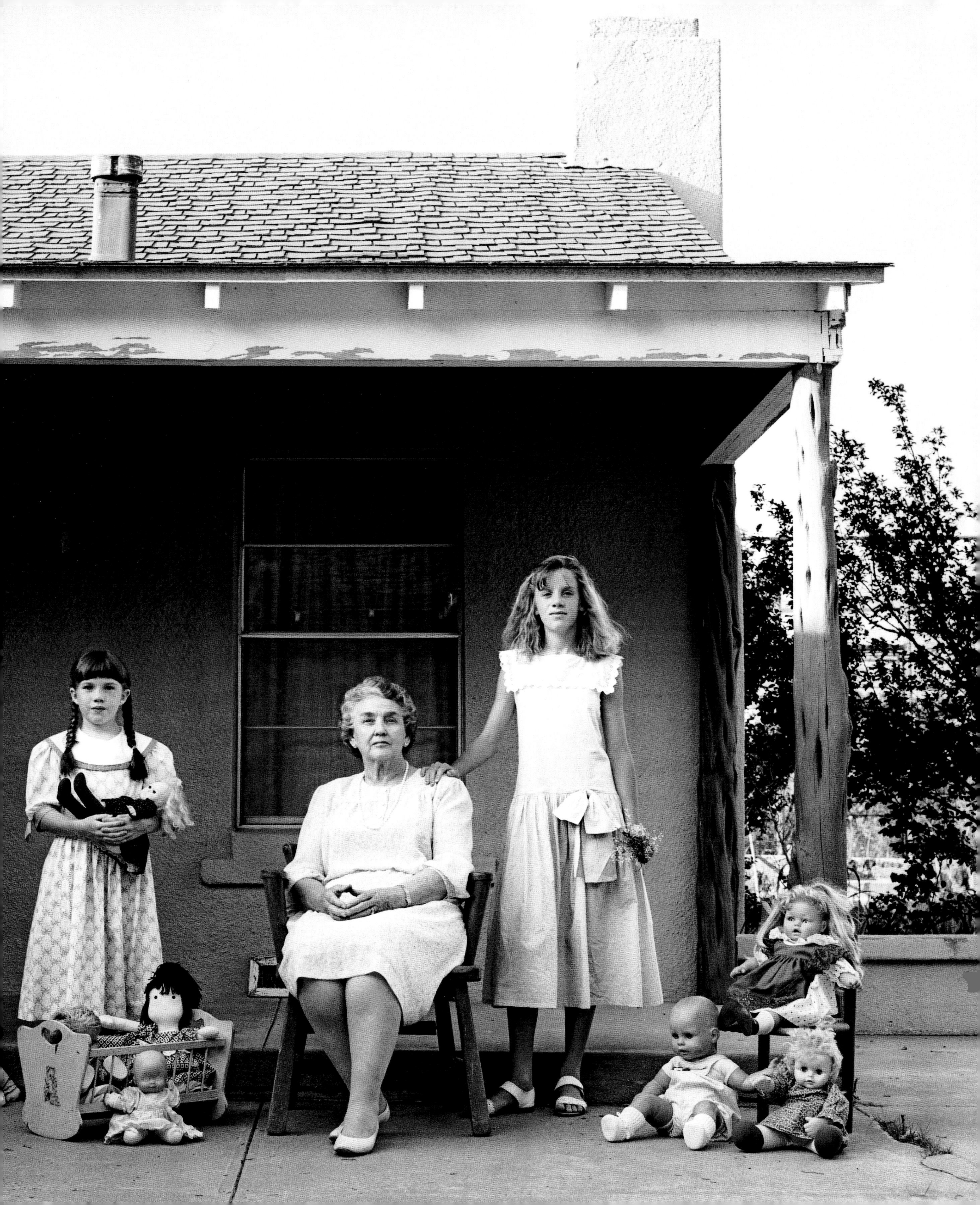

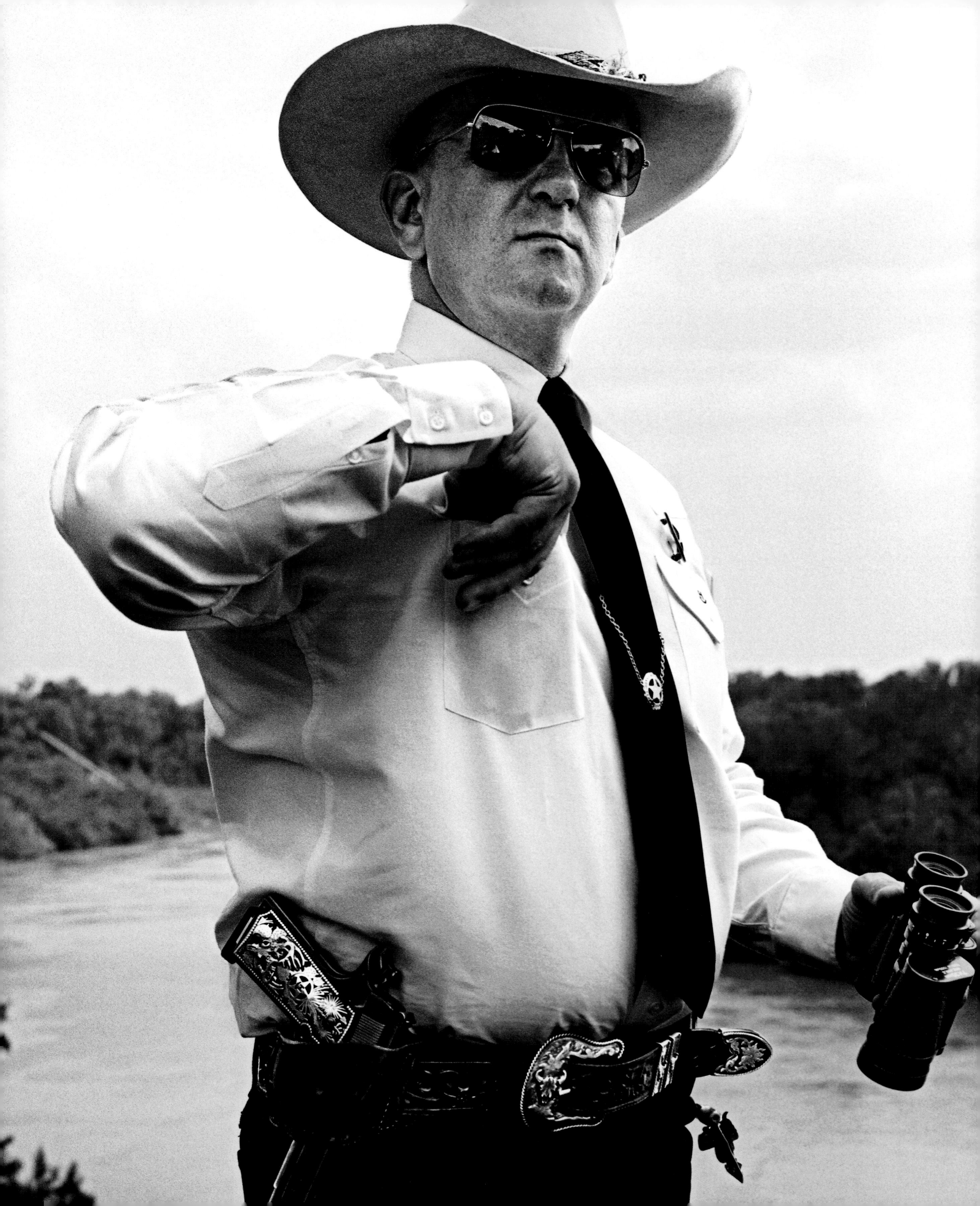

The Border

WEBB COUNTY, TEXAS
MAY 14–15, 1994

I followed Texas Ranger Doyle Holdridge up a bluff overlooking the Rio Grande in Webb County. From that vantage point, Holdridge used binoculars to scan the river and the thorny brush on its banks looking for undocumented immigrants and drug smugglers. The Rangers and Border Patrol have worked for decades to halt the influx of illegal traffic, but it's not easy. The rugged border, 1,954 miles from Brownsville and Matamoros on the Gulf of Mexico to San Diego and Tijuana on the Pacific Ocean, is the most heavily crossed border on earth. It has proved impossible to seal. From season to season, climatic conditions change, and the number of migrants and the smugglers' routes vary accordingly. Even the looping bends in the Rio Grande rearrange themselves in certain areas, making the border fluid. The U.S.–Mexico boundary has always been porous. In spite of billions of dollars allocated for man power, fences, drones, cameras, and helicopters, lawmen like Holdridge know that the border will remain forever permeable. The Border Patrol uses trained dogs to root out drugs in vehicles passing through security checkpoints, and to find people hidden under tarps on trucks in the dark of night. Yet attempts to cross the border are unending, even though only a lucky few are successful. On the same day that I watched a man swim across the river from Nuevo Léon to run into dense brush on the Texas side, I saw another man floating facedown, dead in the Rio Grande.

I've been paying attention to border issues for a quarter of a century now. I've seen Mexico's various attempts to build some kind of democracy fail, and I've despaired at the continuing rise of corruption in the government, enabling narcotics to become that country's primary export. Corruption, collusion, and poverty have combined to make the country incurably unstable and the border with the United States *una herida abierta*, "an open wound."

The writer Gloria Anzaldúa speaks of the border as a place "where the Third World grates against the first and bleeds. And before a scab forms it hemorrhages again, the lifeblood of the two worlds merging to form a third country—a border culture. . . . The prohibited and the forbidden are its inhabitants."

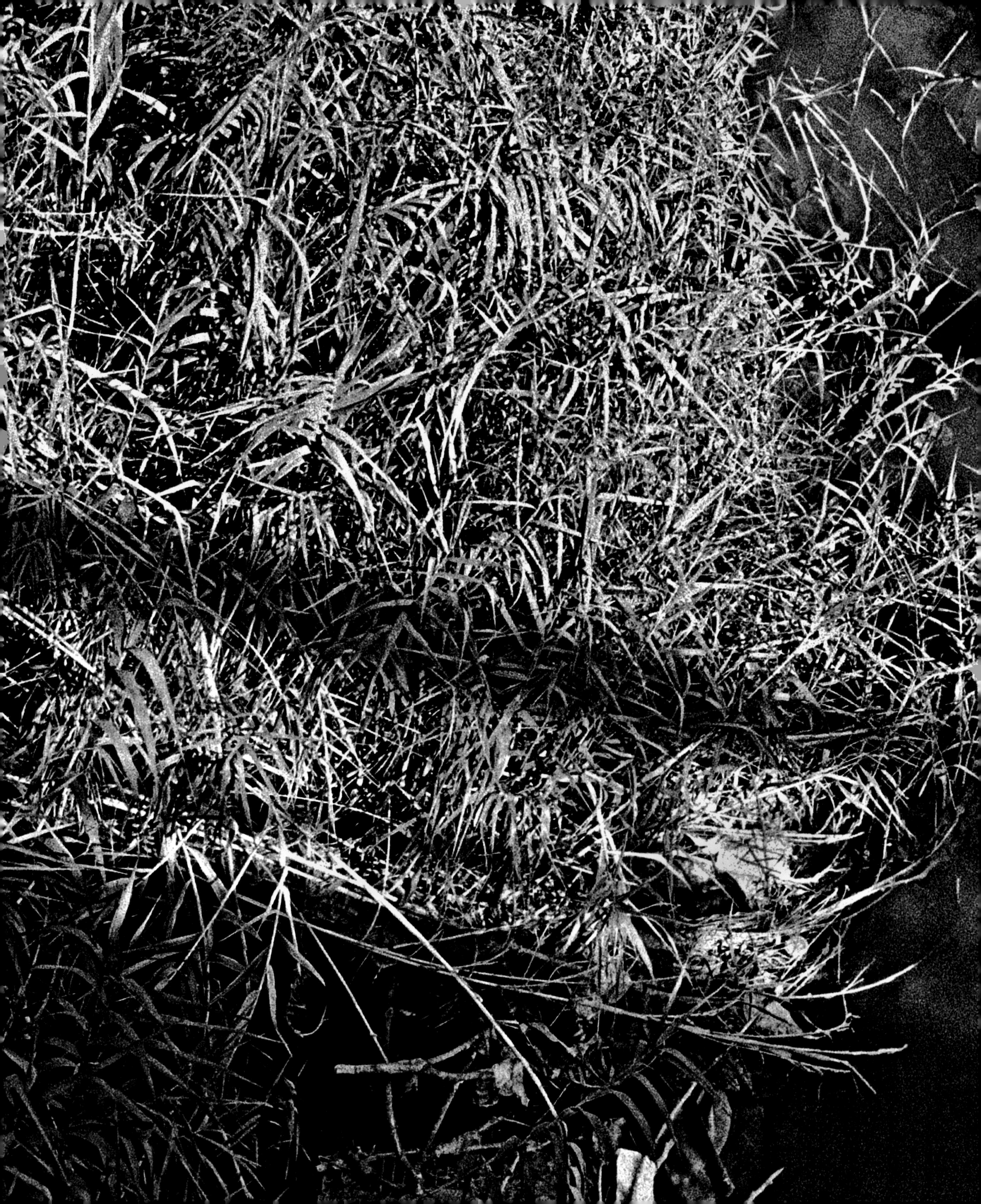

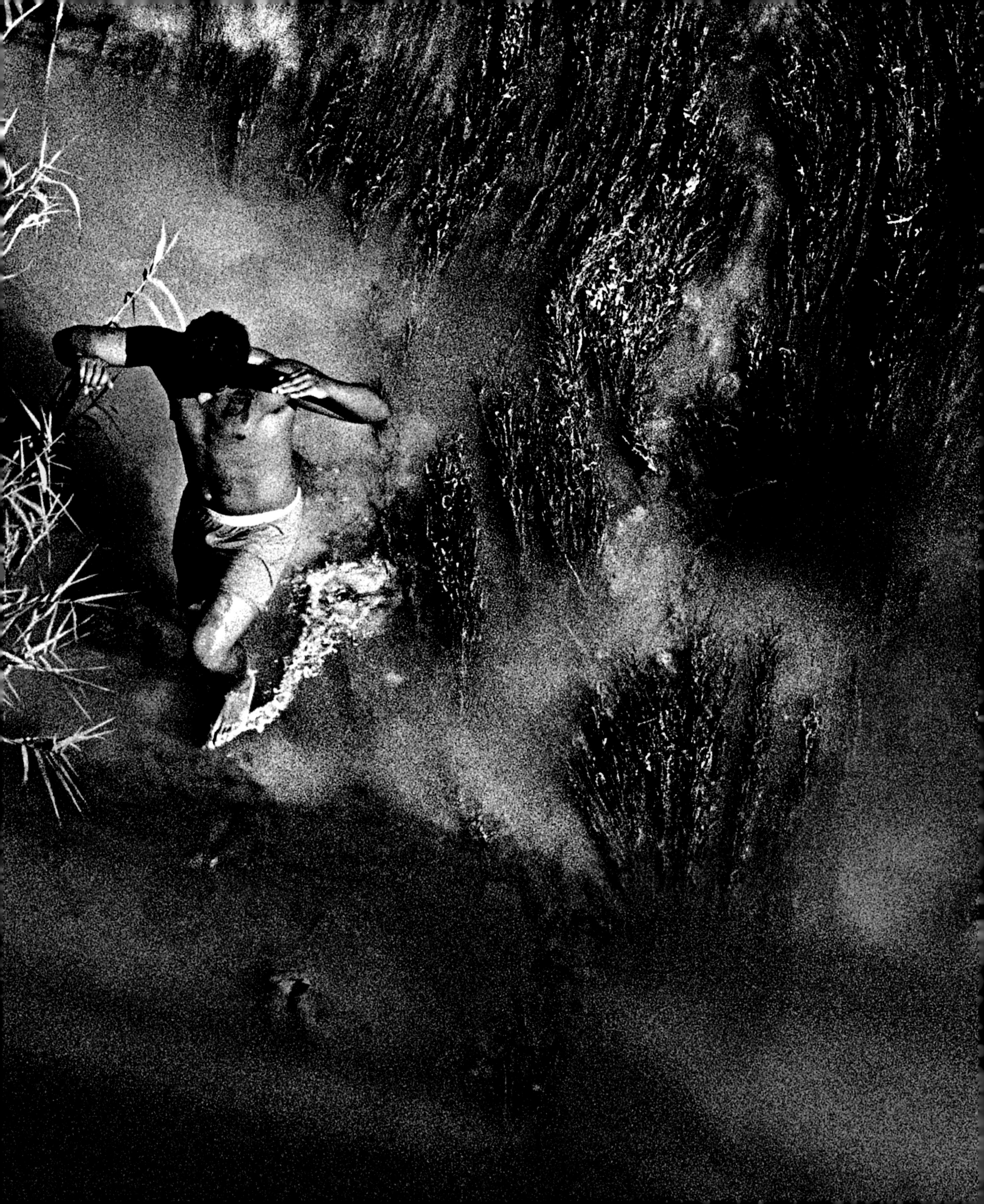

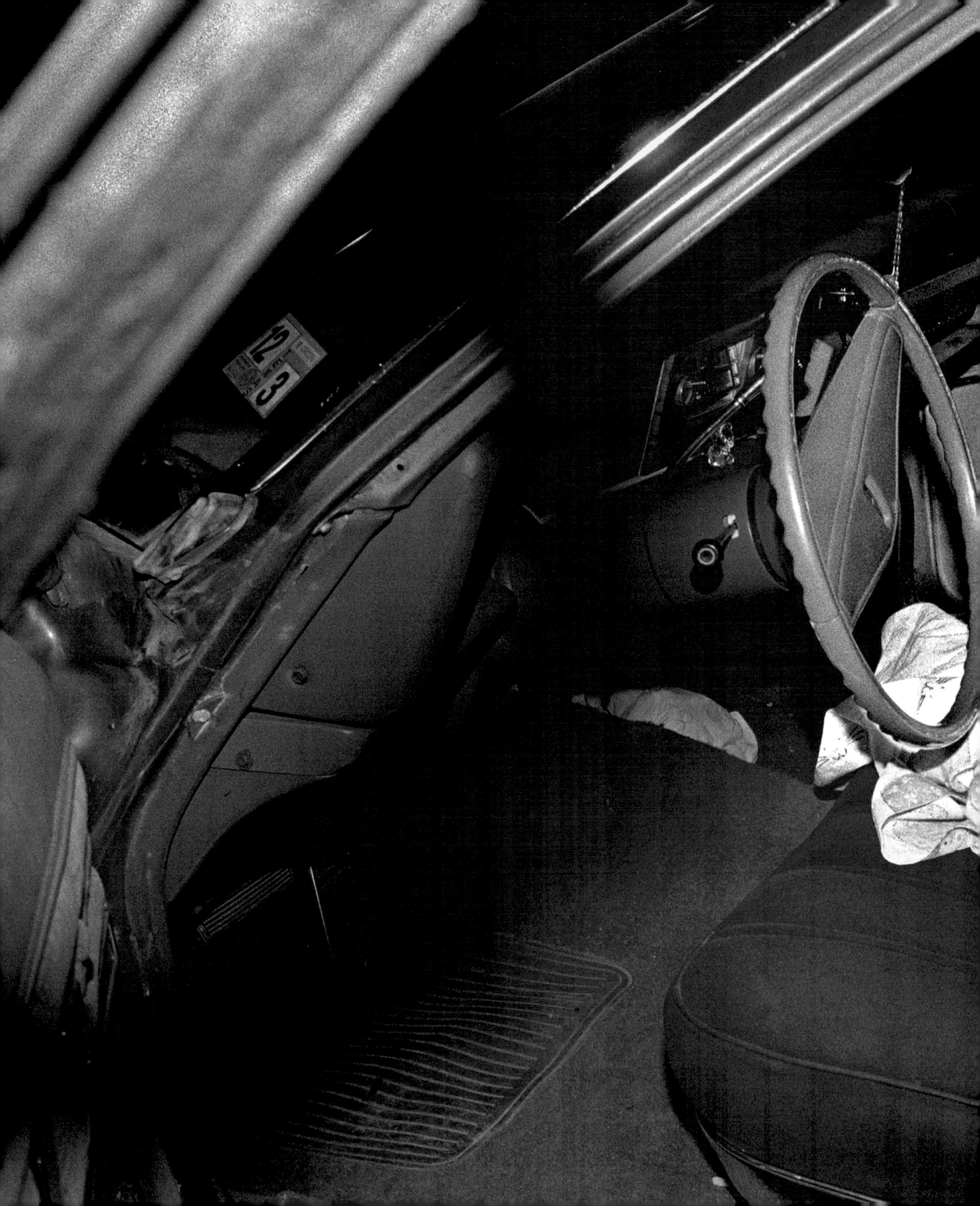
12
3

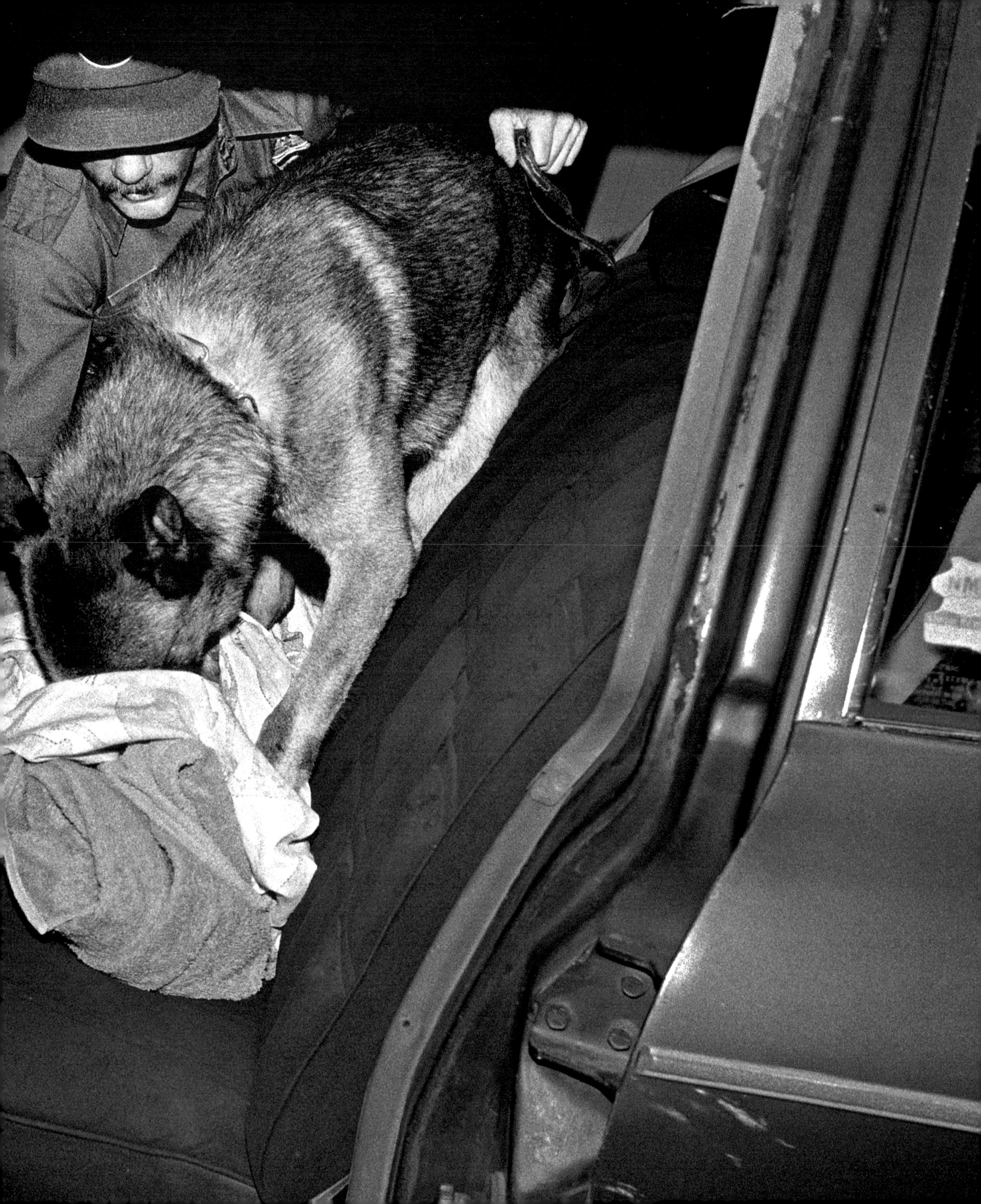

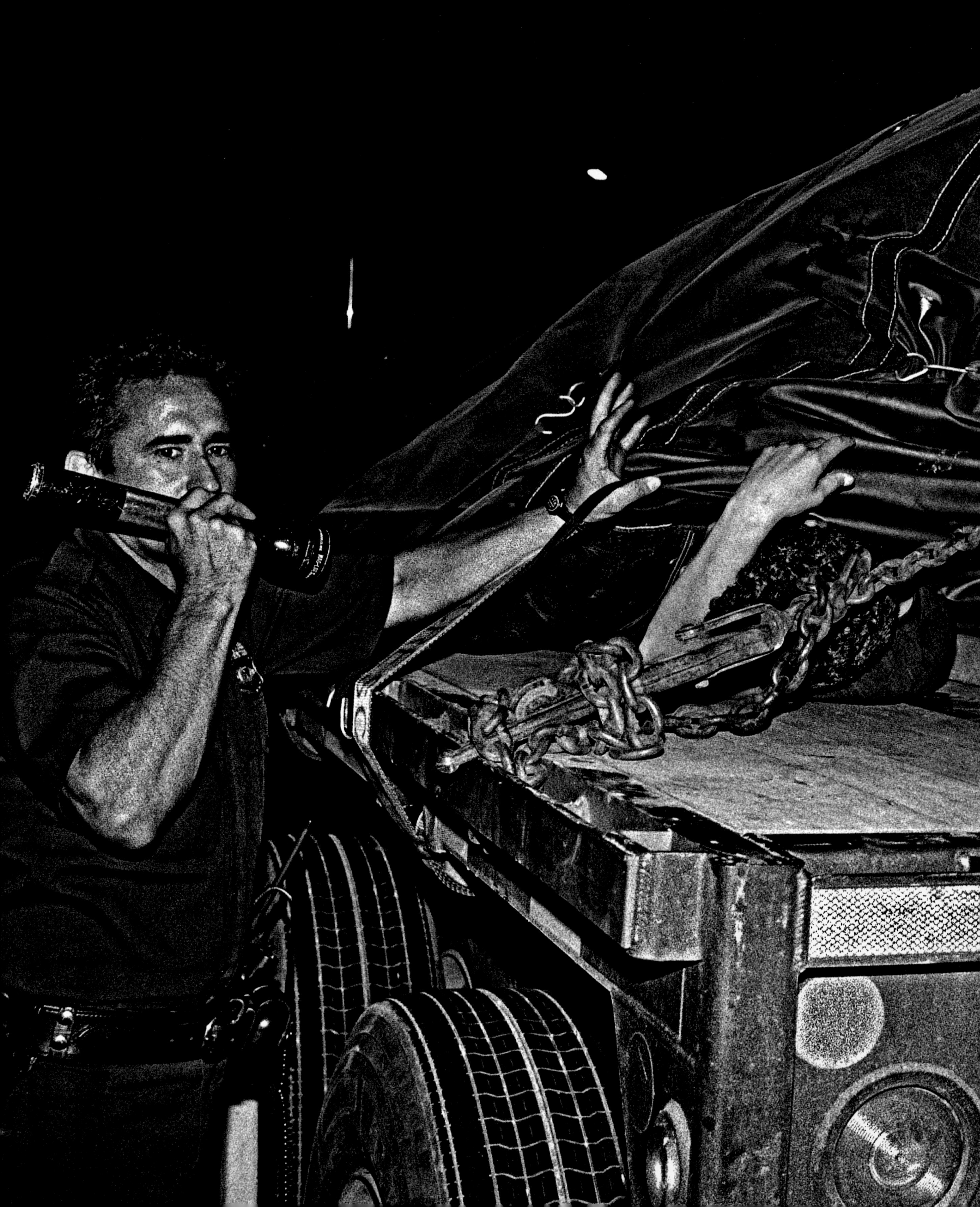

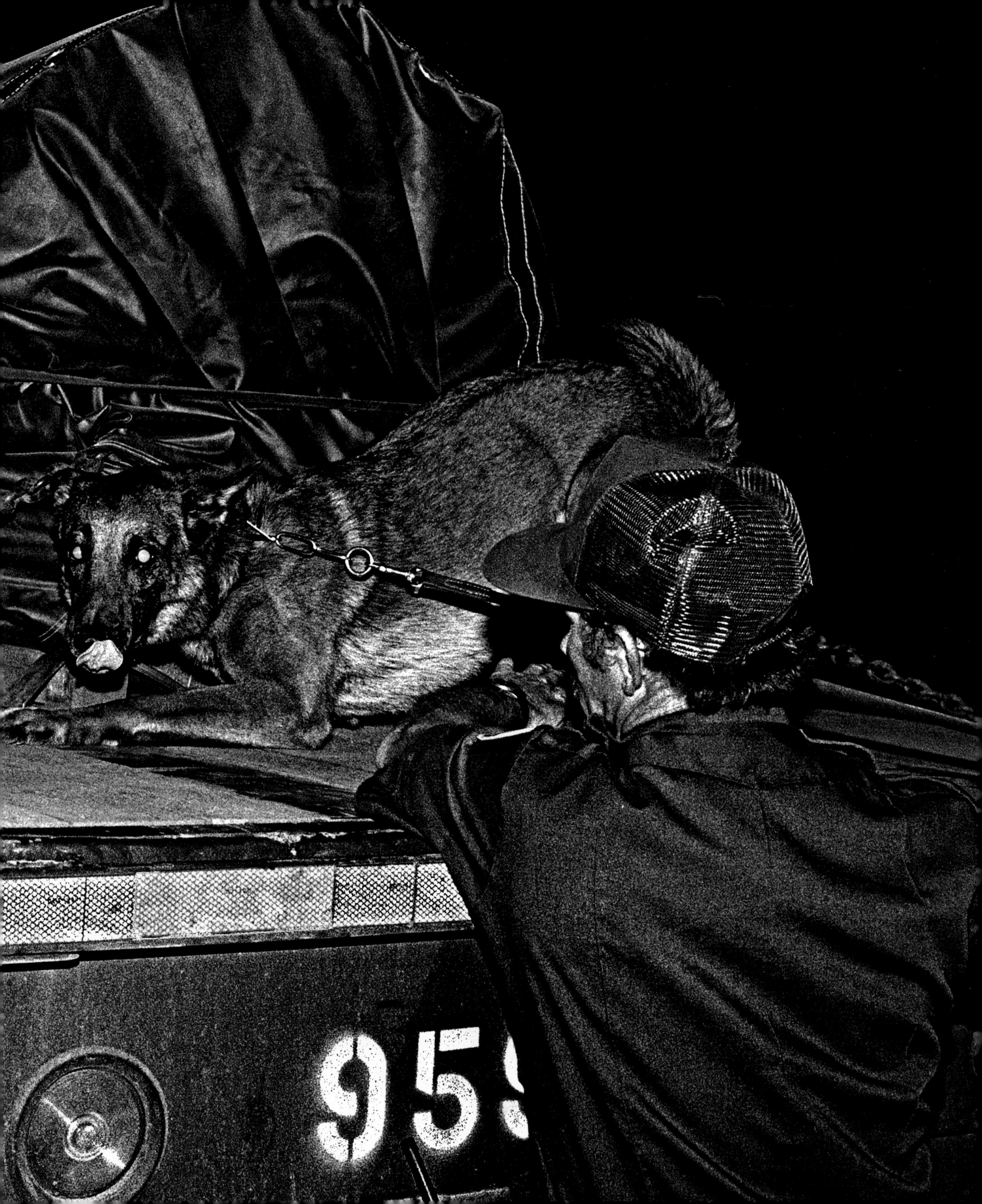
95

Tracking

ZAPATA COUNTY, TEXAS
MAY 11, 1994

Experienced trackers will tell you that when a man tracks another man, he looks for a disturbance to the earth. And the more skilled the tracker, the more subtle the disturbance he can find. Footprints are easy, trackers say. But it takes an expert to track a man over rocks where no distinct prints exist. He'll notice a broken branch, maybe, or a cloth fiber caught on a twig, or a pocket in the ground left by an overturned rock, or even the dislodged stone itself, darker on the underside.

"I'll tell you," said Matt Magoffin, a special agent with the U.S. Customs Service who had tracked men all over the Southwest, "tracking is an art. It has to be developed. The earlier you start, the better you're going to be at it. It helps to know the country—where the water is, the canyons, the gullies, the distance to the foothills. But most of all, you need tenacity. There's some bad country out there. They'll hide in places you wouldn't believe. . . . You put the track between you and the sun. That way you'll get a raking light that causes shadows. Noon is the poorest hour to track. Direct sun appears to flatten tracks. A track is fresh if the edges are crisp, maybe only an hour old. Once the edges round, or the soil lightens, it's older. And if a night has passed, you can tell because critters move at night. Rats or mice or bugs will have moved over the tracks."

"You know how fast a man is traveling by the toe digs," Magoffin continued. "If a smuggler's carrying a heavy load of drugs, he'll dig in deeper, his stride shortens, and he has to rest more often. And you can see that. You can see where he's set down. I'll look for a single fiber off a burlap sack. Smugglers will try to disguise their tracks. They'll wrap rags around their shoes or take a branch to sweep their tracks out, but it all leaves a mark. In the past four years, we've started to see the cartels forcing immigrants to smuggle drugs. Young guys in their teens, out-of-work miners, farmers, or construction laborers, they'll smuggle across the border on foot. They're more dangerous now. The cartels will put pressure on them to protect their loads. They'll smuggle up to I-10. If they make it up to that point, then we've lost 'em."

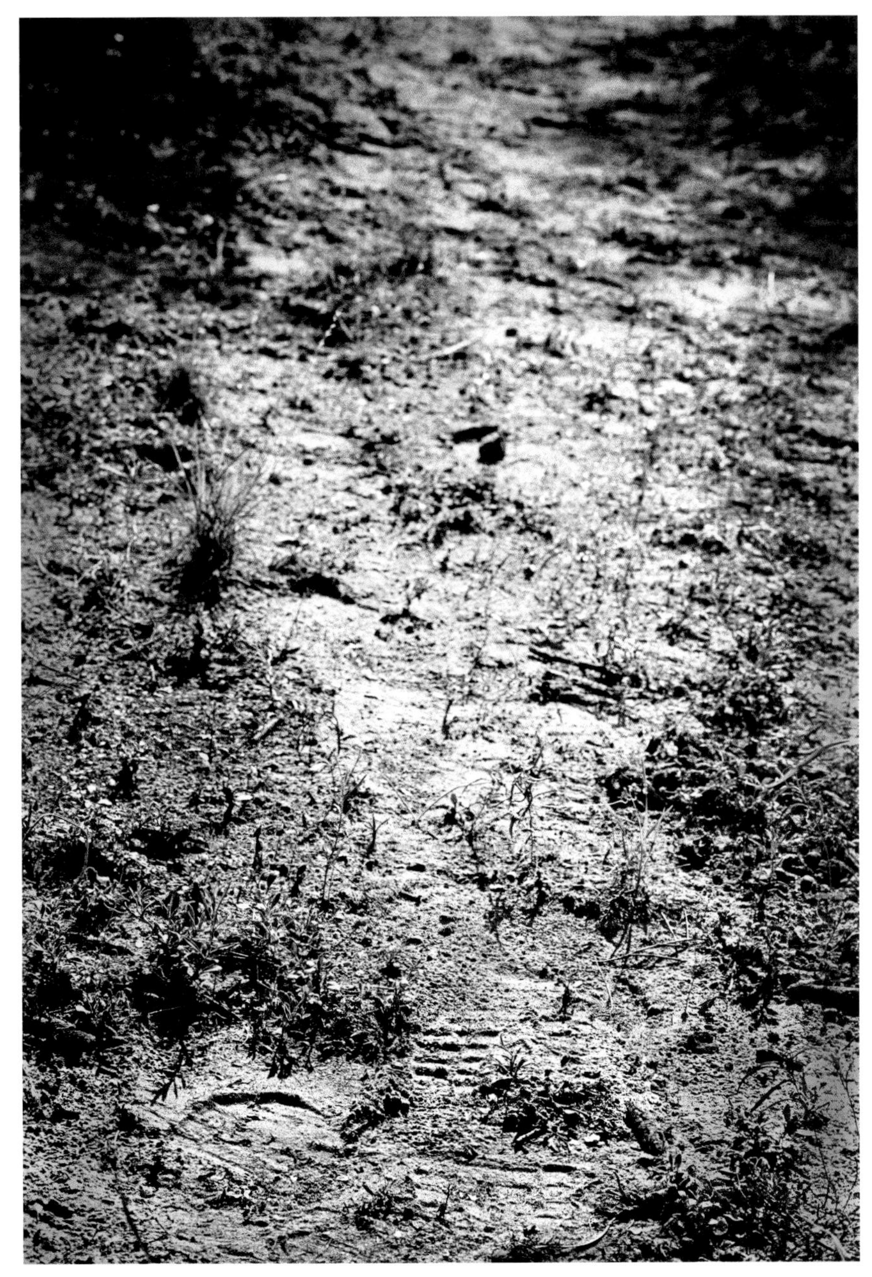

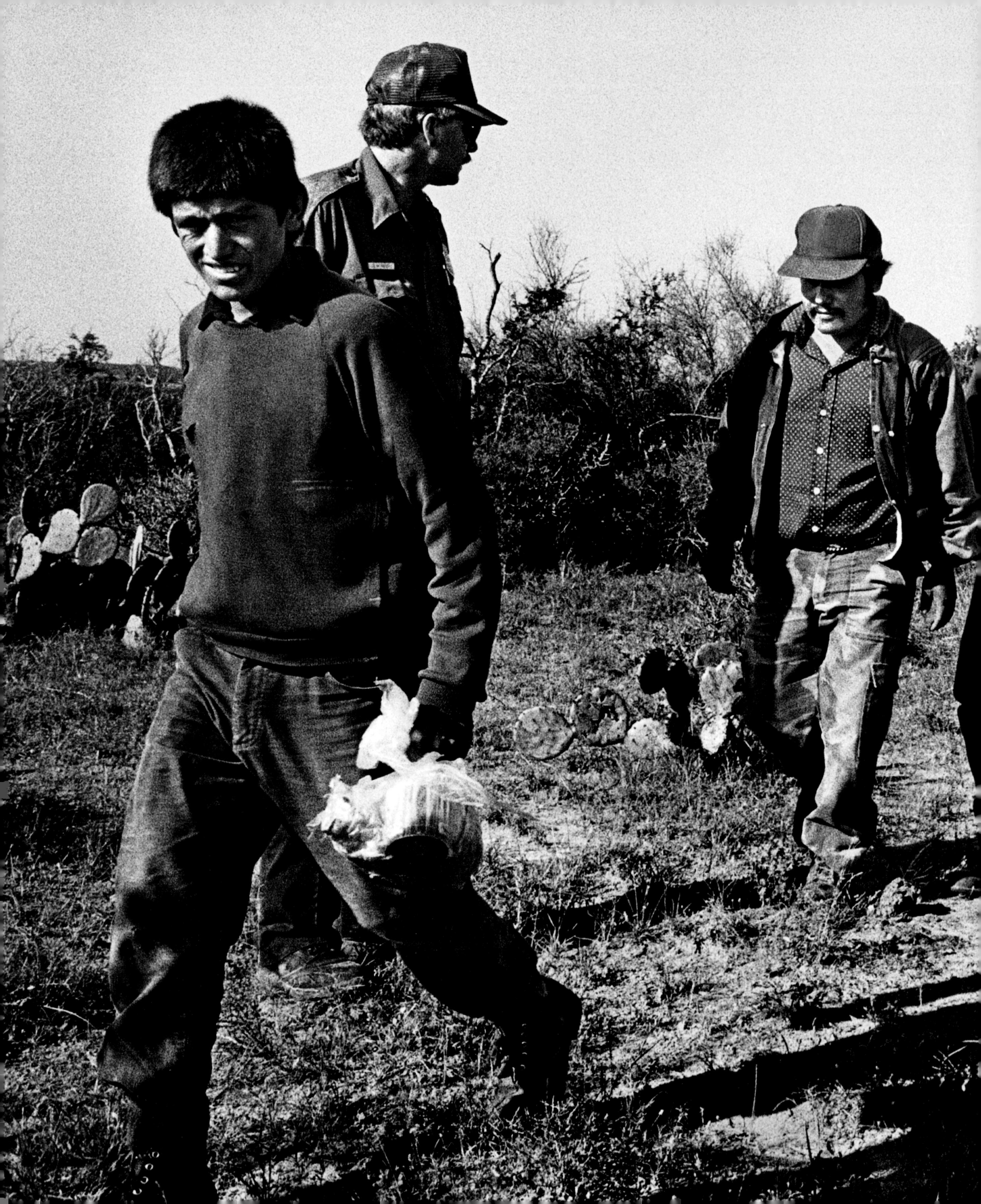

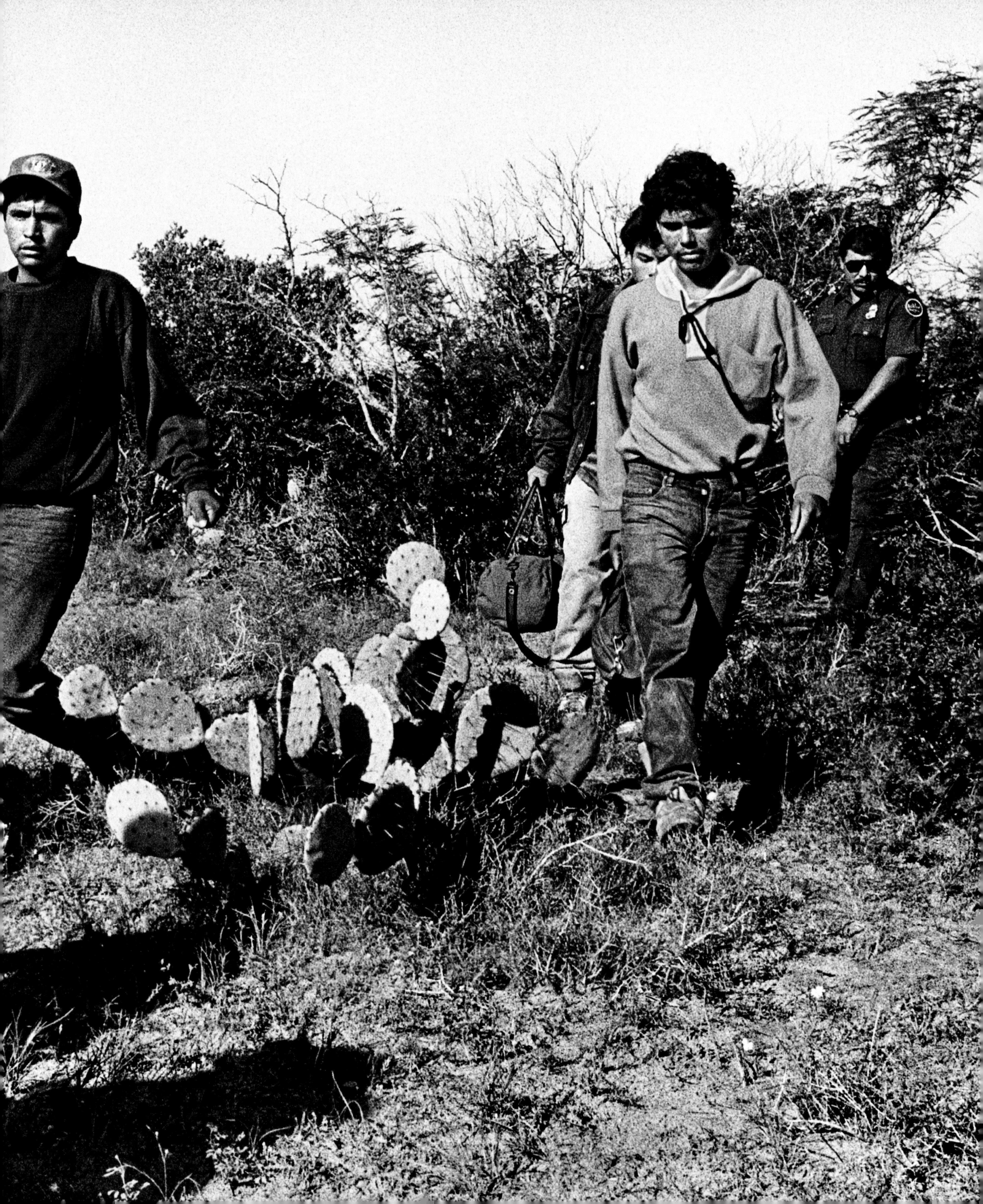

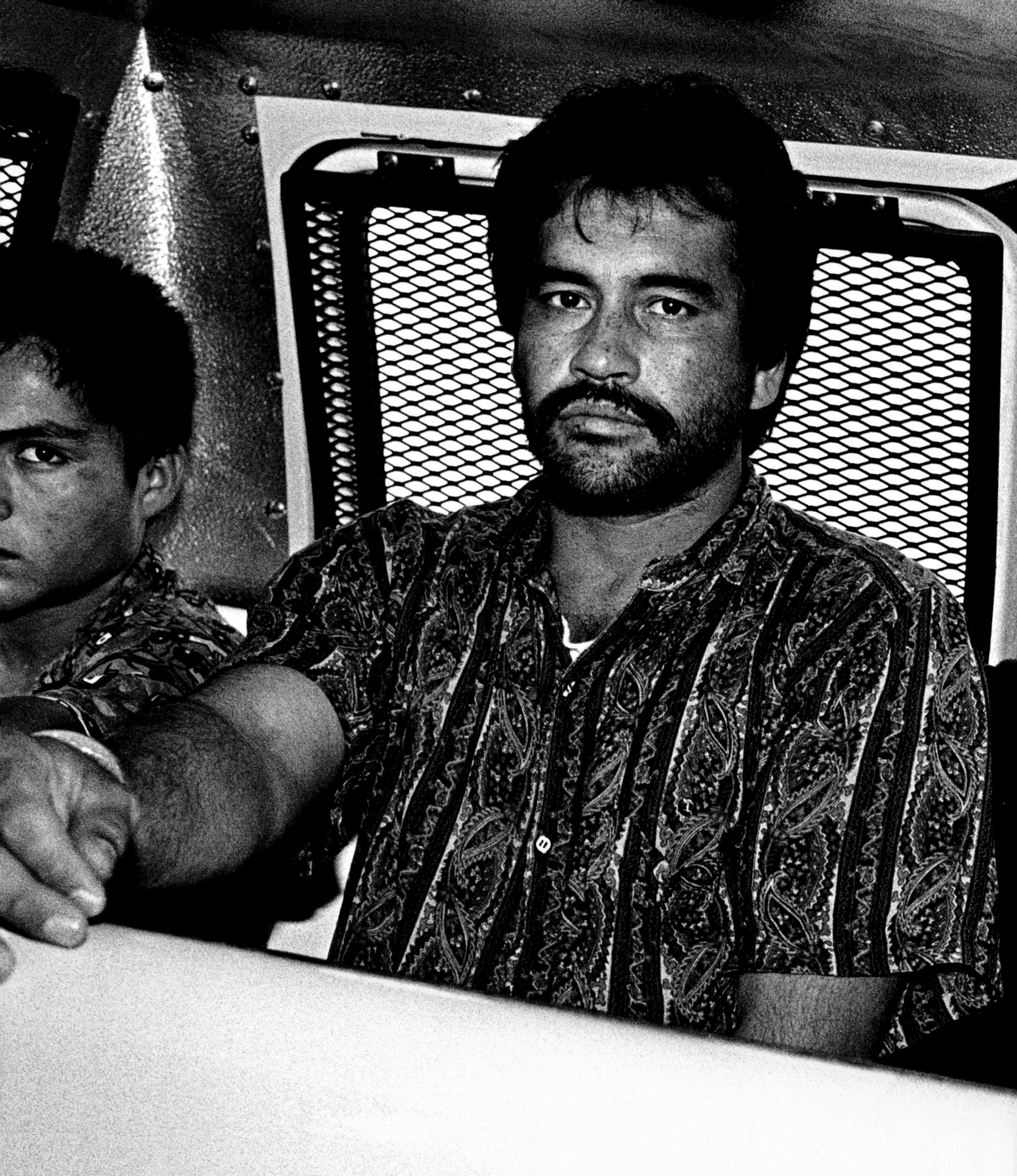

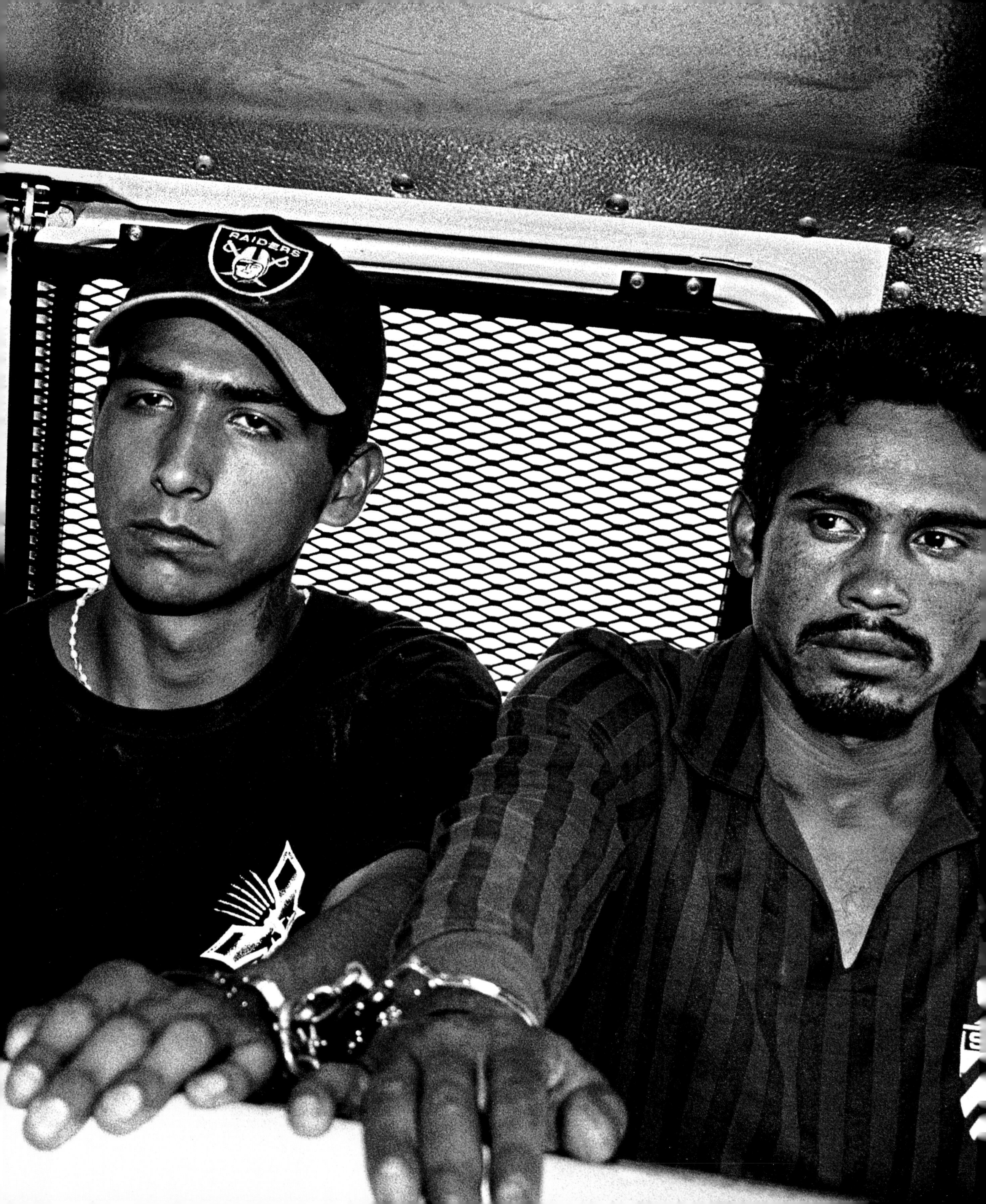
RAIDERS

Dogfighting

COTULLA, TEXAS
MAY 13, 1994

Dogfighting is an underground sport—a bloody, violent battle between two animals driven to frenzy. They are held inches apart, close enough to smell each other to incite aggression, and then returned to the scratch line to be released, tearing into each other, puncturing flesh, and ripping off lips. They fight in a plywood box measuring fifteen by fifteen feet on compact dirt or carpet laid down for traction. The bouts can last ten minutes, thirty minutes, even up to two hours or longer. The most aggressive dogs won't stop. They'll fight until they overheat or die. If they're not killed in the ring, they often die hours or days later from blood loss, shock, dehydration, or infection.

Dogfighting is a felony in Texas, with a possible two-year jail sentence. Even spectators can be jailed for one year for a Class A misdemeanor. Yet, in Texas, this clandestine world thrives. Fights held secretly in barns, suburban houses, or abandoned buildings can attract twenty-five to a hundred and fifty people. But not just anyone can attend; the fights are by invitation only. Other than the dubious lure of blood sport, gambling is the main draw. From what I saw, bets run from $25 or so up to $5,000, $20,000, and $50,000. "Cajun rules" specifying the terms of engagement were enforced at the fight that I witnessed in the countryside, and they are also used in cities such as Dallas, Fort Worth, and Houston. The last of the nineteen rules states that, should the police break up a fight, the referee names the next meeting place.

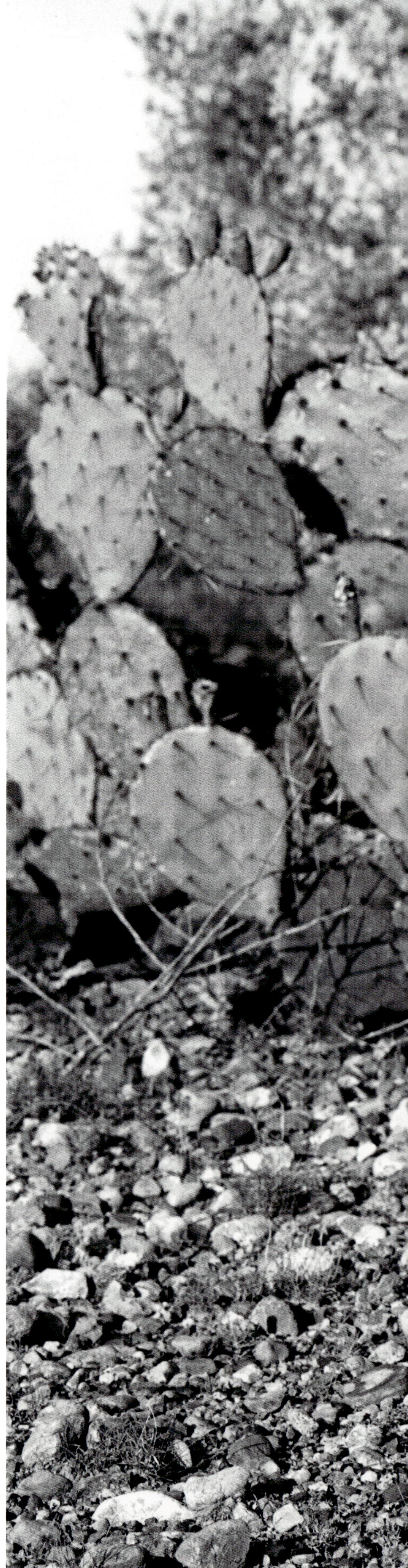

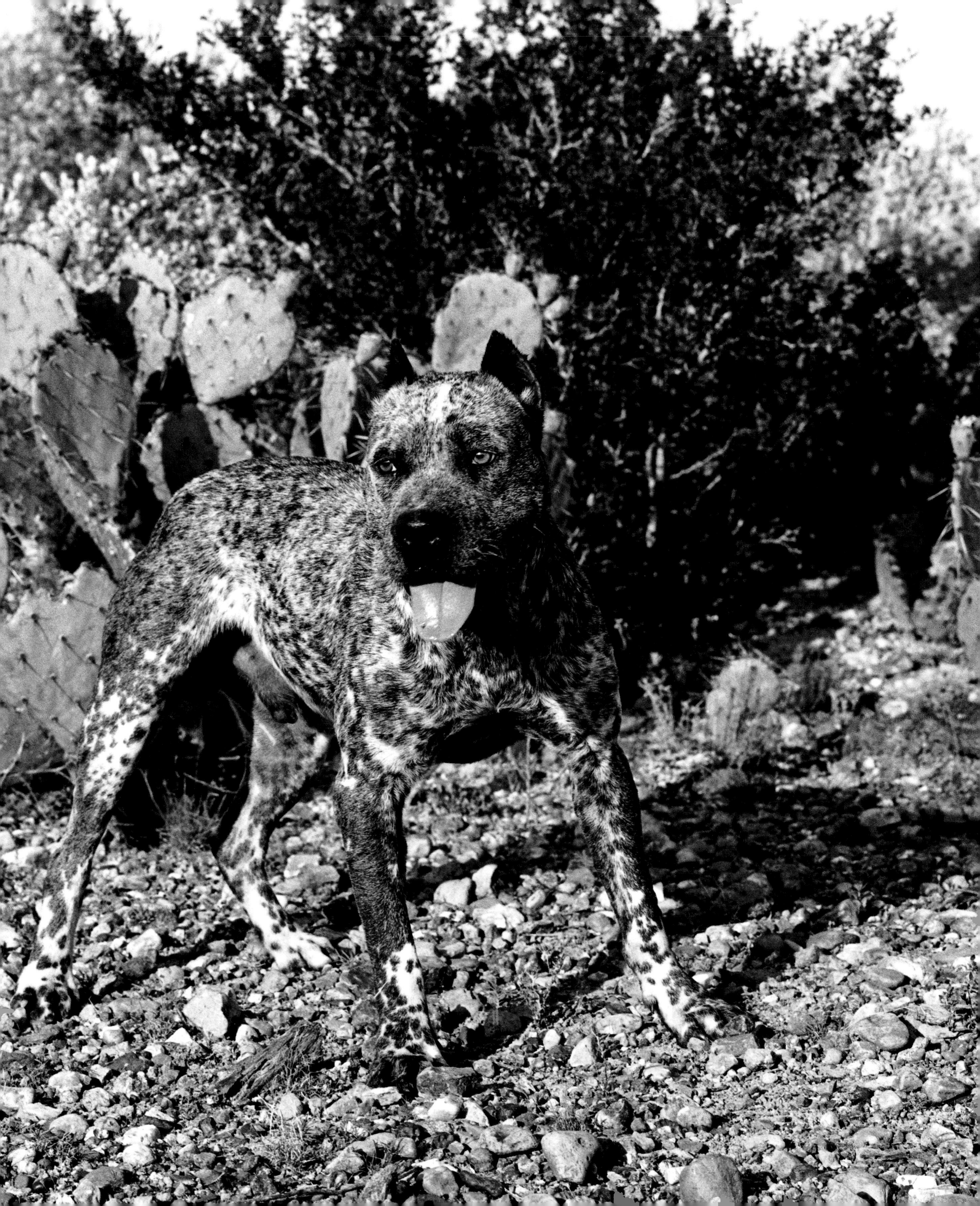

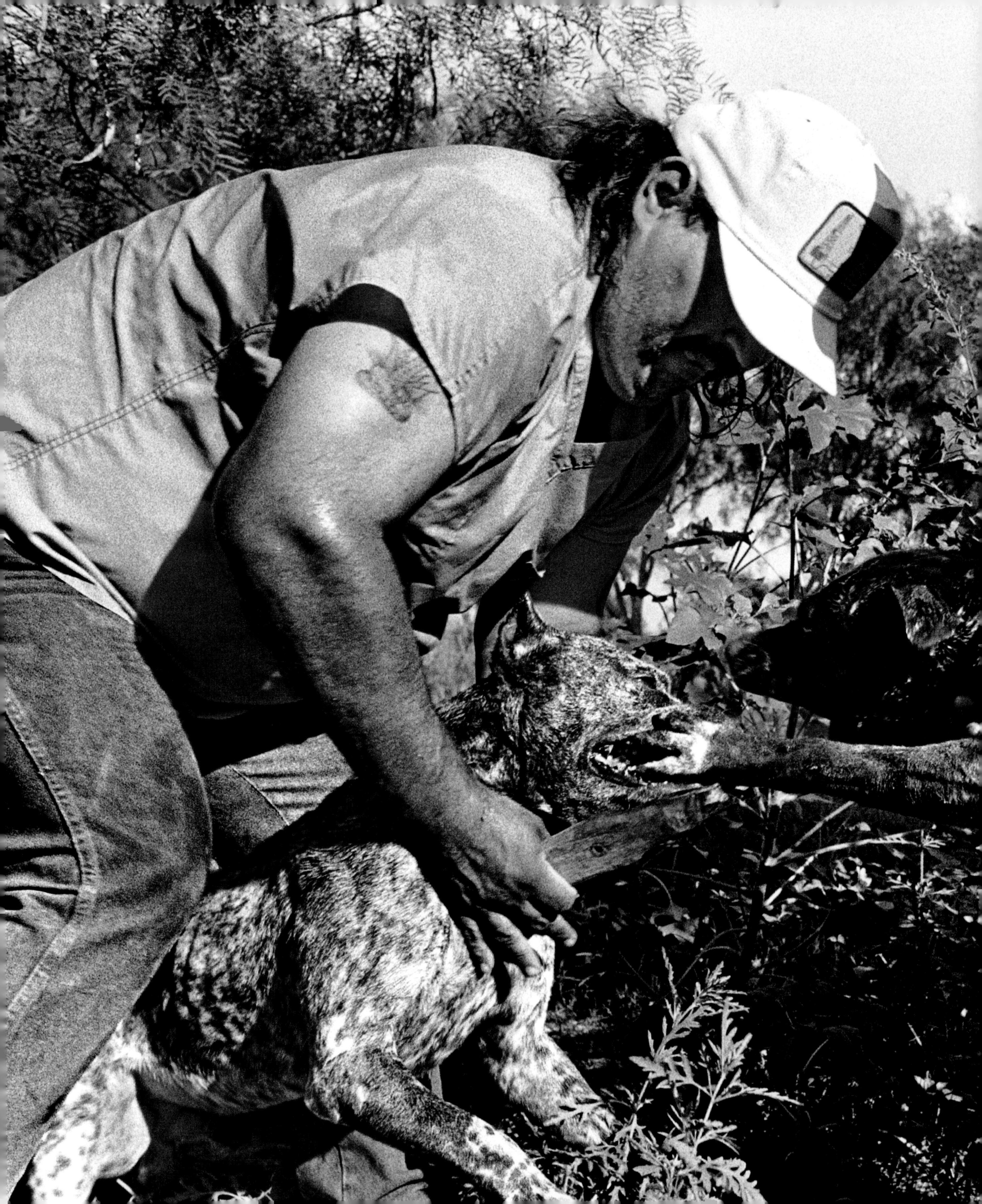

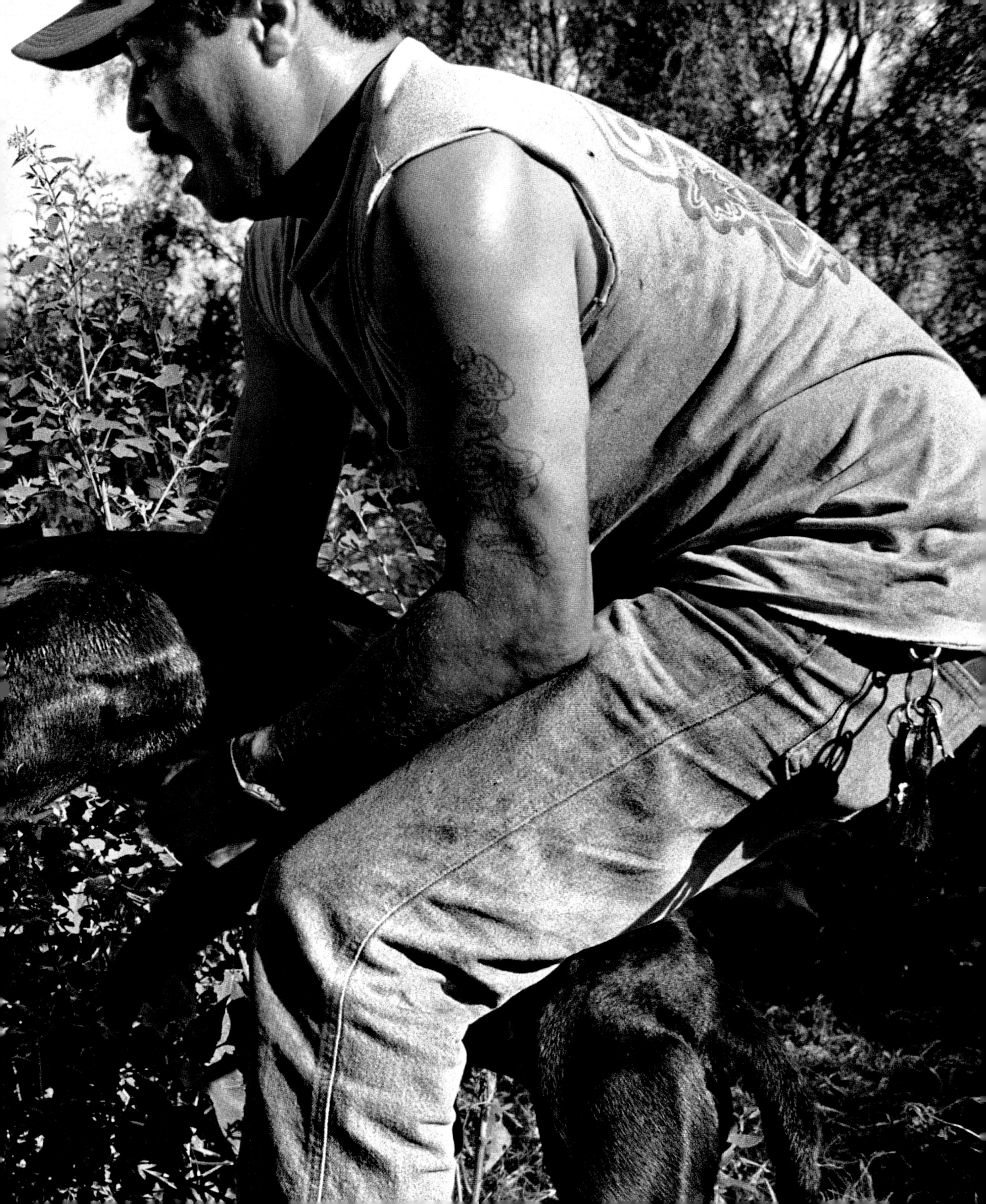

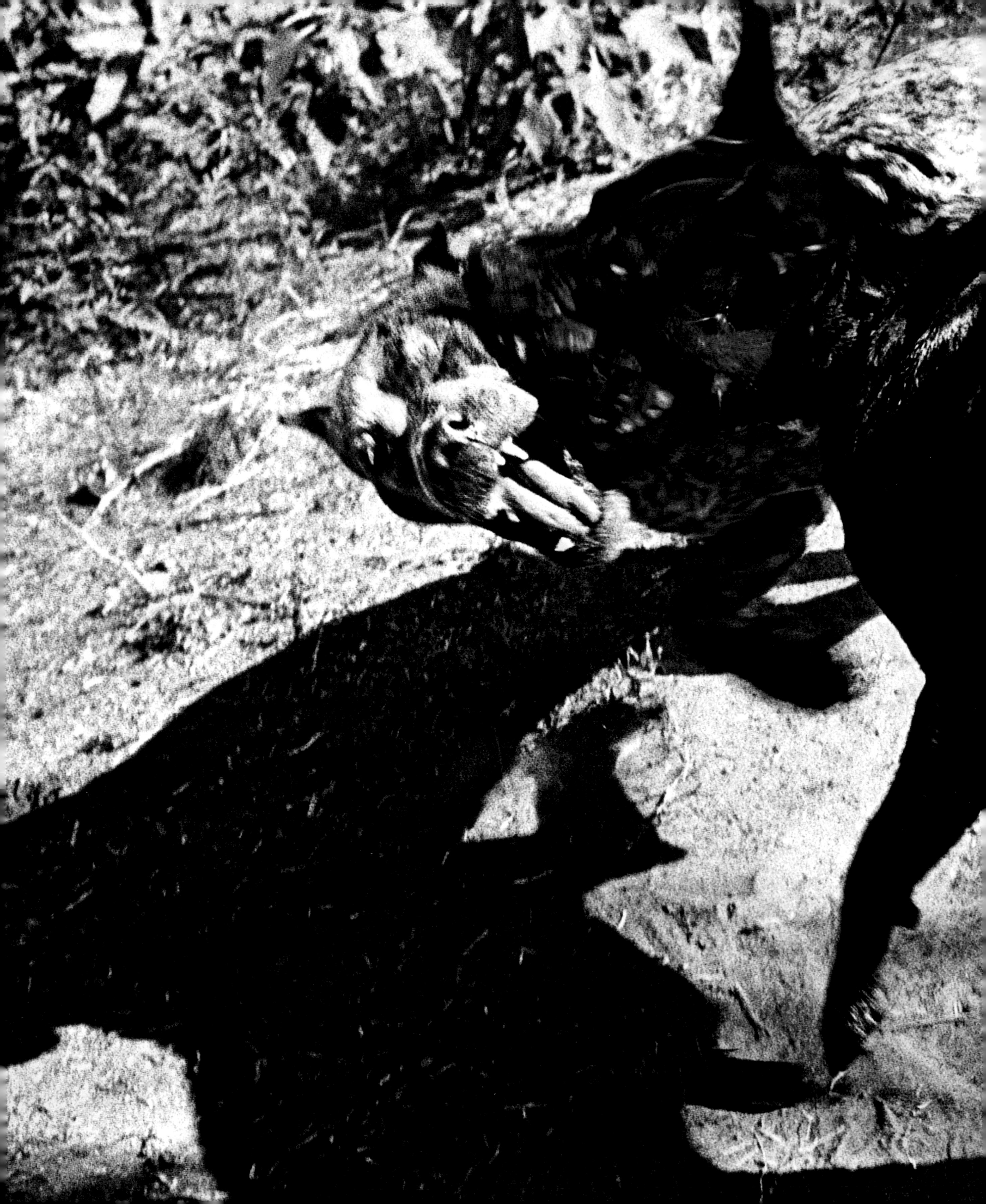

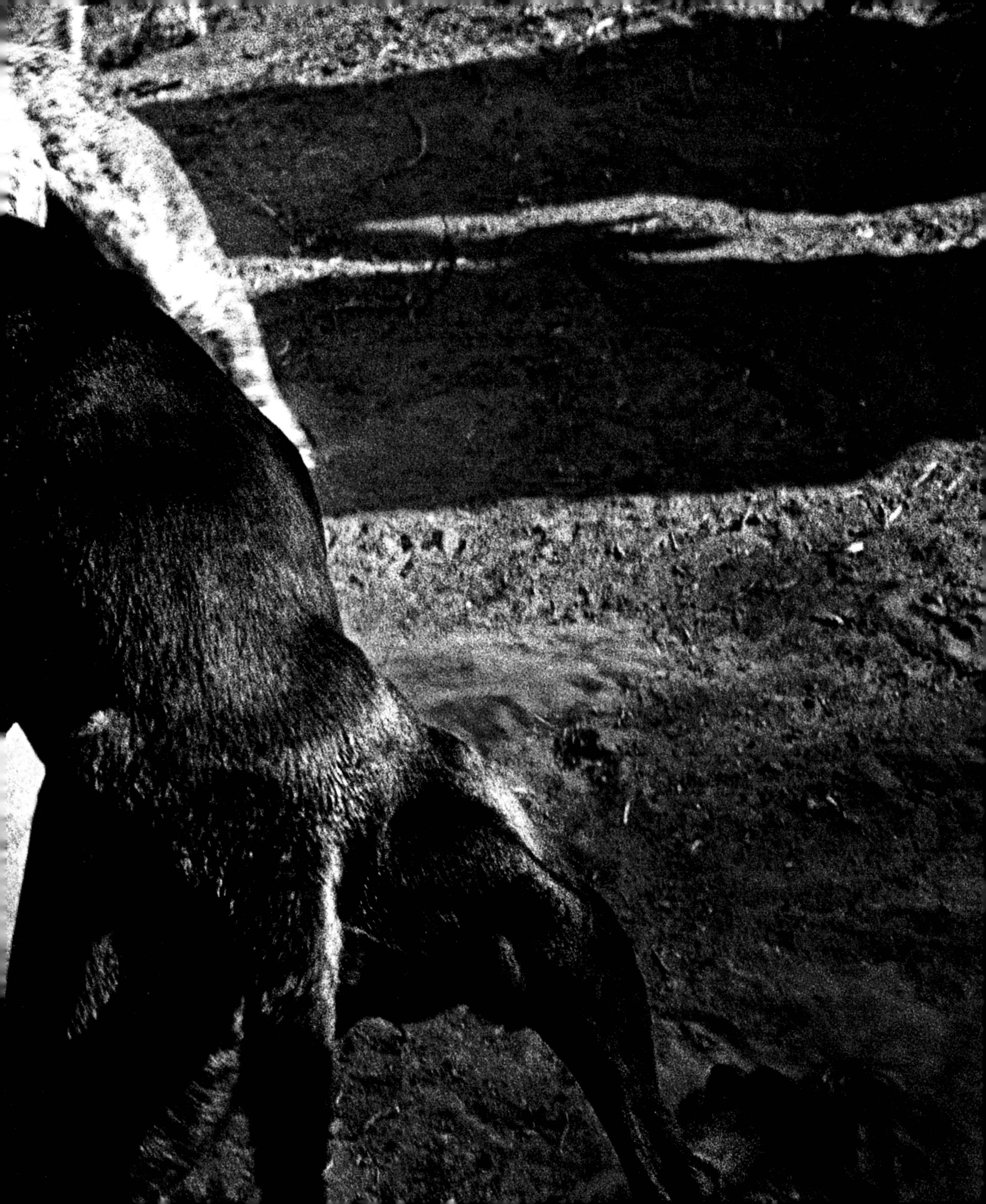

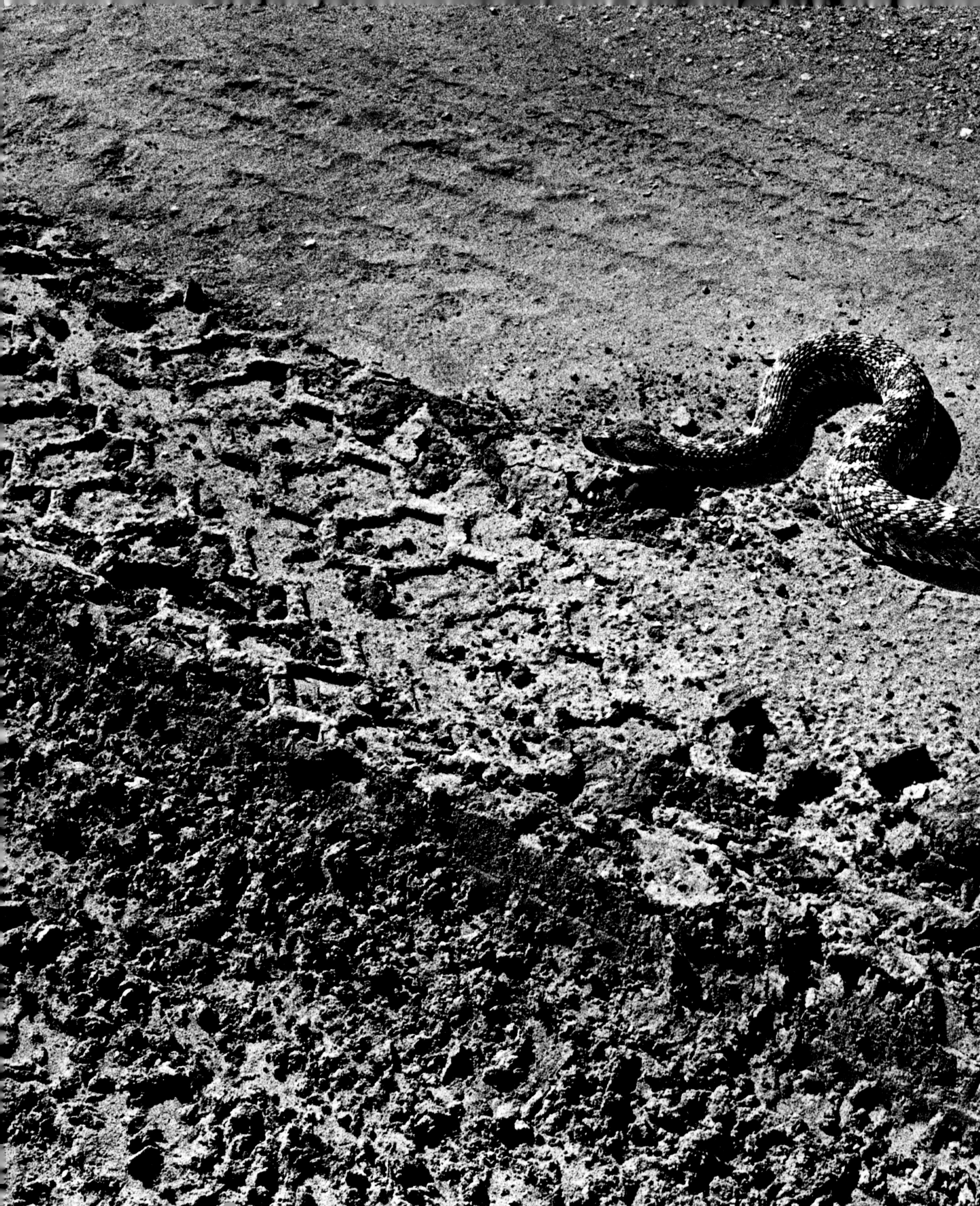

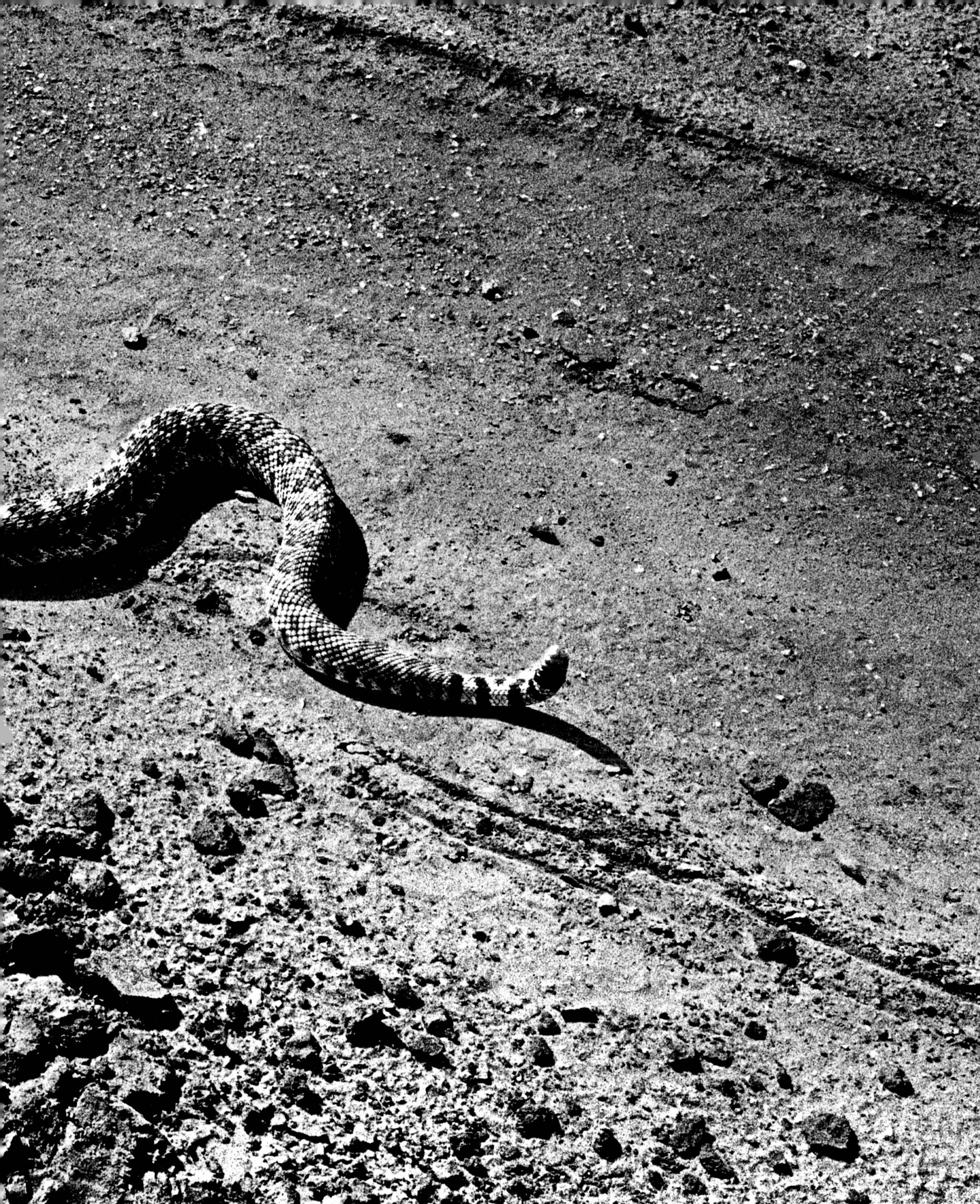

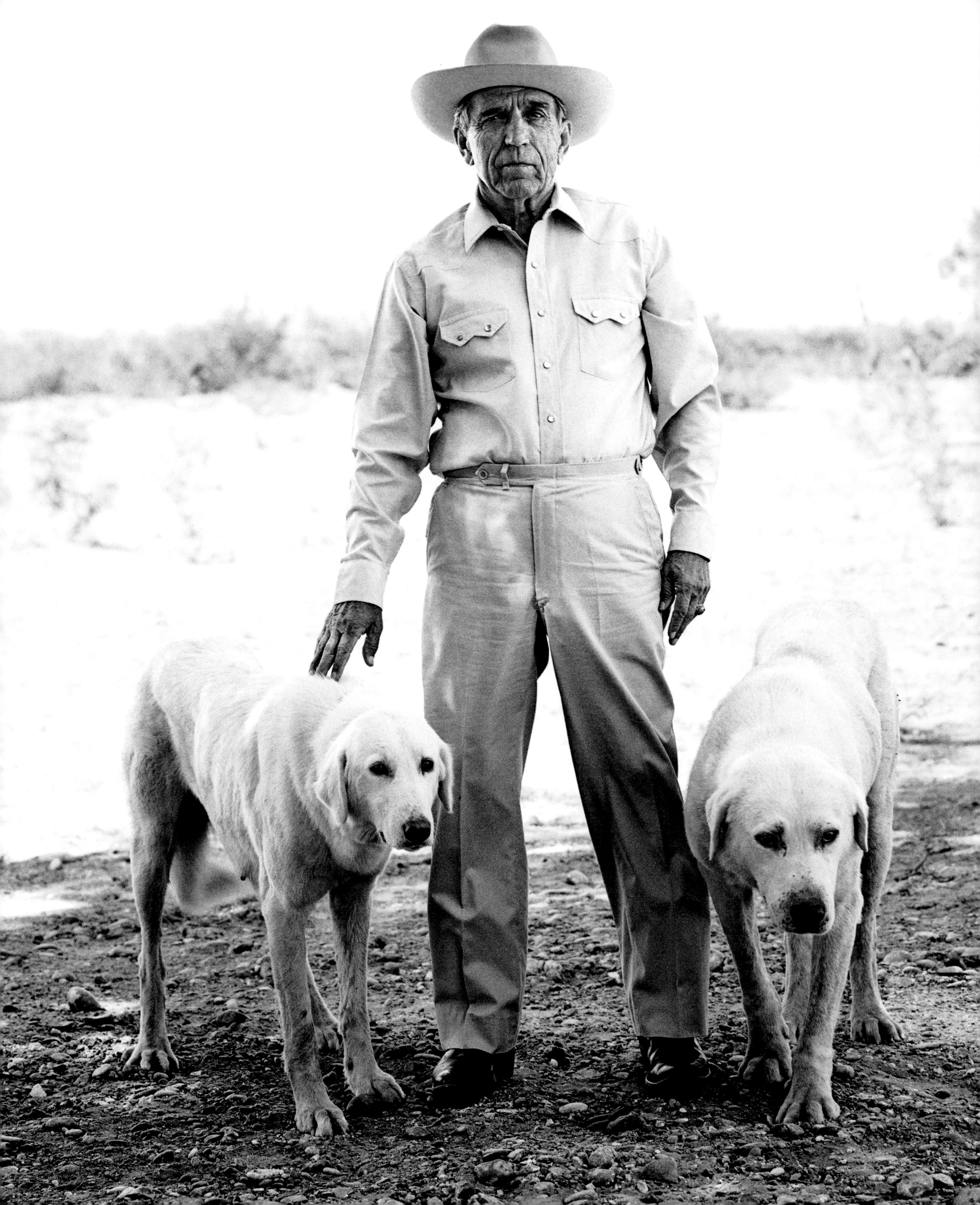

The Longoria Brothers

COAHUILA, MEXICO
APRIL 21, 1993

In the 1950s, the Longoria brothers led one of the most prominent families in northern Mexico. Octaviano, Frederico, Shelby, Eduardo, and Alfredo built a family compound, the Colonia Longoria, in Nuevo Laredo, with a church and gardens and, for each brother, a large house in a different style—Georgian for Frederico ("Quico"), Spanish for Eduardo ("Wayo"), and Colonial for Octaviano ("Chito"). Frederico ran Banco Longoria, founded in 1929 by their father, Octaviano, Sr. Prudent and shrewd, Frederico grew the bank to more than fifty branches across northern Mexico, from Matamoros to Tijuana, and, with his brothers, seized opportunities to diversify. Their company Empresas Longoria expanded into real estate, cotton, cattle, lumberyards, butane distribution, movie theaters, ice plants, car dealerships, soap, and lard production, operating primarily in Mexico but also across the border in Texas.

"My dad, Frederico, was gentle and quiet," Maria Christina Longoria told me. "I remember people coming to our house on Sunday afternoons. My dad would go out on the porch to talk. He'd help them with personal problems, give them money. He always tried to help."

Sylvia René Longoria also spoke of her father, Eduardo Longoria, who operated the family's hundred-thousand-acre ranch in Coahuila on the Rio Grande (Río Bravo). His mother had named a large portion of the ranch the "Saint Eduardo," for her son. Sylvia, remembering, said, "Whenever I think of my father, I still see him on the ranch, standing out in the rain, smiling. To this day, even though I live in Houston, just the smell of rain excites me. In that dry, parched land, I know grass will grow, cattle will graze, and my father will be so happy."

NUEVO LAREDO, MEXICO
APRIL 20, 1993

By the time I photographed the Longoria brothers, only Frederico remained in the Colonia Longoria compound. Eduardo had been kidnapped on March 17, 1986, at 7:30 in the morning as he got out of his car in the parking lot of his office in downtown Nuevo Laredo. Three armed men threw him into a van, blindfolded him, and drove away. In those days, cars with megaphones on their roofs were driven throughout the city, announcing sales at various stores. Even blindfolded and stuffed in the back of the van, Eduardo, listening, was able to keep track of his location. The kidnappers demanded a ransom but kept changing the location of the payment drop-off to different towns, making it difficult for the family to know where Eduardo was being held. A family attorney was instructed to drive the payment to a hotel near Monterrey. Finally, after midnight, Eduardo walked into his own house, his mouth and hands covered in black electrical tape. Soon after, he moved his family across the border to an unassuming house in Laredo without saying a word to the Mexican police. The day I photographed him, I asked why he hadn't reported his kidnapping. "The police," he said, "were in on it."

Eduardo died at age ninety-one in 2004. Frederico died at ninety-four in 2001, and his daughter Maria Christina Longoria told me in 2015, "I'm glad my dad's not alive now. He was so proud of the city, the people. He'd be devastated by the drug cartels, the killings, the way they've taken over Nuevo Laredo."

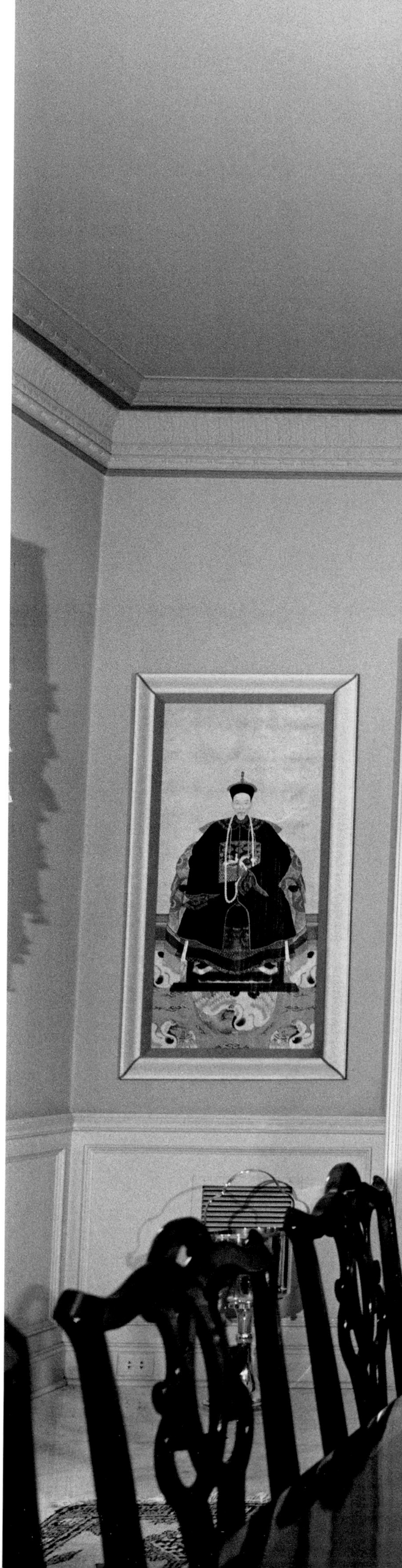

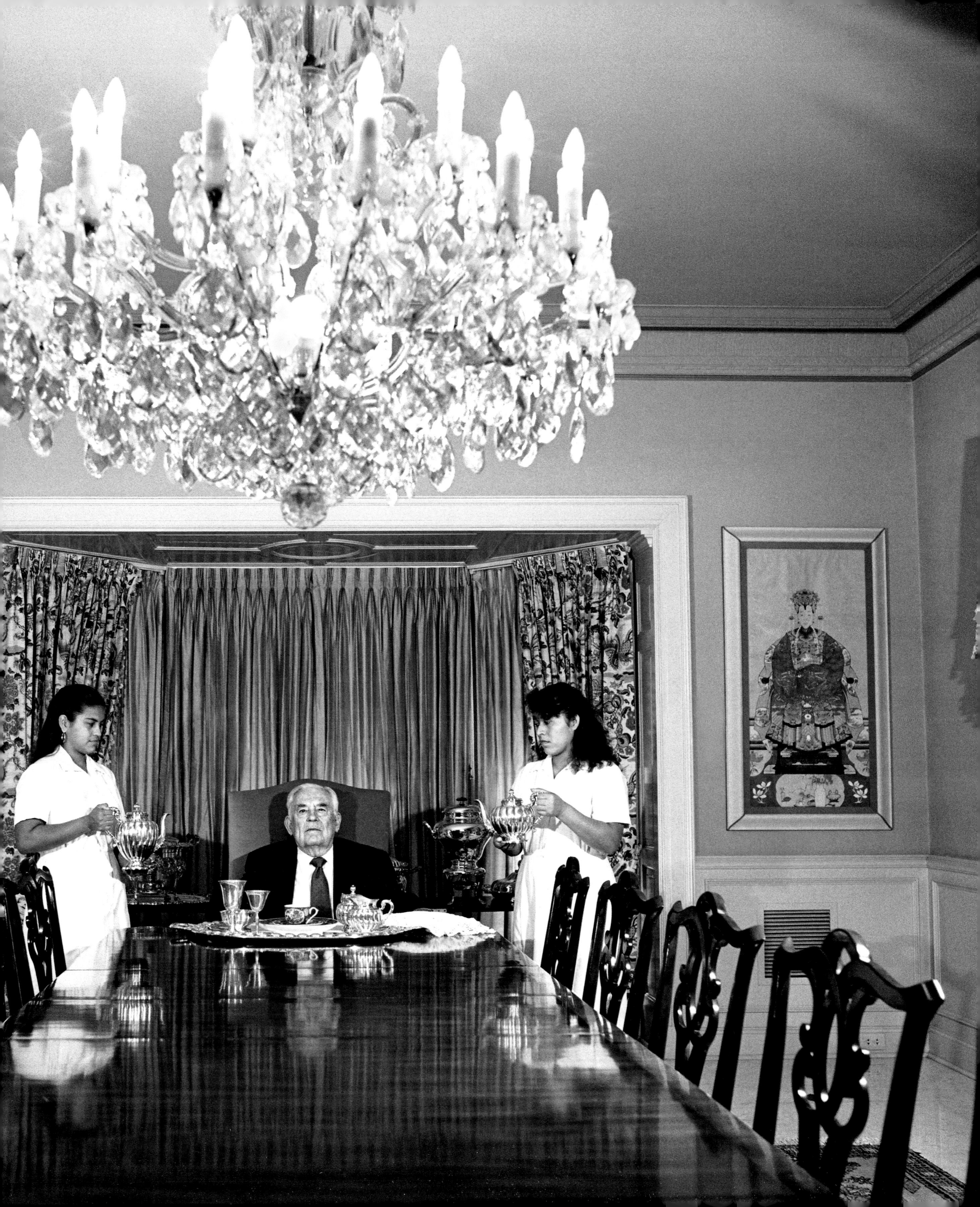

Debutante Cotillion

LAREDO, TEXAS
FEBRUARY 17–18, 1994

As the crow flies, Laredo is fifteen hundred miles from the Virginia home of our first First Lady, but distance did not prevent the women of Webb County, seventy-five years ago, from founding the Society of Martha Washington on the Texas–Mexico border. Today, the society's members continue to assert their Americanism with the lavish Colonial Pageant and Ball during the weeklong celebration of George Washington's birthday in a land that still seems to belong to Mexico. For two Februaries, I photographed the seventeen or so debutantes presented at Laredo's most lustrous event. The young women wear dresses that can take a year to make and are embellished with pearls, crystals, silk flowers, silver cord, gold sequins, tiers of taffeta ruffles, and beaded lace. The dresses can cost as much as thirty thousand dollars and weigh nearly a hundred pounds.

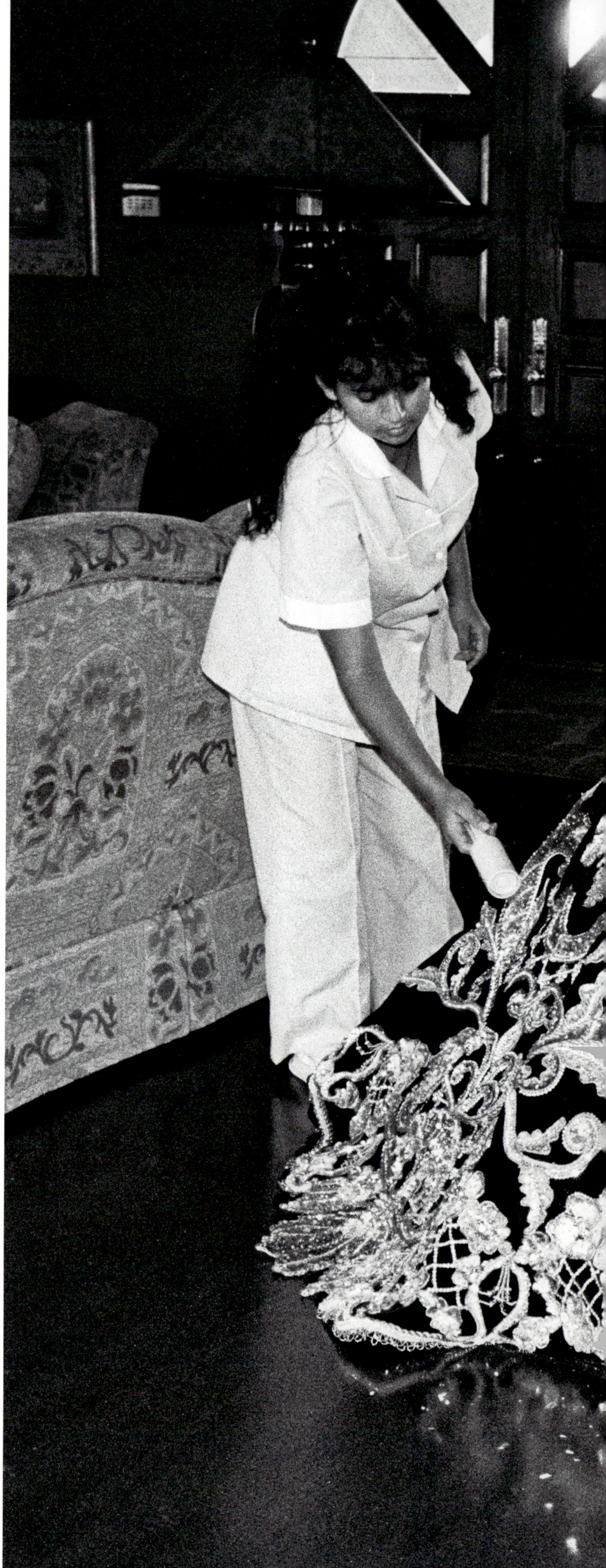

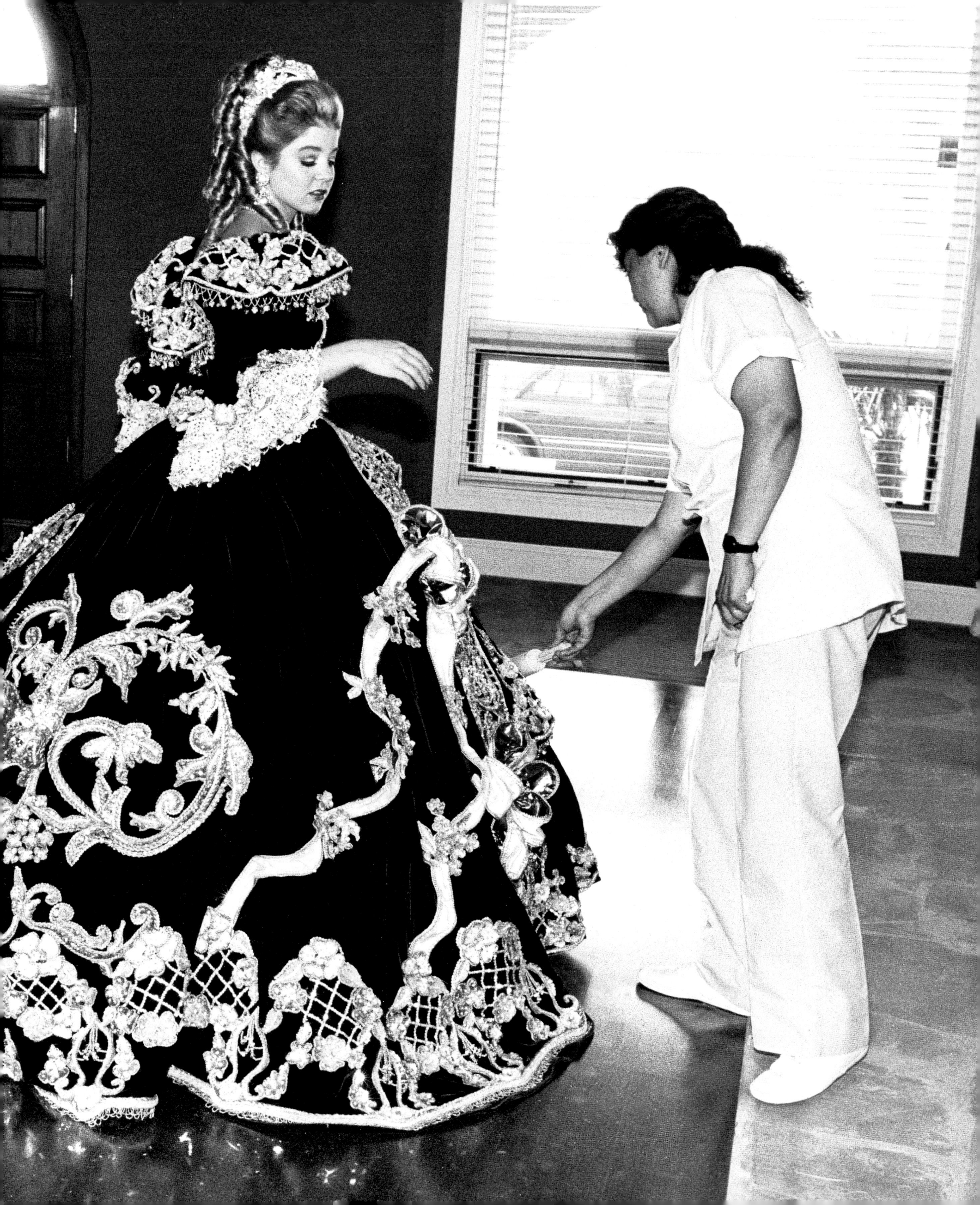

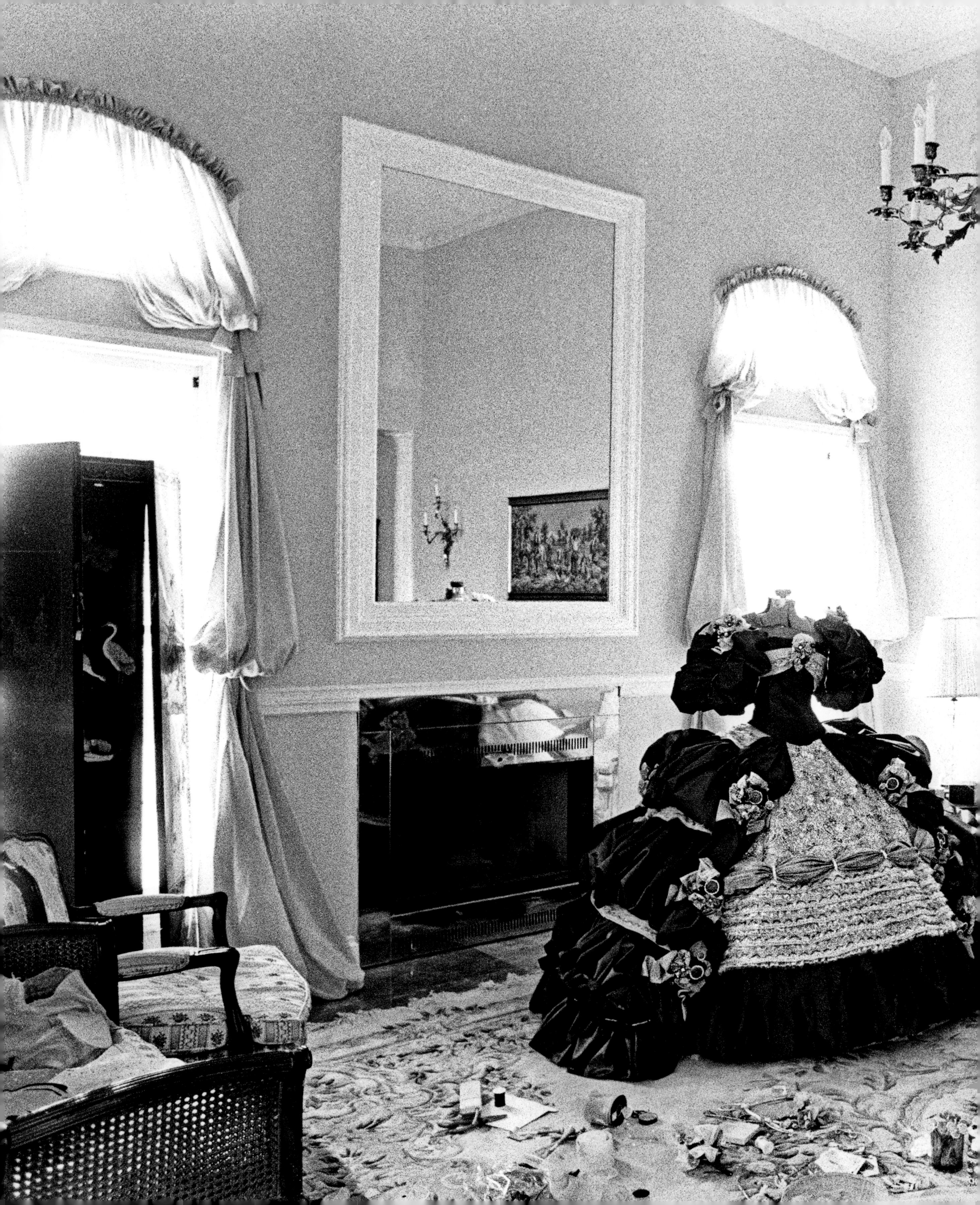

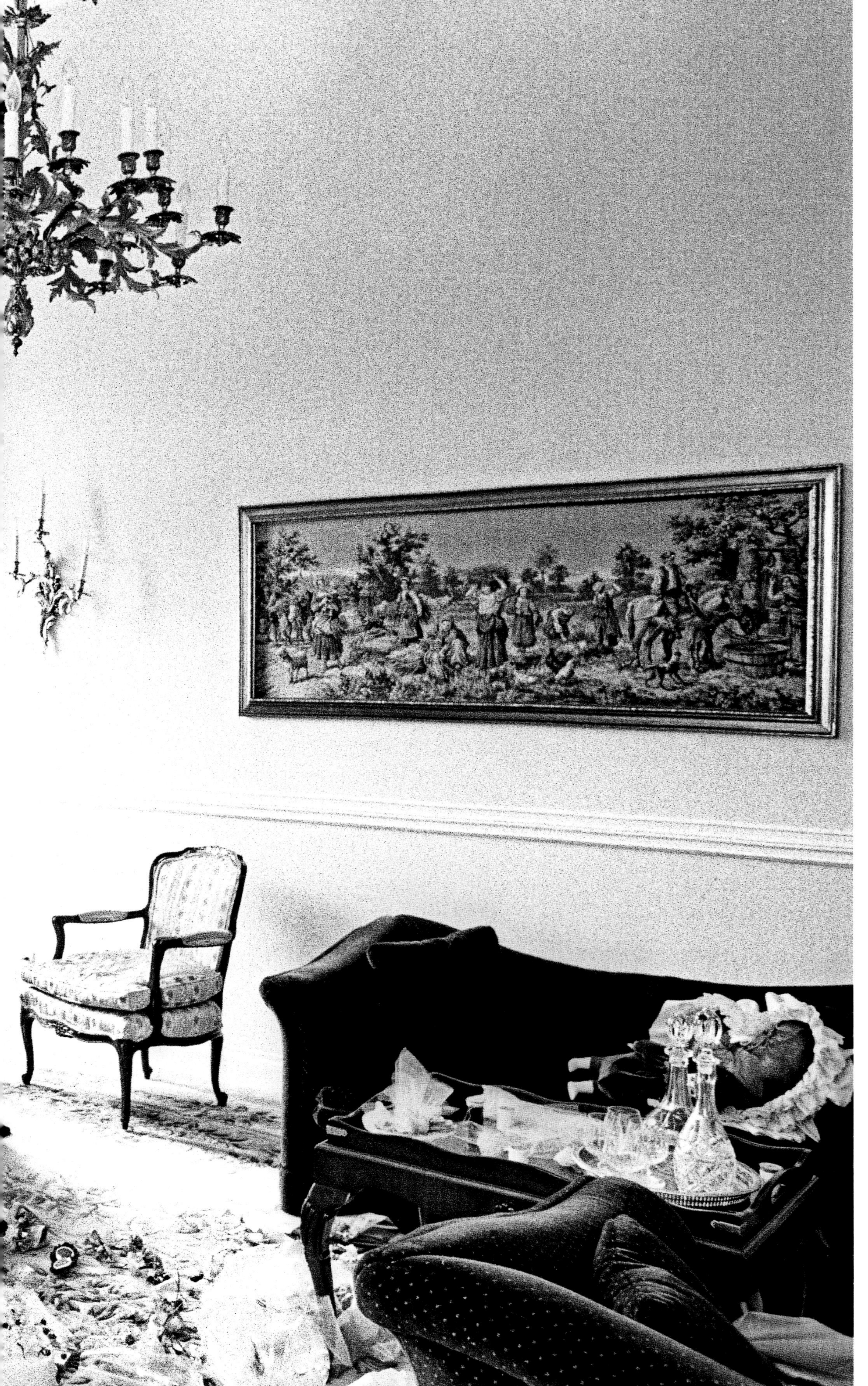

LAREDO, TEXAS
FEBRUARY 19, 1993

The circumference of these rigid, heavily beaded skirts is so great that debutantes cannot travel to the ball by car, limousine, or van. Instead, they use eighteen-wheel moving vans, with the debutantes strapped in like racehorses, three or four to a truck.

The girls presented at the Colonial Pageant and Ball each year are high school seniors and usually the daughters and granddaughters of "the Marthas," as the women of the two-hundred-member society call themselves. A few carefully selected girls from other parts of Texas are also invited to make their debut. The Marthas are mostly descendants of the founding families and old money of Laredo and Nuevo Laredo. They are unexpectedly diverse, including women of Spanish, Mexican, Jewish, and Anglo heritage. The ball is a chance for the sons and daughters of these families to connect and maybe marry, with the hope of preserving family money and land.

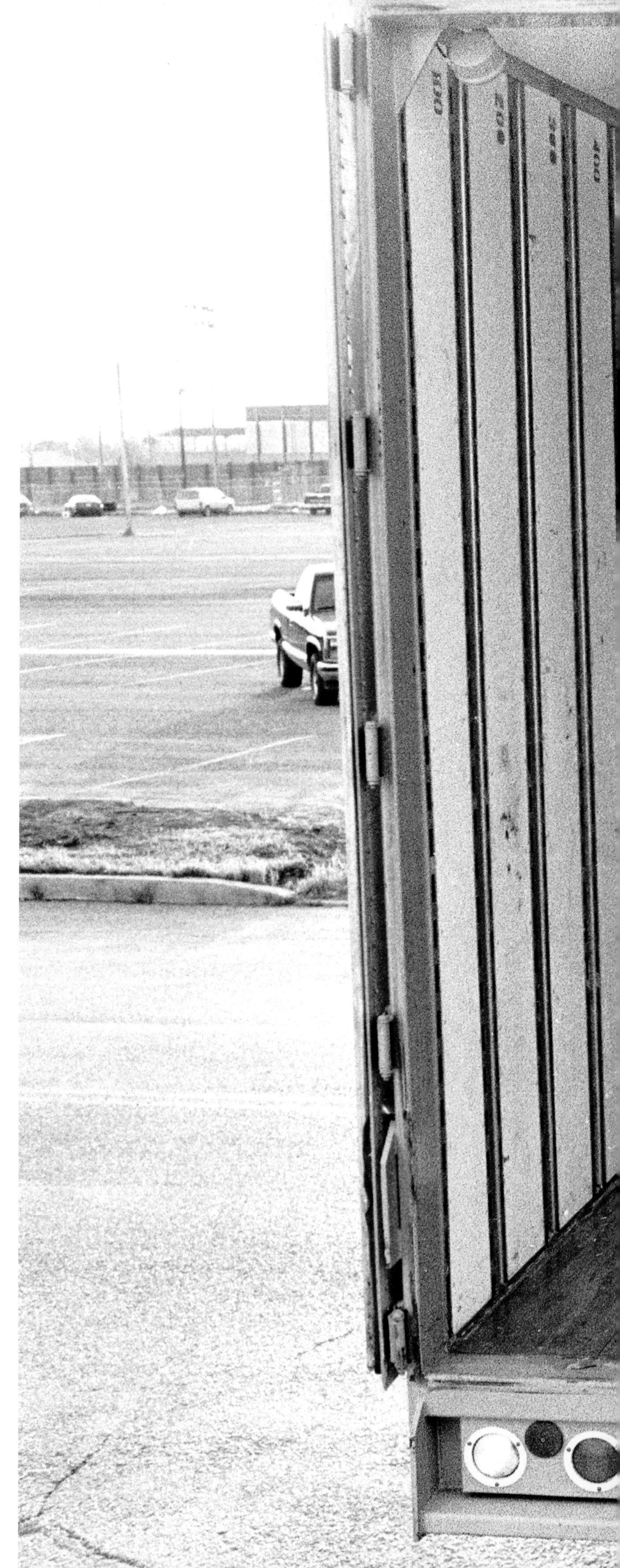

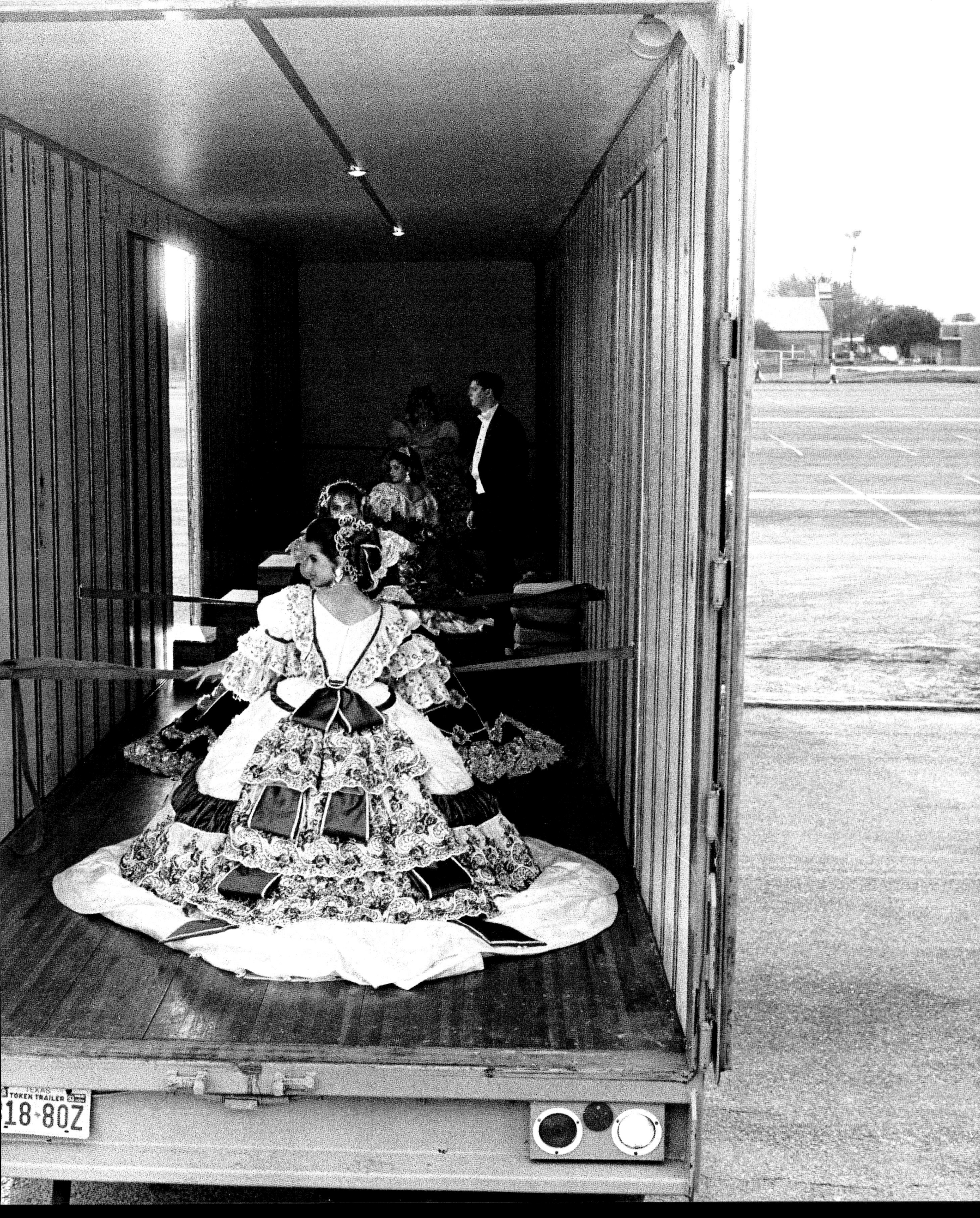
TEXAS
TOKEN TRAILER
18 80Z

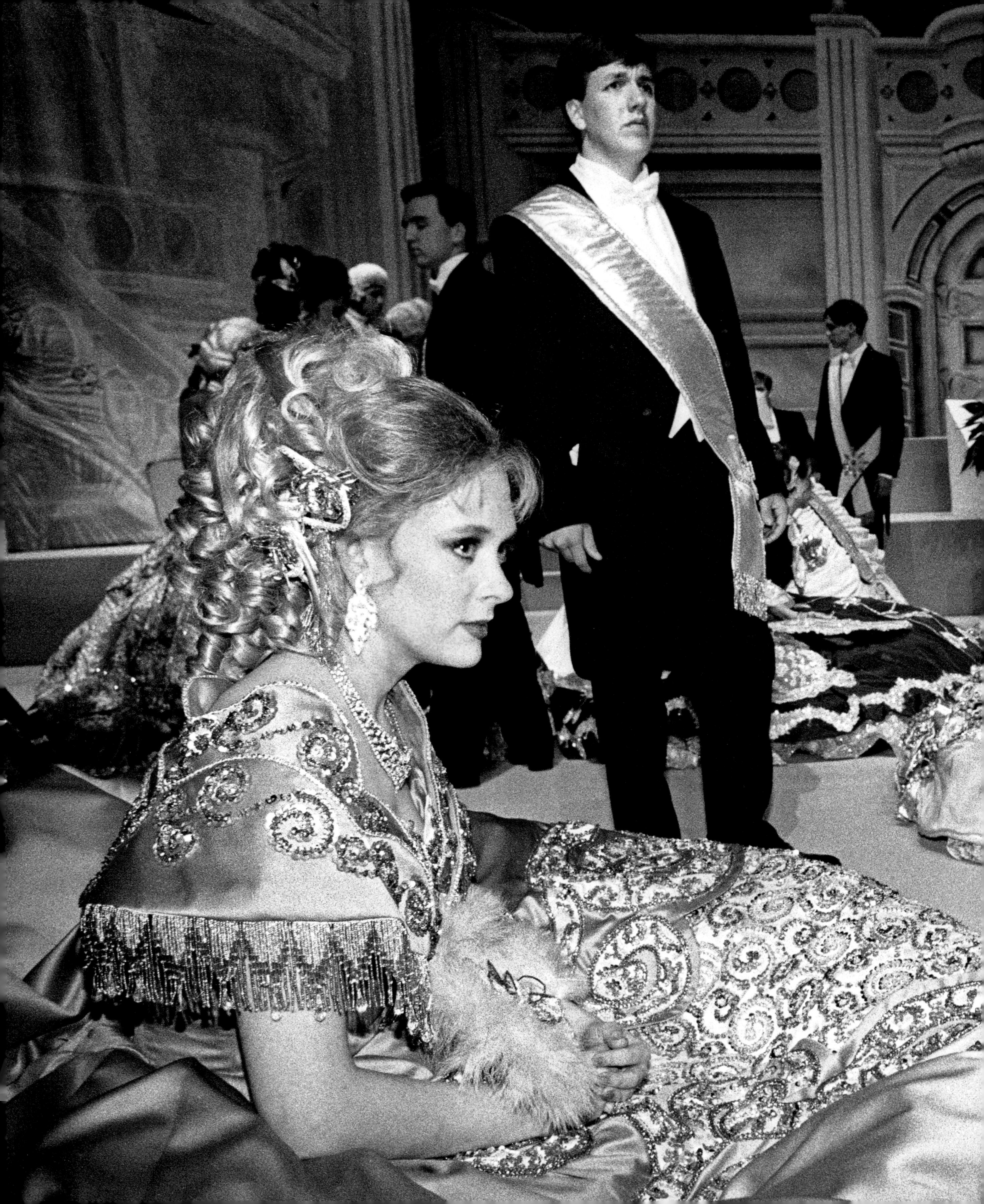

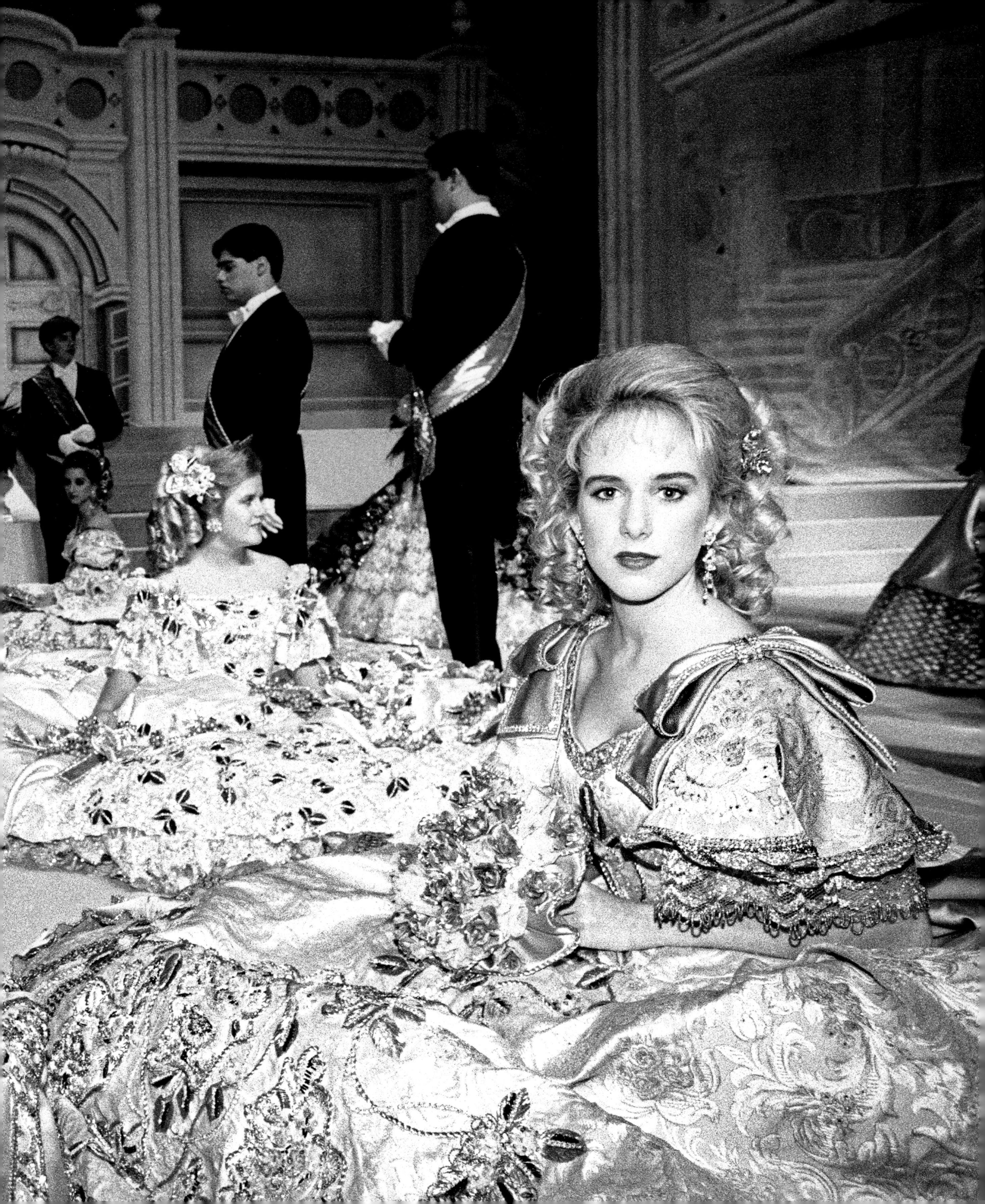

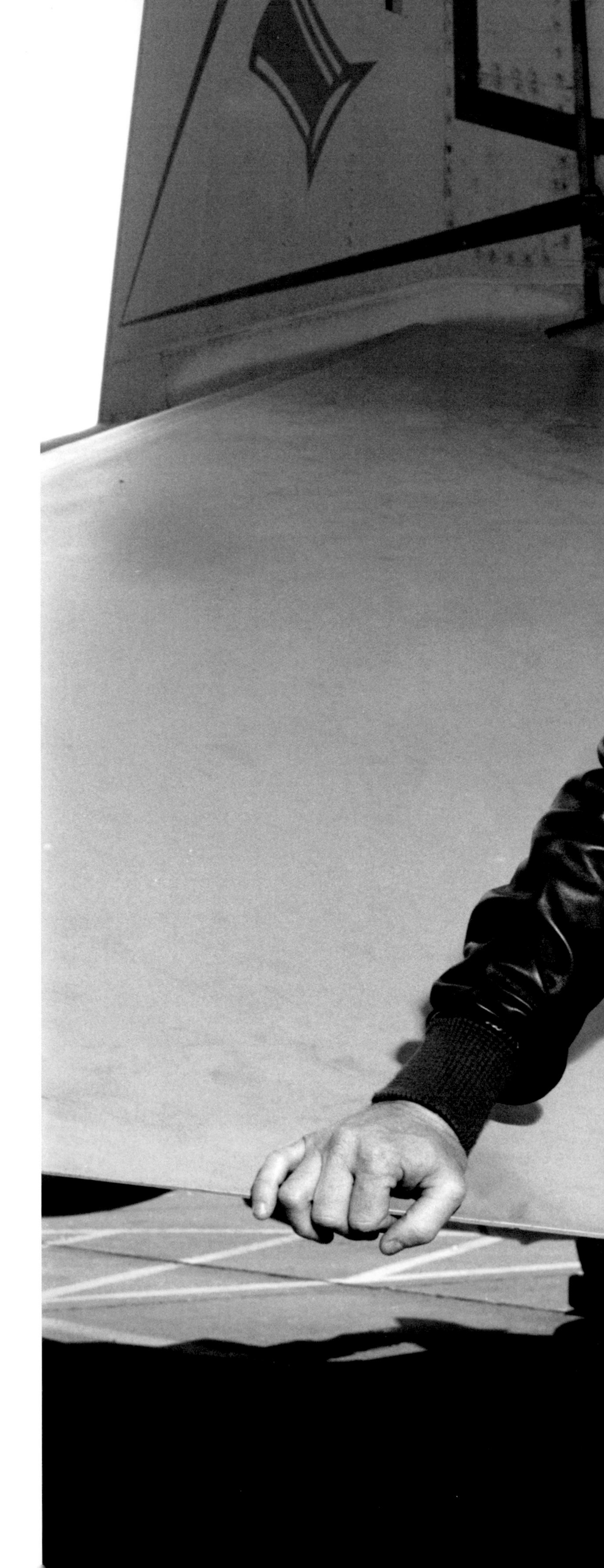

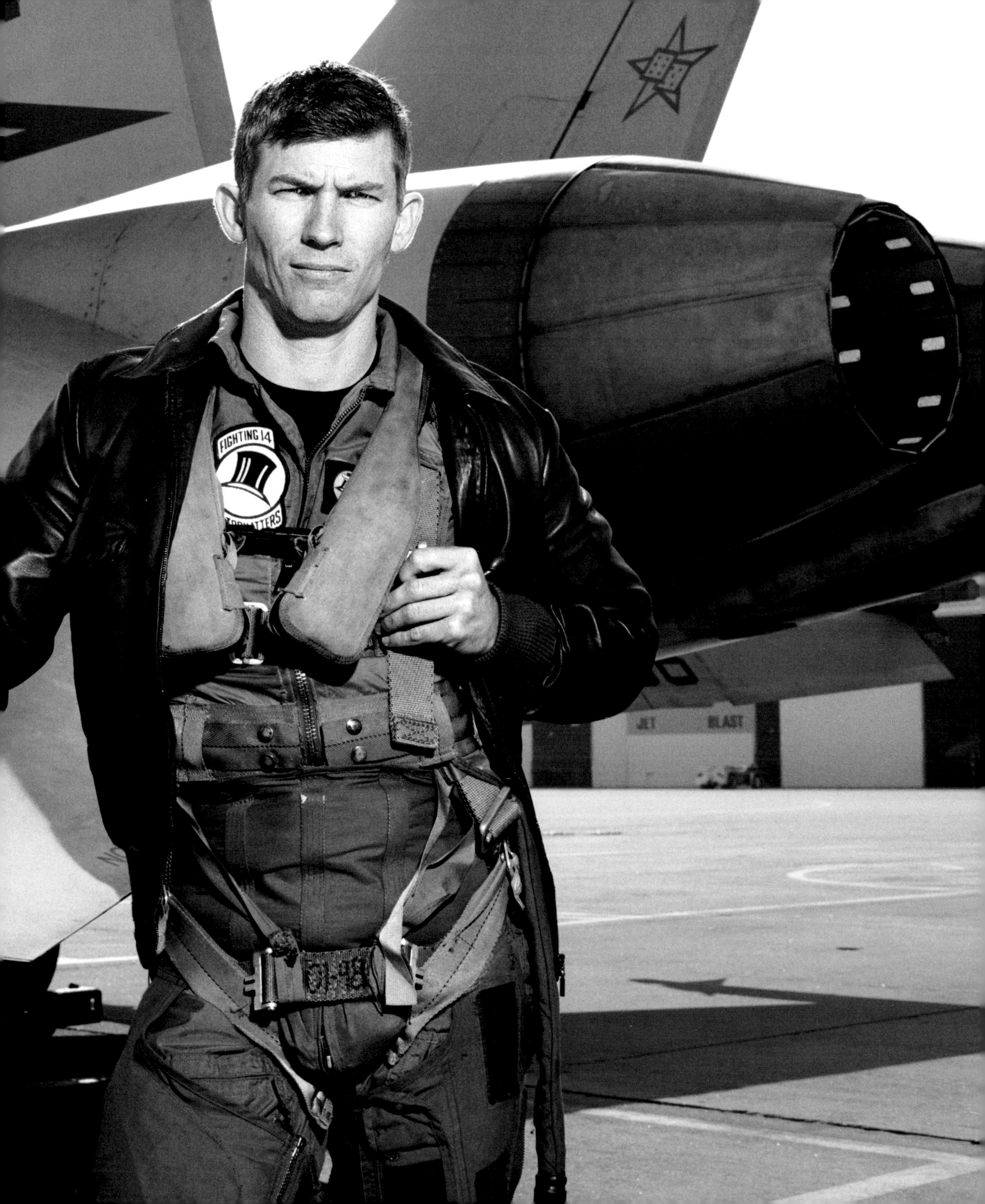
FIGHTING 14
JET
BLAST

Fighter Pilots

FALLON, NEVADA
JUNE 15–16, 2004

"You can kill yourself faster in a single-seat jet fighter than anywhere else on the planet." That's what Jake Ellzey told me. Both smart and cocky, Ellzey possessed the classic traits of a competitive fighter pilot. He grew up in the Texas Panhandle and was valedictorian of his high school class. After graduating from the U.S. Naval Academy, he honed his obsession to become a fighter pilot and ended up flying in the opening strike of the war in Tora Bora, Afghanistan, in November 2001.

The first fighter pilots I ever met were on the USS *Carl Vinson*, an aircraft carrier patrolling the Pacific Ocean in 2001. I sat in on a night briefing and was startled by how young the pilots were. The ship, longer than three football fields, had a crew of five thousand men and women who served to sharpen the "tip of the spear"—the hundred and twenty pilots on board. We went out on the flight deck in the freezing night, and I watched as each pilot climbed into a sixty-five-million-dollar F/A-18 Super Hornet to be catapulted off the deck at a hundred and fifty miles an hour in less than three seconds. But hurtling down the greasy, fuel-soaked flight deck and ascending into the dark sky for night maneuvers was nothing compared to the challenge of returning to the carrier. That was the tricky part—the dangerous, nerve-wracking return to the carrier, which pilots say looks like a postage stamp being tossed on a black, tumultuous sea.

Some fighter pilots are quiet, some are cocky, and some are women, but all are extraordinary. They form a group of highly intelligent, aggressive, quick-thinking, athletic perfectionists. They are, generally, firstborns with strong father figures. They tend to avoid introspection. They think of themselves as invulnerable. Imagine the nerve necessary to enjoy the thrill of a thirty-five-hundred-foot dive at five hundred miles an hour, necessitating a hundredth of a second reaction time with no margin of error. When I visited the naval air station at Fallon, Nevada, I saw these fighter pilots horsing around at the Officers' Club. In the evenings they sat around the bar, drinking and joking and blowing off steam by recounting their exploits, bragging about who "shacked the target" and who "John Wayned his strafing run." They bonded—members of an elite brotherhood.

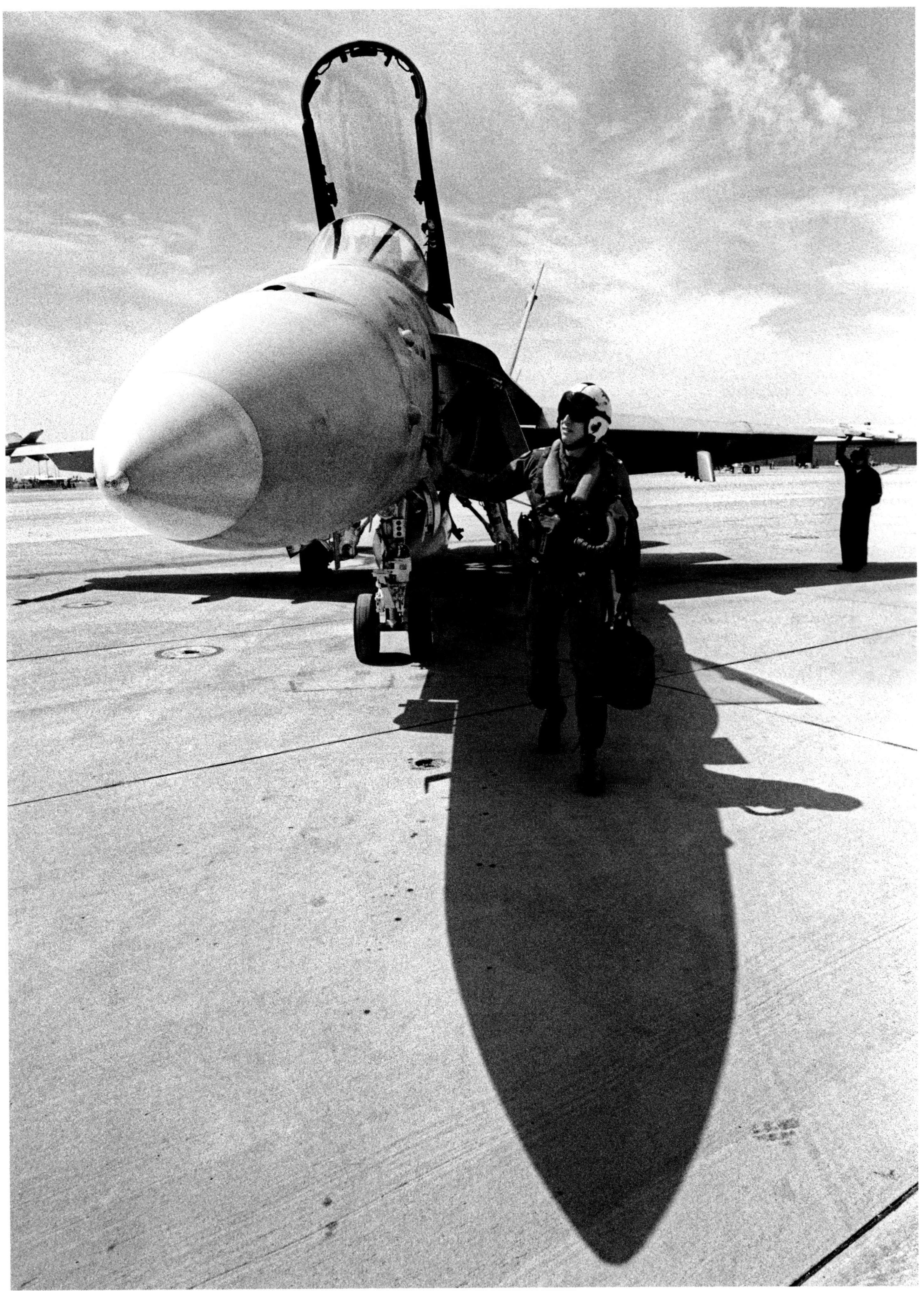

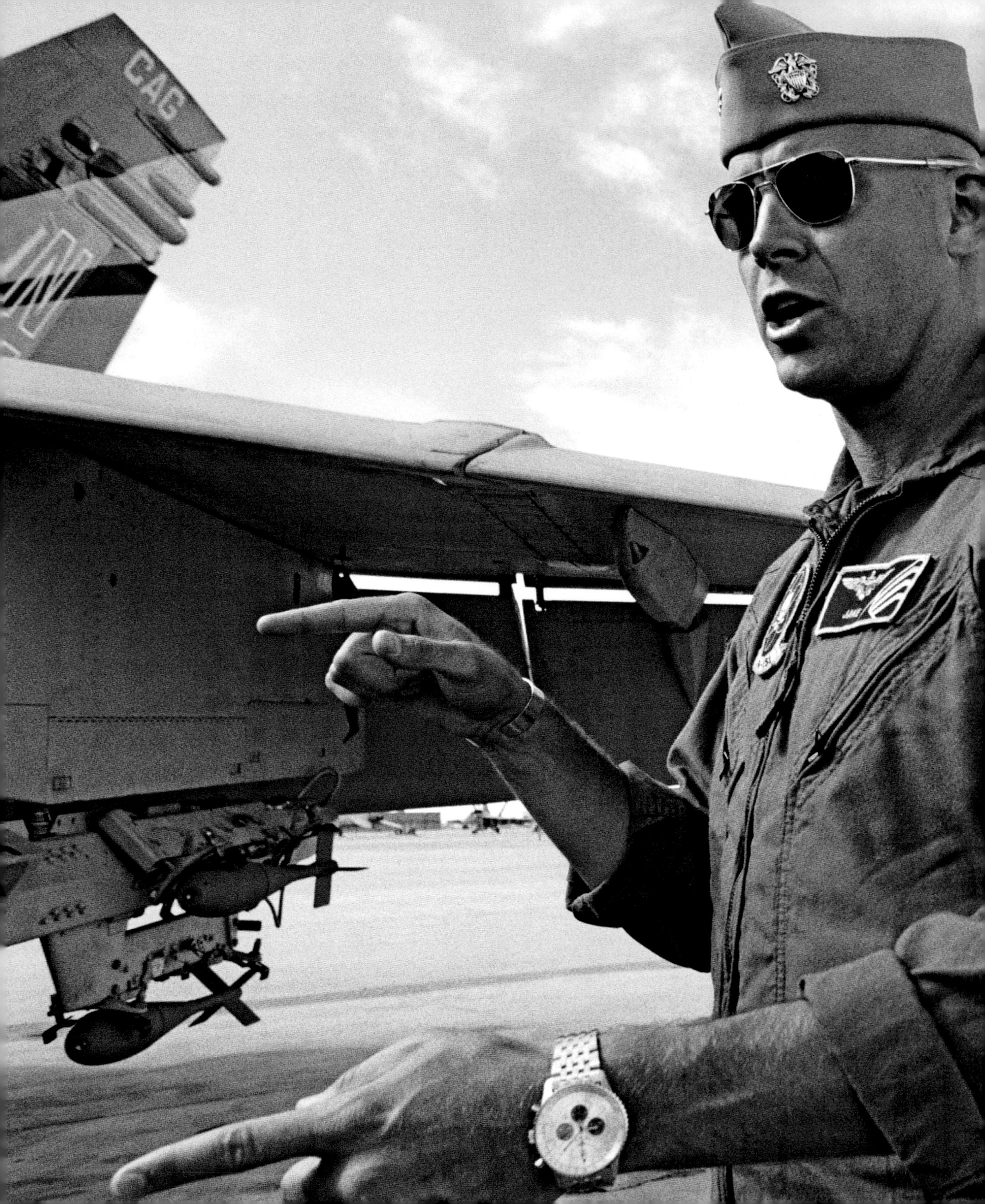
CAG

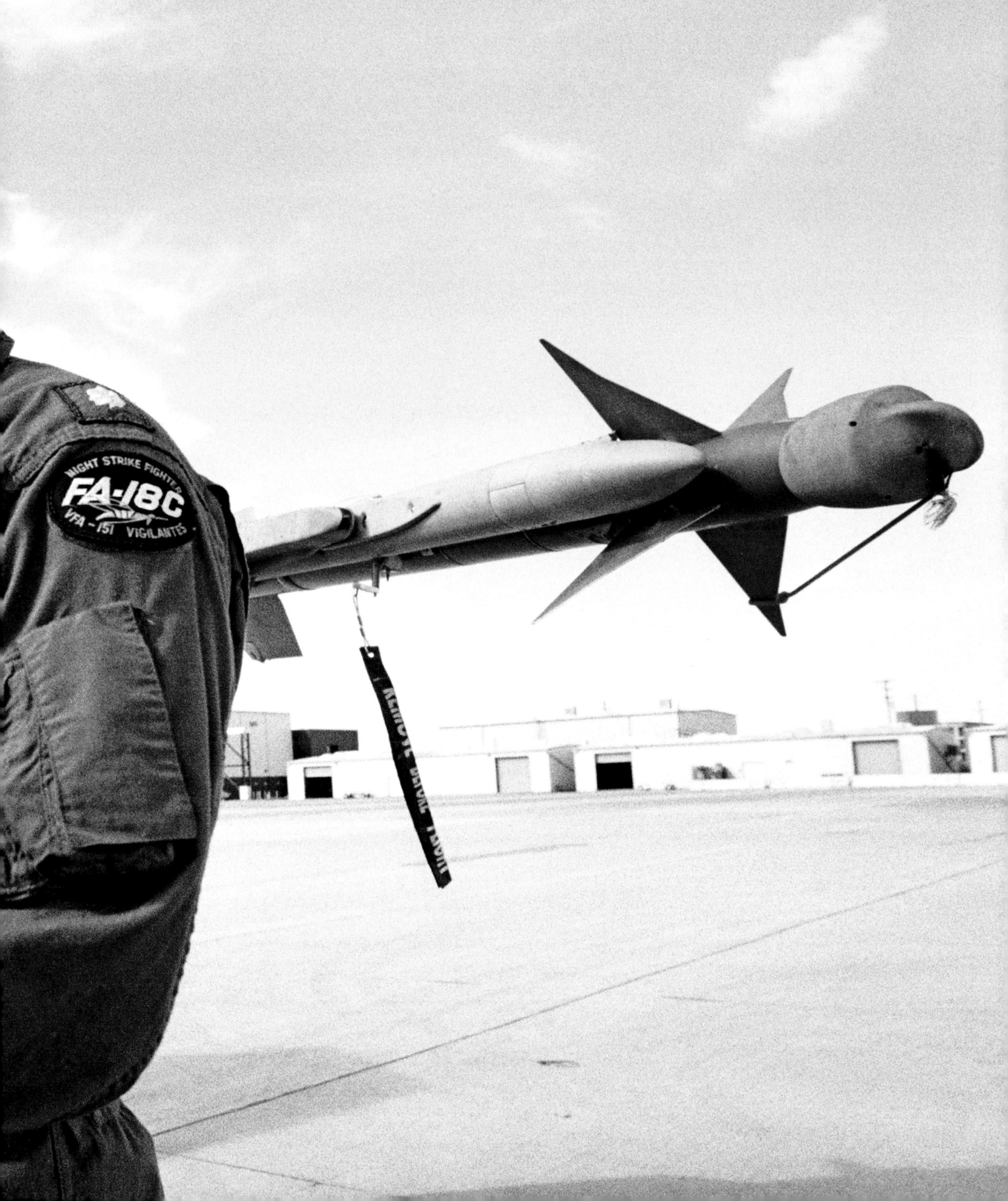
NIGHT STRIKE FIGHTER
FA-18C
VFA-151 VIGILANTES

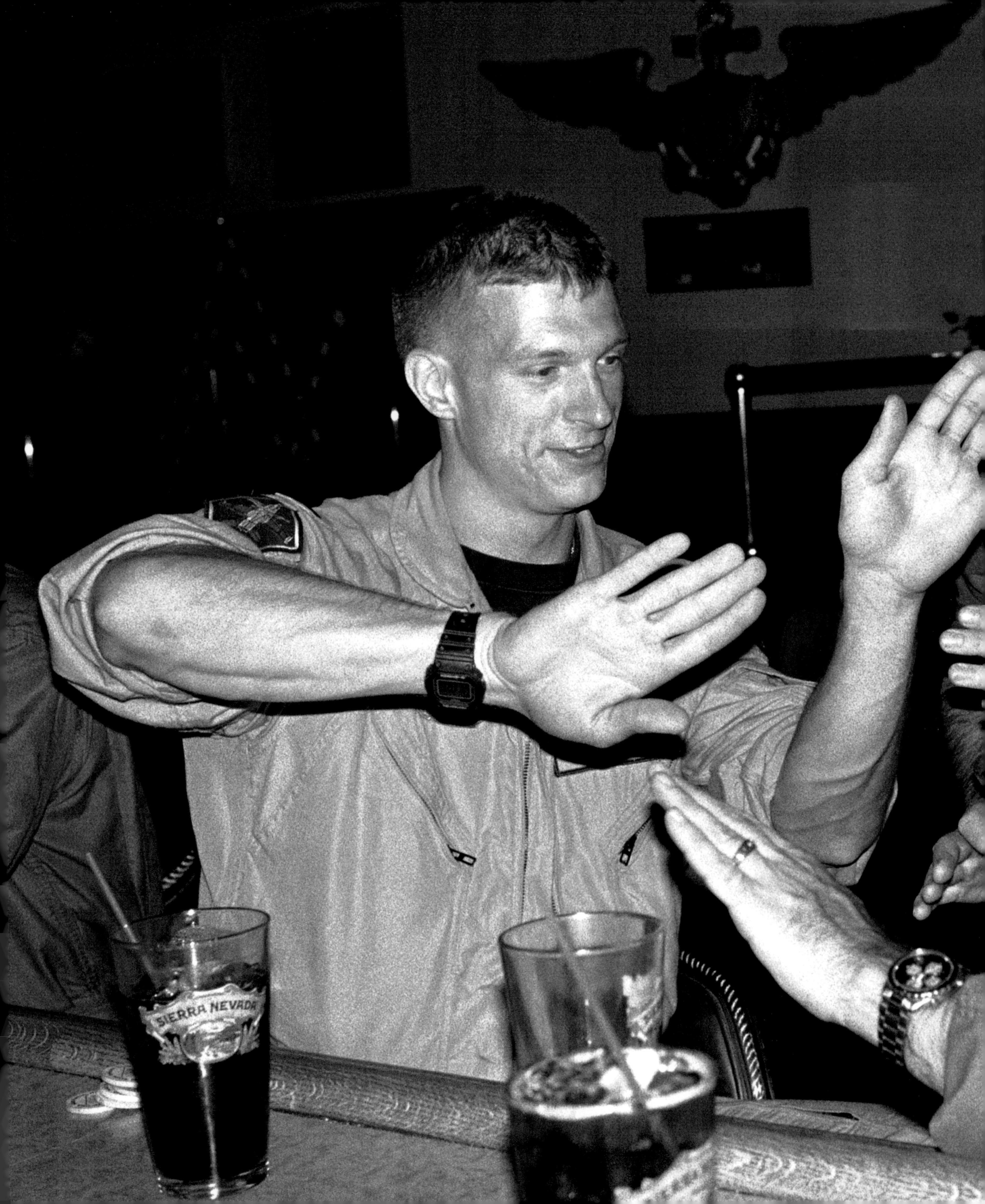
SIERRA NEVADA

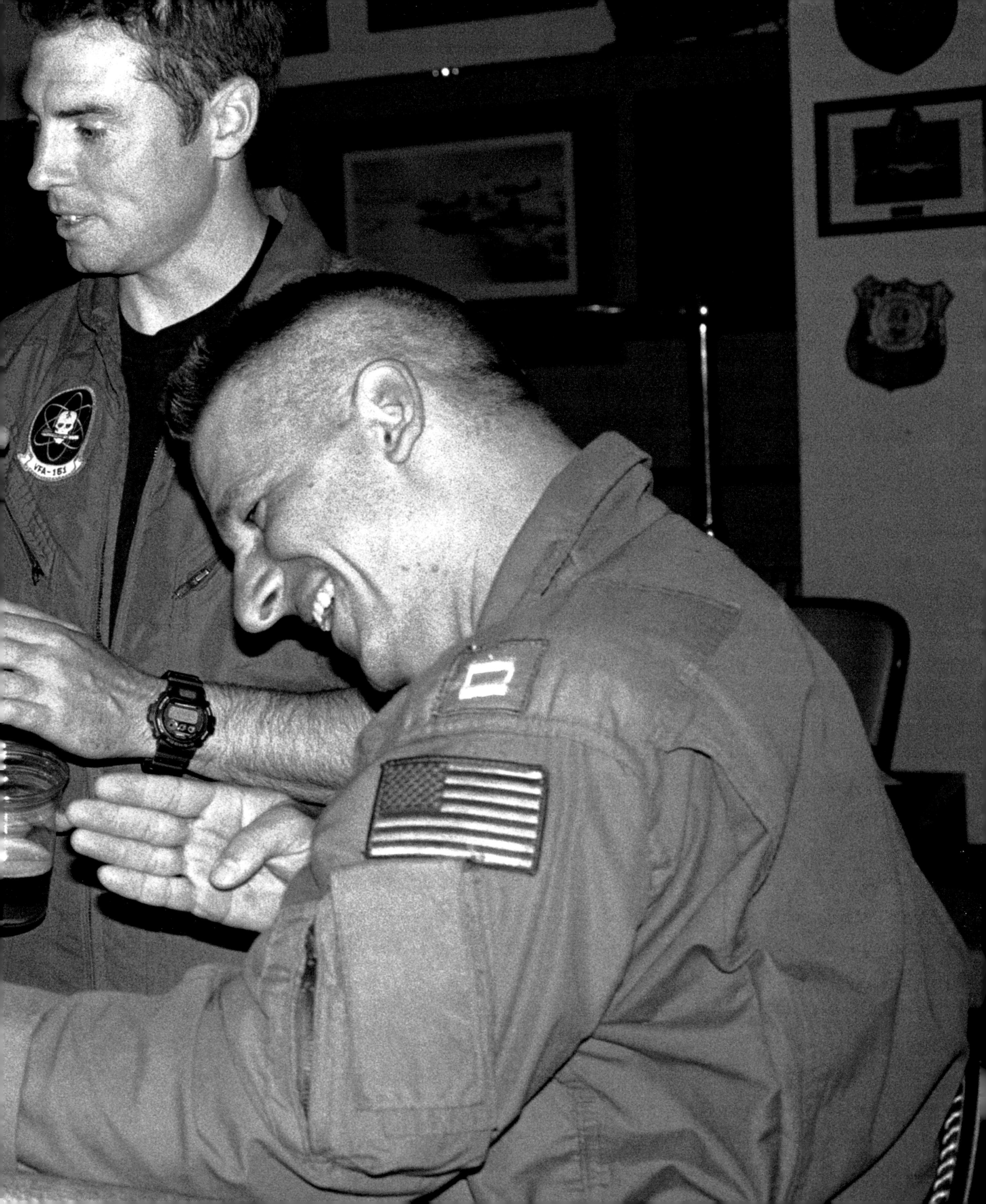

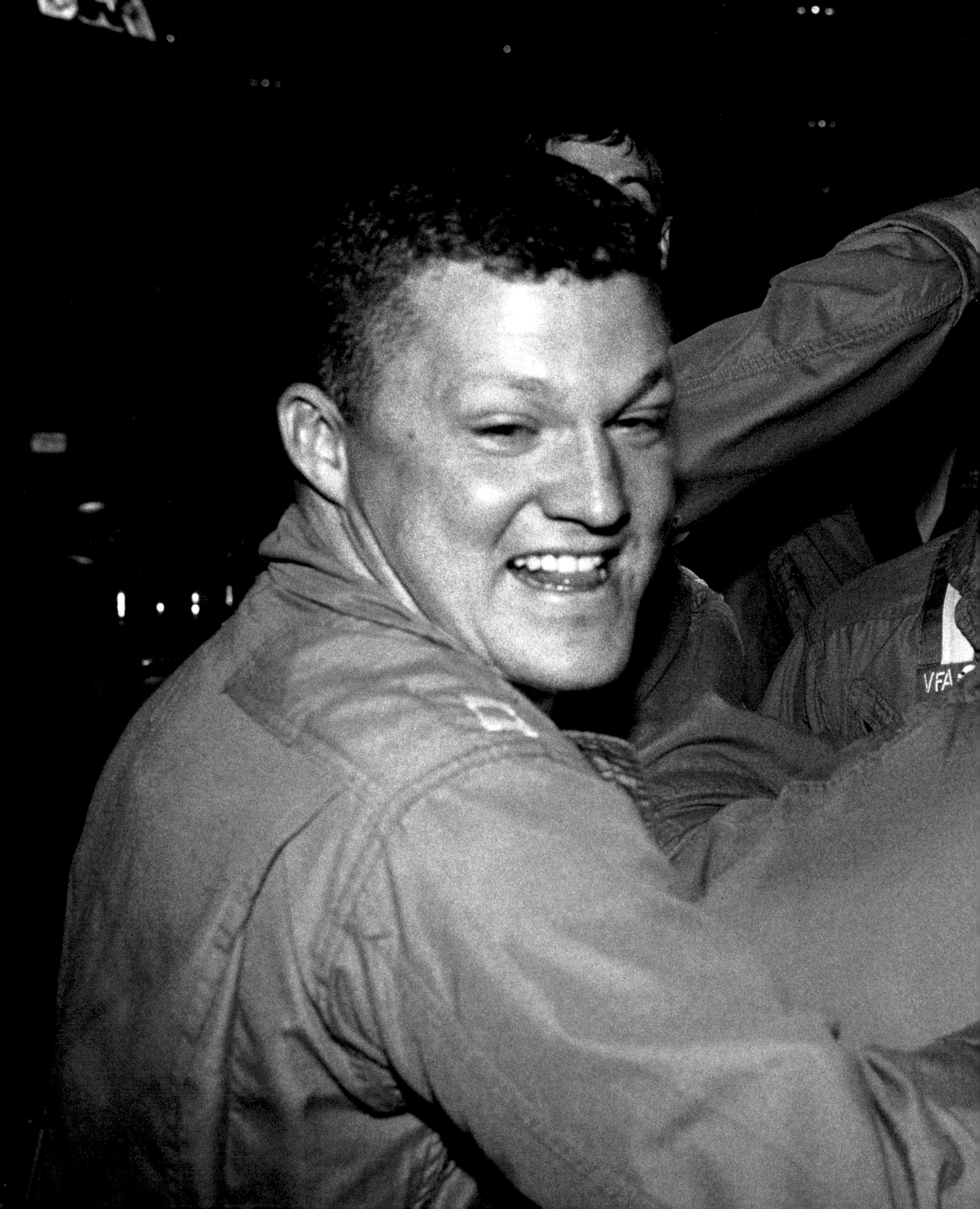
VFA

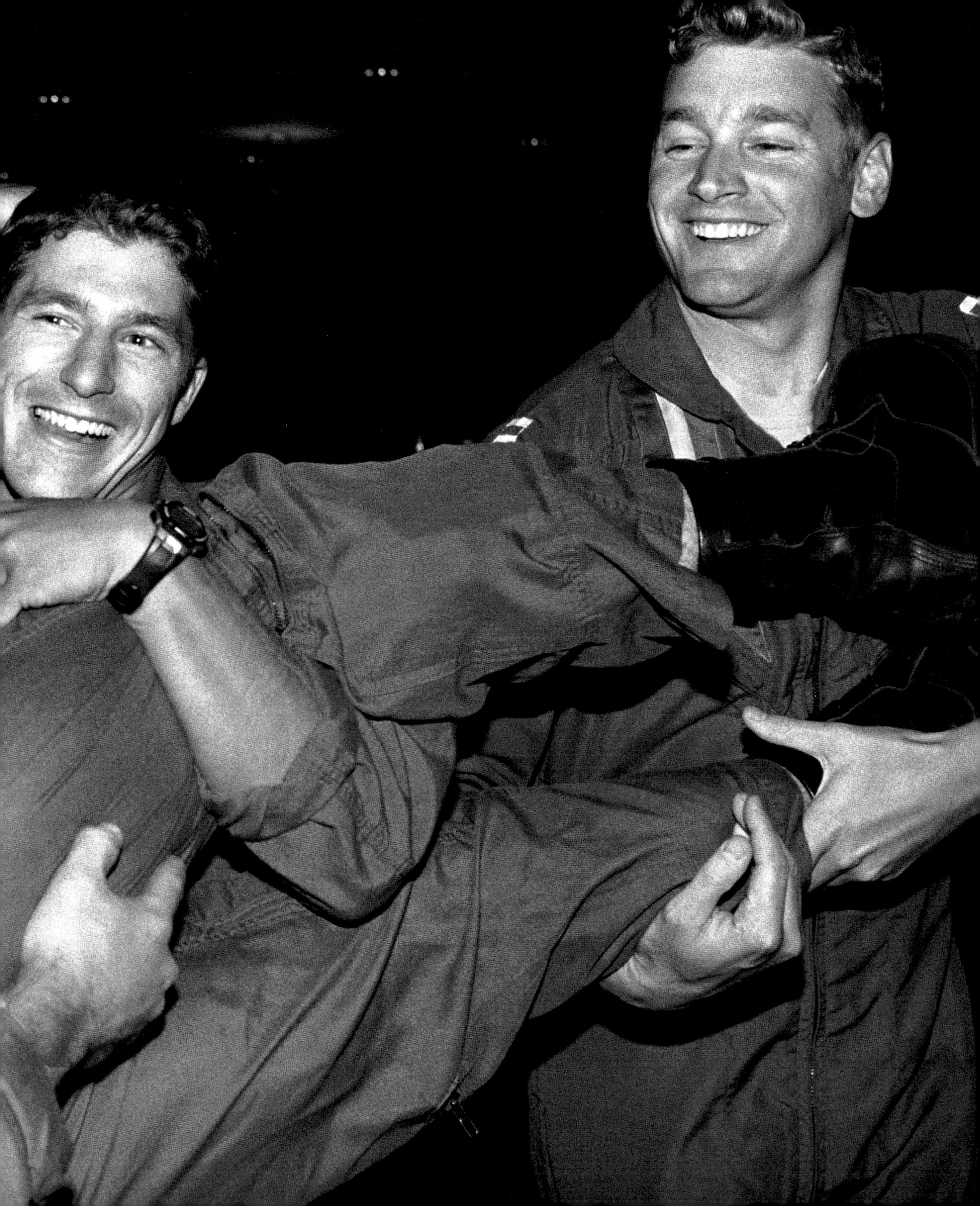

Cockfighting

WEBB COUNTY, TEXAS
MAY 12, 1994

The vicious and illegal sport of cockfighting is thriving among furtive, tight-knit groups of people in rural Texas and Oklahoma. It's now against the law to own birds with the intent to fight them. Even to possess the gaffs and spurs used as weapons on a bird's legs is a legal offense. For a fight, two roosters that have been bred for the ring are fitted with the razor-sharp steel gaffs designed to slice, puncture, and mutilate. The birds are often drugged to heighten their aggression. The carefully vetted spectators yell out their bets before the birds are tossed into battle, where they fight to the death in an enclosure from which they cannot escape.

On July 2, 1994, I drove north from Dallas across the Red River to a farm near Ardmore, Oklahoma. At that time, cockfighting was still legal in the state. I had learned of the fight and its location when a man from South Texas invited me to photograph him and his birds over a two-day period. When I arrived at the Oklahoma farm, I found the man next to his pickup. He was cordial, friendly even, as he tended to his birds. Without my cameras, I walked around the large field, looking at all the people arriving in trucks with their roosters in plywood boxes. It was a social event. Beer and soft drinks were for sale. I headed into a barn where the cockfighting was taking place. Immediately, I was stopped at the door, questioned, and taken to a small room in another building. Two tough locals continued the questioning. The atmosphere was hostile. Who was I working for? Was I a reporter? If not, why was I there? I told them that the man from South Texas had invited me. He was called into the room. "Do you know her?" he was asked. "No, I've never seen her," the man replied. My wallet was searched. My camera bag was searched. I was not allowed to leave. An hour passed. More questions. The sheriff was called. A deputy arrived to remove me from "private property" and escort me across the field, now packed with vehicles, to my car. In my notes for that day, I wrote, "disaster trip to cockfight in Oklahoma."

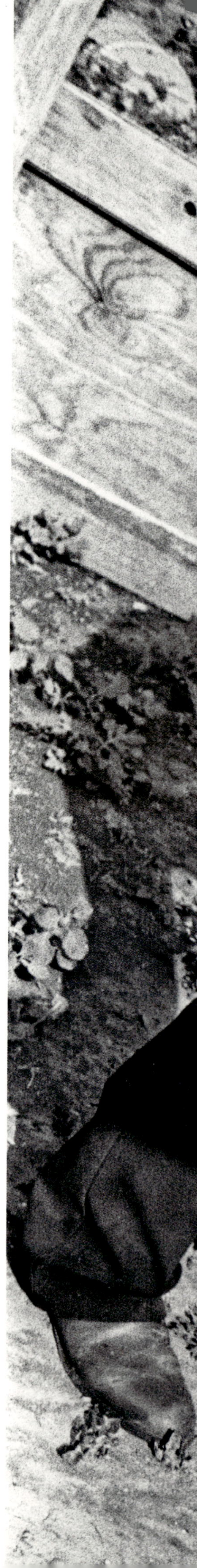

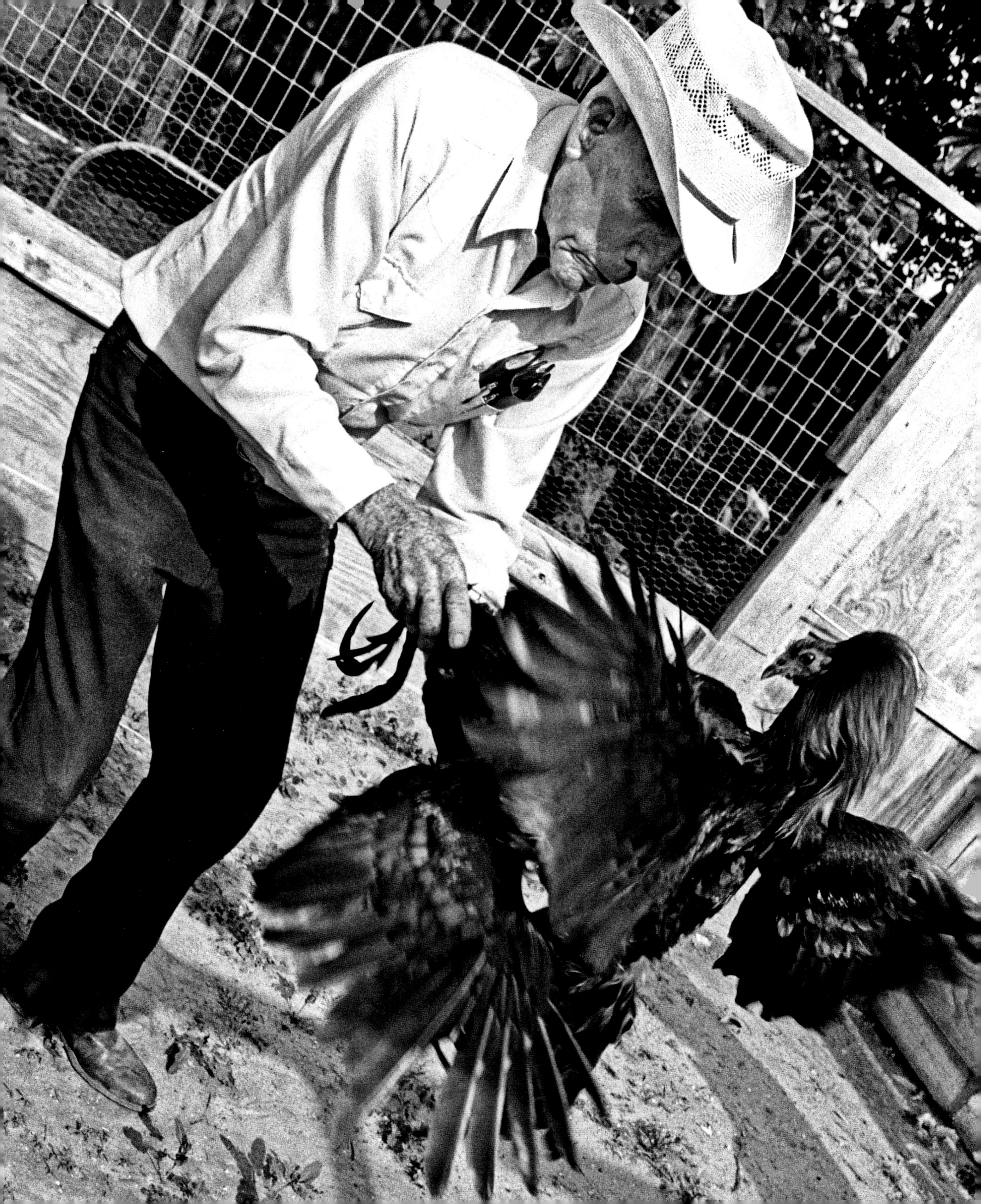

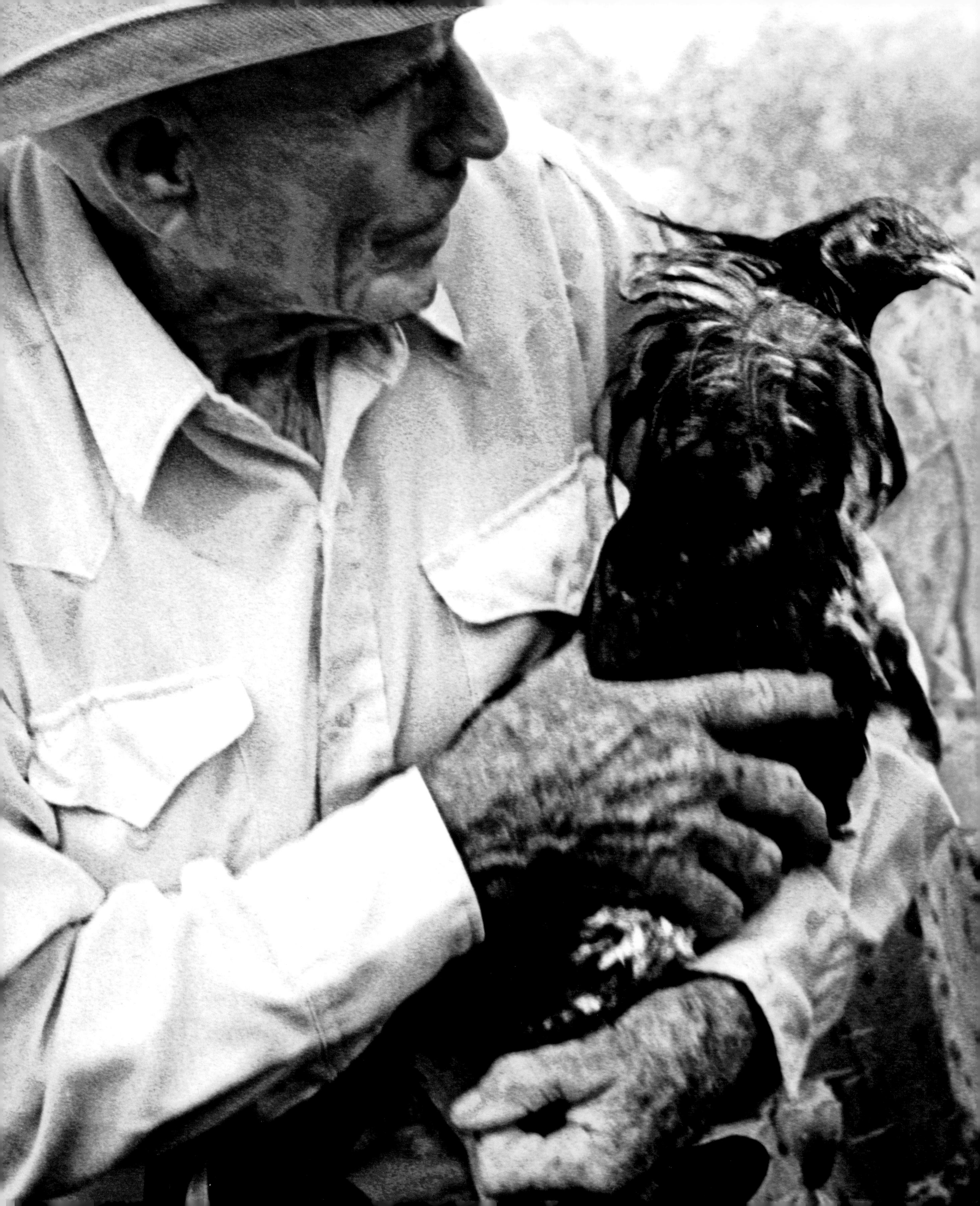

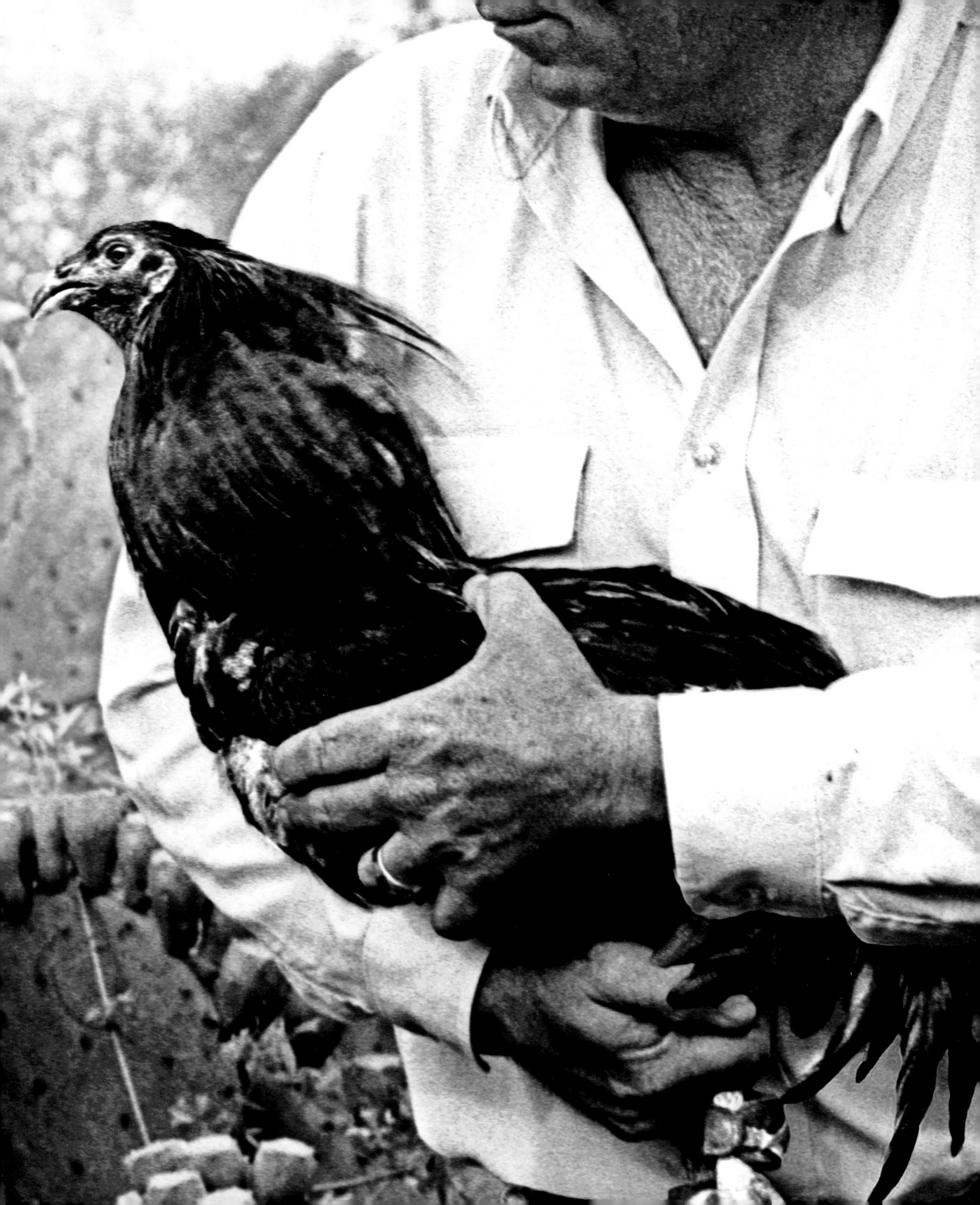

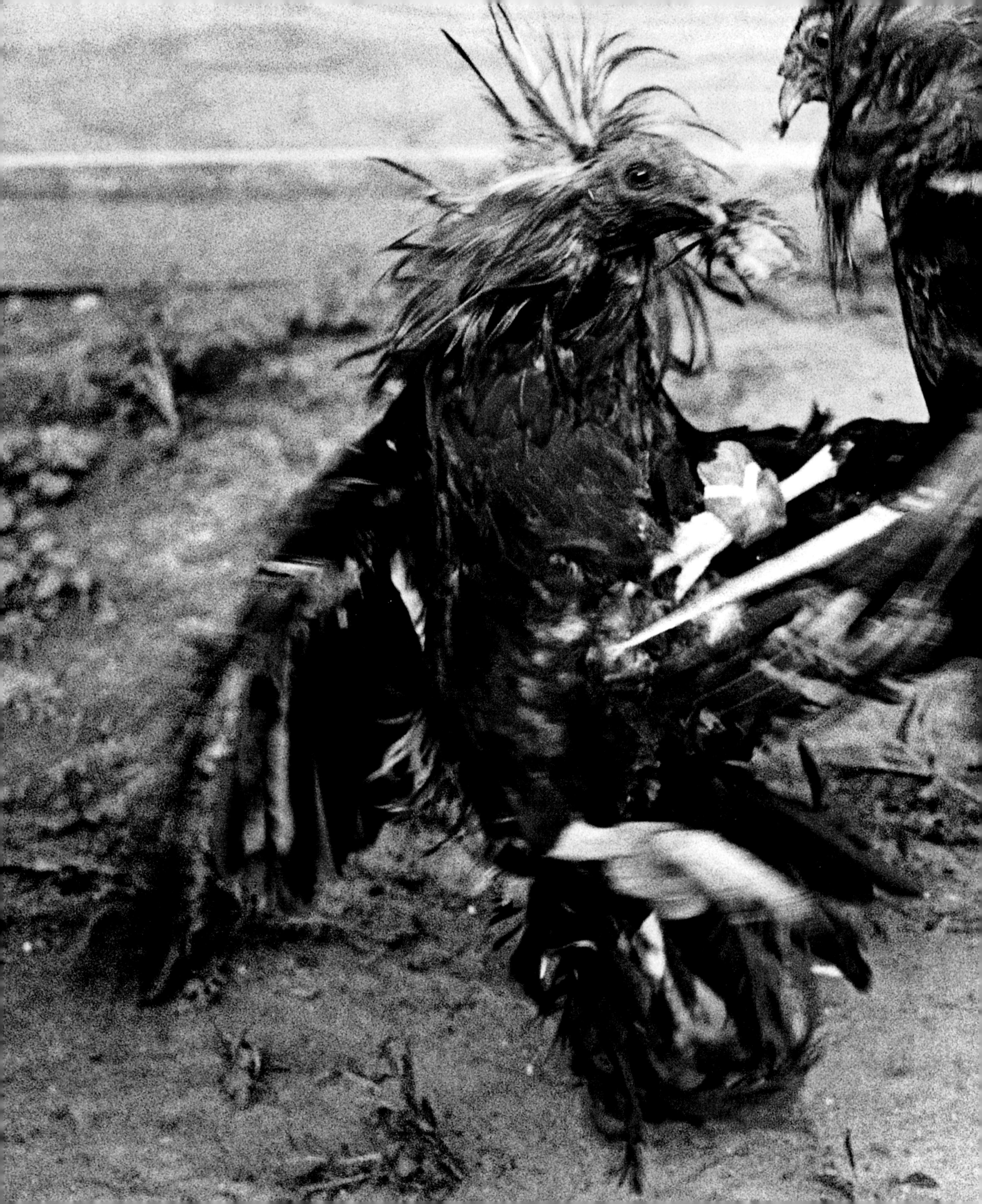

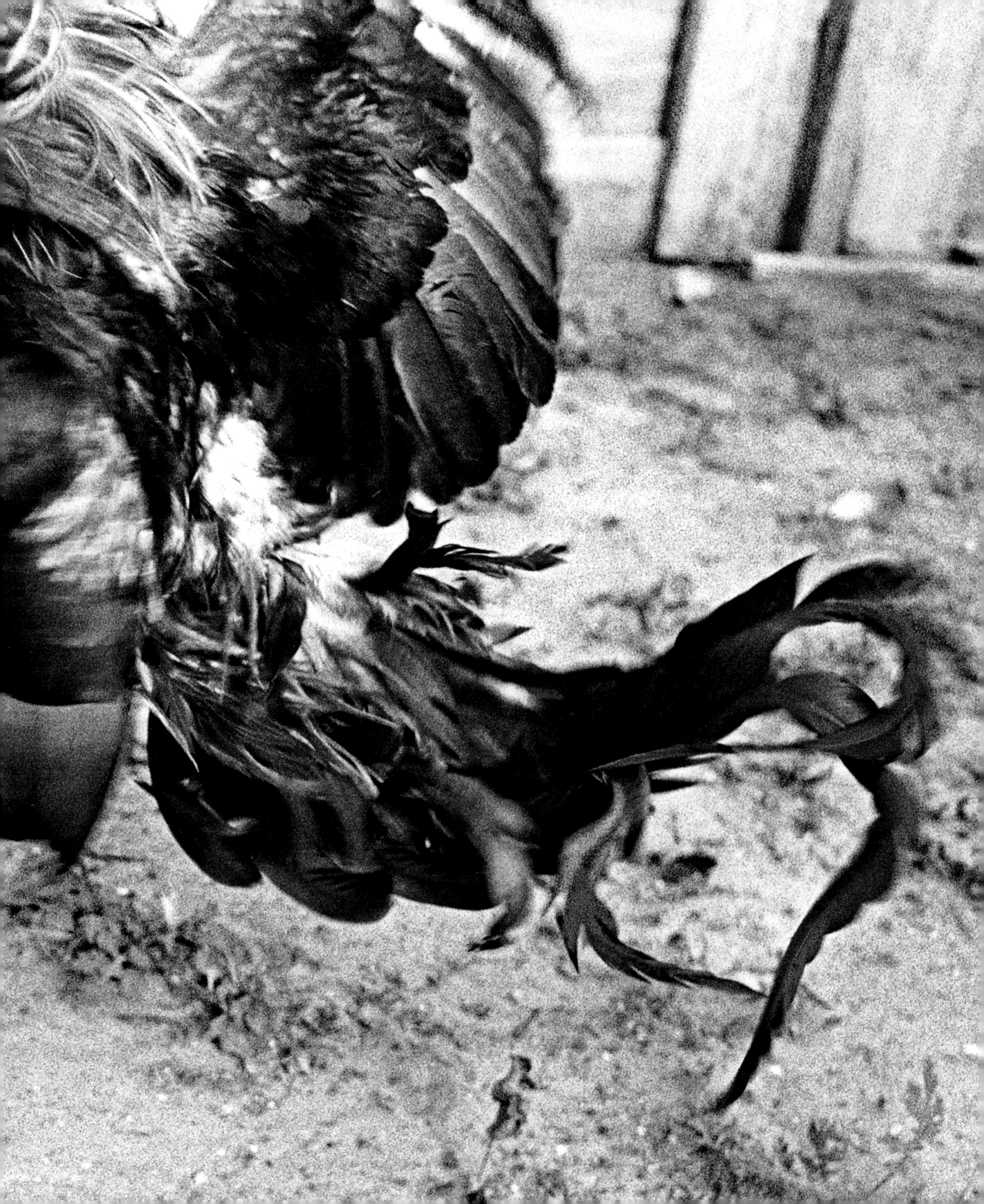

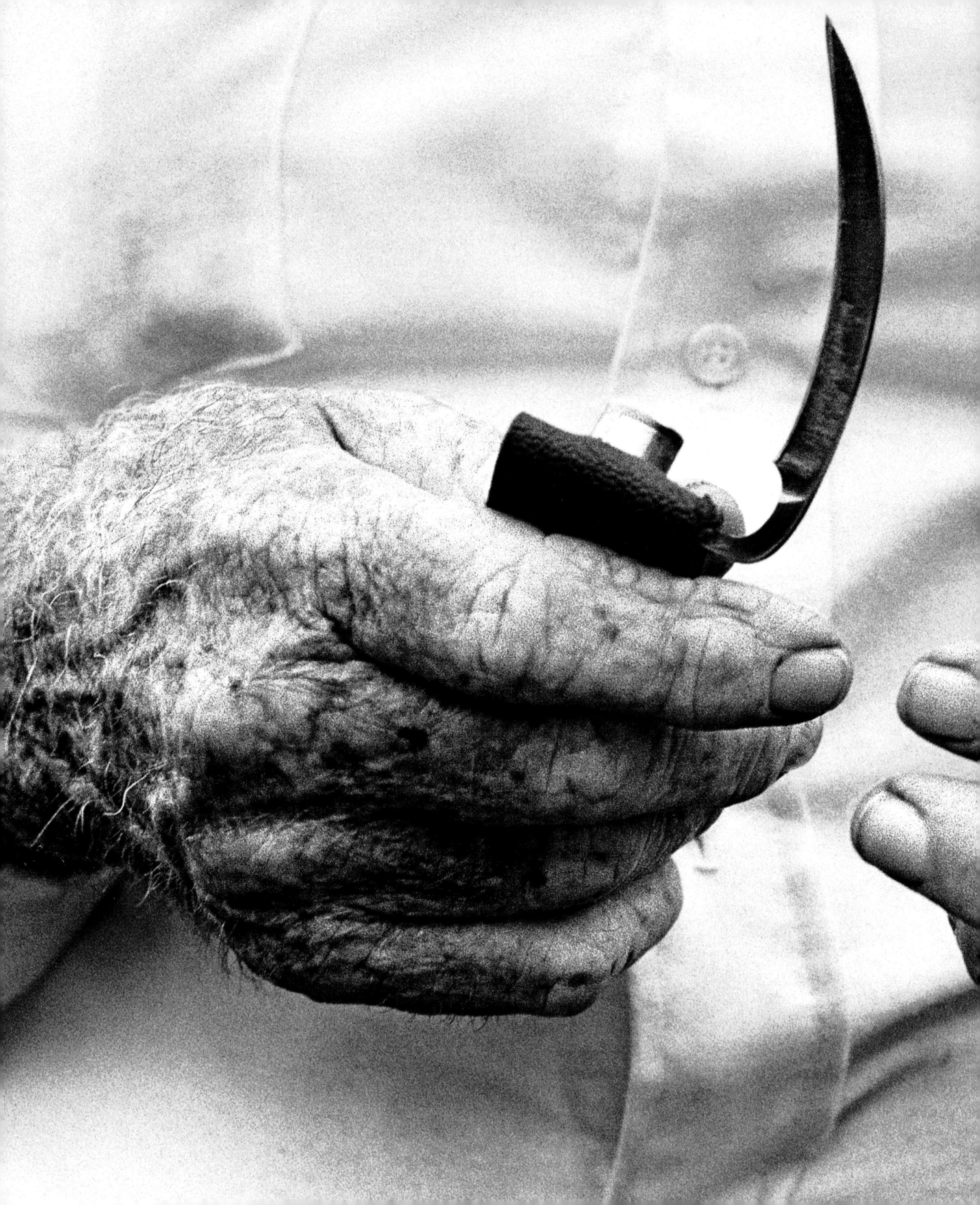

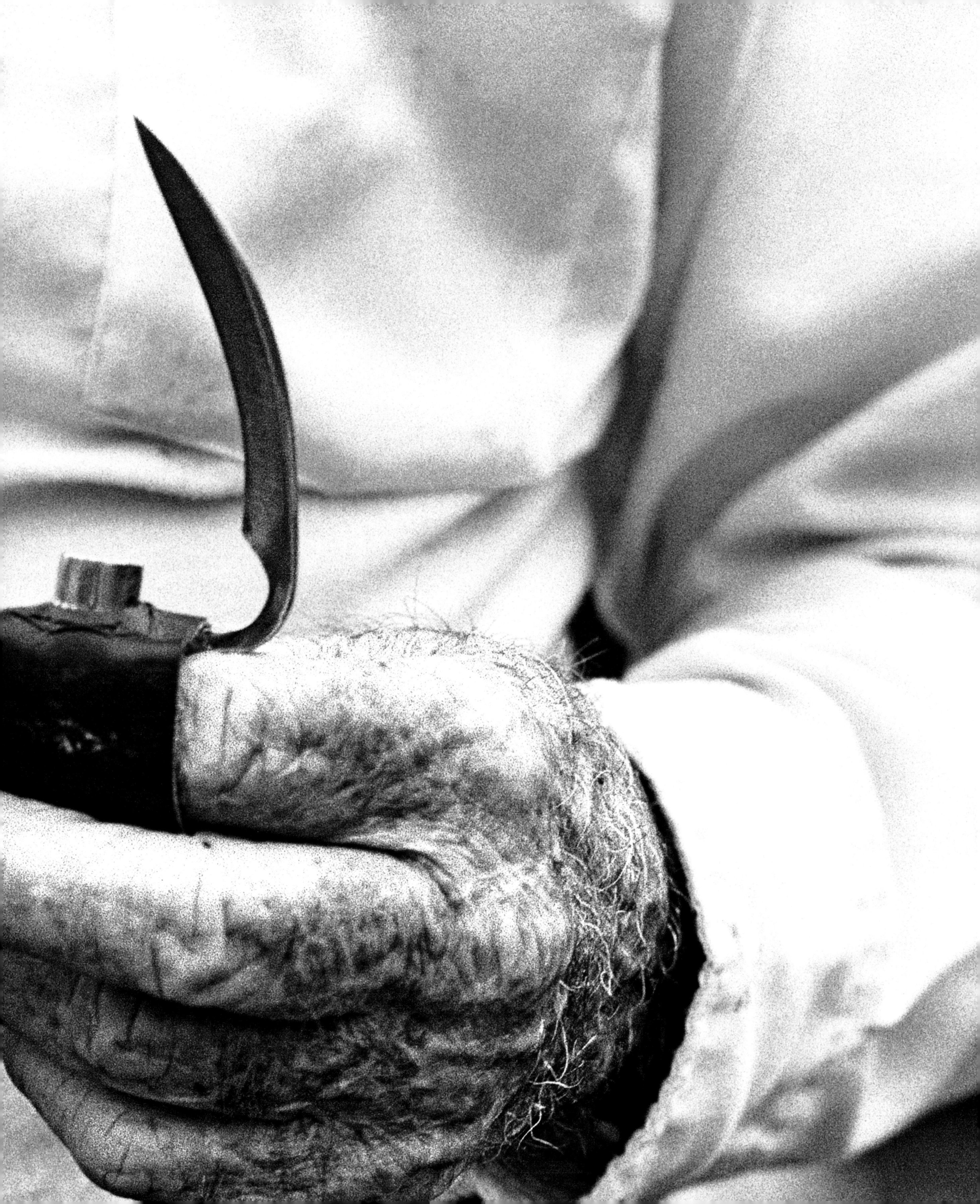

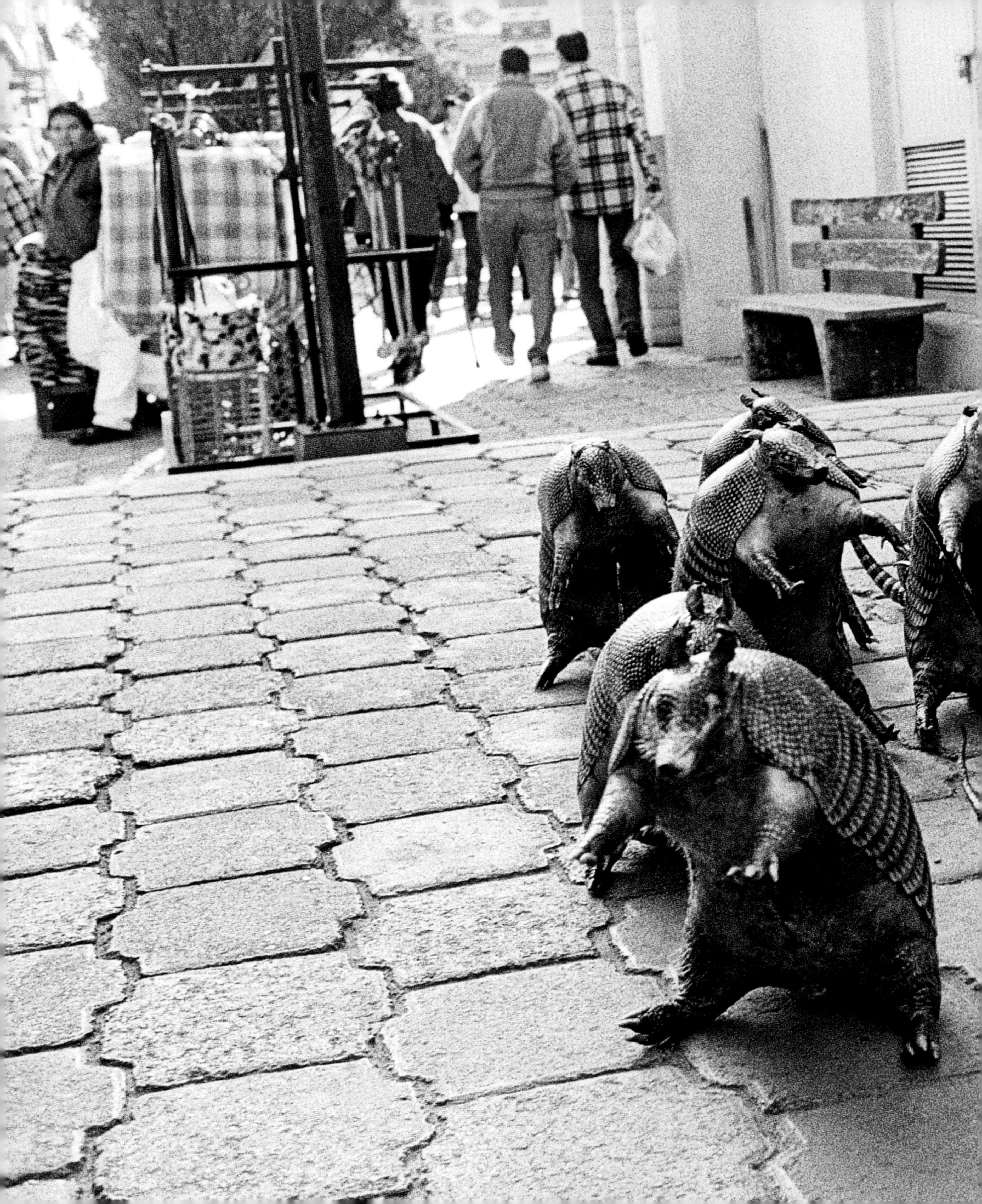

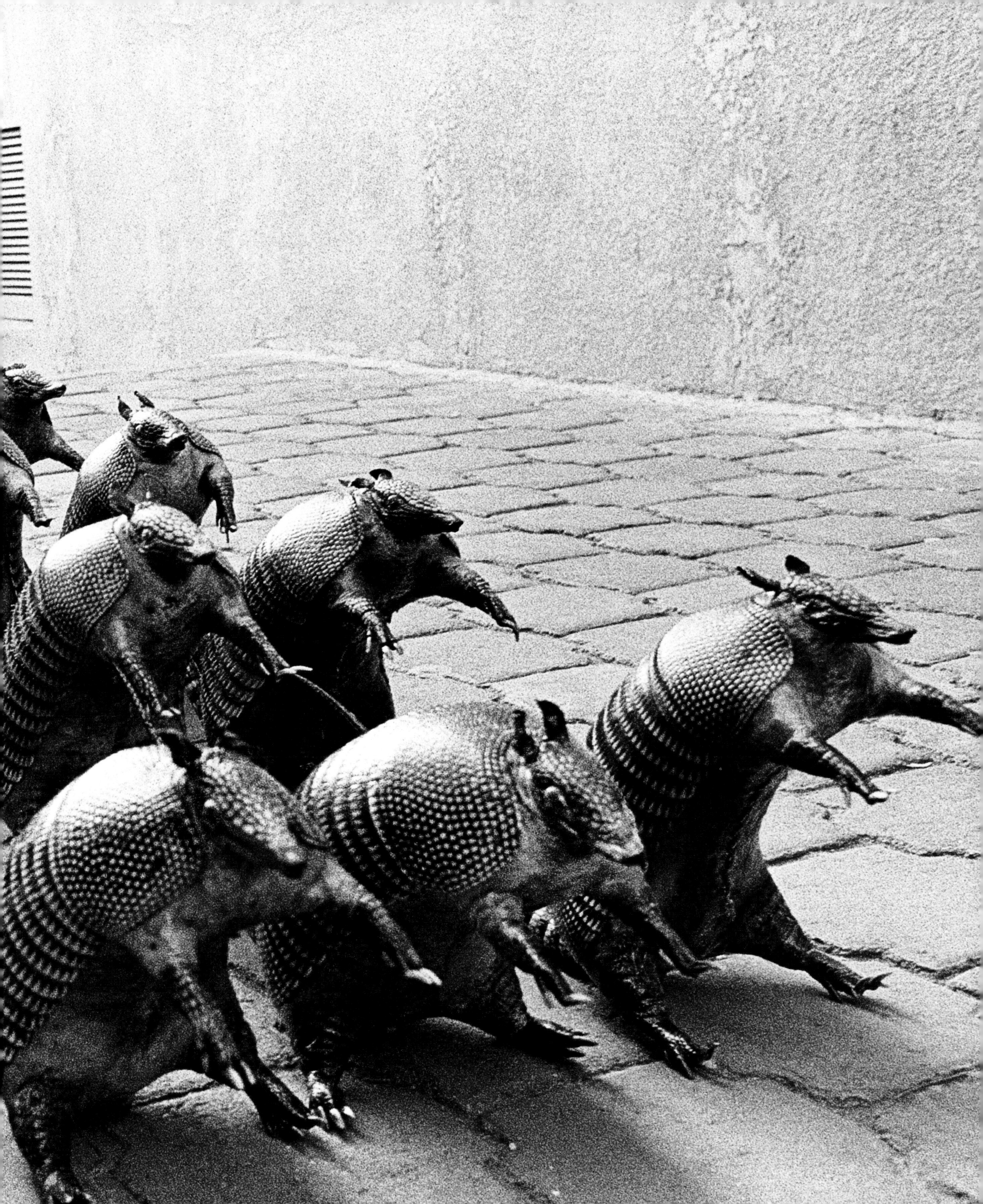

How can life on the border be other than reckless? You are pulled by different ties of love and hate.

—Graham Greene, English novelist, 1904–1991

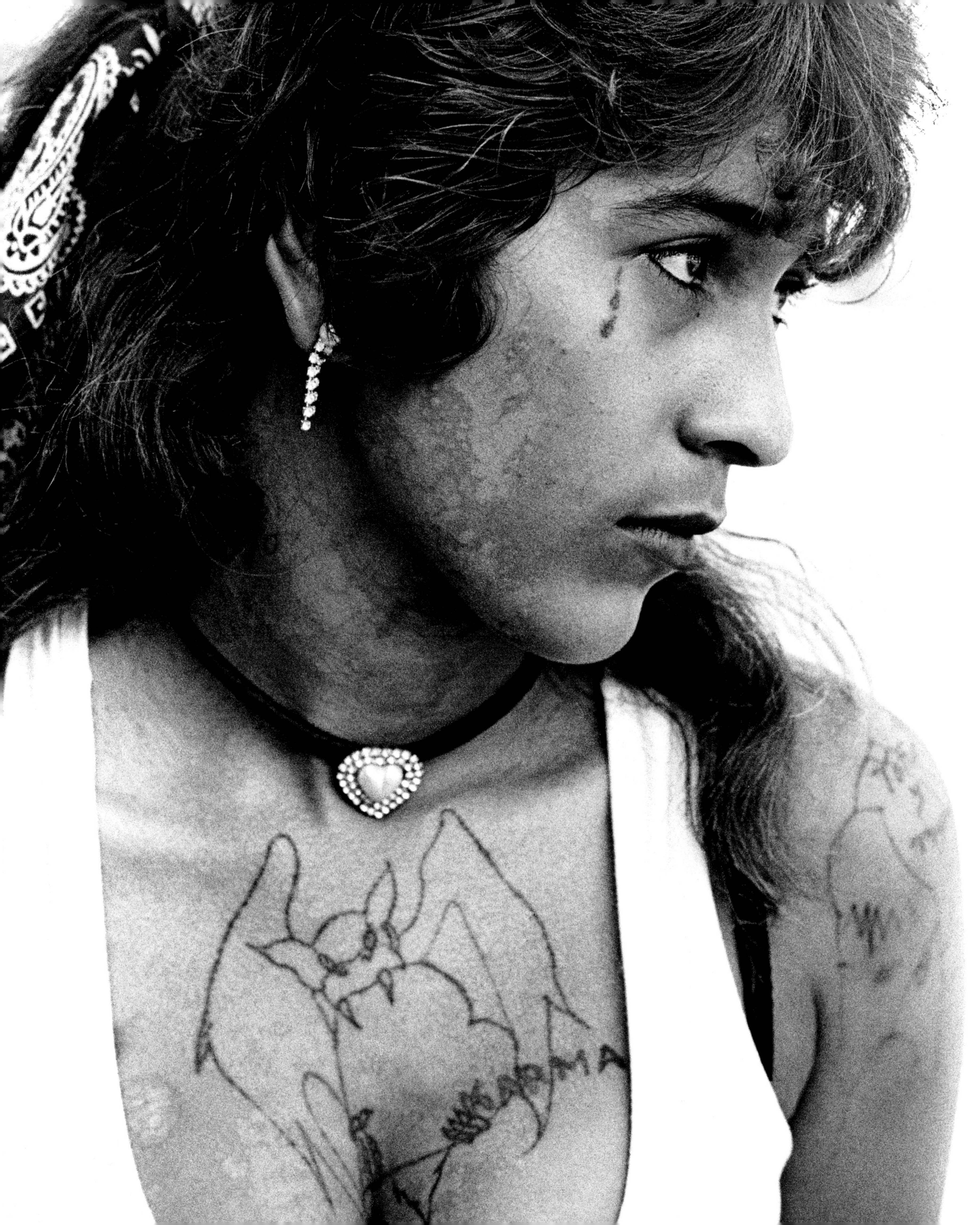

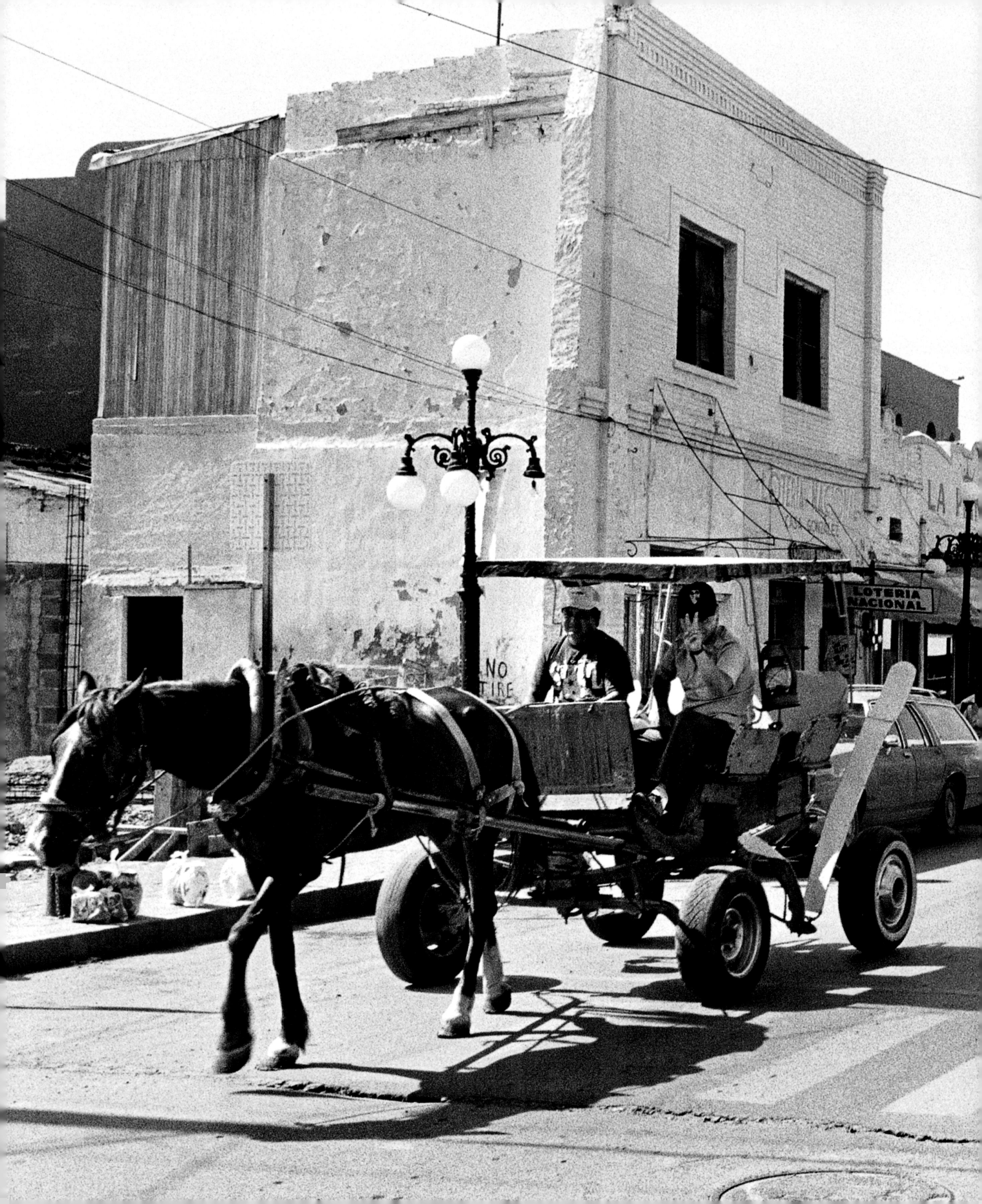
NO
TIRE
LOTERIA
NACIONAL

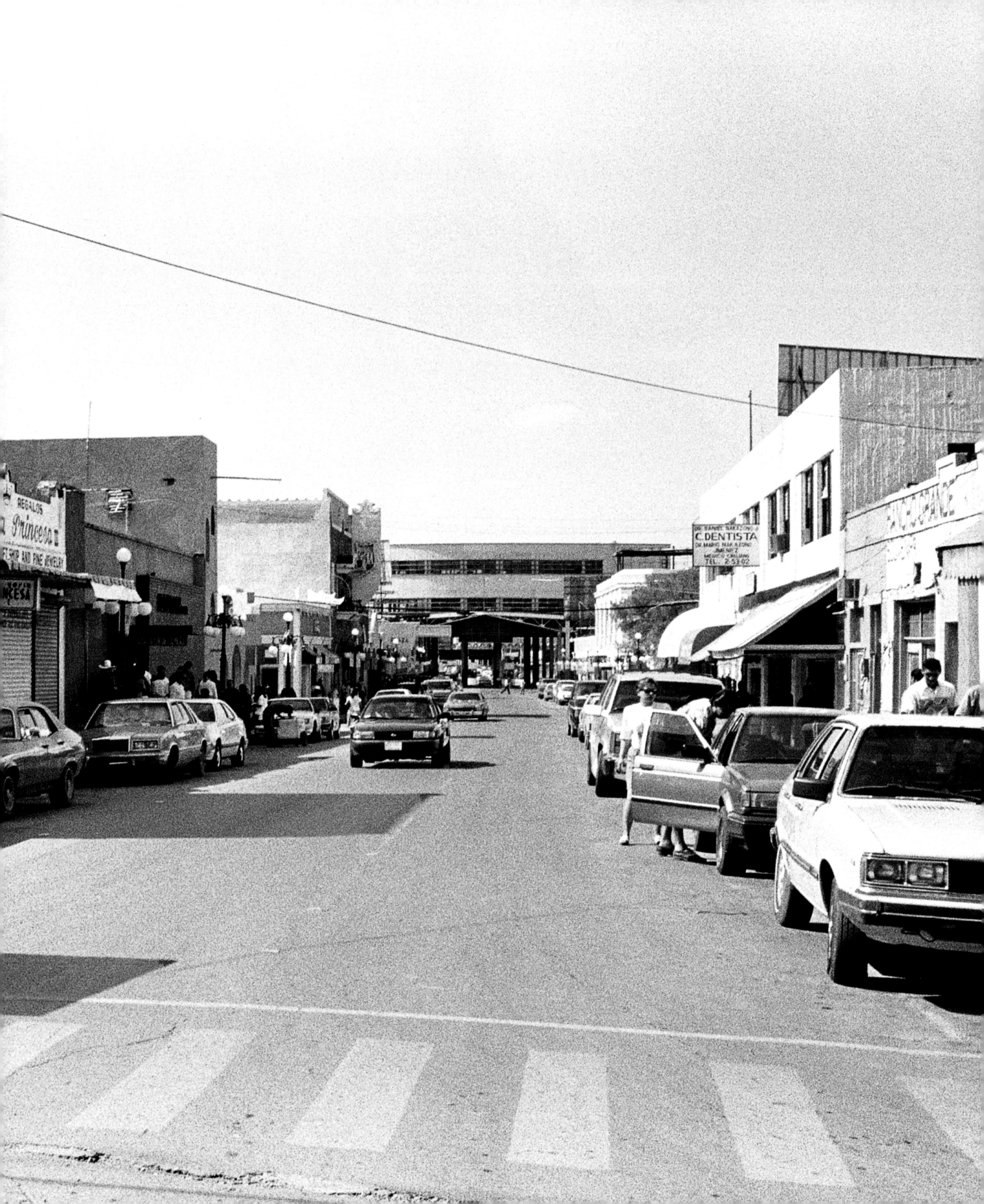
REGALOS
Princesa
AND FINE JEWELRY
C. DENTISTA
TEL. 2-53-02

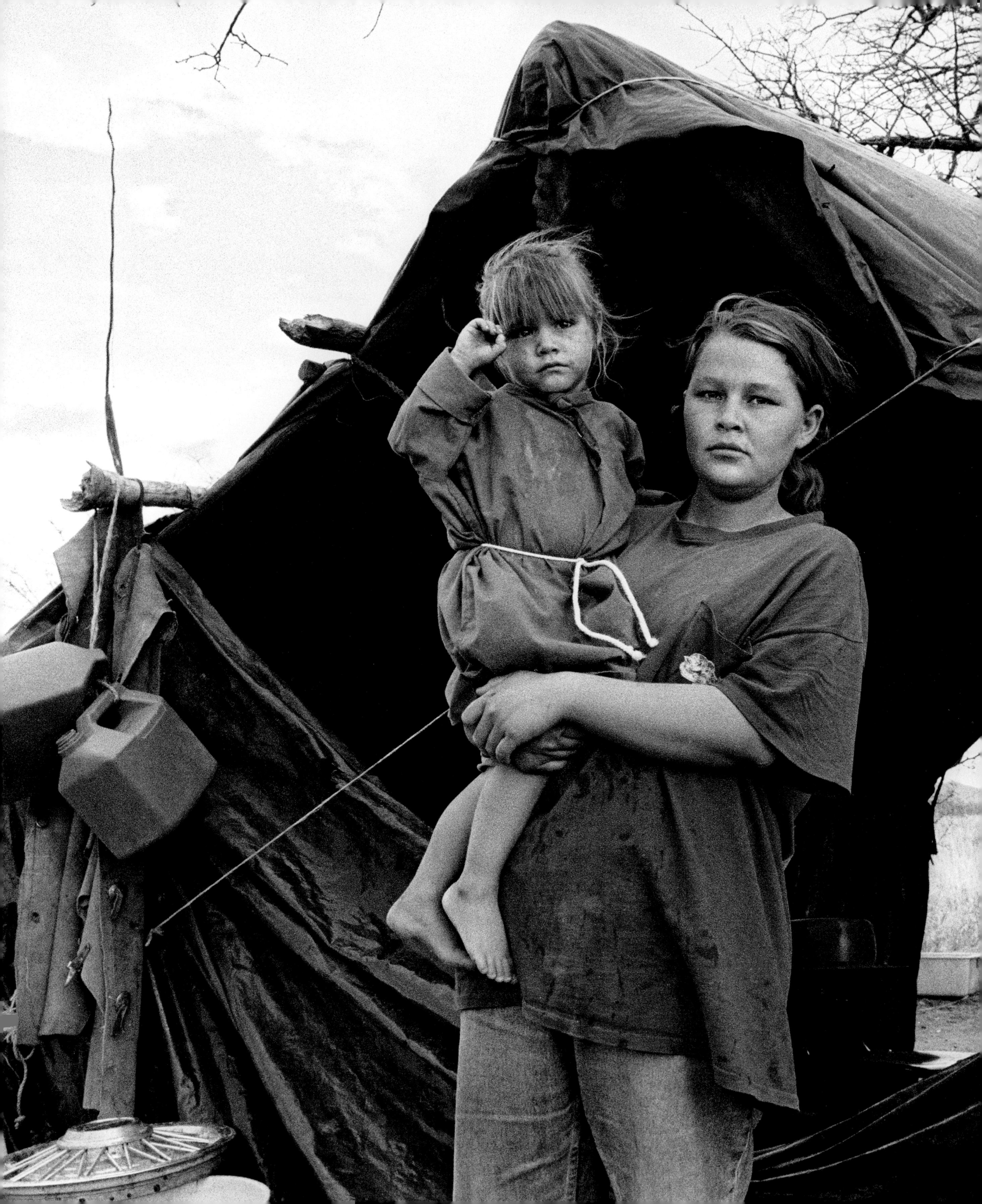

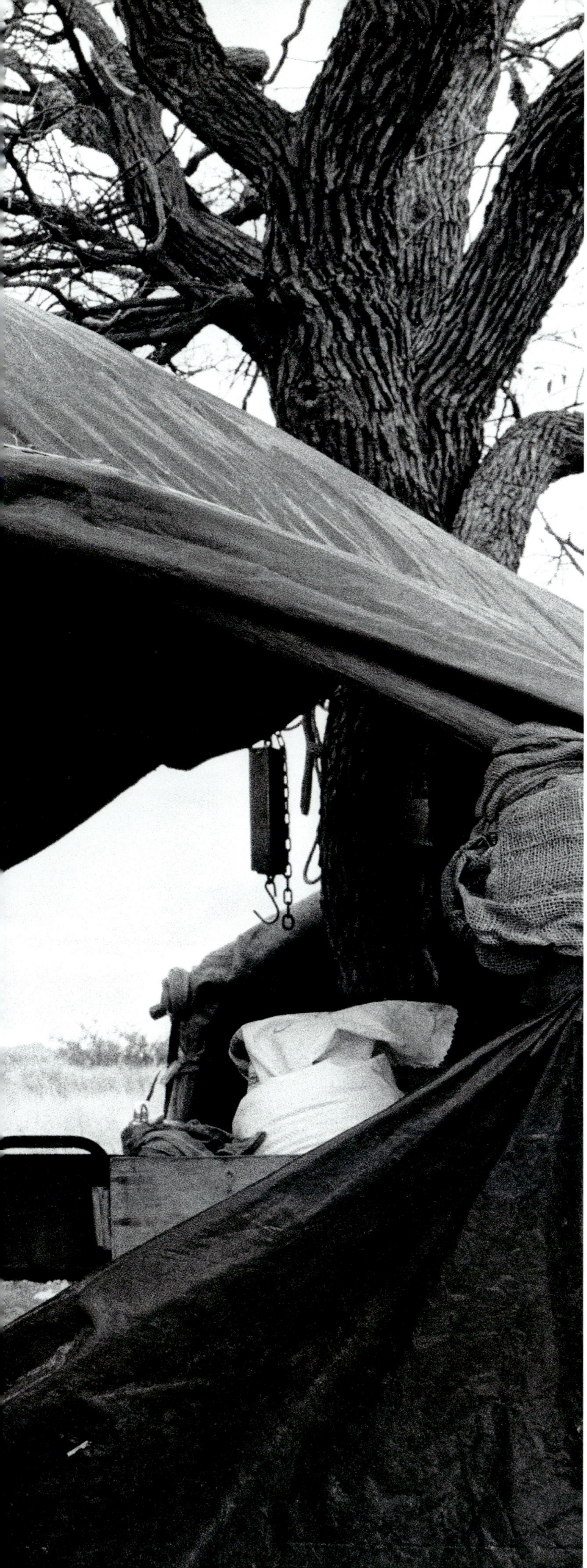

Border Camp

SONORA, MEXICO
JUNE 30, 2000

In the late afternoon, we came upon a camp of *palmilleros*—men who cut beargrass on border ranches in Arizona and in Sonora, Mexico. Mexicans call this fat, heavy grass *palmilla* or *sacahuista* and gather it to make brooms or chair seats. For hundreds of years, Indians used the thick grass to make fires because it burns hot and slowly. The day we stopped to visit with them, the men were gathering beargrass for a big broom factory in Sonora. This young woman was cooking for them.

Today, the palmilleros have all but disappeared, bringing an end to a form of manual labor for many poor people. A trade that once meant sustenance for generations has died out. The brooms and chair seats are now, for the most part, made of plastic.

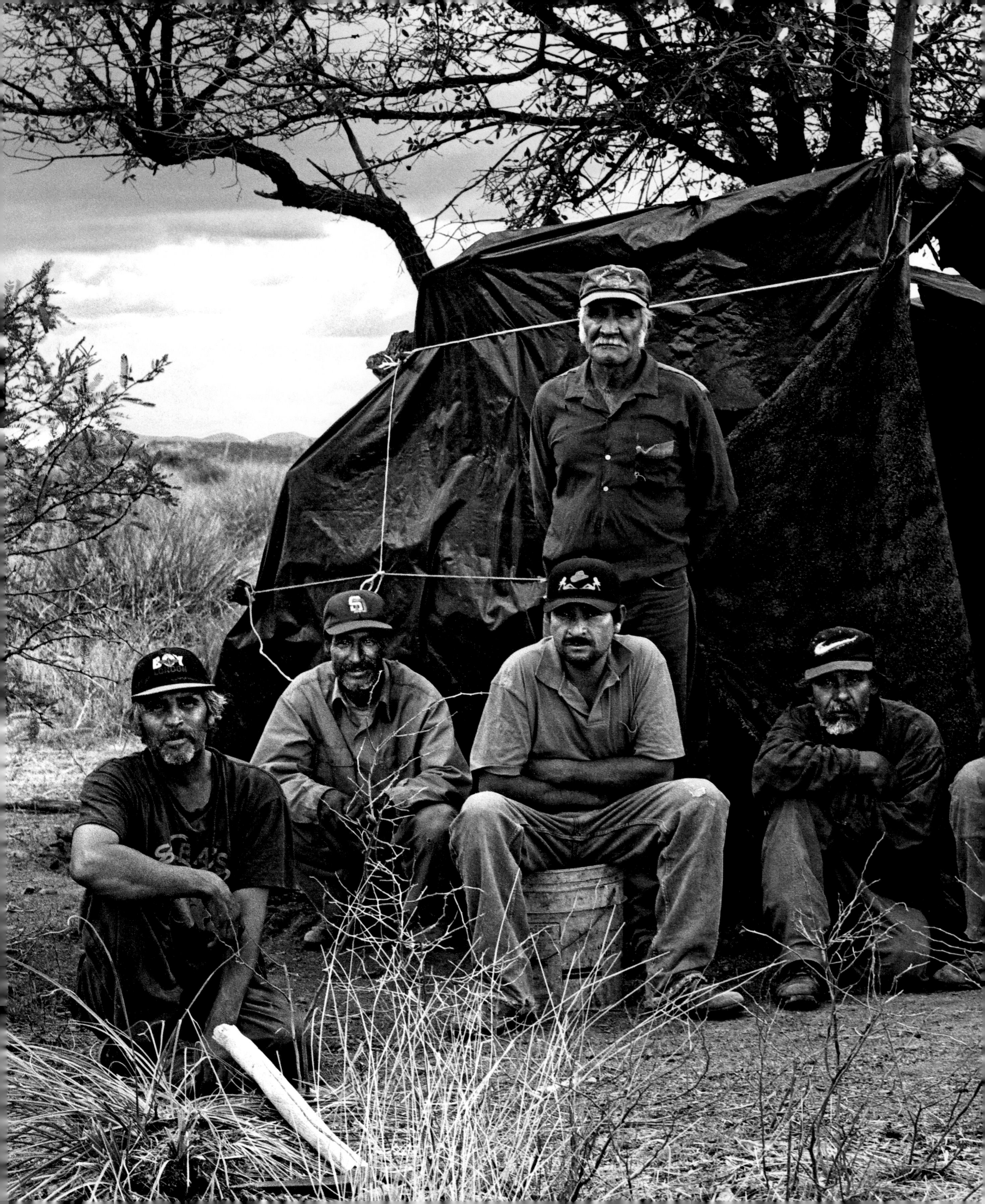
BOY
LONDON

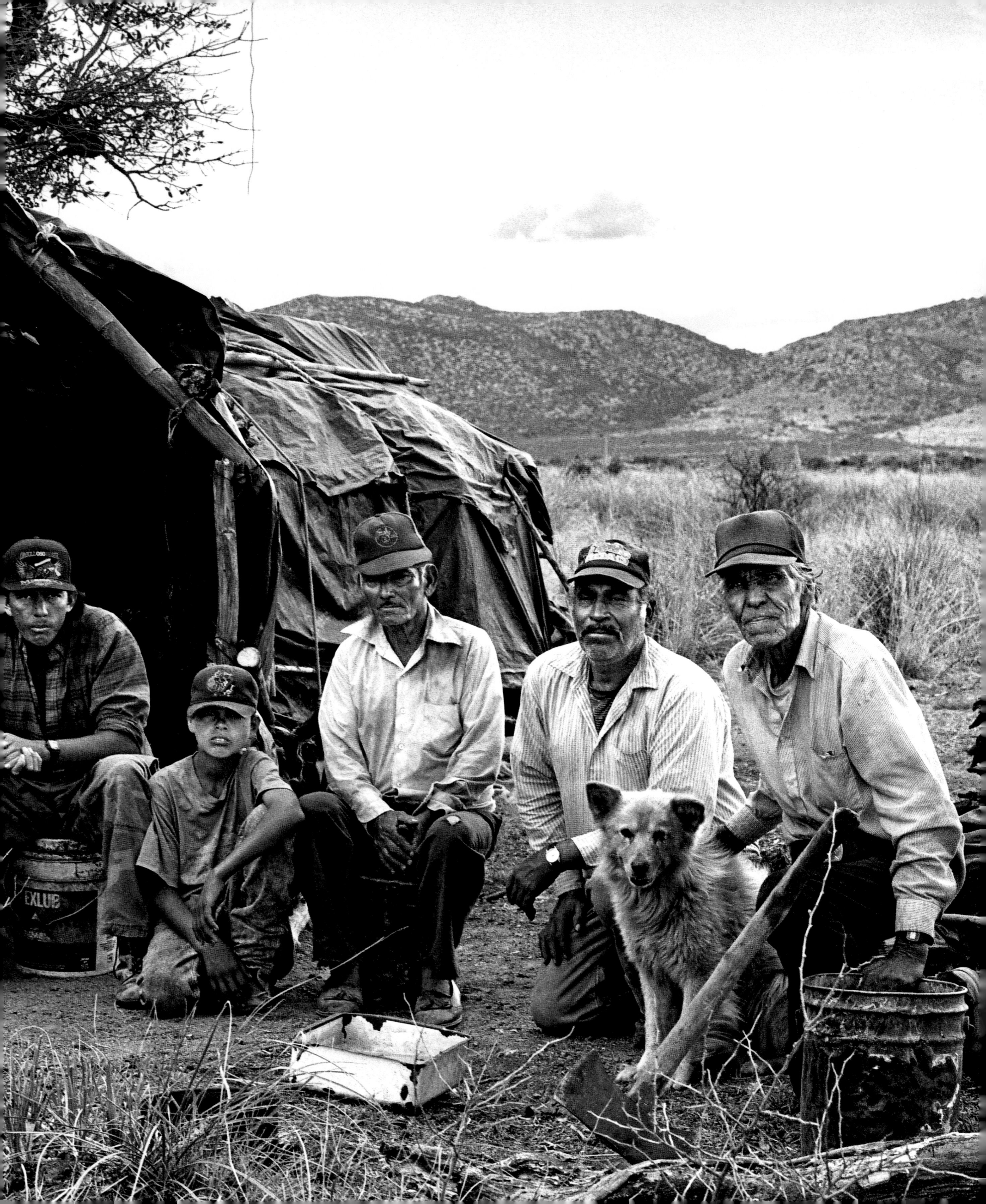
EXLUB

Hacienda de San Diego

CHIHUAHUA, MEXICO
JUNE 29, 2000

Driving north from Mata Ortiz, Mexico, across the Chihuahuan Desert toward the Arizona border, we came upon a grand ruin under a dark, lowering sky: the Hacienda de San Diego, built in the late 1860s by Luis Terrazas, the governor of Chihuahua. Terrazas was a big operator, with ranches covering more than seven million acres. Benito Juárez, president of Mexico for five terms in the mid-nineteenth century, confiscated many of those acres from the Catholic Church and passed them along to his friend Terrazas. When marauding Apaches and Comanches rode down from the western territories of the United States, Terrazas, along with other hacienda owners, needed protection. They encouraged military settlements on their ranches in exchange for defense. Once the Indians were subdued, the landowners forced out the military, which made the jilted soldiers ripe for Pancho Villa's revolution in 1910. As a result, Terrazas was ruined, his cattle and money taken, and his land given away to the country's peasants, *campesinos*—a few descendants of whom still live in one corner of the hacienda today.

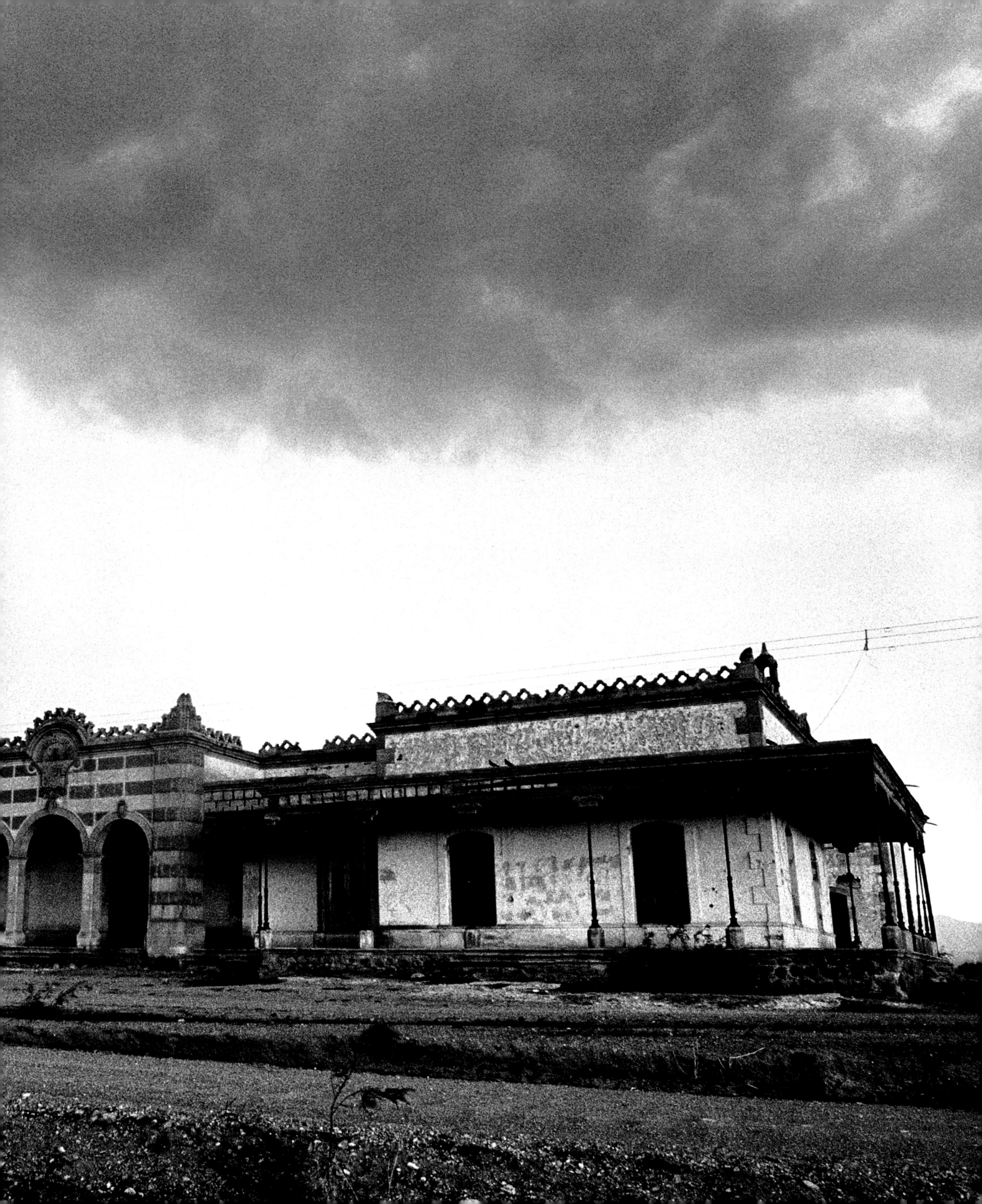

Colonias

NUEVO LAREDO, MEXICO
APRIL 19, 1993

The little girl couldn't have been more than seven years old, maybe younger, and I don't remember her name, but the expression on her face and the way she stood have stayed with me. She was one of a hundred or so people living in makeshift shacks on unclaimed land in a *colonia*, one of several on the outskirts of Nuevo Laredo, Mexico. Her house, a one-room plywood box, like the others in this squatters' community, had no running water, no electricity, and no sewage treatment. Medical care was not available. All categories of disease, even blindness, were common here. The people scavenged for food, and for scraps of metal, wooden planks, cinder blocks, and "whatever the hell they could find," Odie Arambula, the former editor of the *Laredo Times*, told me.

Many people in these colonias came from the interior of Mexico to the border area to find work, but jobs were scarce. So they waited, hoping to get lucky, hoping to cross the Rio Grande and make their way to Austin or Dallas or Houston. But for more than two decades, Mexico's drug wars have scorched these poverty-stricken colonias, scaring off most of those who, in the past, had come to help. Volunteers from Texas used to bring food and clothes, and church groups set up an orphanage, but most people don't dare cross the border anymore.

Like the rest of the border country, the colonias have come under the control of drug cartels. According to Arambula, children from the colonias are used by the cartels as "watchdogs." They are armed with cell phones to facilitate kidnappings or to move drugs from one neighborhood to another. When I look at an old photograph, particularly this one, I often wonder what's become of the person in the picture.

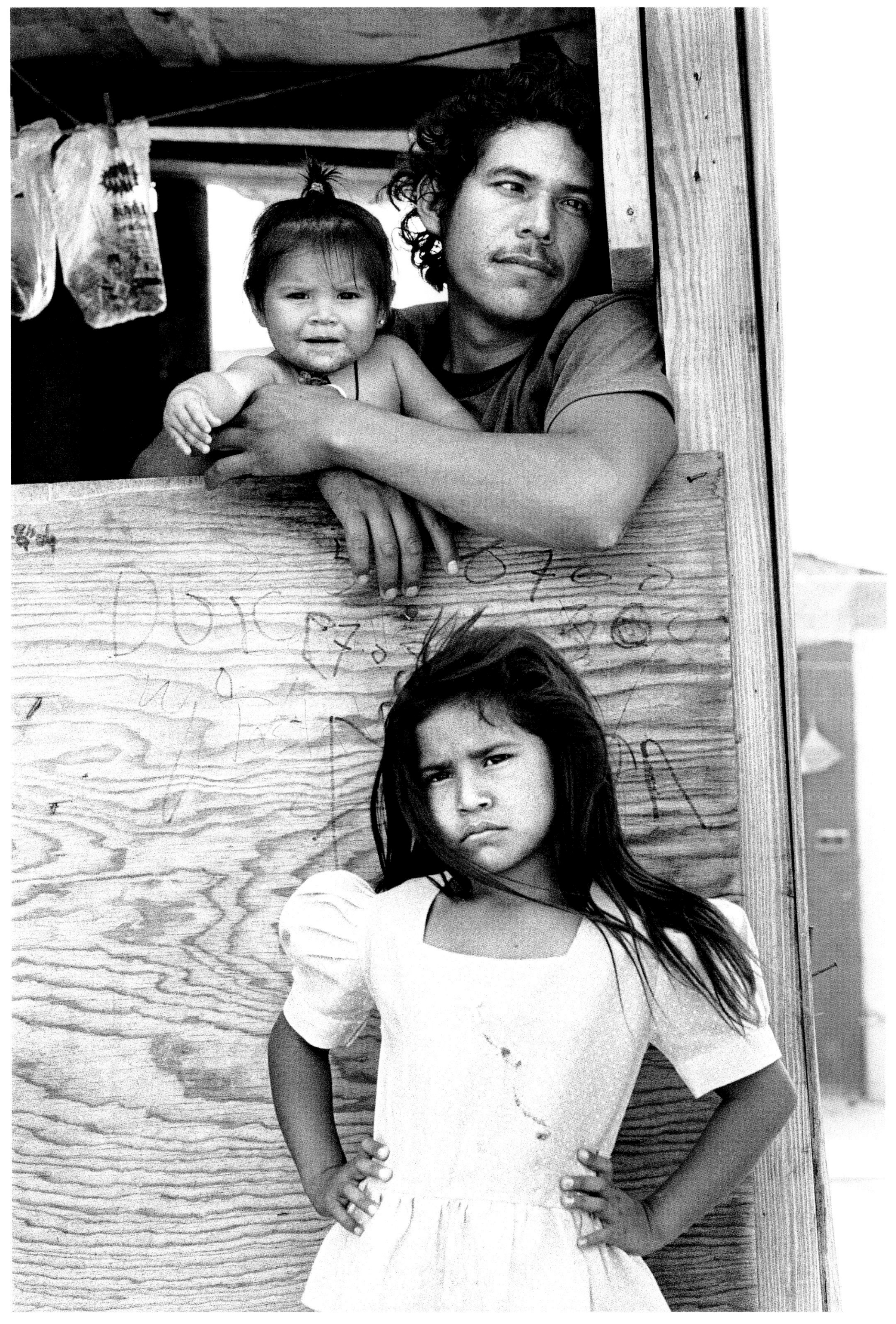

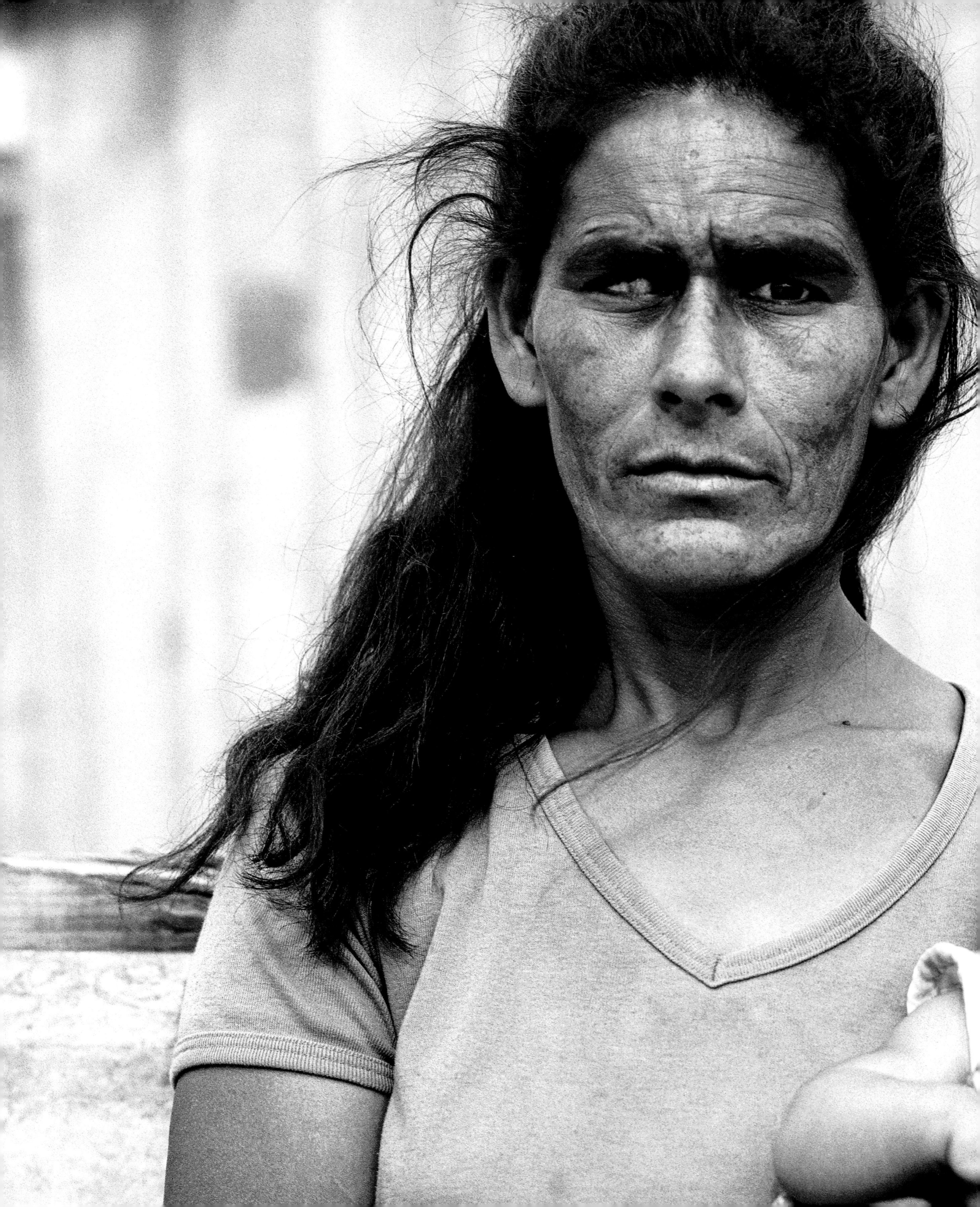

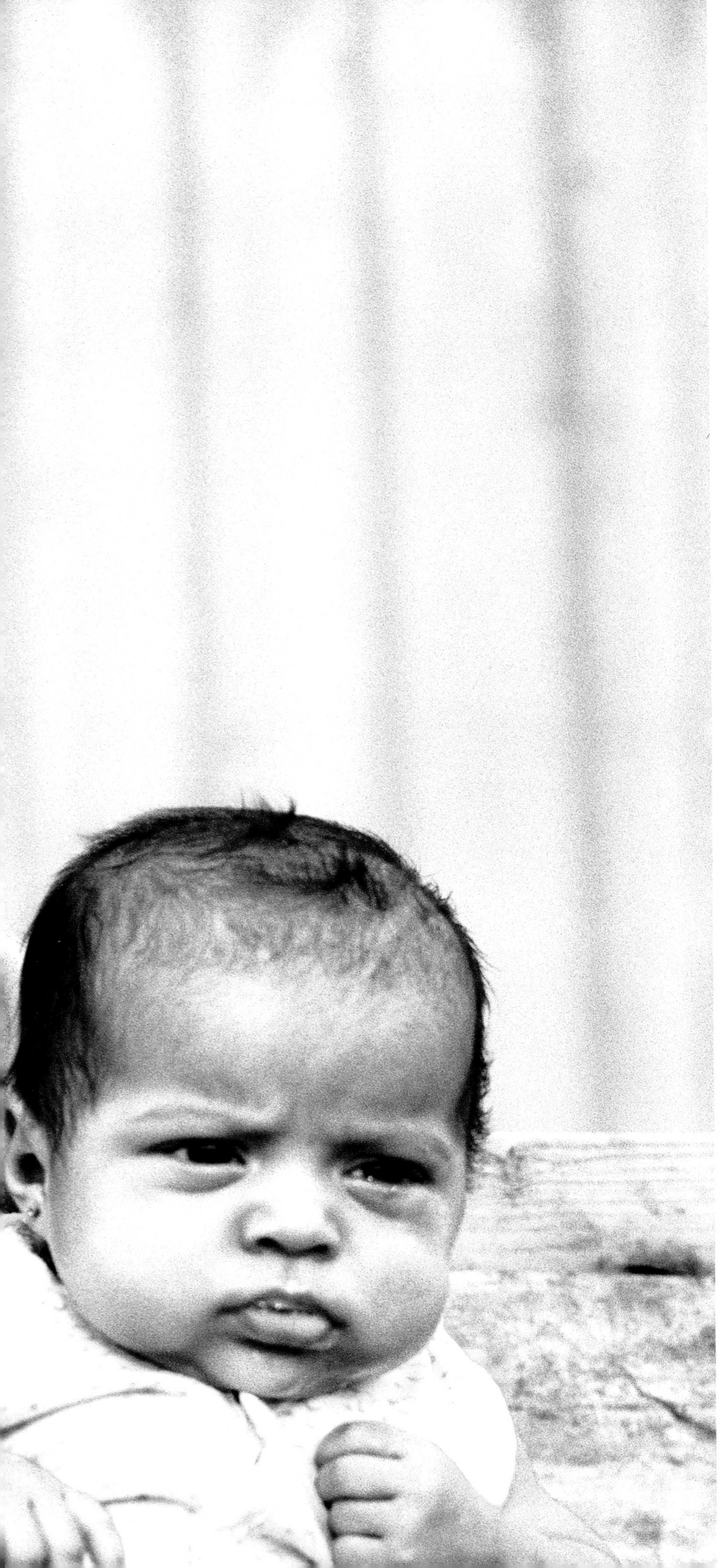

Buffalo

FREDERICKSBURG, TEXAS
MAY 5, 1996

Wild plains bison (buffalo) once formed the greatest assemblage of mammals that ever roamed the earth. Tens of millions grazed the plains of North America until the mid-nineteenth century. Mike Phillips, a Montana state senator and restoration ecologist, told me, "We are the most selfish species. We're the most unaccommodating." In less than fifty years, we drove the buffalo to the edge of extinction; just two hundred wild bison were left, saved by the fact that they lived in the area that became Yellowstone National Park. Even there, poachers had killed all but about twenty-five by the 1890s. "We just completely dominated the Great Plains," Phillips said. "We got rid of anything in our way—bison, wolves, Indians, elk."

The science of wildlife management grew out of these depredations. Today, populations of elk and wolves are being rebuilt. And yet, the greatest mammals on the plains are being left behind. The bison have never recovered from the slaughter. There are now perhaps only five or six thousand genetically pure bison remaining, and those are contained on the narrow reservation of land that is Yellowstone National Park. When they numbered in the millions, they were natural conservationists, migrating south along one route and, to avoid overgrazing, north along another, their hooves aerating the prairie soil. Now that the bison are confined in Yellowstone or on ranches in the West, Phillips explained, "Their ecological role is functionally extinct."

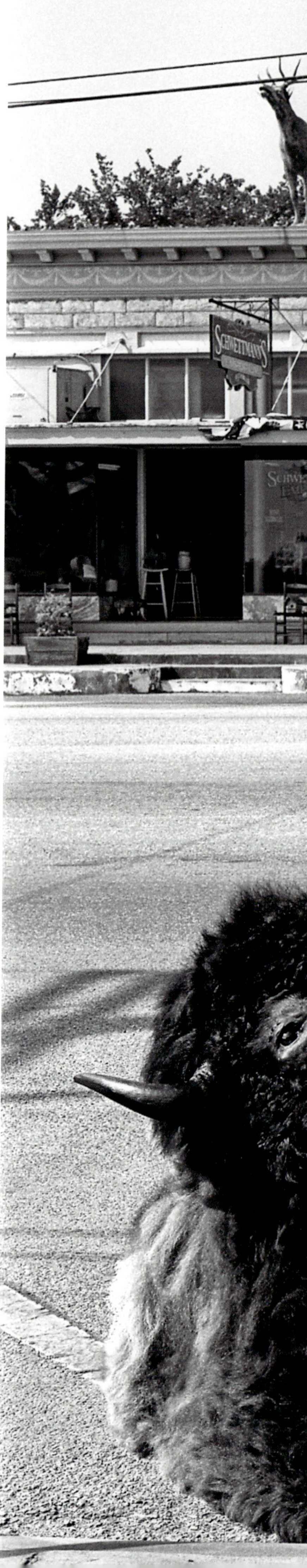

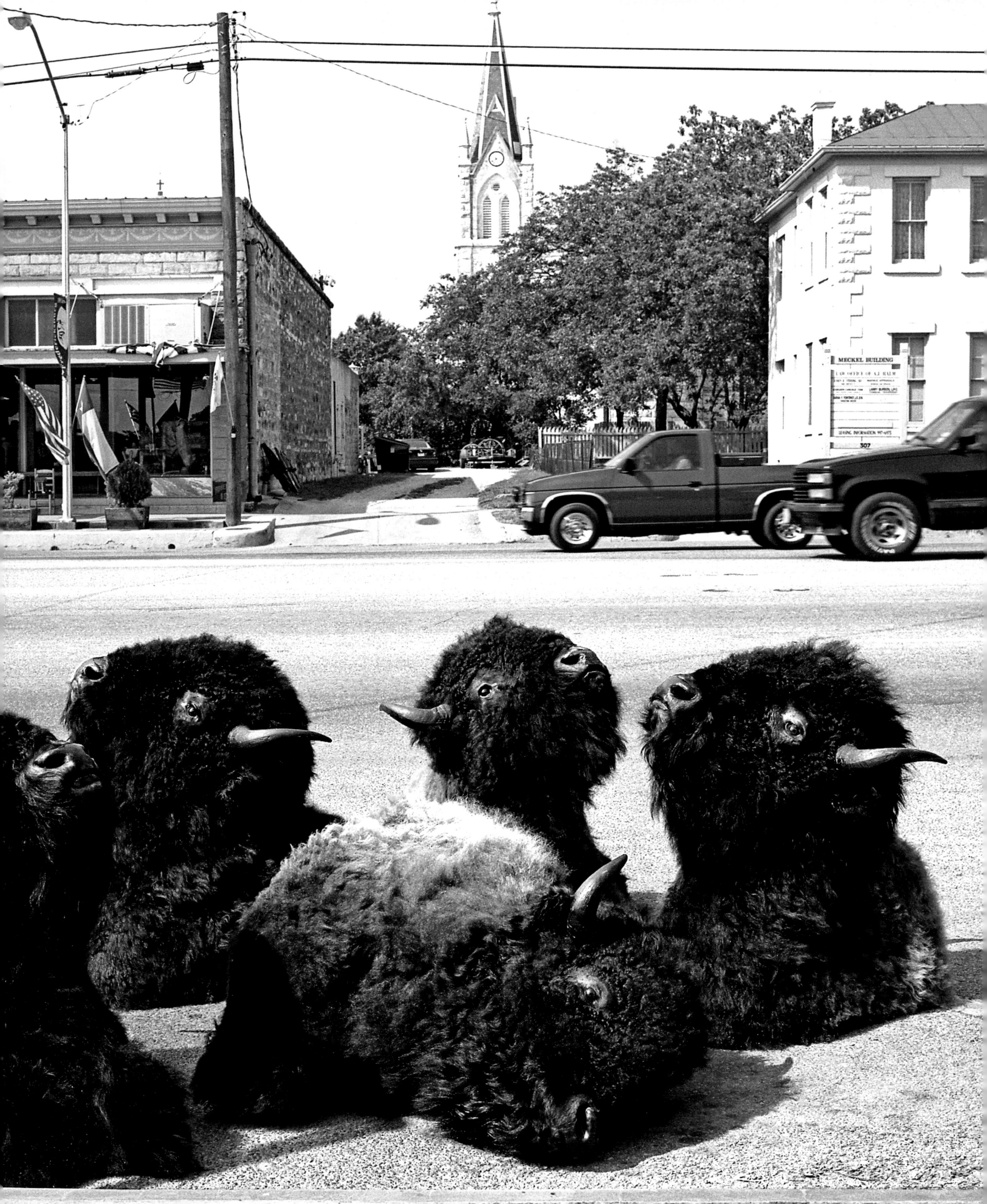
MECKEL BUILDING
307

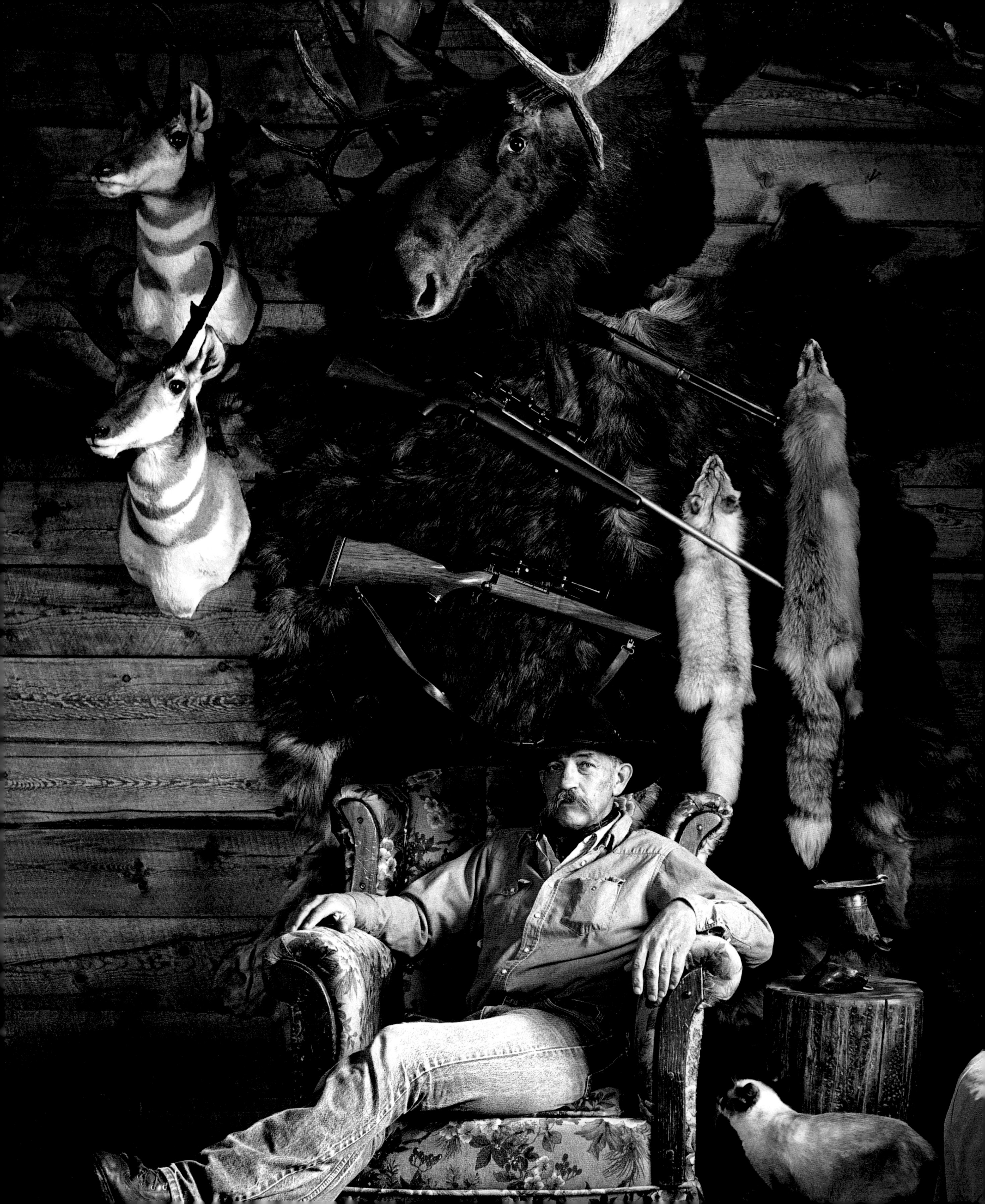

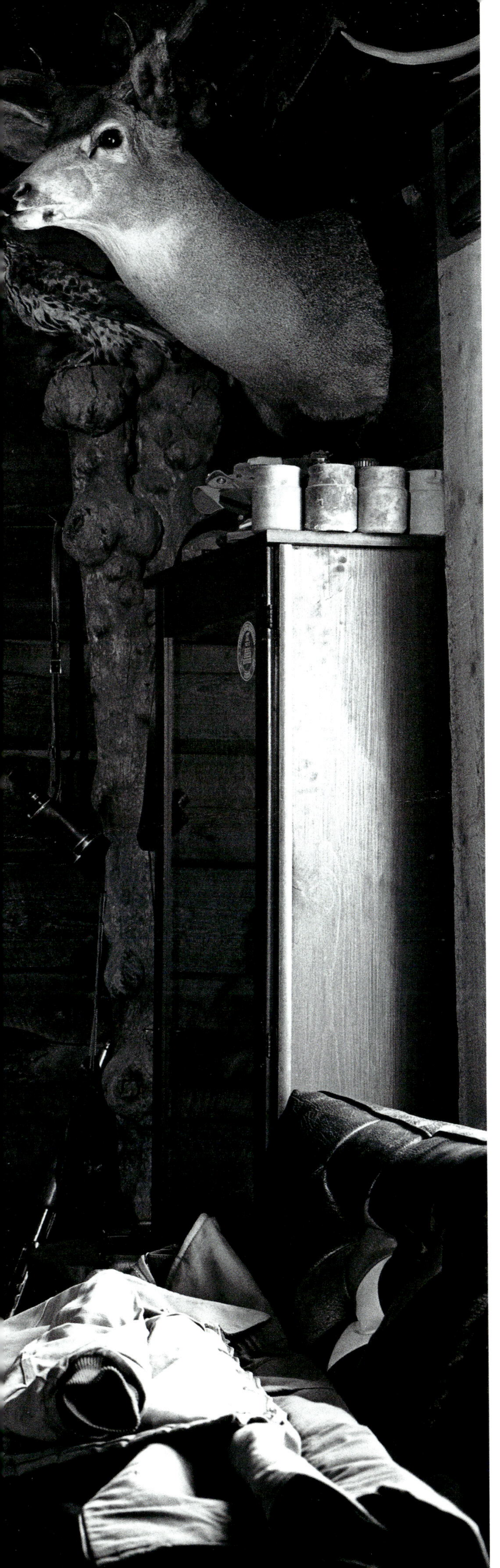

Outfitter

BONDURANT, WYOMING
FEBRUARY 21, 1996

Deep winter had settled on the Hoback Basin, south of the Gros Ventre Wilderness, when I traveled to Bondurant, Wyoming. Heavy snow covered the open, broad, rolling hills. The brilliant whiteness in all directions of the undulating landscape made the sky seem so close, as if I could reach up and touch it.

One morning during a thick snowfall, I stopped at a little corner store to warm up. Paul Crittenden sat at the counter with his coffee. Crittenden is a professional hunter, an outfitter licensed by Wyoming to take people into the backcountry to look for elk, moose, deer, antelope, even bear. He's paid to supply all support needed for a weeklong hunt. After talking with Crittenden that day, I realized that the most valuable thing people could gain from such a hunt is the rare experience of being a small part of a functioning wilderness landscape.

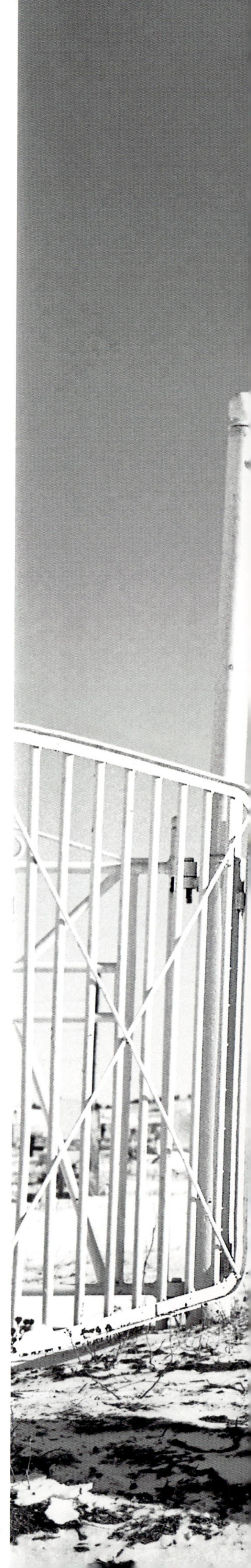

Brother Simon, Society of Jesus

PINE RIDGE, SOUTH DAKOTA
DECEMBER 12, 1996

Brother Simon had gone up to the cemetery to walk among the graves. When he turned toward me in his long, dark cassock and old Pendleton jacket, he looked like one of Chief Red Cloud's "Black Robes." In 1868, the chief had specifically requested that Jesuits come to teach the Oglala Lakota Sioux as part of the Treaty of Fort Laramie. Brother Simon had lived on the Pine Ridge Indian Reservation for thirty-seven years. In that time, he had developed a deep knowledge of the indigenous art of the native peoples and collected examples of their beadwork, textiles, and pottery. In 1982 he established the Red Cloud Indian School's Heritage Center to share his collection and raise awareness of Lakota artists. On the cold, bright morning when I photographed Brother Simon, I worried that he might grow peevish as I fiddled with lenses and f-stops. But he was patient, and, in a slight stutter, quietly told me about his efforts to nourish cultural pride on the reservation.

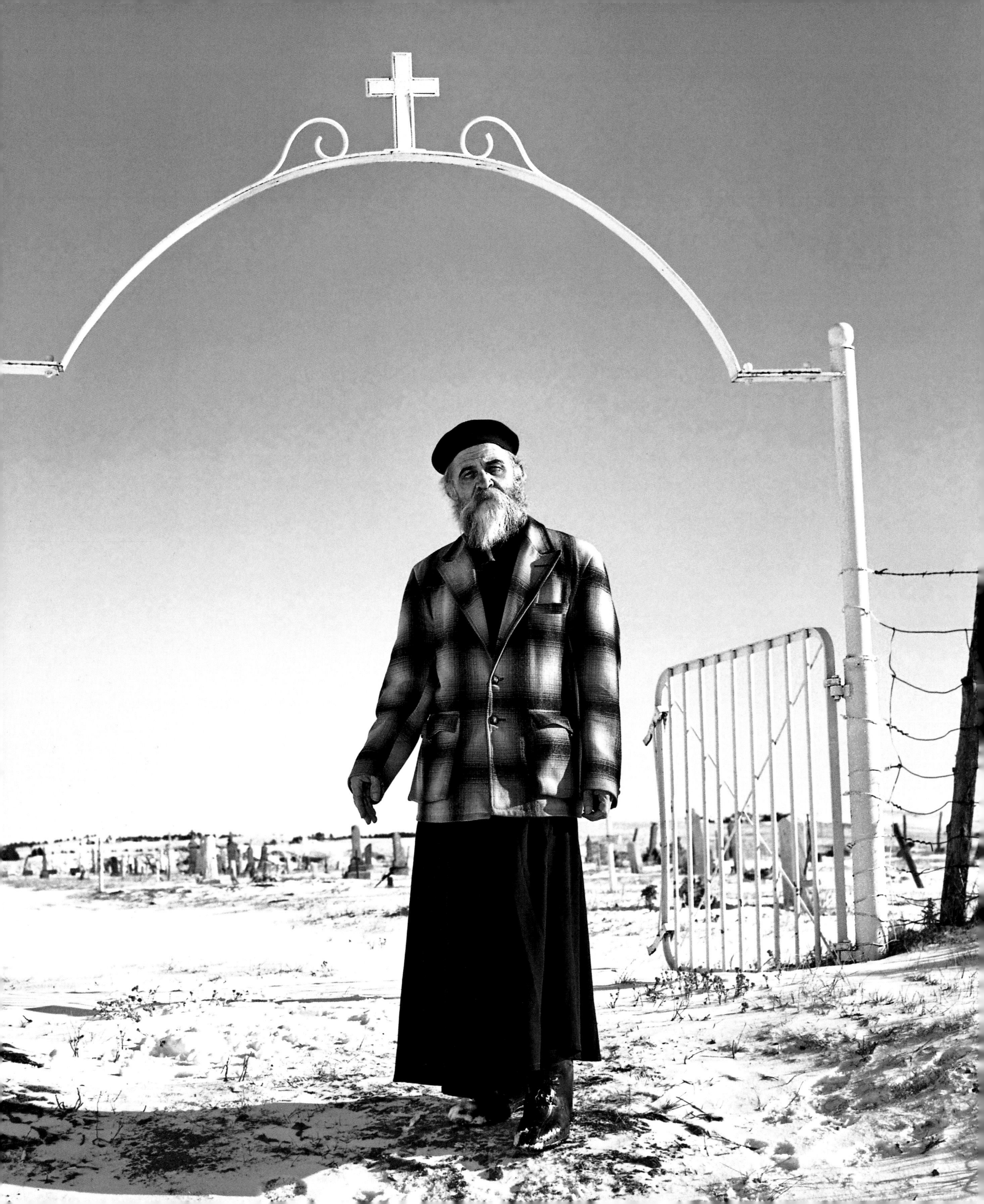

Bill Richardson

RICHARDSON'S TRADING COMPANY
GALLUP, NEW MEXICO
JANUARY 14, 2008

You know you're getting close to Gallup when you pick up the news and road conditions on KTNN AM 660 spoken in Navajo. Gallup lies like a lizard along old Route 66 parallel to I-40 in the heart of Indian country. This tough western town swells to twice its normal size on weekends when Navajo, Hopi, and Zuni come in from reservations to shop and trade. Bill Richardson was ninety years old when I photographed him that day inside one of three vaults in Richardson's Trading Company and Cash Pawn:

"The Richardson brothers, my dad and his brother, Hubert, come into Winslow [Arizona] in 1912. Nothing to do but pick cotton in Texas, so they come out here. They walked across the Colorado River. Their brother-in-law, McAdams, was here in 1890. They learned his business, became traders, good ones."

"I was a trader kid. I played with Indians, speaking Navajo. We dug in caves, jumped in rivers. There'd be four hundred to five hundred Indians in an area. They'd bring in cattle, sheep, lambs, and ewes, on horseback with dogs. We'd drive 'em to the railroad, ship 'em to California. Indians'd bring in hundreds of sacks of wool—one hundred pounds, a hundred and fifty to two hundred pounds. We'd give 'em twenty-five cents a pound. They'd sell piñons [pine nuts] to us for ten cents a pound, and we'd sell 'em for twenty-five cents a pound to mom-and-pop stores. The Indians'd trade for flour, baking powder, sugar, salt, salt blocks, canned tomatoes, canned peaches, canned pears, coffee, Levis, shoes. We couldn't sell guns and bullets. We'd sell 'em piece goods, cotton, sateen, velveteen, frying pans, cast-iron pots."

"There's almost three hundred thousand Indians on the Navajo reservation today. We take in half a million a month. Now they bring in rugs, pottery, jewelry. They need to buy tires, batteries. They've got kids in school. They might say, 'I need $500 on this belt.' I can go $300. Maximum we'll go on an item is $2,000."

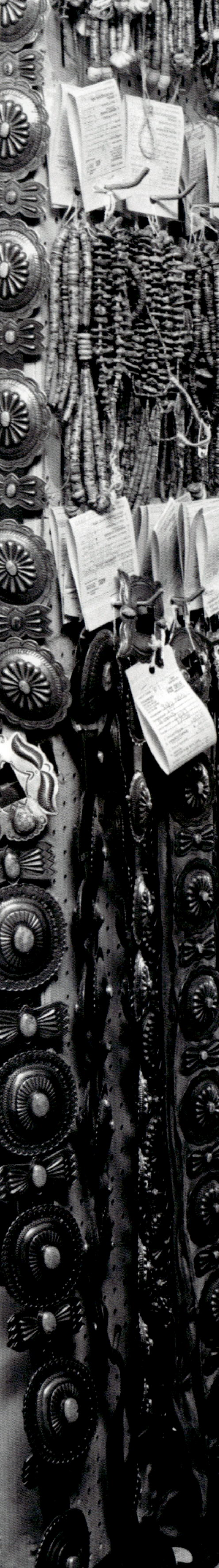

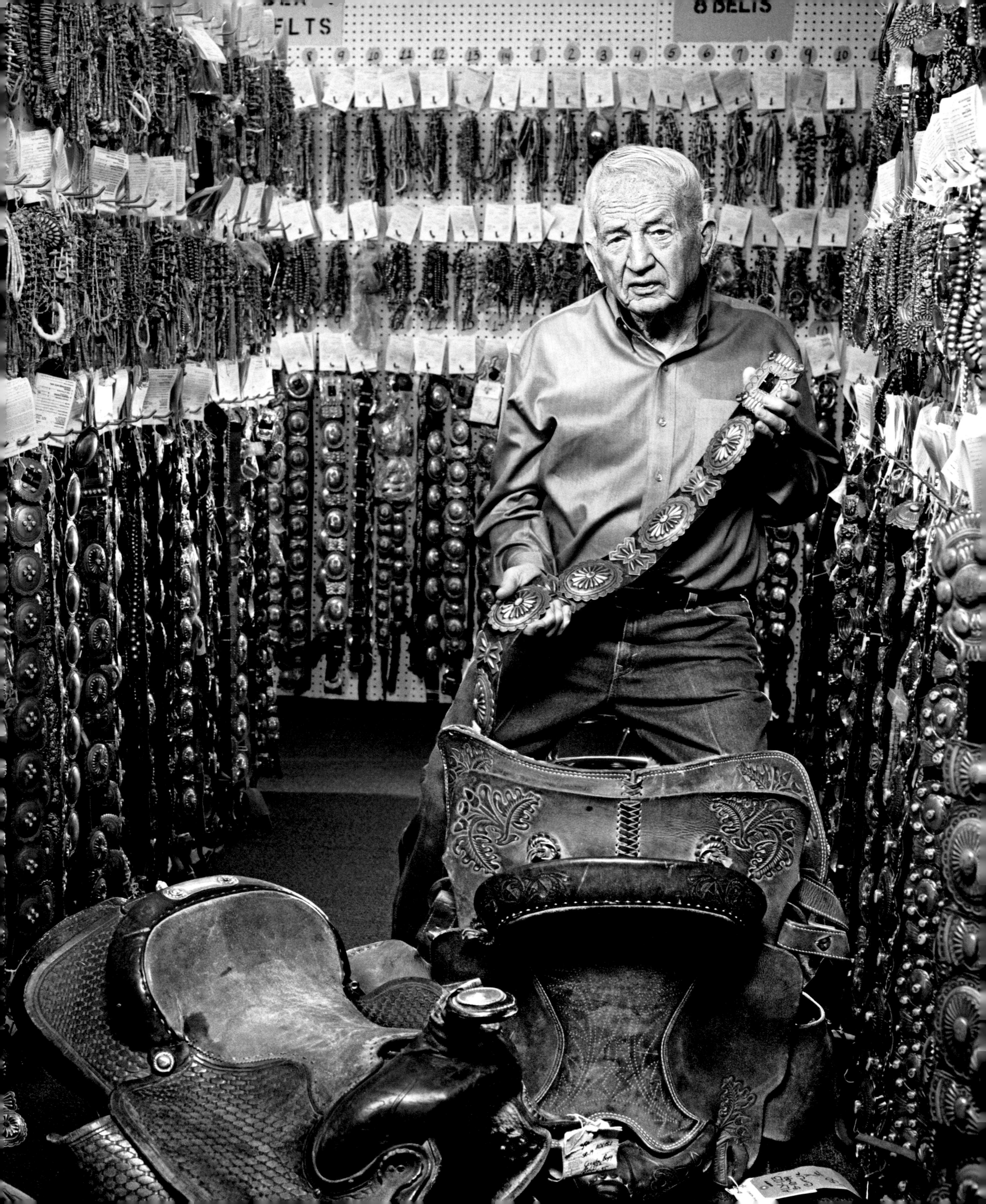
8 BELTS
8 9 10 11 12 13 14 1 2 3 4 5 6 7 8 9 10

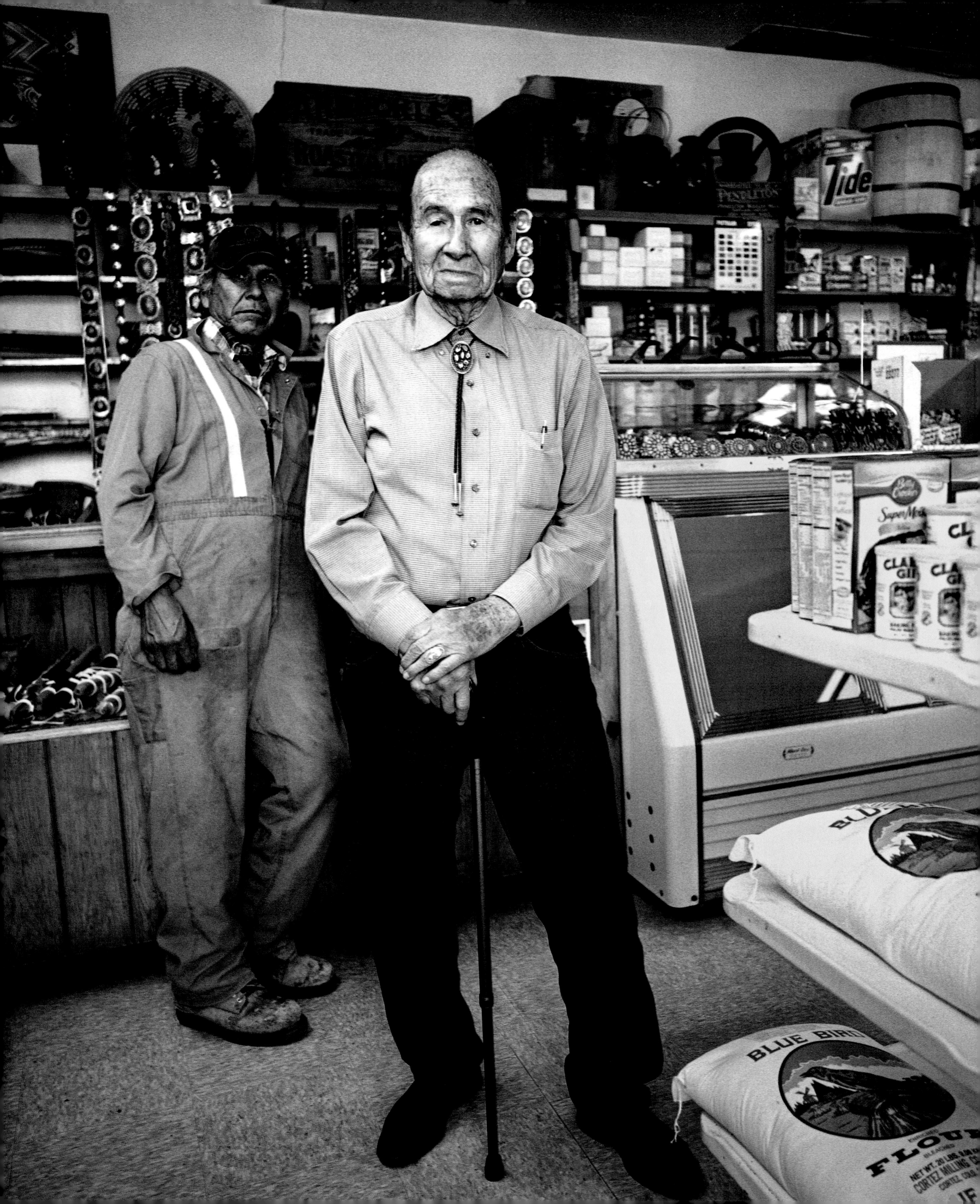
Tide
BLUE BIRD

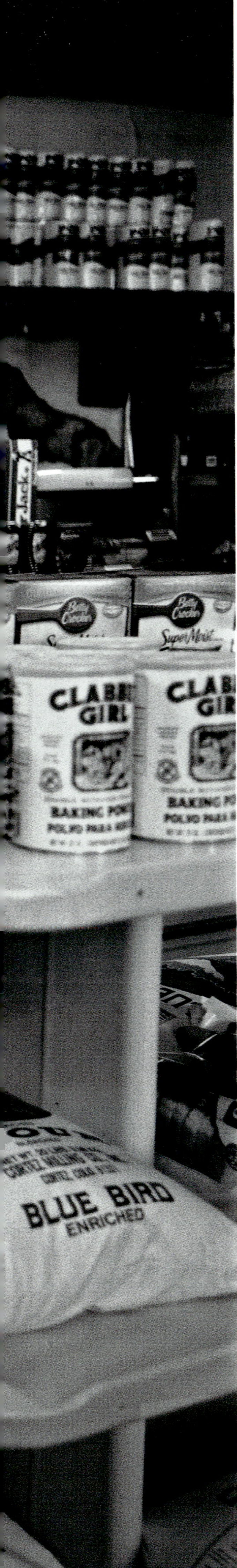

Stuart Hatch

HATCH BROTHERS TRADING POST
SAN JUAN RIVER
FRUITLAND, NEW MEXICO
NOVEMBER 16, 2009

I drove west from Albuquerque, New Mexico, through Grants to Gallup, then straight north on to the Navajo Nation, past Tohatchi, on up to Shiprock, then followed the San Juan River east for about fifteen miles. There, in a small two-room trading post under cottonwood trees at the river's edge, I met Stuart Hatch. This is what he told me that day: "My mother was part Navajo, part Paiute. My dad was an Anglo from Arkansas. I was born on the San Juan River, not far from Shiprock, in 1919. My dad was in the Indian trading business all his life, and I just grew up in it. I speak Navajo and Paiute. We dealt with what the Indians had to sell: cattle, horses, rugs, sheep, wool, jewelry."

"I've enjoyed most of all the people I've dealt with. Indians are just nice people, nice to deal with. Navajo, they got a different attitude, more considerate of one another. Seems that way to me. My whole life has been good living here by the river. I'd do it over again. The rugs, jewelry, the livestock—it all is interesting to me."

Lion Hunters

FORT DAVIS, TEXAS
AUGUST 1, 1991

Big Jim Espy and his son, Jim, are from a pioneer family in the Davis Mountains of far West Texas. They're known as "good stockmen." They, along with other ranchers in this rugged country, have a long history of hunting mountain lions. "These lions are solitary, hard to find," Jim Espy, Jr., said. "They prey on livestock, the younger ones mostly—calves, sheep, goats, horse colts." The Espys use "lion dogs," mixed-breed hounds that are trained to track a scent eight to fifteen hours old in the high desert country.

Billy Pat McKinney, who often hunts mountain lions, told me, "A good lion dog is independent. They're not trained up like a bird dog. Lion hounds are a rough, rowdy bunch and hardheaded. The hunt is 75 percent dogs and 25 percent the man managing the dogs. They'll bark on scent, and they've got strong voices. You've got to ride to keep up. It's a test of stamina for you and the dogs and the animal you're after." Most hunters prefer to ride a mule rather than a horse because mules have tremendous stamina. A cross between a female horse and a male donkey, a mule has a hybrid vigor that makes it tough and agile. "After a hard ride, a horse might take one or two days to recover, but a mule will rally overnight," McKinney said.

An experienced hunter knows where mountain lions travel, knows they like rough country, canyons, and bluffs. Lions prey heavily on deer, so where deer country and lion country meet is an excellent place to start. A hunter will look for a kill or a scrape—or, since lions are nocturnal, he'll look for a place where a lion might have crossed during the night. The hunter rides with dogs working out in front to locate a scent. The dogs might strike a track, and the hunter will follow, working his way across rough country and up a canyon, listening for his dogs' frenzied bark. When he hears that sound, he knows the dogs have "bayed up" a lion—either treed or trapped it on a rockslide or cliff. The experienced dog won't attack a lion but will hold it in place. To reach the lion, the hunter might have to go on foot to climb slick rocks or limestone too steep for his mule. "I like my hands free," McKinney said. "So I use a sidearm, a pistol. A rifle's too hard to carry in that country. I want to get within ten feet of the lion. . . . But I don't know. That's a beautiful, majestic animal. Now I've kinda moved to tracking and preserving them."

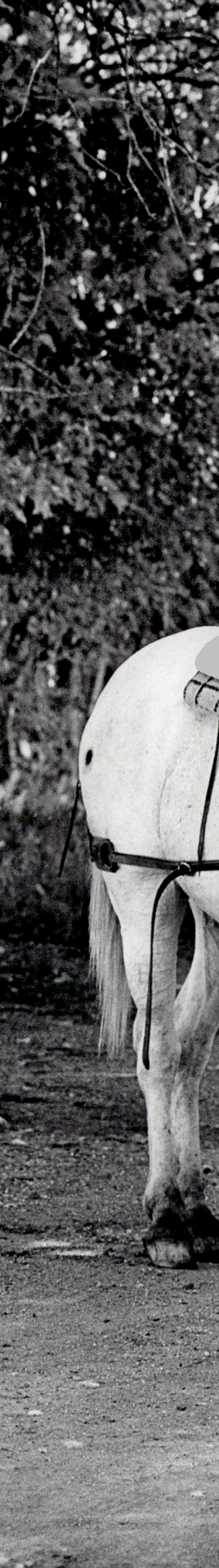

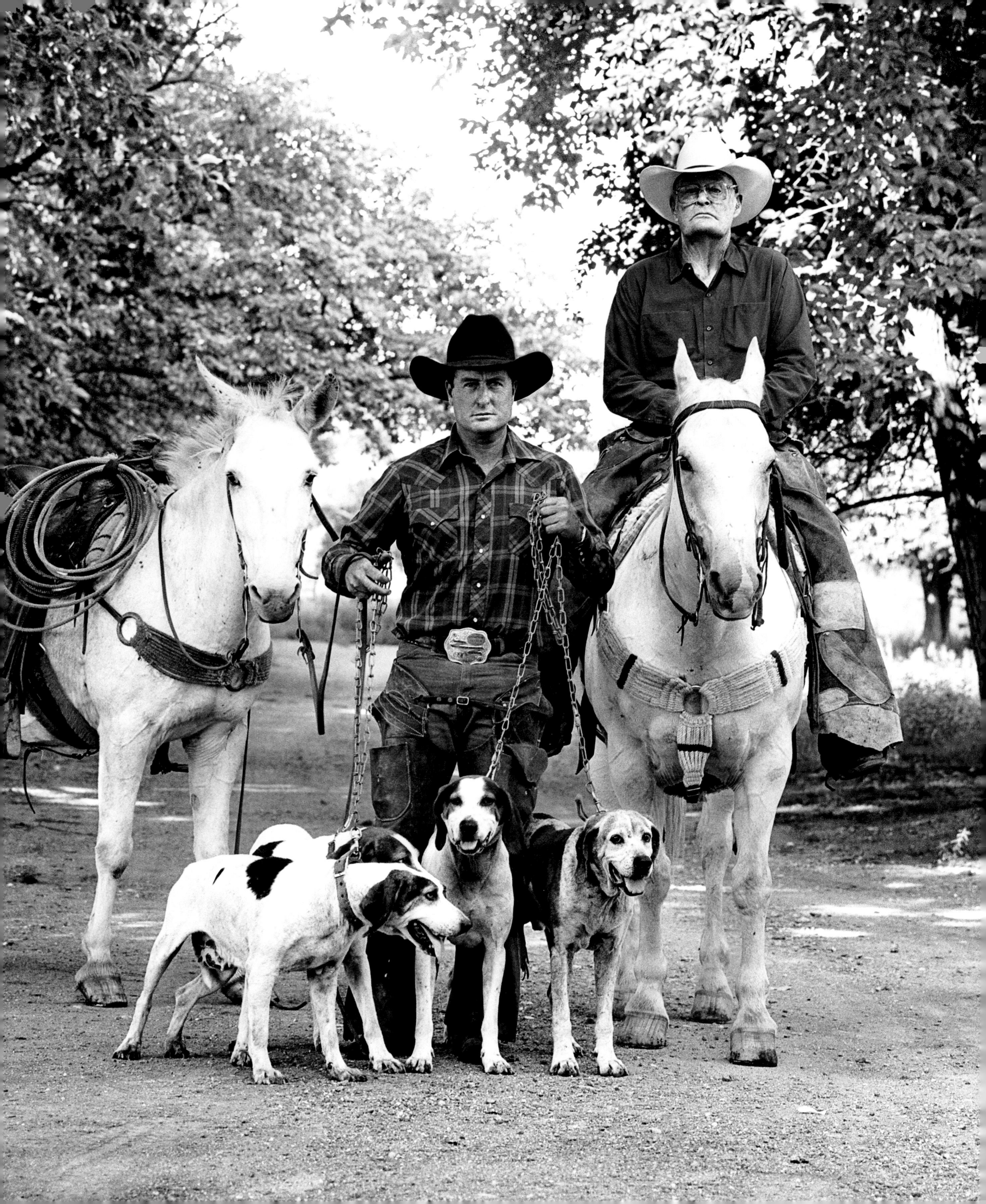

Sheriff

SAN AUGUSTINE COUNTY, TEXAS
AUGUST 4, 1993

Nathan Tindall had been the law in San Augustine County, Texas, for forty years. It was unusual, even in East Texas, to elect a twenty-one-year-old sheriff. "Hell, I was just as settled at twenty-one as I am now," the sixty-nine-year-old Tindall explained. At fifteen, he had been a "mule skinner," wrestling logs in the hardwood forests near the poor tenant farm where he grew up. In 1943 he joined the Navy, was wounded in the Pacific, and returned home on a wave of goodwill to run for sheriff. A local veterinarian remembered, "There wasn't a scared bone in his body. He was strangely even-tempered. Almost unnaturally so."

Sheriff Tindall had never, in all his forty years, carried a gun. He always maintained a good relationship with both black and white citizens. He was known to call up a suspect, even one accused of murder, on the telephone to say "meet me at the jailhouse." But he was no pushover. Occasionally, and only reluctantly, he used a famously effective knock-out punch. He told me his long reign was due to two things: "First, I had the vote of every mother in this county 'cause when their kids got in trouble, I always treated them with respect, even the ones I put in jail. And second thing was, I had good relations with my black constituents." Tindall was no "whip-snappin' sheriff," a local newspaperman recalled. "He was a practical man livin' with poor practical people."

But even a good man can't be good at everything, not in this altogether different day and age. Tindall was defeated in his bid for reelection when drugs became an incendiary issue in San Augustine County. I asked him what he thought of the man who had taken his place. In a calm, factual manner, he said, "I'll tell you one thing, he's so dumb he couldn't even track an elephant bleedin' to death in the snow."

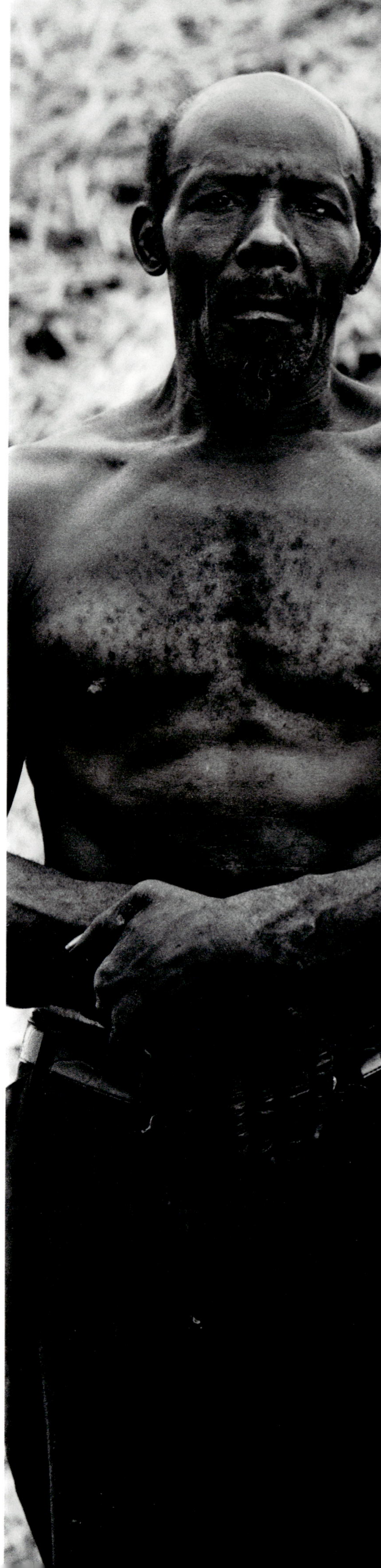

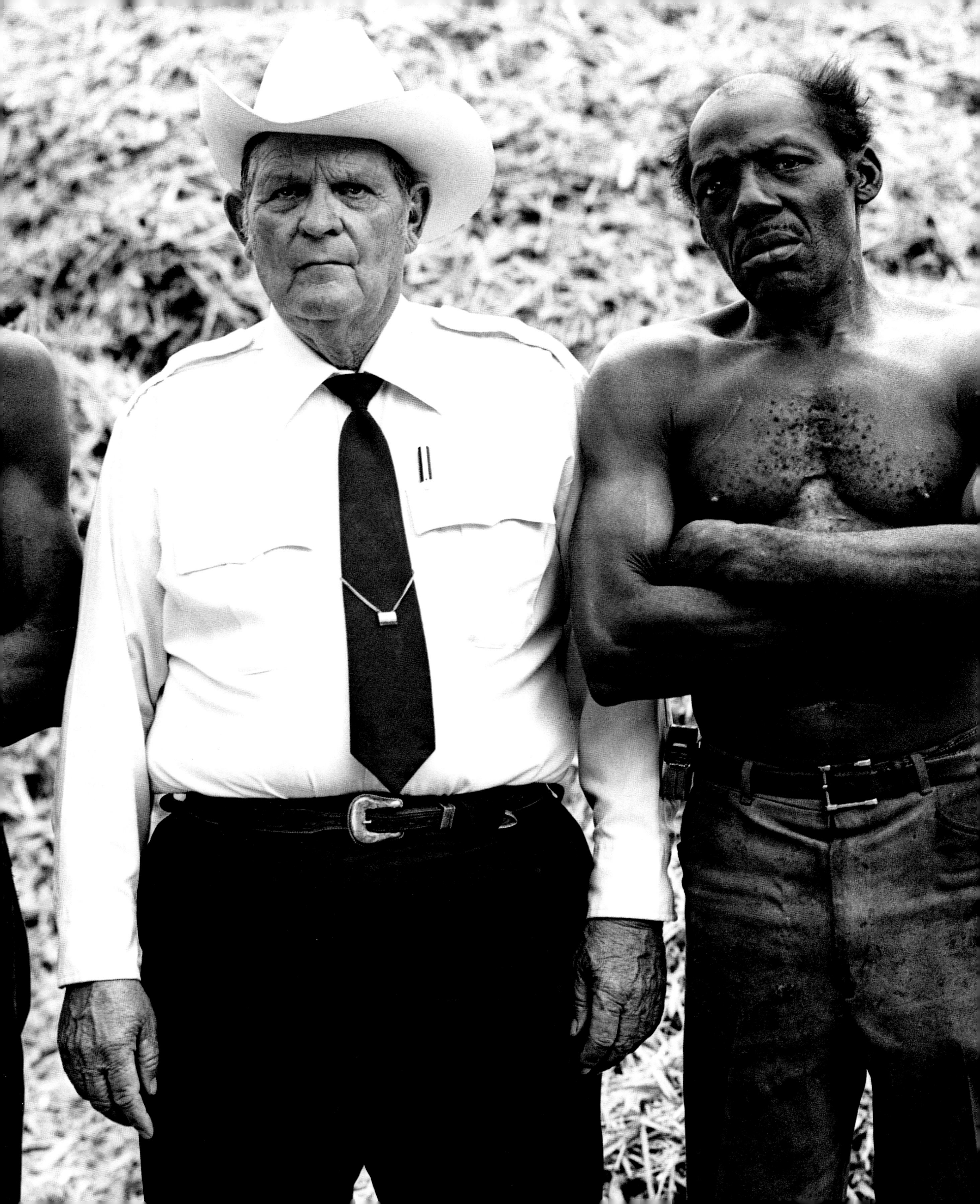

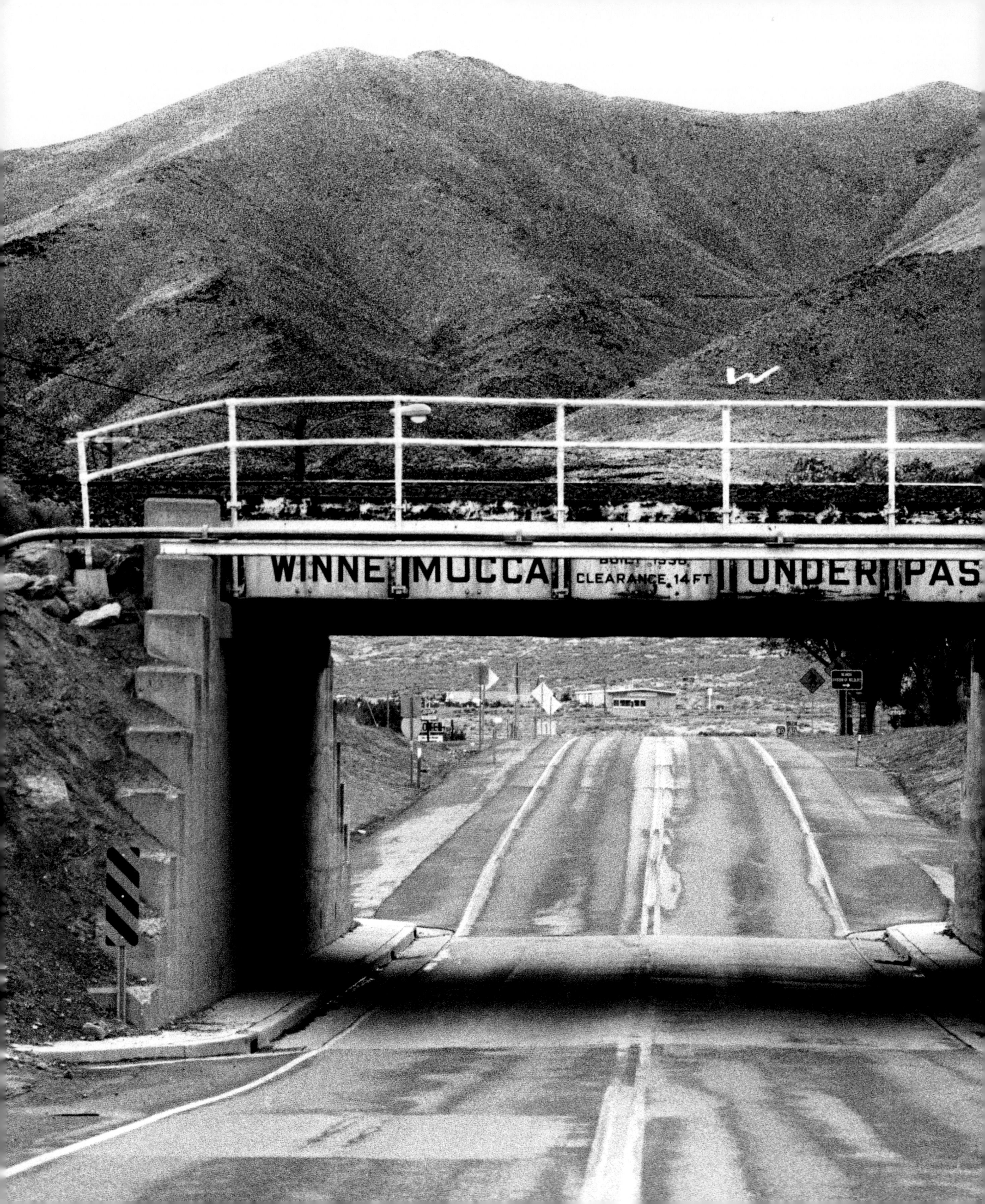
WINNE MUCCA
CLEARANCE 14 FT
UNDER PAS

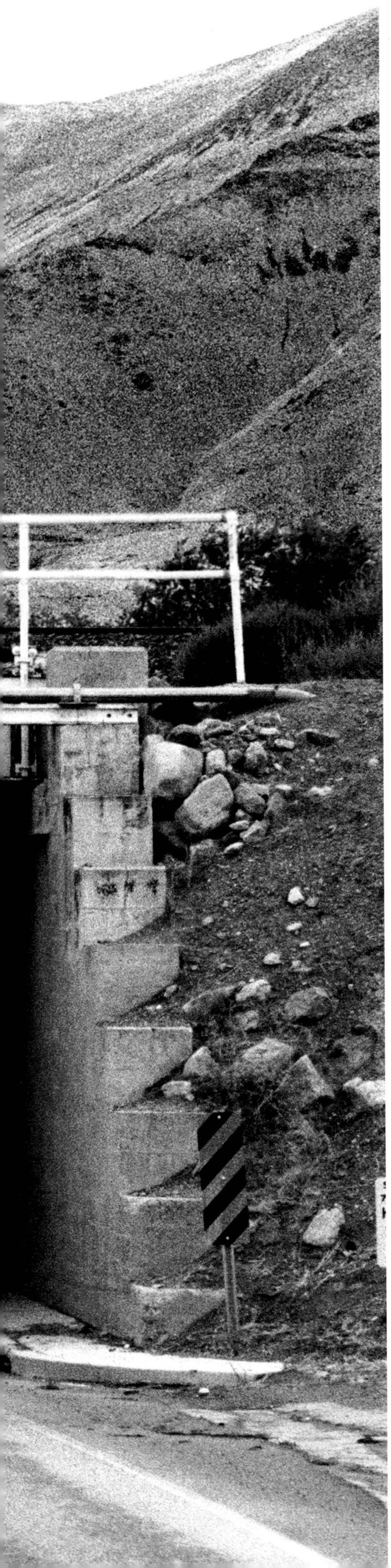

They leave Winnemucca in a hurry
The Father stuffing a thousand-dollar
jackpot in his pockets
The Son begging to hold a Silver Dollar
Just to touch the Eagle
The Father asking the son to call it heads
or tails
as they roar down Highway 80

The Son calling it tails as it comes up tails
Slap in the middle of the map of Nevada

8/10/80
Winnemucca, Nevada

—Sam Shepard, American playwright, b. 1943

Sam Shepard

SANTA FE, NEW MEXICO
ARROYO HONDO, NEW MEXICO
JUNE 29, 2012

On a bright, chilly spring day in 2011, I joined Sam Shepard and about eight scientists for lunch outside in the warmth of the courtyard of the Santa Fe Institute. Shepard and one other writer were "in residence" at the institute, mingling with thirty physicists, mathematicians, and biologists. The theory behind this odd coupling was that the scientists might benefit from exposure to the creativity of first-rate writers. The conversation was lively and spirited, fueled by the scientists' wide-ranging curiosity. I left the luncheon happy to have met the physicist Murray Gell-Mann, whose most famous discovery was named for a word in James Joyce's *Finnegans Wake*—the quark. This just goes to show what can come from a lunch of blue-corn tortillas.

Shepard left a day or two later to cross continents and oceans for work on plays and movies. It was another year before I was able to take this portrait of him back at the Santa Fe Institute. He had just finished writing the final lines of his play *Heartless*. He filled out a FedEx form and sent the play off to New York, where it would go into production two months later. Shepard was in good spirits, free for the afternoon to be photographed. He and I stopped at his adobe house, ten miles outside of town, where he showed off a fancy new fly rod, casting here and there over the dusty, dry land, demonstrating the rod's special capabilities to an audience of me and a forlorn lawn chair. Not a drop of water was to be found at any point on the compass for as far as the eye could see.

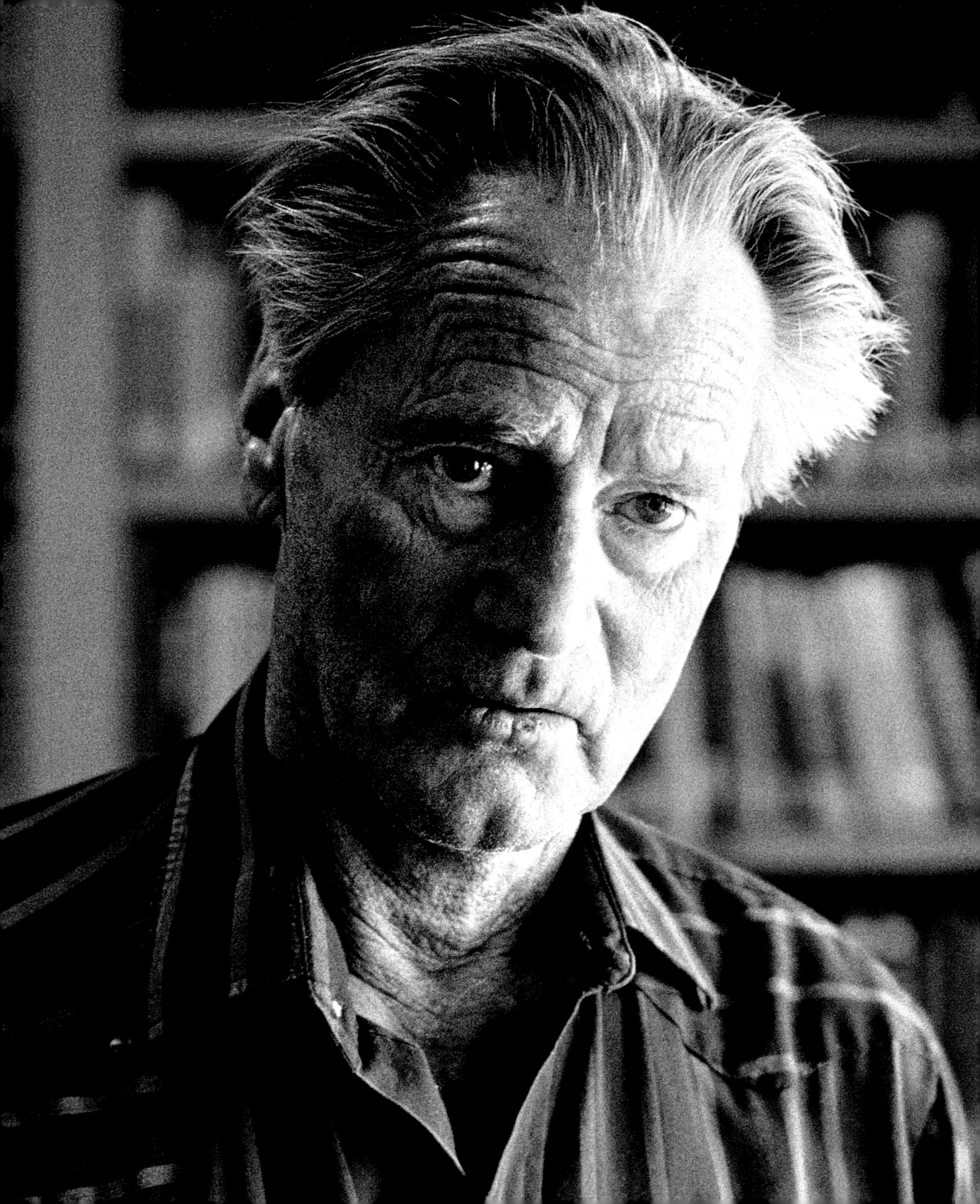

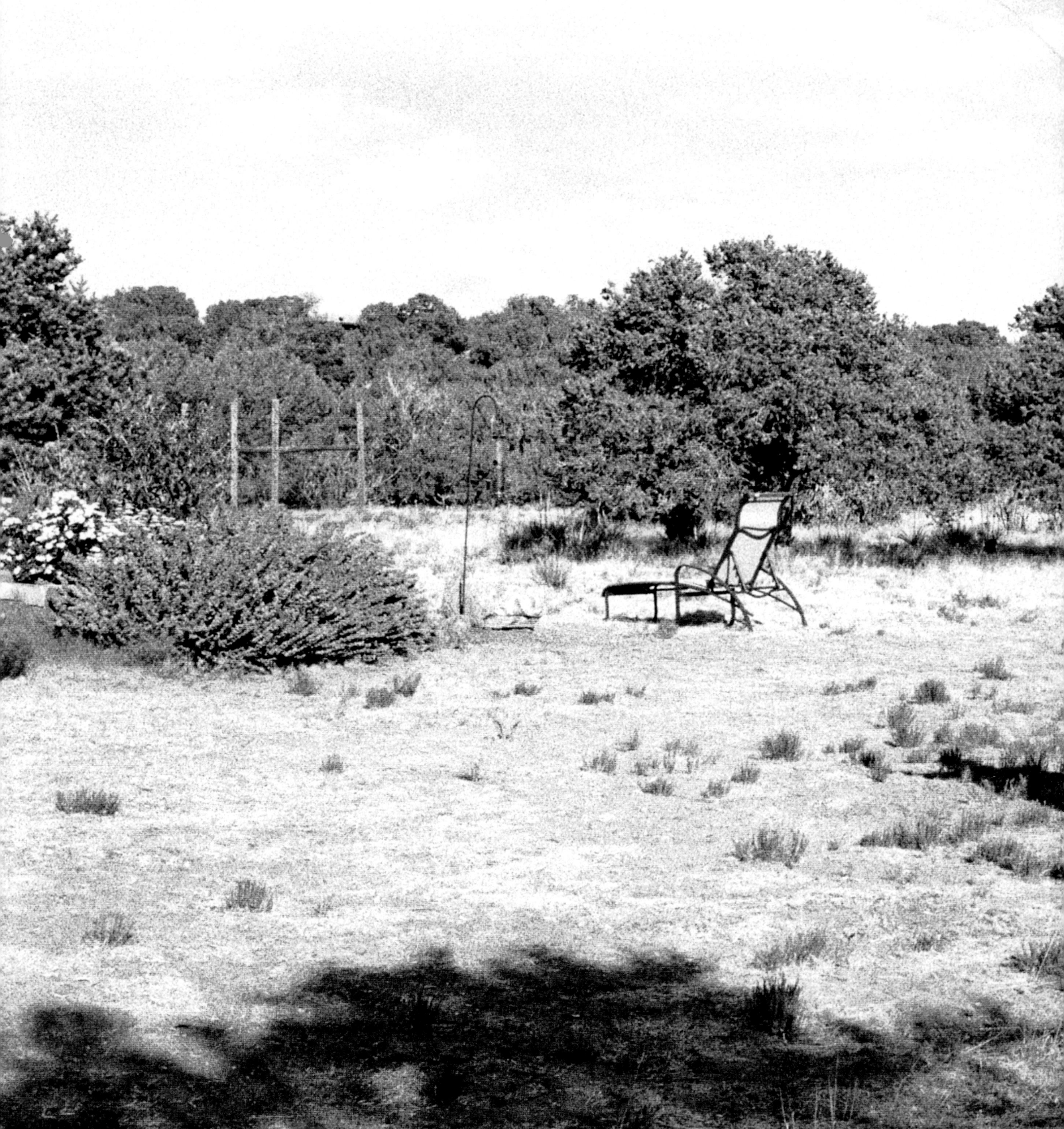

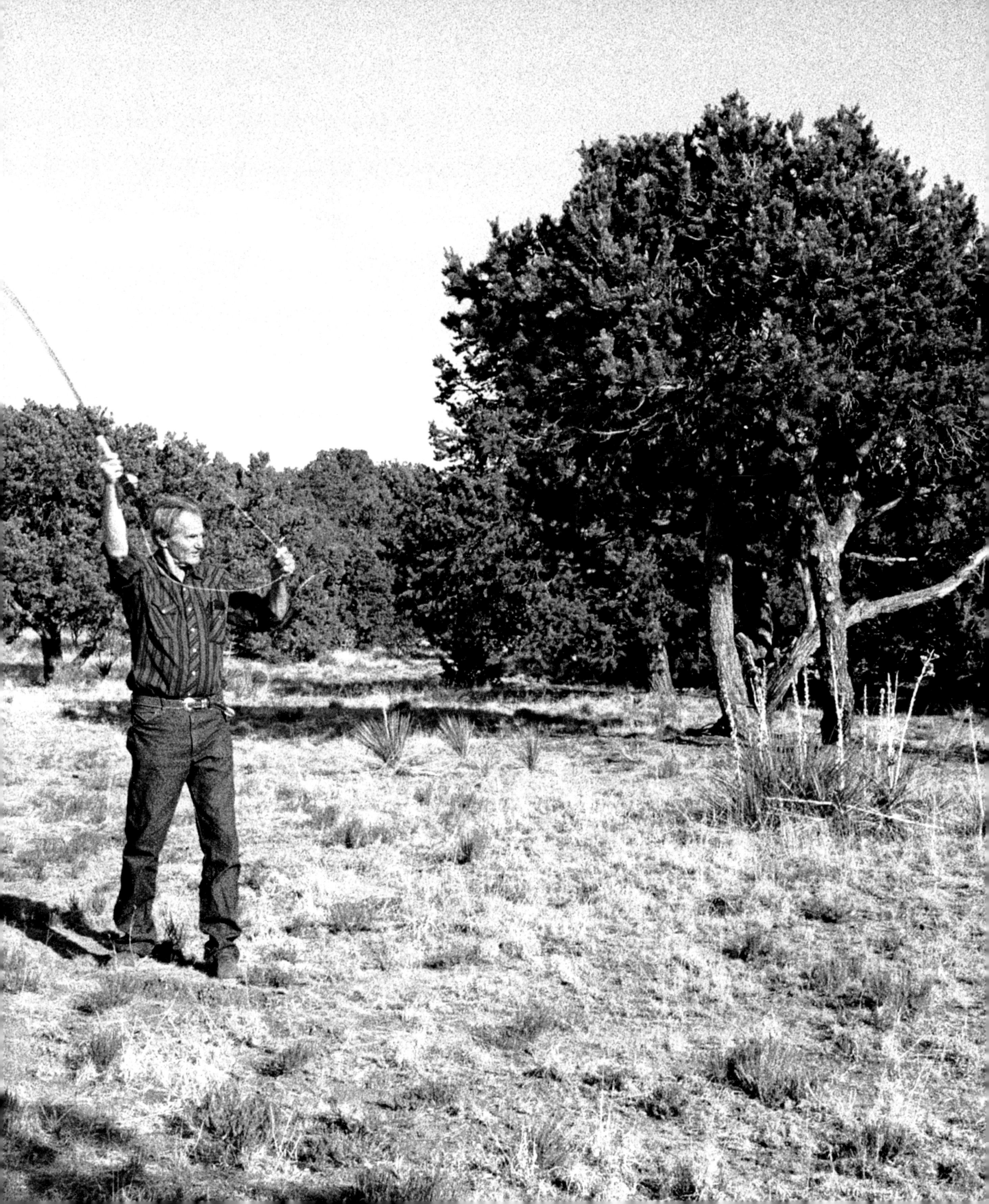

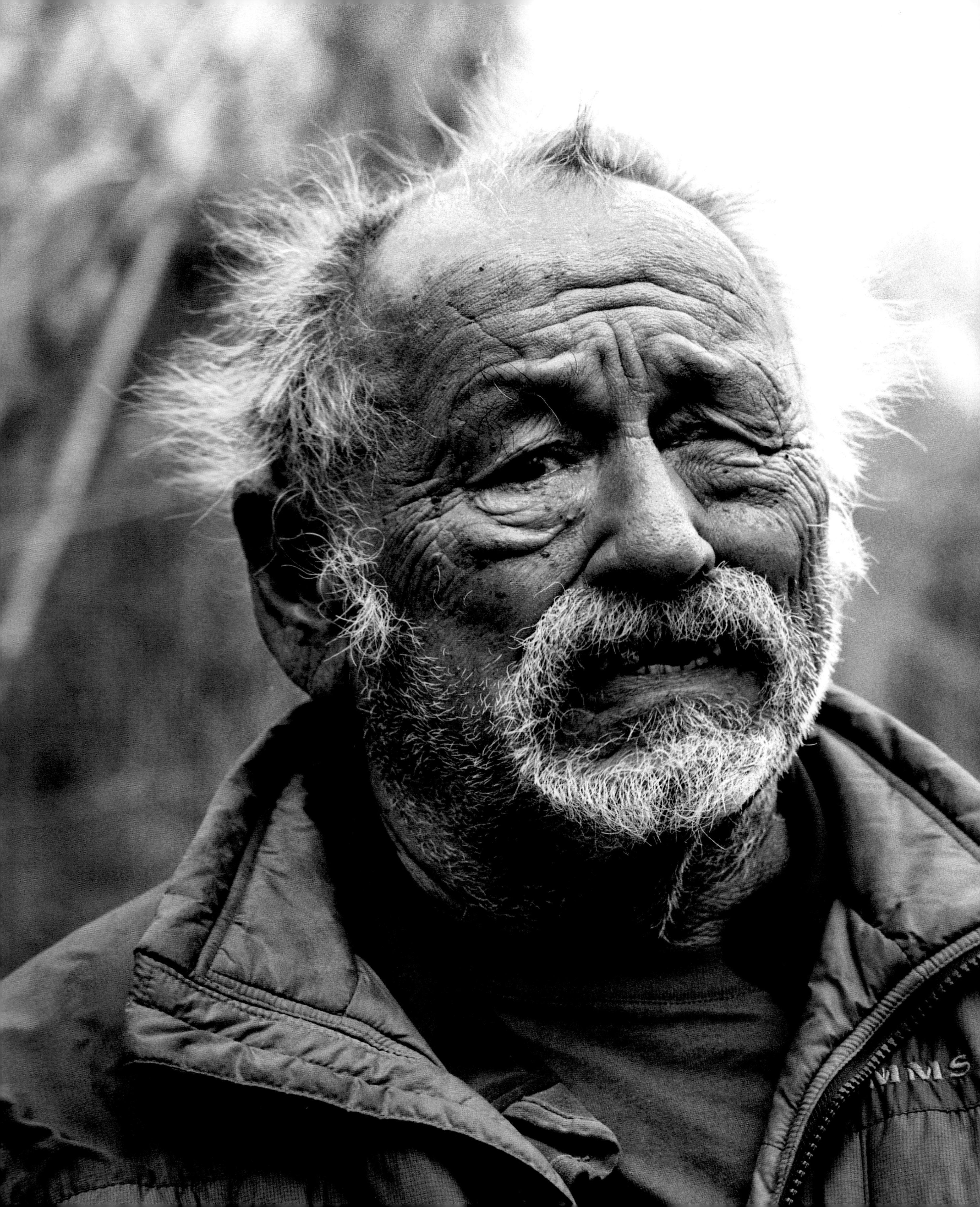

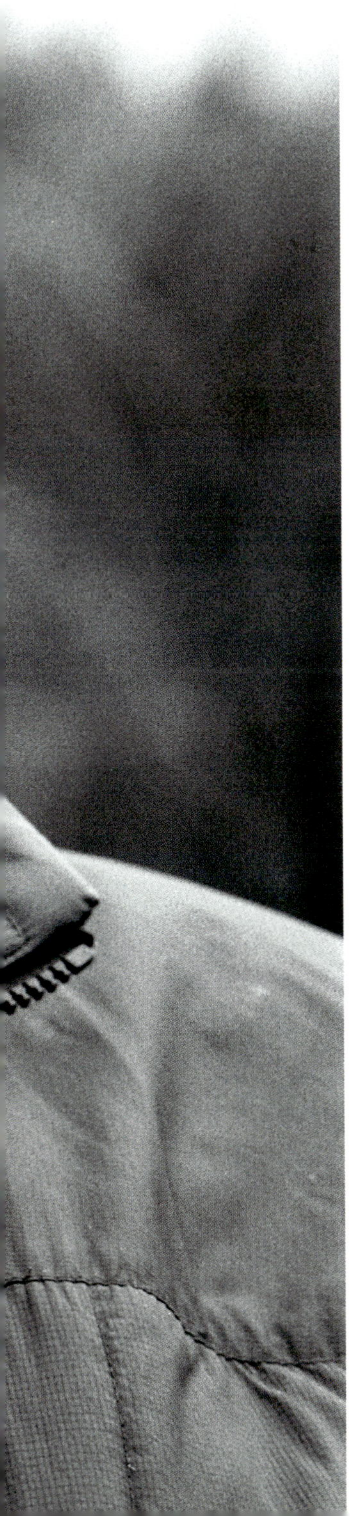

Jim Harrison

PATAGONIA, ARIZONA
MARCH 19, 2012

A big storm flailed away in Patagonia, a tiny enclave of artists, writers, and snowbirds in southern Arizona, eighteen miles from the Mexican border. The wind and rain subsided just as I knocked on the door of the writer Jim Harrison's house. His wife, Linda, answered my knock with a pleasant welcome, but from within another voice growled, "You're two minutes late." It was Harrison. "No," I said, "I'm three minutes early." With this exchange clearing the air, we settled into a good afternoon of photography. He was sly and charming. He has had a lifelong appreciation for women, although he lost his left eye in a quarrel with a neighbor girl at age seven. I photographed him outside his house while he talked about writing poems for Jack Nicholson to read to Diana Vreeland on her deathbed. He quoted W. H. Auden as we made our way through wet grass and mud for pictures alongside a creek, but we had to stay on high ground because he had worn his bedroom slippers. As I fumbled with what I thought was a malfunctioning camera, he suggested I remove the lens cap. Throughout the afternoon, Harrison's double-barreled intake of alcohol and cigarettes alarmed me, yet Harrison was unfazed. He even suggested ending the session in the Wagon Wheel Saloon to top off a day of wine and photography with a vodka.

Jimmie Dale Gilmore

BEE CAVE, TEXAS
NOVEMBER 9, 1995

Jimmie Dale Gilmore grew up in Lubbock, Texas, and has an old-fashioned, rural tenor voice—a voice with a nasal quality that is a perfect fit for his fusion of honky-tonk and traditional country. His lyrics are often inspired by Eastern mysticism, and this atypical combination has contributed to his reputation and celebrity. But that day in Bee Cave, Texas, where I photographed him, he had tacked a simple yet descriptive note to the screen door of his small, wood-frame house:

> Laura,
> Sorry I couldn't reach you. I'll be back before 2 o'clock—Make yourself at home.
> The dogs are very friendly but rowdy. The white one is Lyra, the wiry-looking one is Vega, and the smooth-haired black one is Maia. I'll see you soon.
> Jimmie Dale Gilmore

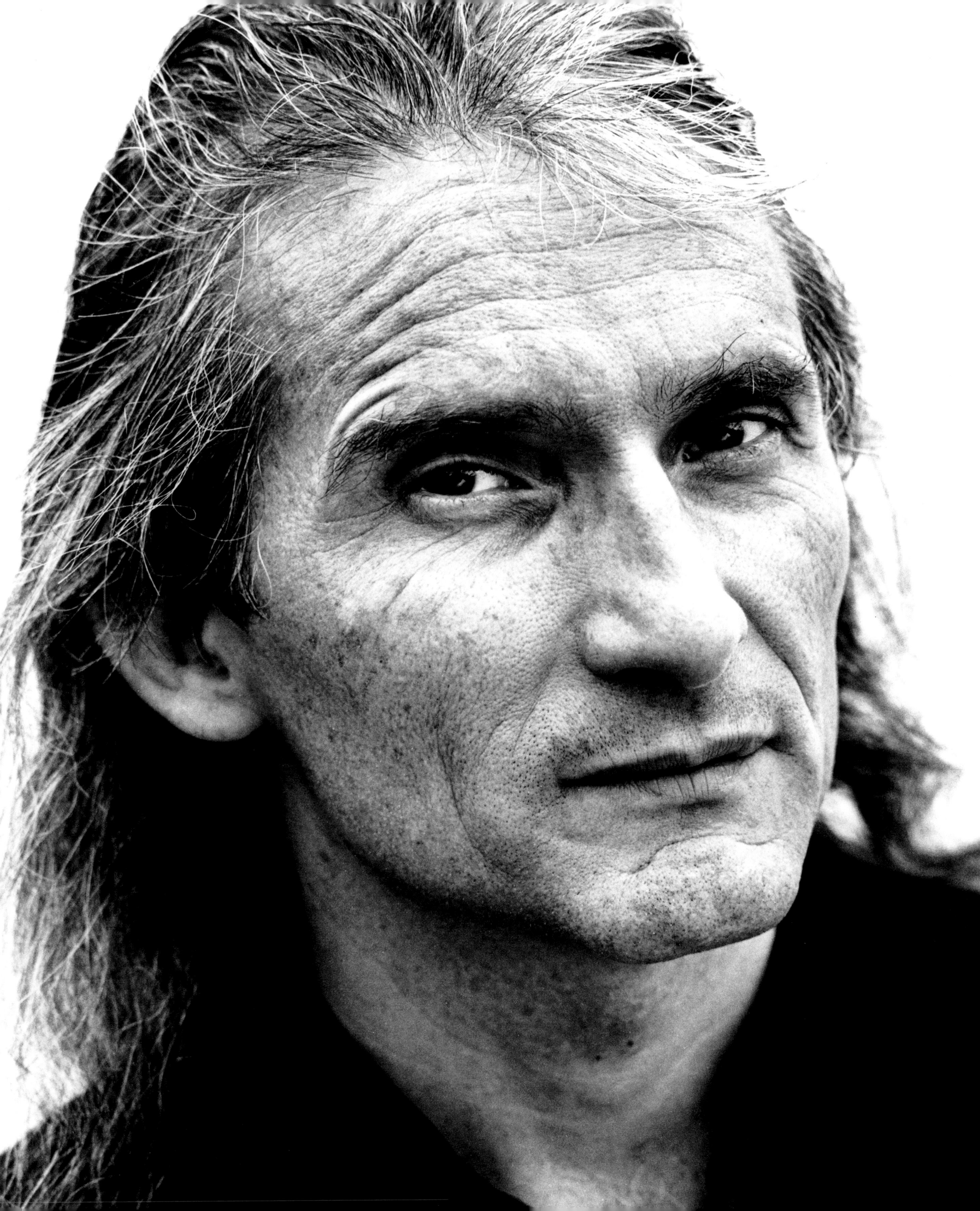

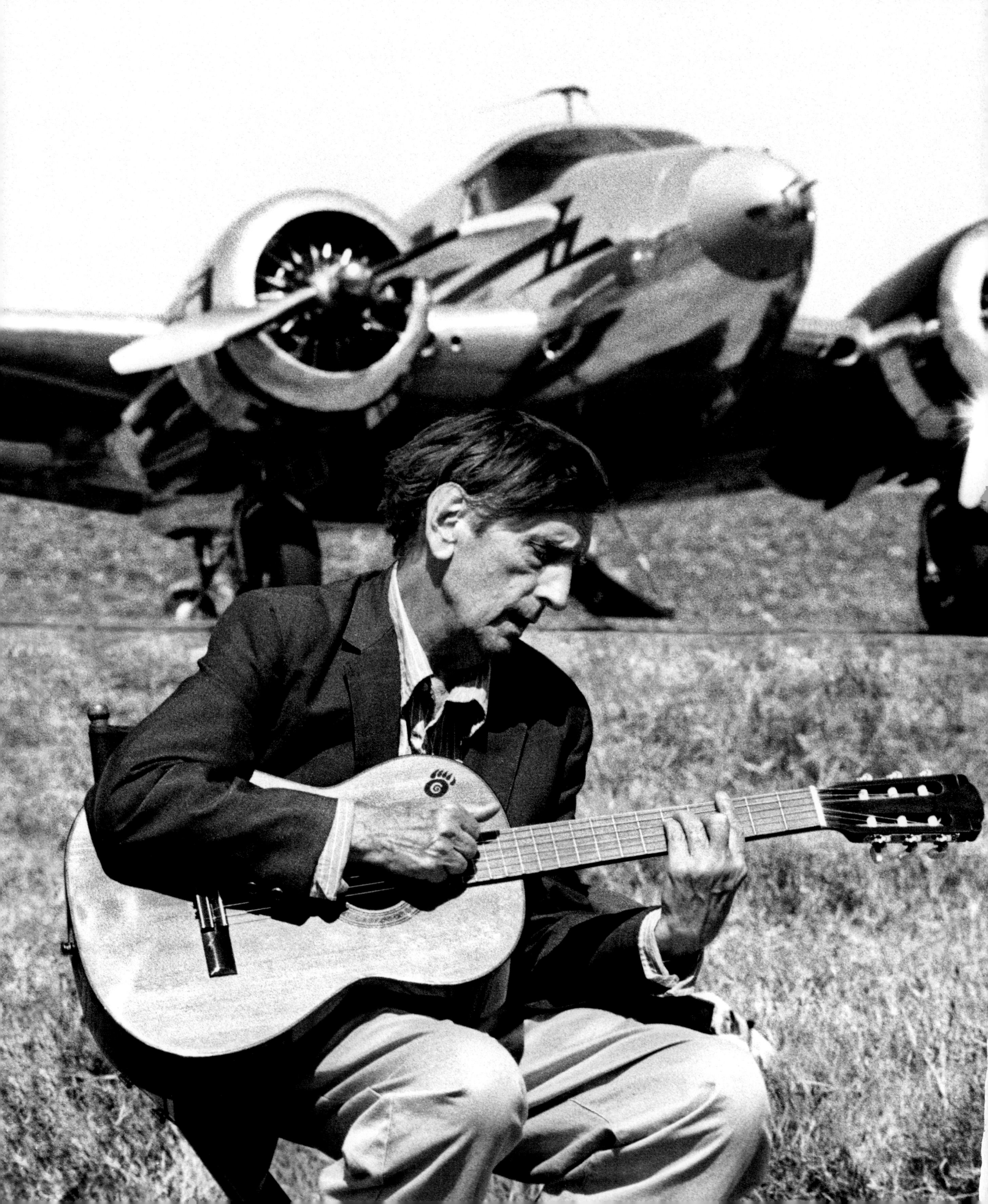

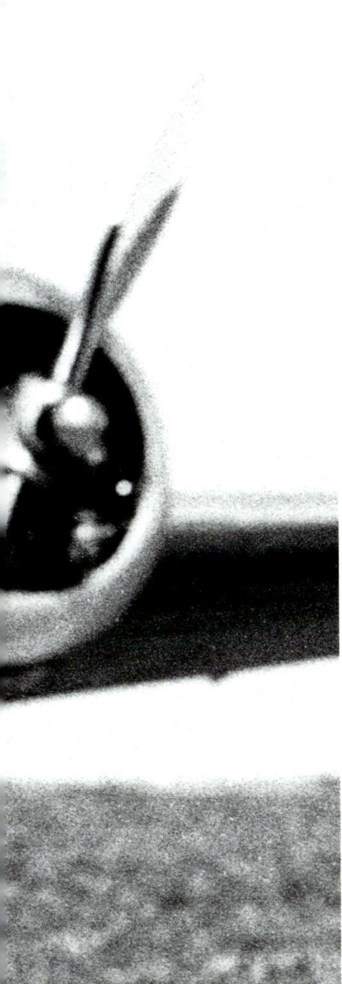

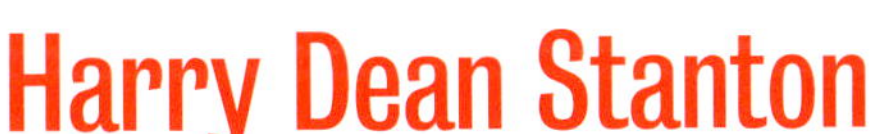

Harry Dean Stanton

CIRCLEVILLE, TEXAS
SEPTEMBER 22, 2003

It was no later than midmorning in Circleville, Texas, but nonetheless another September scorcher. Harry Dean Stanton, oblivious to the heat, waited near a beautiful Beechcraft Model 18 plane for the next scene in *The Wendell Baker Story*. He sang one of his favorite tunes, "Canción Mixteca," the story of a man filled with longing for his homeland of Oaxaca, Mexico. Stanton has appeared in more than two hundred films over the past sixty years, and he has been known to sit and play mournful Mexican ballads while the film crew works around him. He has the same strong, haunting voice that he had nearly a quarter century ago when he sang "Canción Mixteca" for Wim Wenders in the film *Paris, Texas* and, before that, when he sang "Just a Closer Walk with Thee" to fellow convicts, including Paul Newman, in *Cool Hand Luke*.

Stunt Cowboy

VENTURA COUNTY, CALIFORNIA
FEBRUARY 20, 2007

I think nowadays, while literary men seem to have neglected their epic duties, the epic has been saved for us, strangely enough, by the Westerns . . . has been saved for the world by, of all places, Hollywood.

—Jorge Luis Borges, *The Paris Review*

The Western movie may be the most American of art forms. From its first flicker on the silent screen in 1903 (*The Great Train Robbery*) through its Technicolor heyday with John Ford and Howard Hawks, up to the Coen brothers' *True Grit,* the Western has had a secure purchase on our imagination. Throughout this long sweep, one key ingredient has always been present—the stunt cowboy. How else could you have runaway stagecoaches, attacking Indians, breakaway horses, charging cavalry, and wrecked wagons without the skills and daring of stunt performers?

Richard Bucher grew up in a ranching family in California, where he learned to ride jumping and bucking horses. His mother's family had homesteaded in Ventura, California, in the 1860s. Bucher recalled that he became interested in training horses to fall "because no one my age was doing it. I learned the stunt business from old-timers, soaked up as much information as I could. I learned their secrets. I'm fortunate that I've been pretty successful. I've worked on every Western made for twenty years." Horse work, of all stunt work, is the most taxing on the body. According to Bucher, "You've got to remember that with a horse, something that size—just the weight ratio—if something goes wrong, you're going to lose."

Experienced stuntmen specialize today in cars or motorcycles or fires or fight sequences, but as Bucher told me, "You can't say you're a stuntman unless you've done a Western. There're only about ten of us left. It's dying out. And we're all still looking for that one last, great, cowboy adventure."

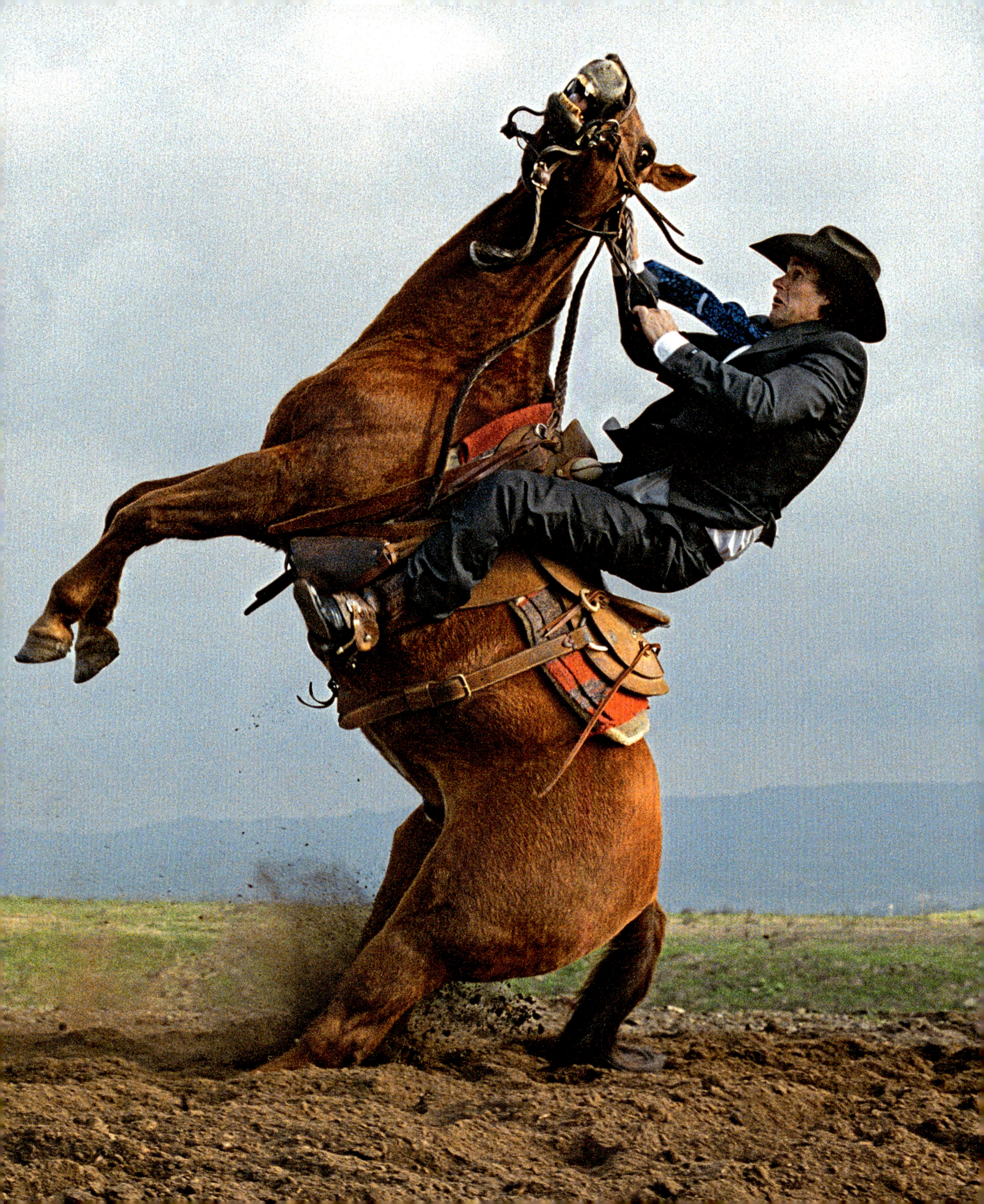

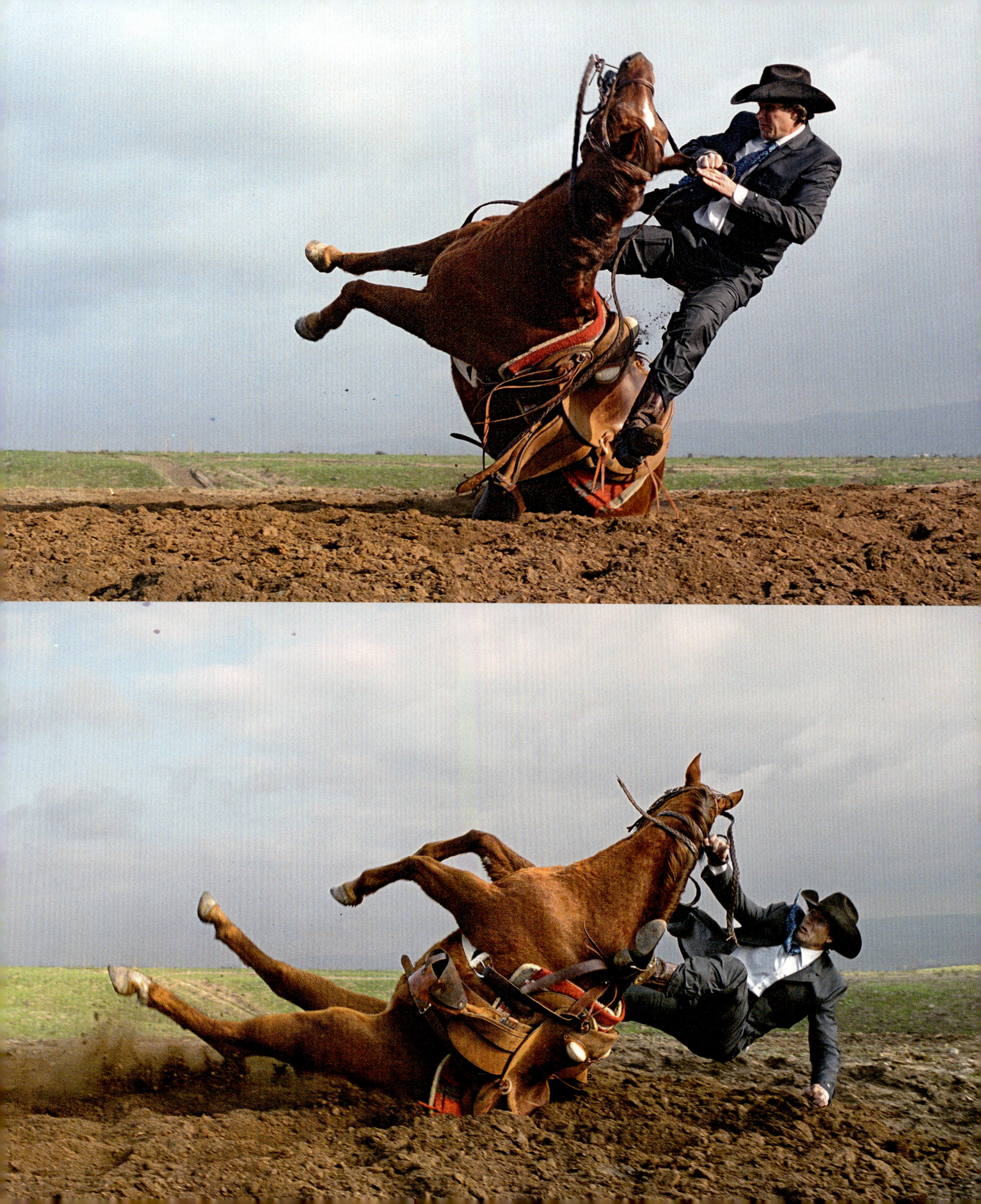

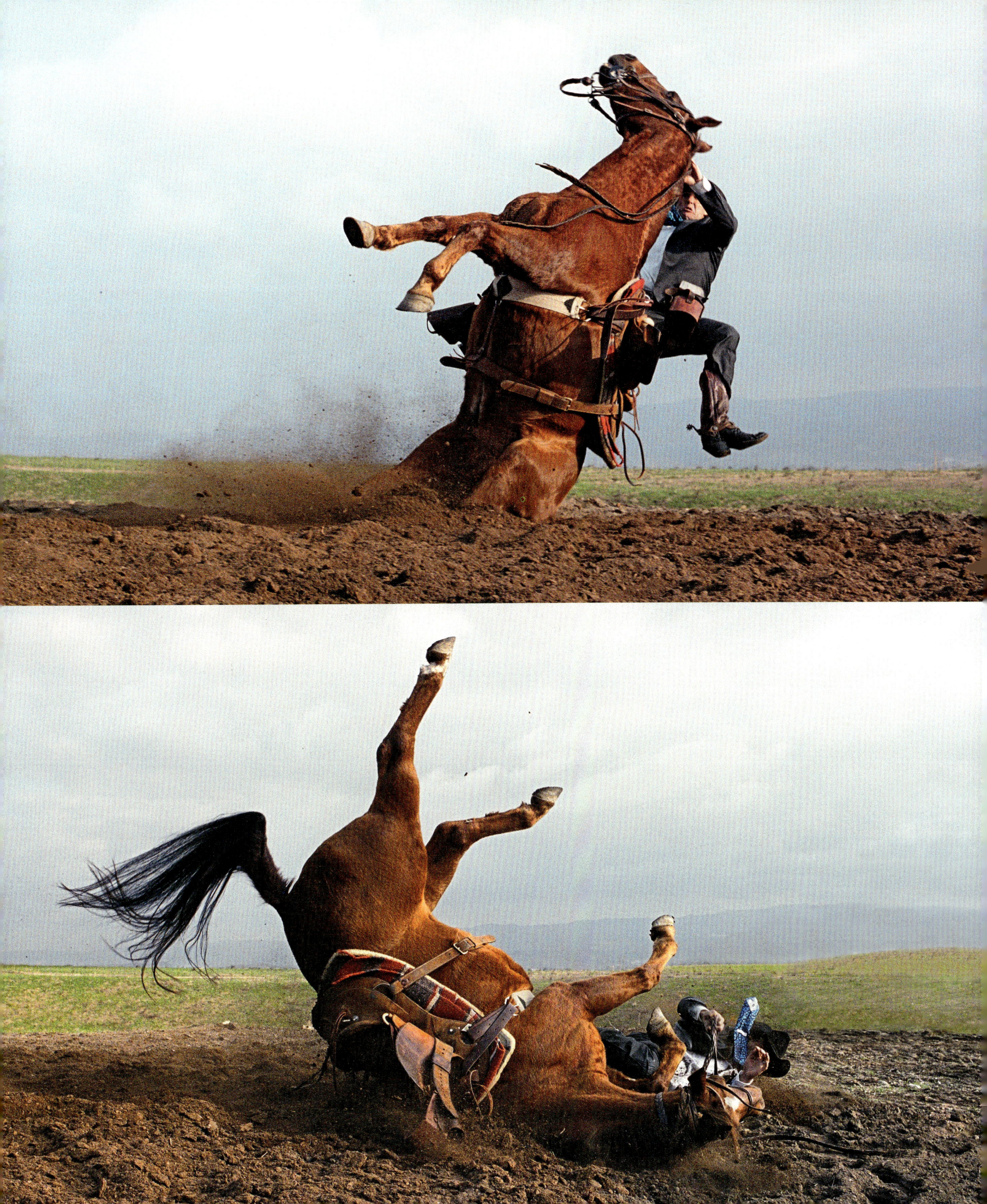

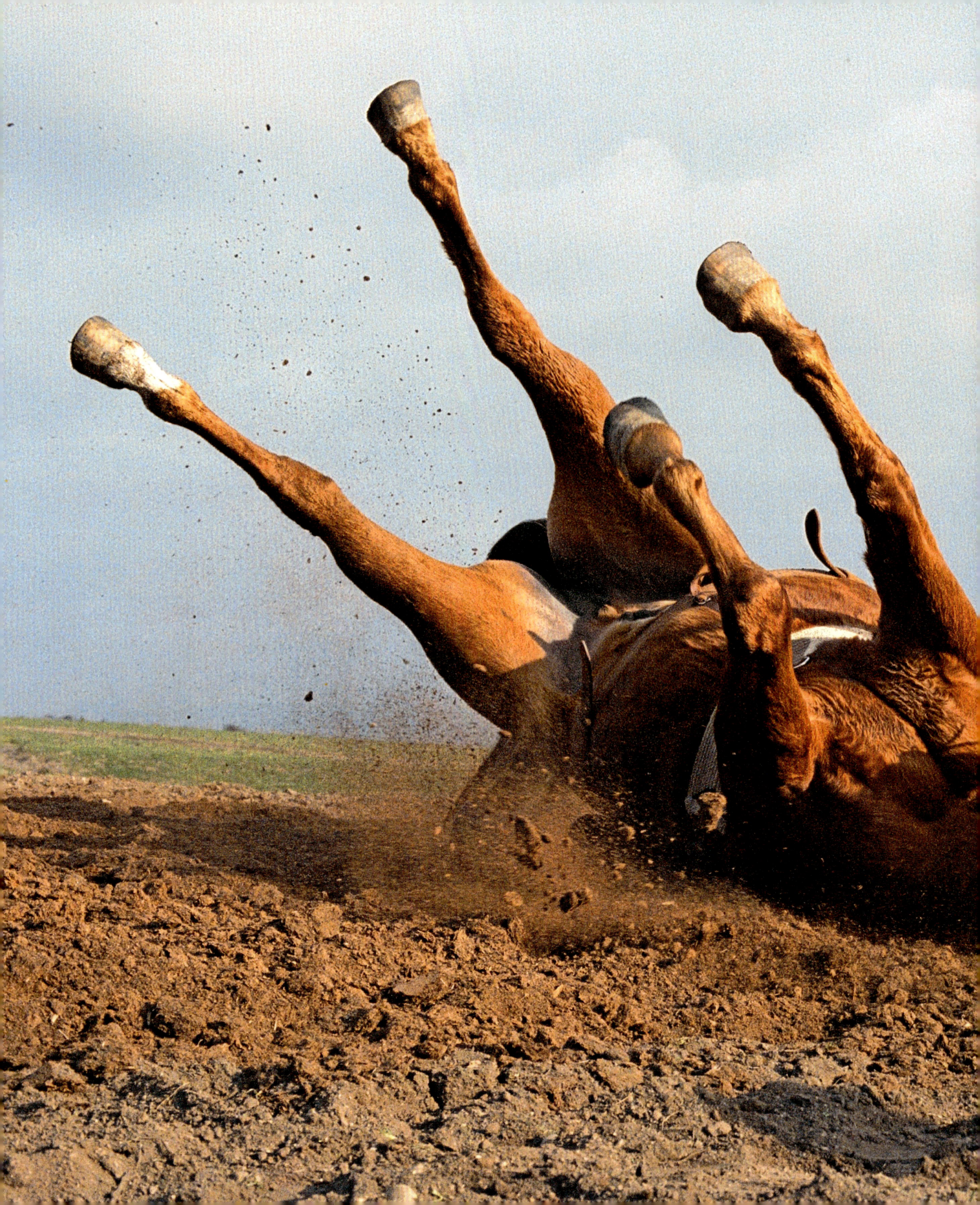

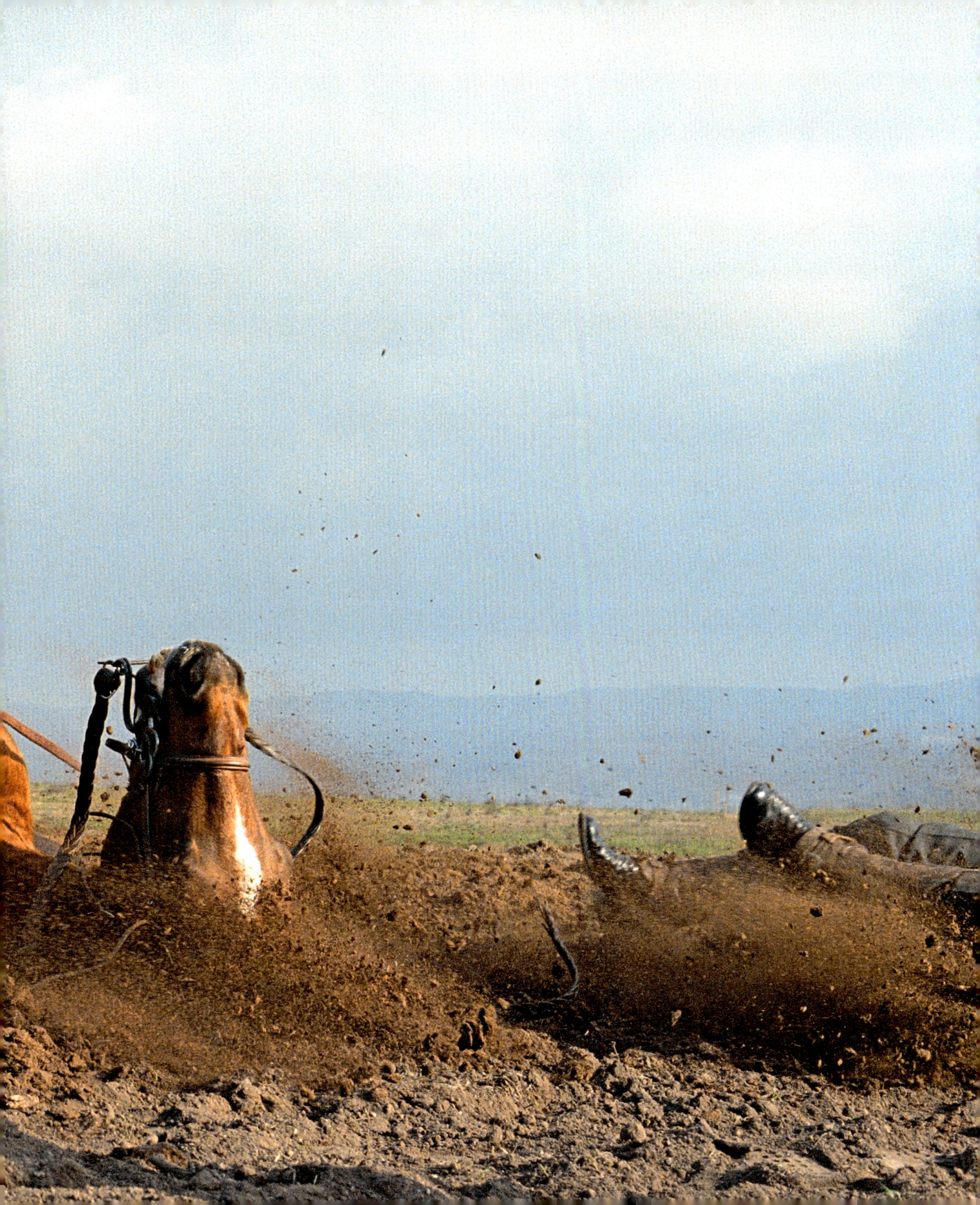

Trick Riders

FORT WORTH, TEXAS
FEBRUARY 1, 2001

Three girls in shiny, sequined costumes standing high on fast, running horses sped into the rodeo arena. The crowd cheered, the horses rocketed on, and the girls vaulted and flipped and hung from their saddles. They threaded themselves beneath their galloping horses to come up on the opposite side, smiling and waving. Their showmanship made their daring stunts look easy and fun.

After the performance ended, I went behind the chutes to arrange to photograph Niki Cammaert, one of the three trick riders, during a practice session the next afternoon. It was only then, in the clarity of daylight in a small outdoor arena, with no music and no lights, that I saw the real hazards of trick riding. Cammaert came toward me at a full gallop, balancing at a right angle off the side of her horse, her body jerking and swaying with her head not three feet from the ground. I was startled to see the strength and toughness necessary to perfect stunts on a horse rising and dropping at a lunging gallop. Later that same afternoon, Cammaert's horse misjudged a turn, smashing her hard against an iron fence. She got up gamely, though she had to have a four-inch gash stitched at the hospital. Cammaert had been trick riding for four years. But that afternoon, on the way home from the hospital, she admitted, "To push the limits of horsemanship at the speed I like to do it, really fast, I have to trust my horse, rely on him with my whole heart. My life depends on his judgment. It's very dangerous."

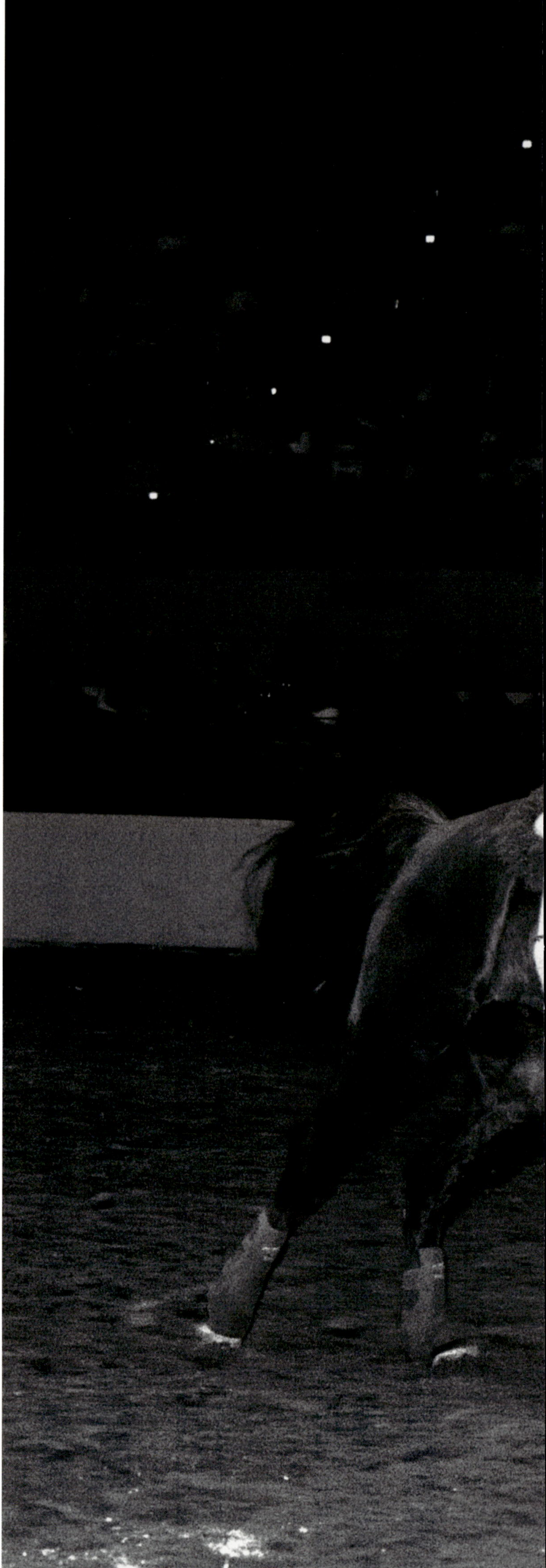

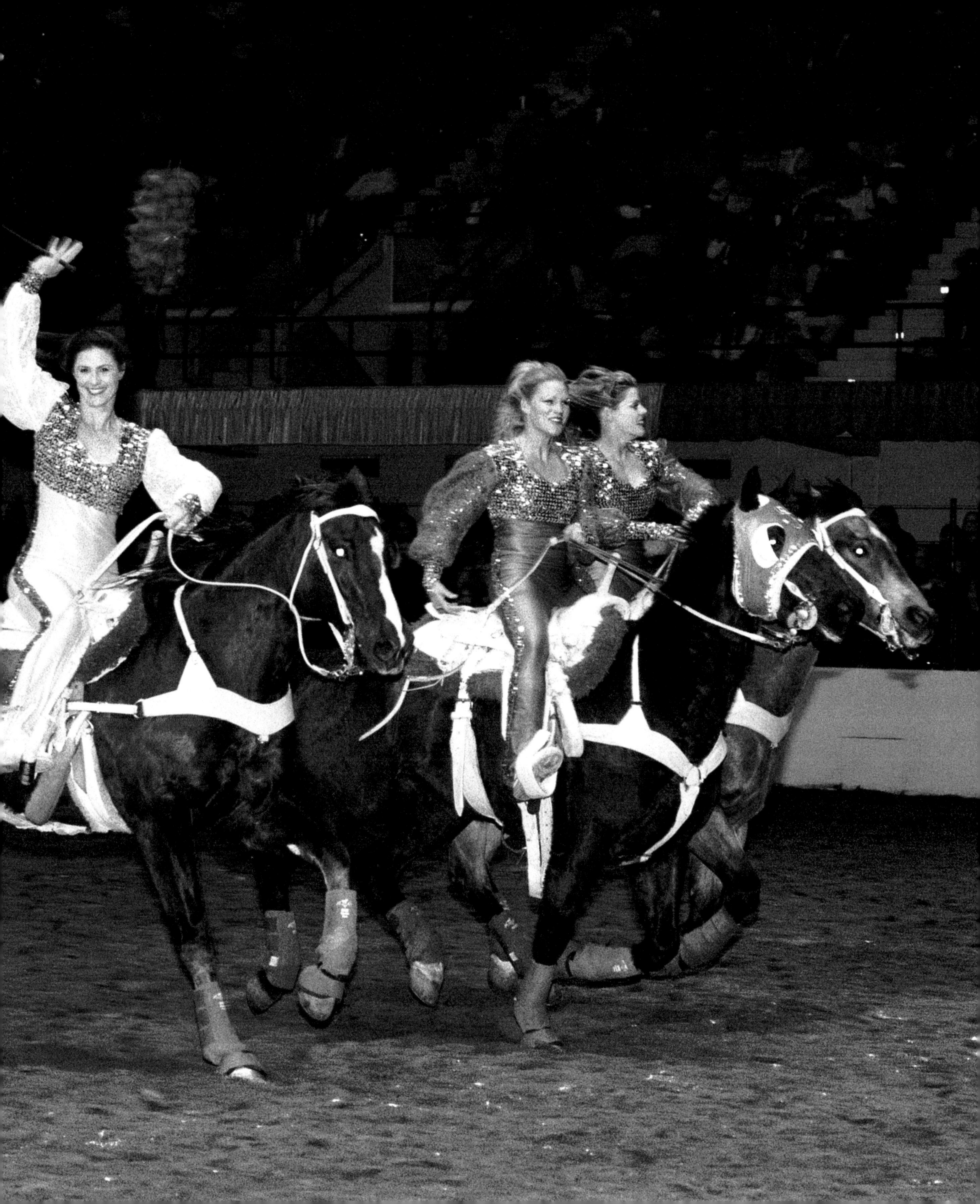

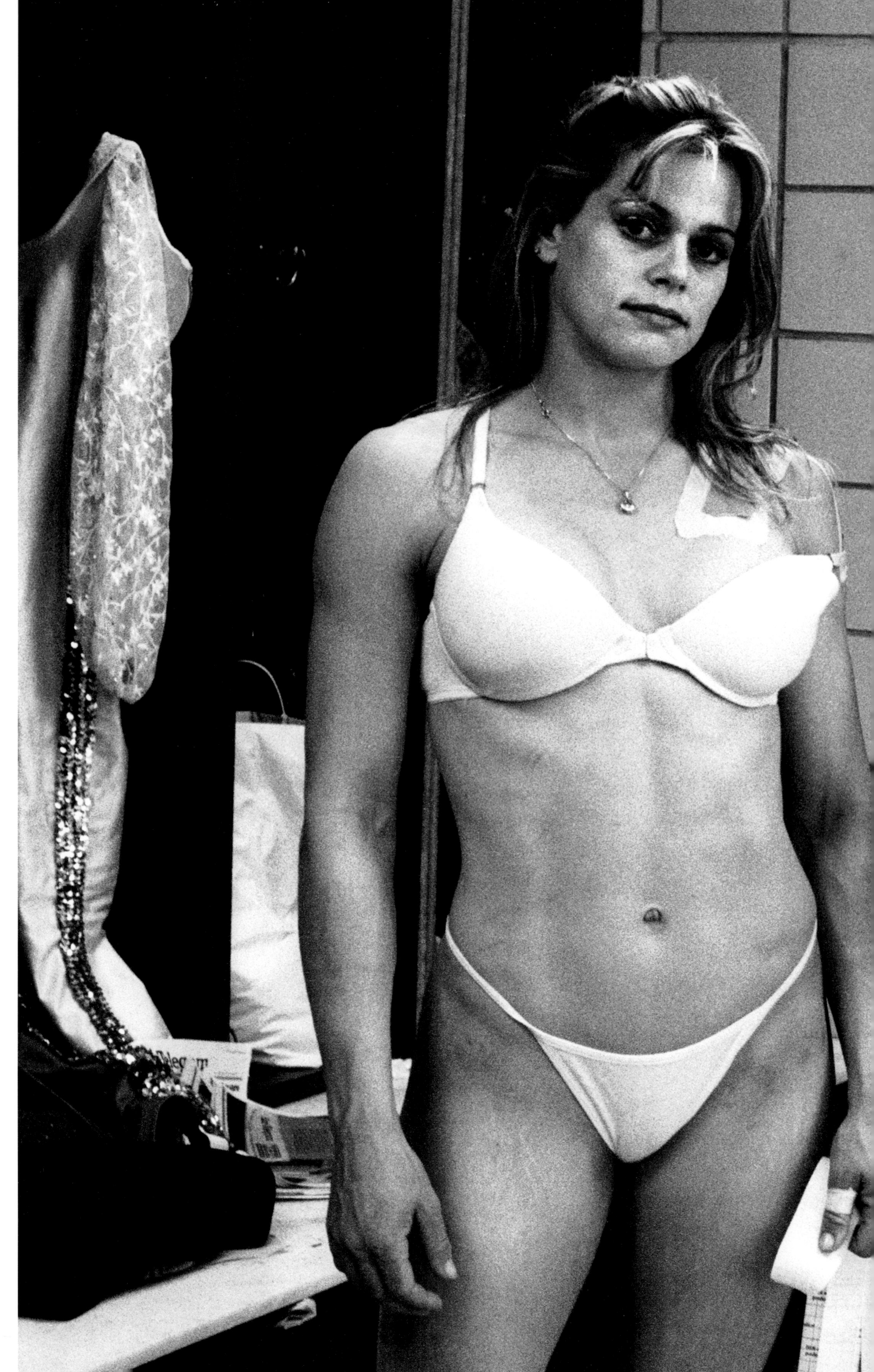

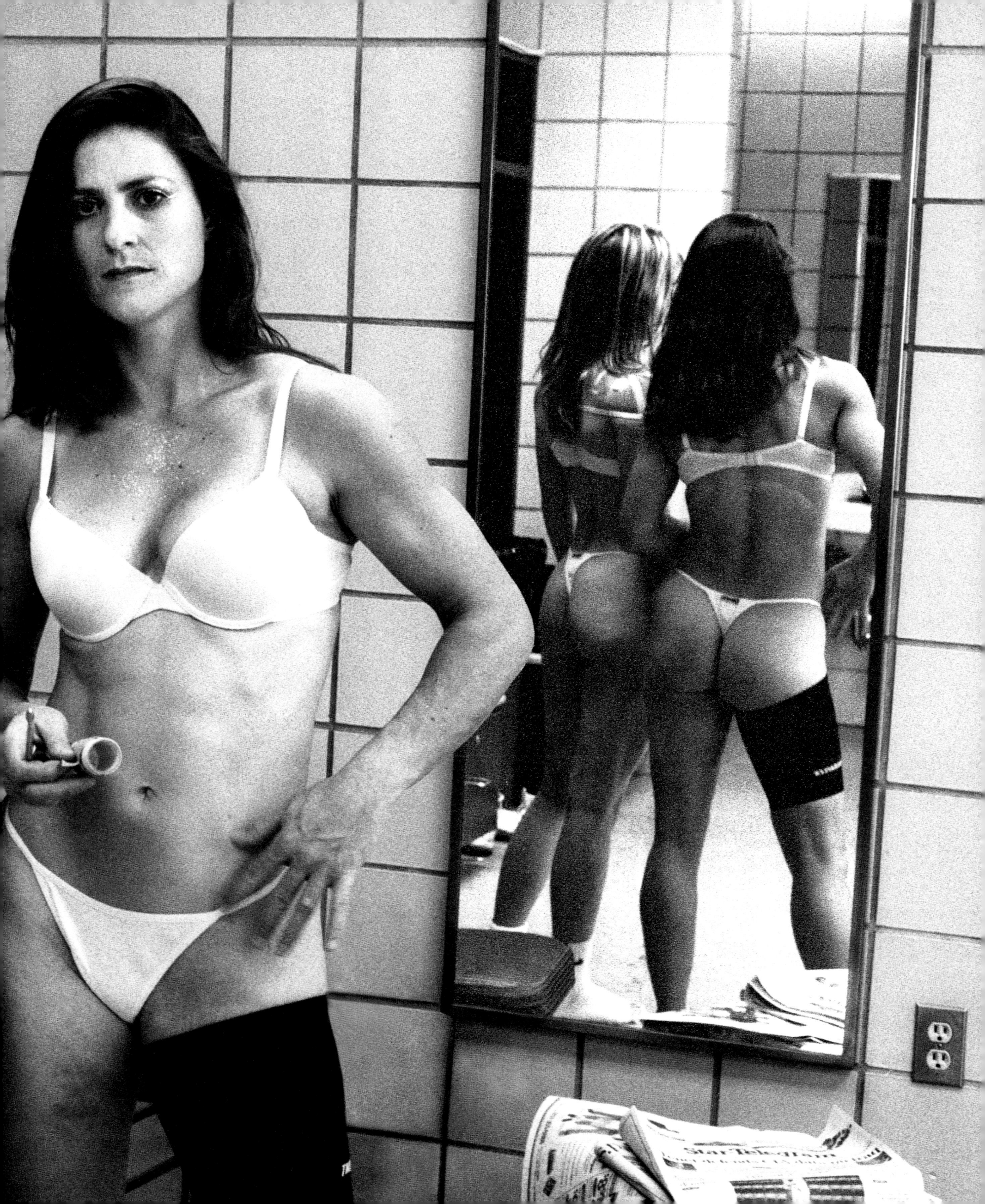
Star-Telegram

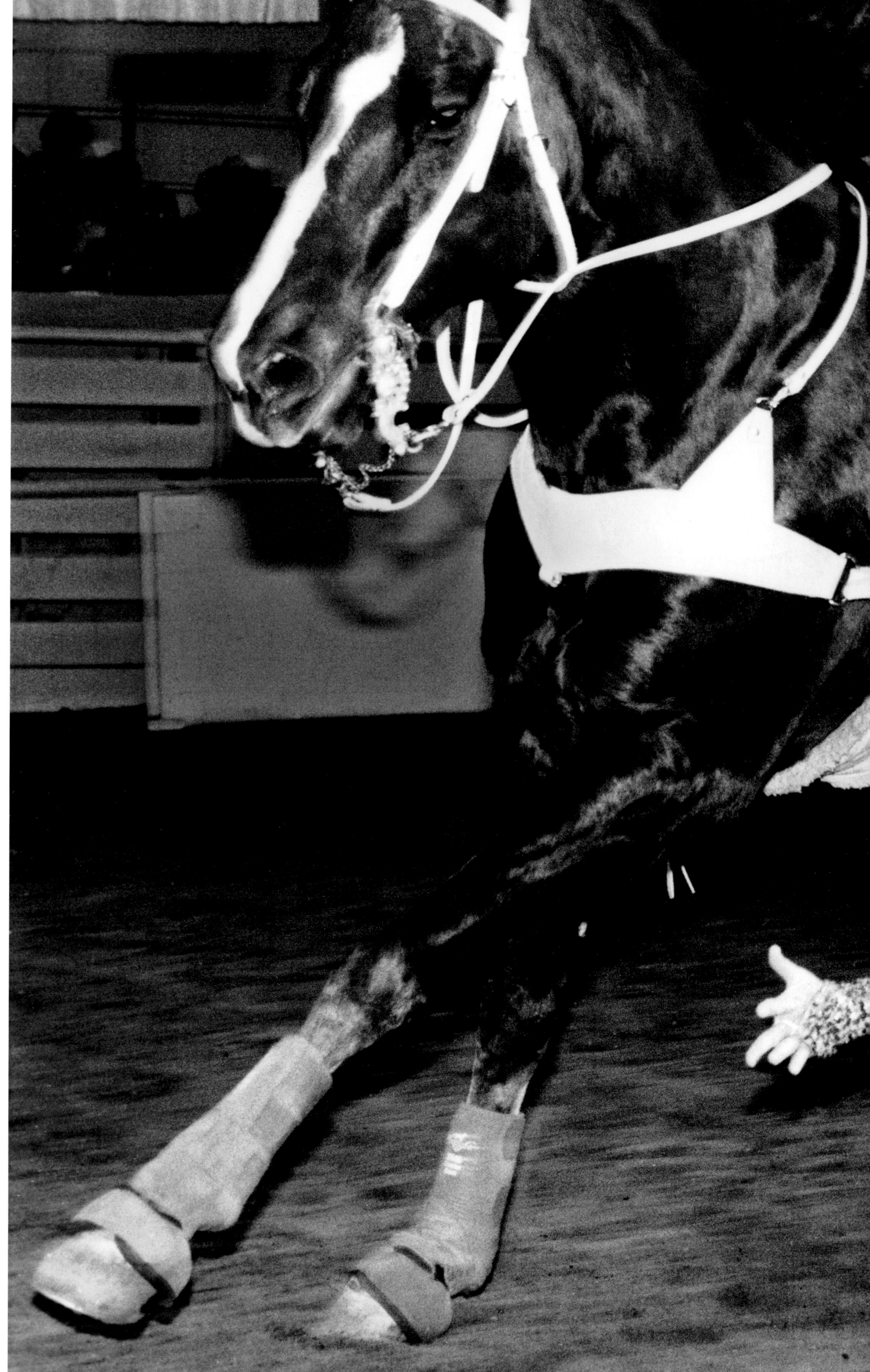

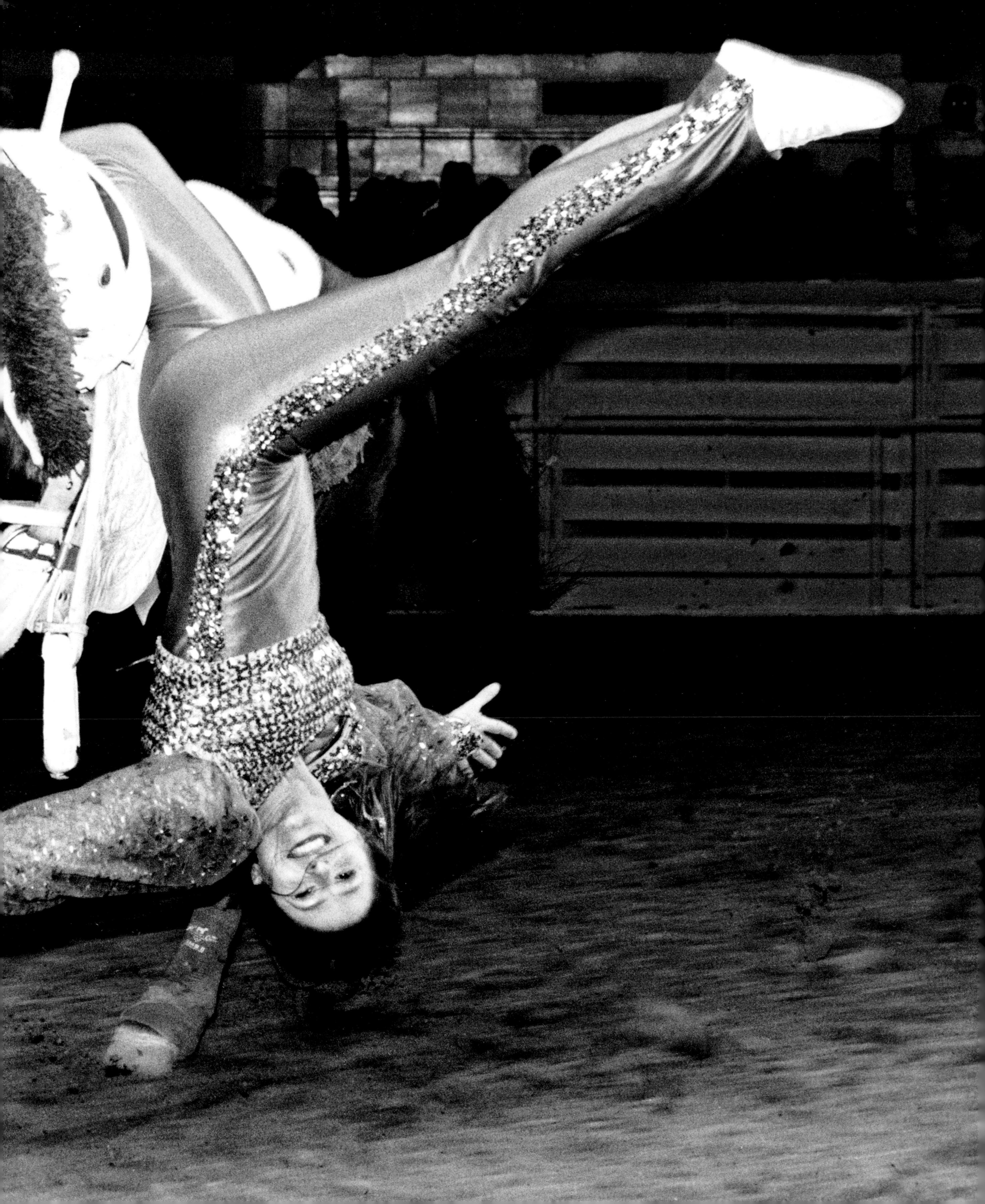

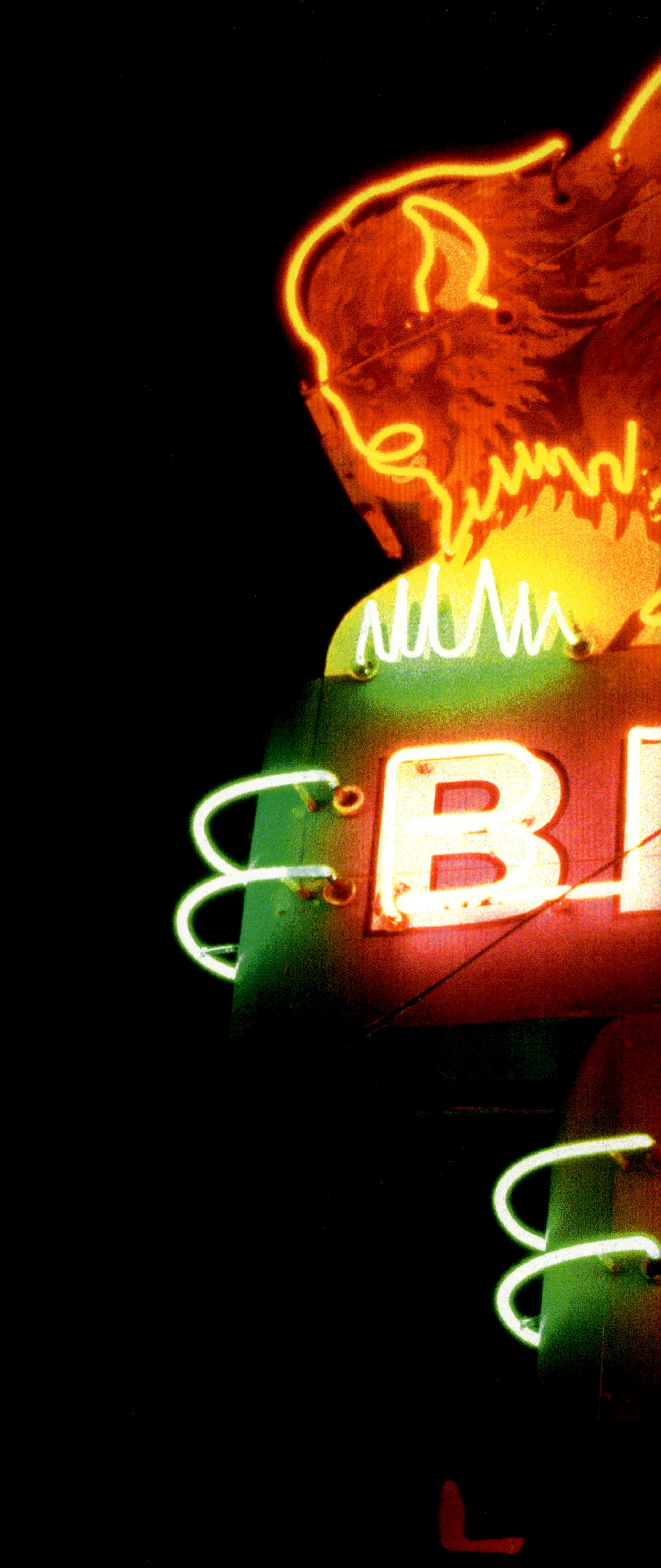

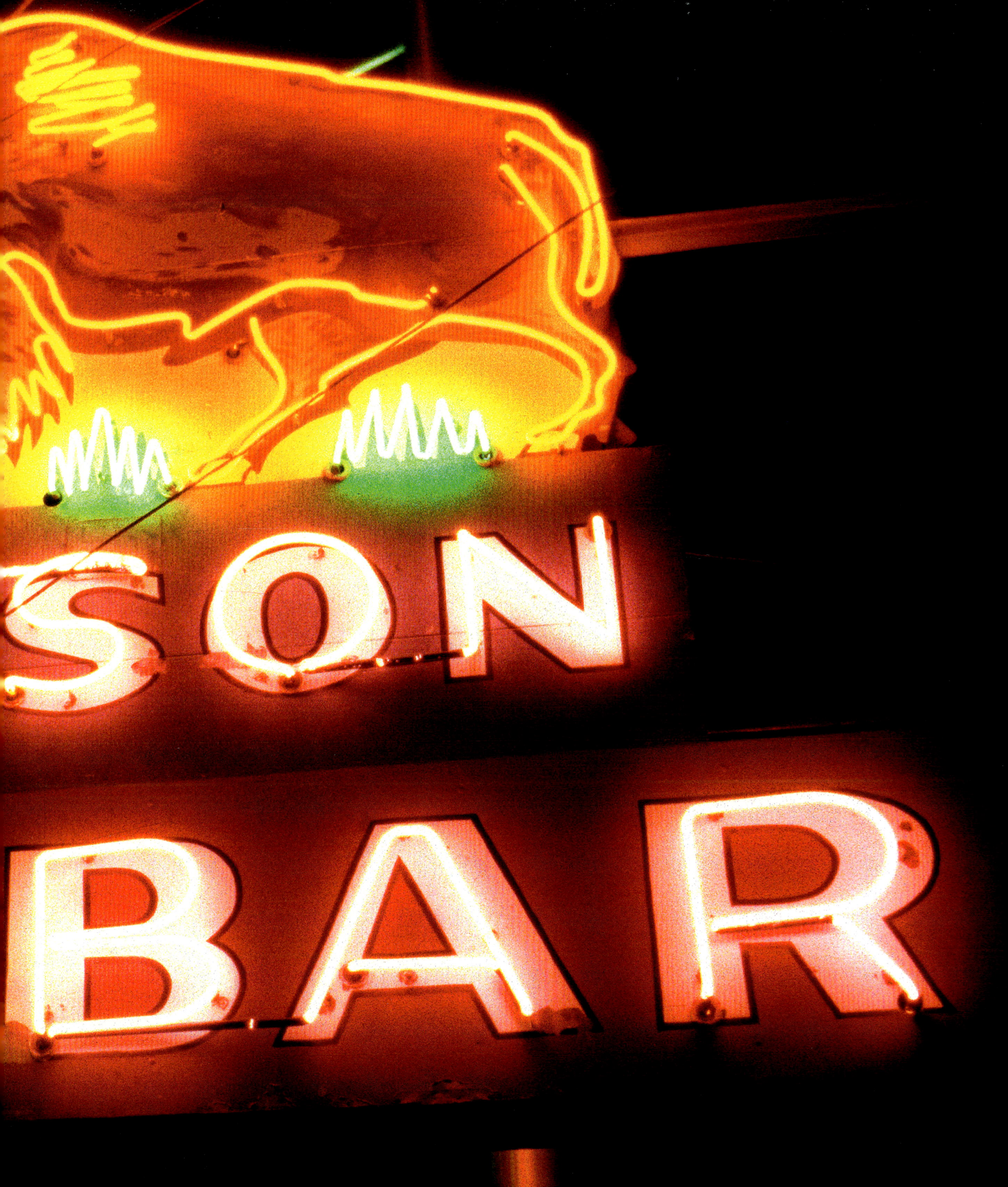
SON
BAR

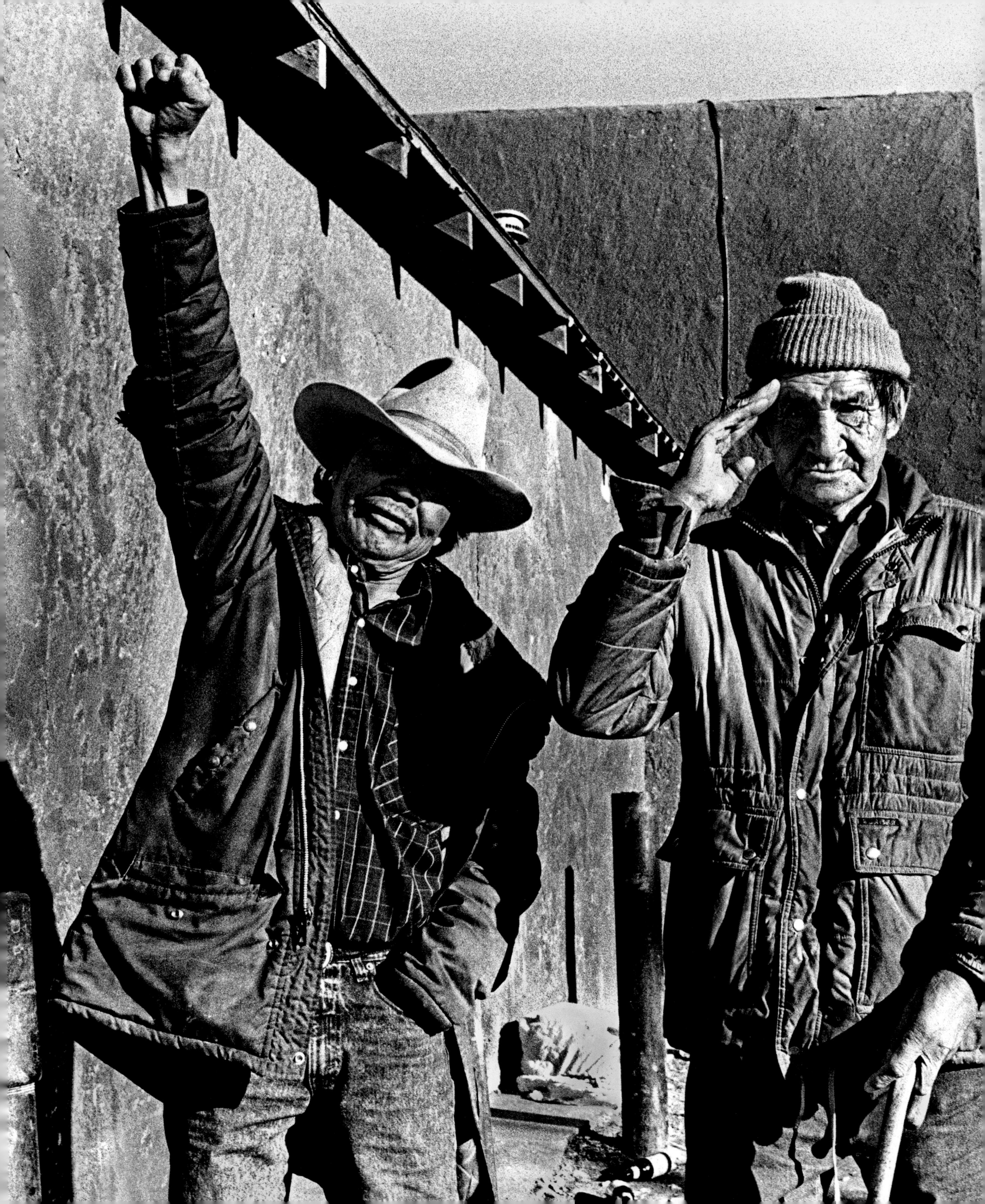

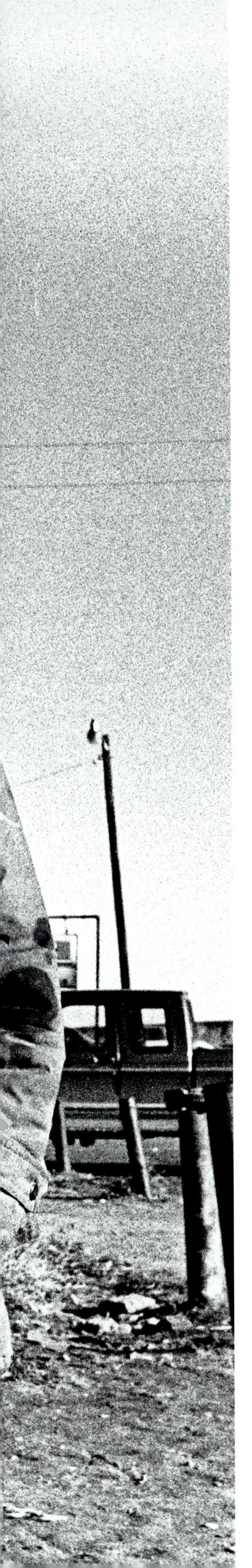

Oglala Sioux

WHITECLAY, NEBRASKA
DECEMBER 13, 1996

The Pine Ridge Indian Reservation in South Dakota bans the sale of liquor, and yet it is plagued by alcohol problems. Crime rates and health problems due to drinking are disproportionately high. In a particularly hellish confluence of desire and commerce, the town of Whiteclay, Nebraska, seventeen miles south, across the border from the reservation, has four stores that together sell thirteen thousand cans of beer and malt liquor each day. Whiteclay has a population of about ten people. The Pine Ridge Indian Reservation has a population of almost forty thousand.

I went with Milo Yellow Hair, an Oglala Sioux tribal leader, to Whiteclay, where he slowly drove his pickup down the main street. A woman wearing a Dallas Cowboys jacket approached the truck. She was young and clearly alcoholic. She leaned into the cab, begging Milo to give her husband a job. She said that twenty people in her family lived in one house. The house had no heat. It was February. The young woman told him that she had a month-old baby with fetal alcohol syndrome. "I'm the drunk in the family, Milo. My husband, he's a good man," she said. "He's at home now, taking care of the kids. Help him."

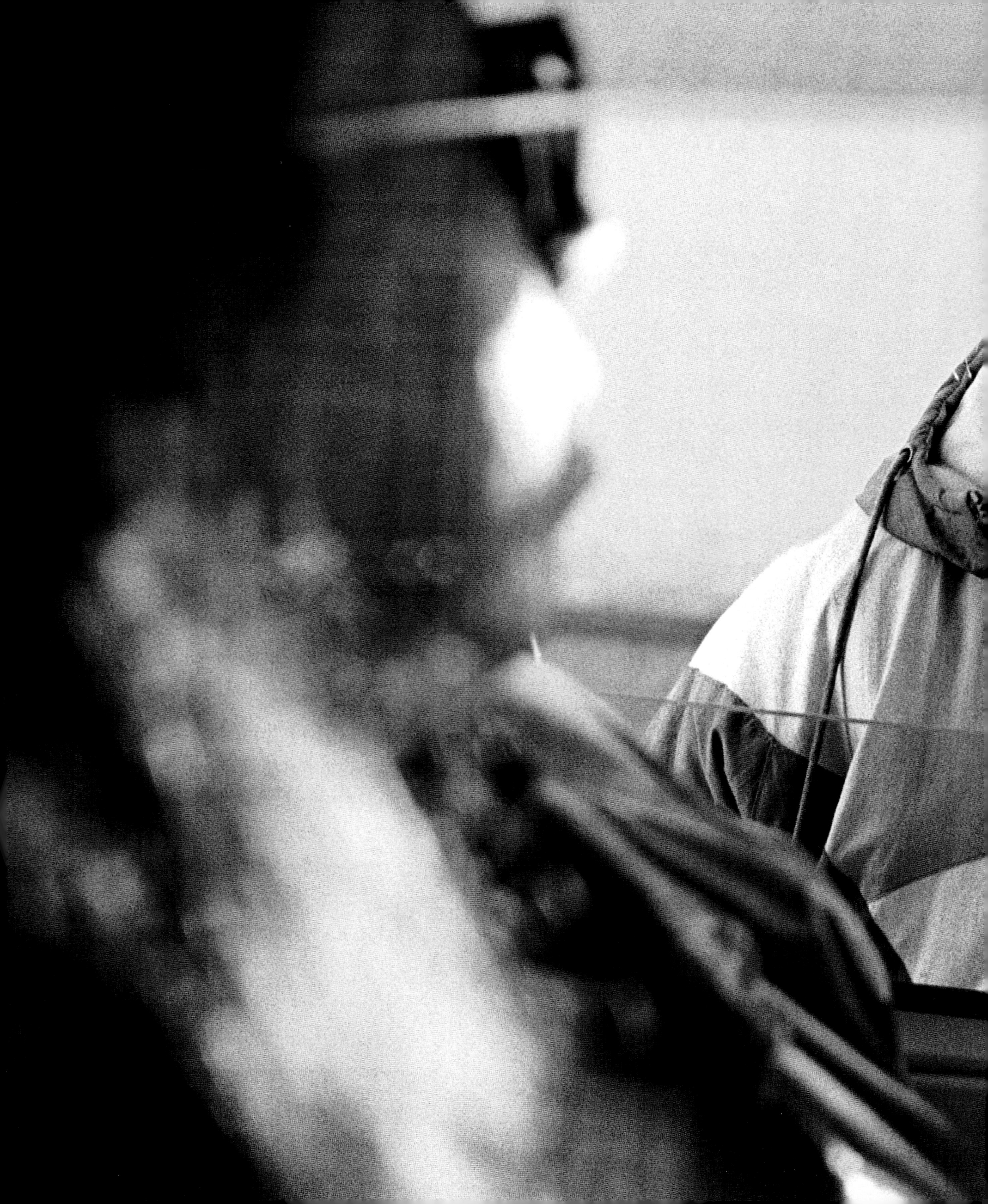

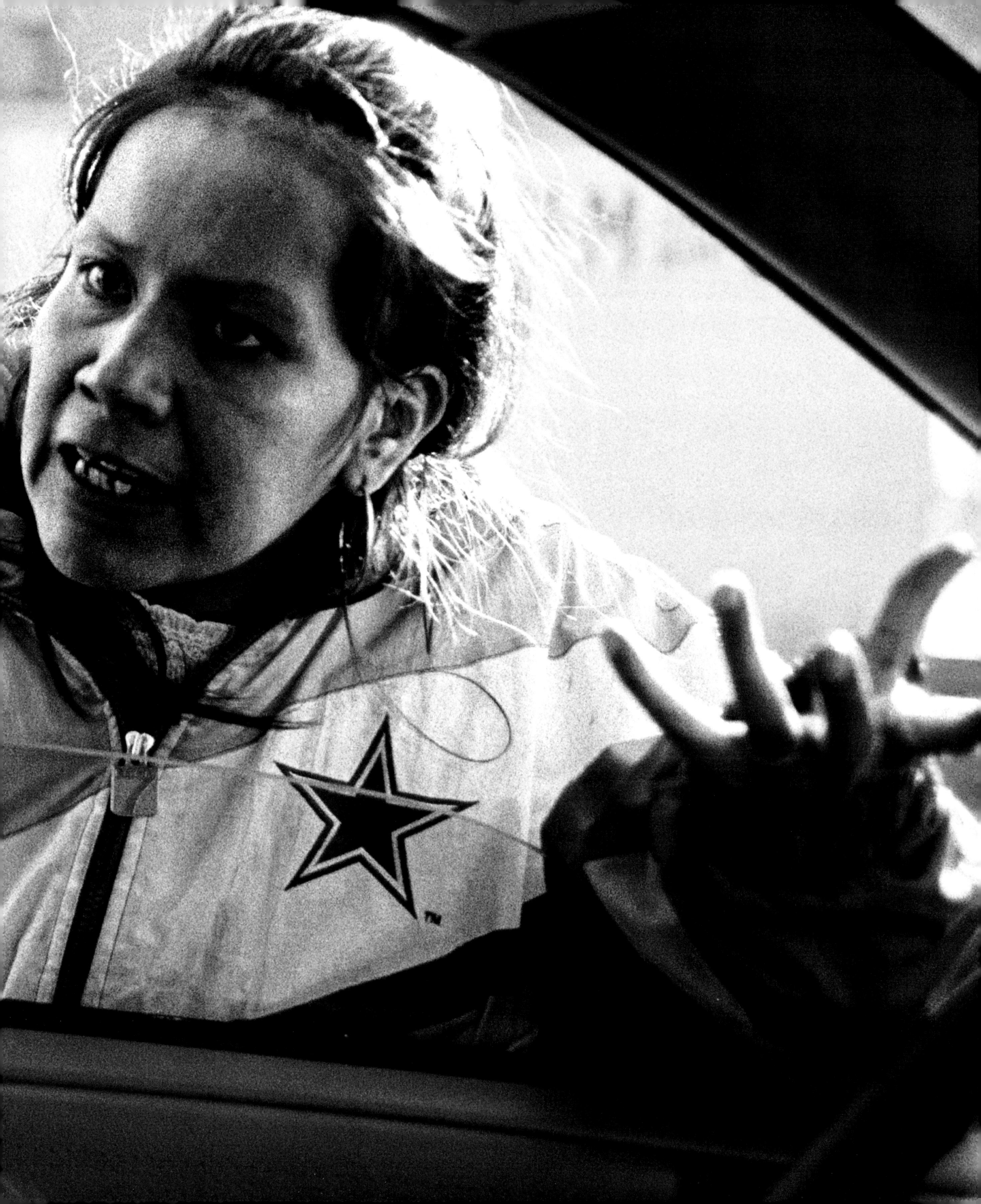

PINE RIDGE, SOUTH DAKOTA
DECEMBER 14–15, 1996

When you are on the Pine Ridge Indian Reservation in South Dakota, you cannot help but feel a sense of desperation. This reservation, in one of the poorest areas of the United States, is sparsely populated and far from urban job opportunities. With 80 percent unemployment, the prospects for those with hopes of breaking out of seven or eight generations of profound poverty are slim. Alcoholism affects eight out of ten families; one in five babies is born with fetal alcohol syndrome.

For more than a hundred and fifty years, both the federal and tribal governments have tried a series of often conflicting and seldom successful ways of improving living conditions among the Oglala Sioux. Today, the Pine Ridge Indian Reservation is still burdened by those same problems—generational poverty, chronic unemployment, and rampant alcoholism. When this series of photographs was first published in the *Washington Post Magazine* in 2007, the editor rejected many of them for being too difficult and upsetting for readers of a weekend magazine. Yet they show the truth of reservation life. If we can't even look at these problems, then how will they ever be solved?

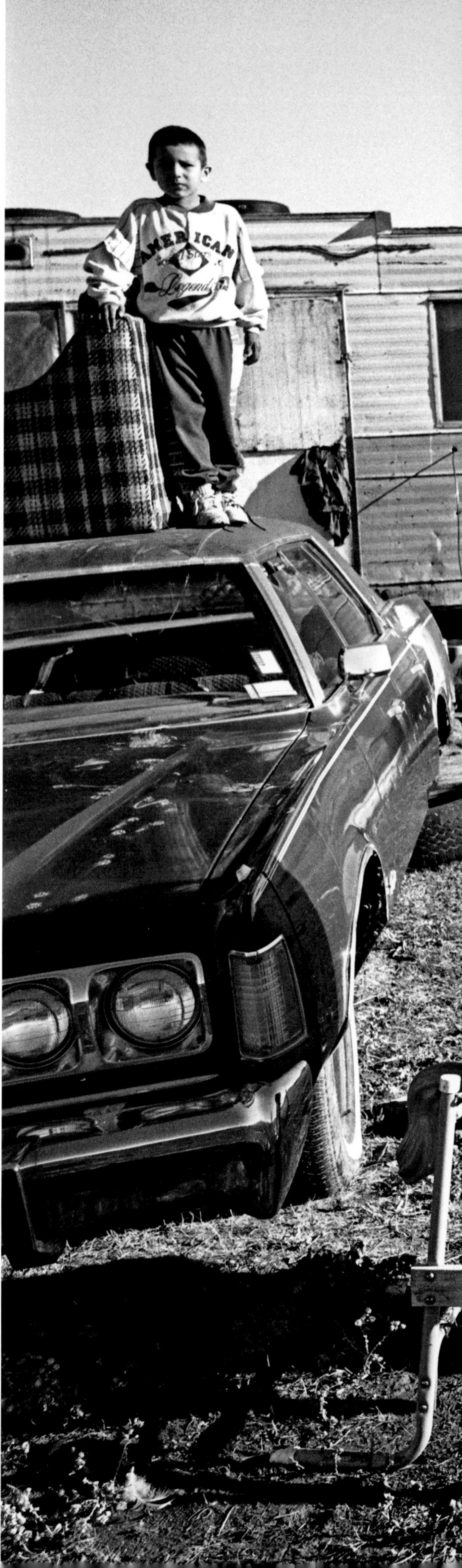

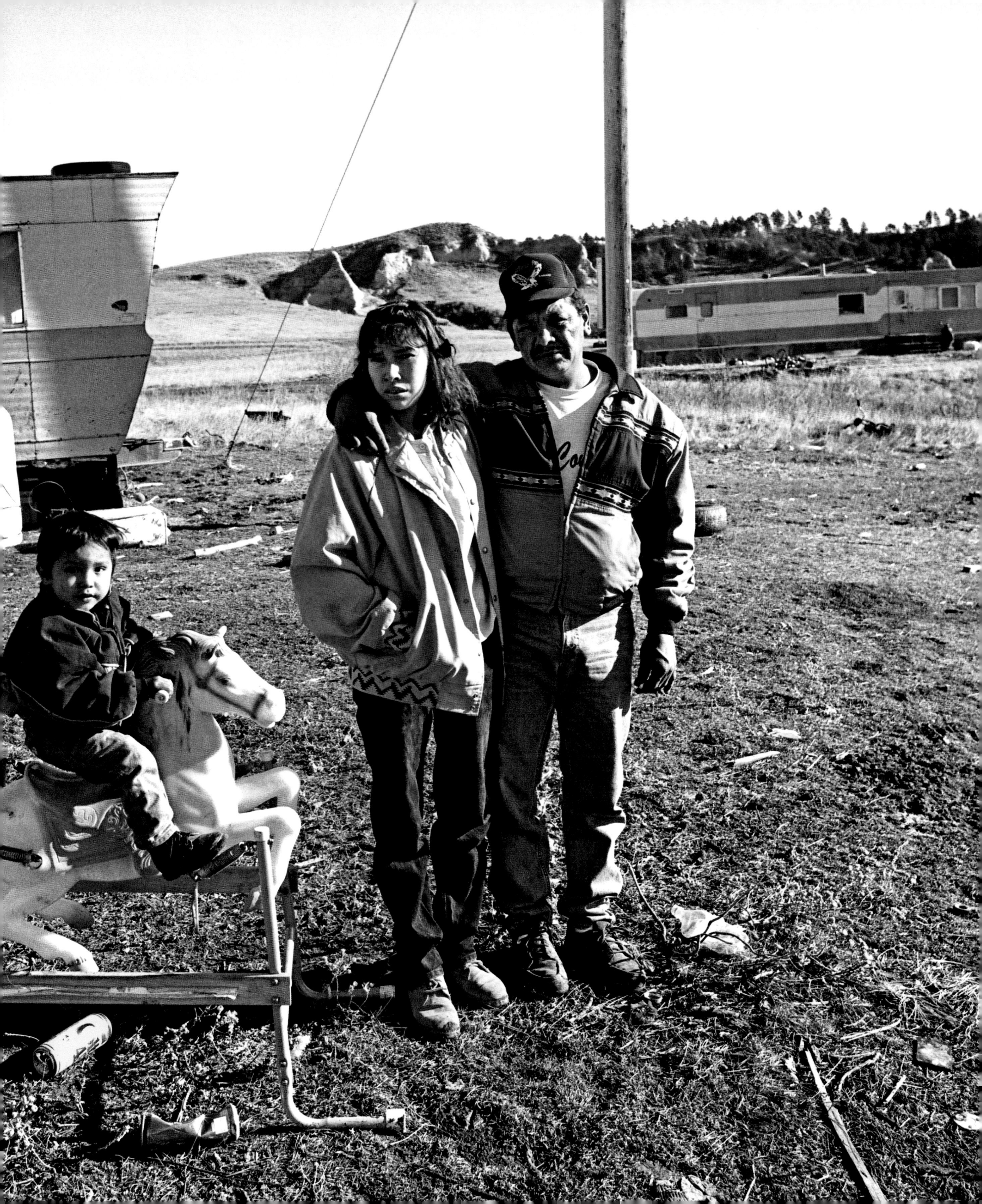

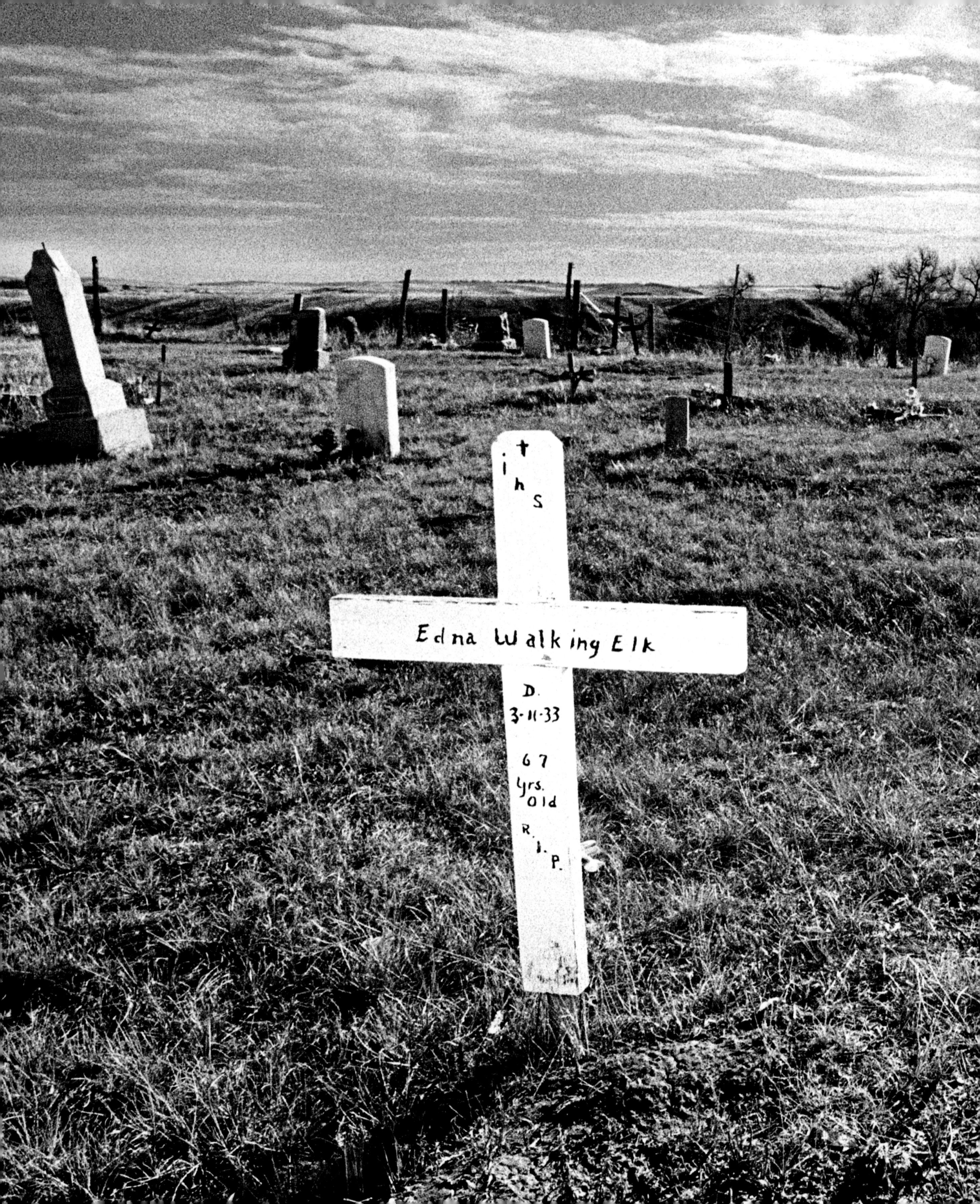

ihs
Edna Walking Elk
D.
3-11-33
67
yrs.
old
R.I.P.

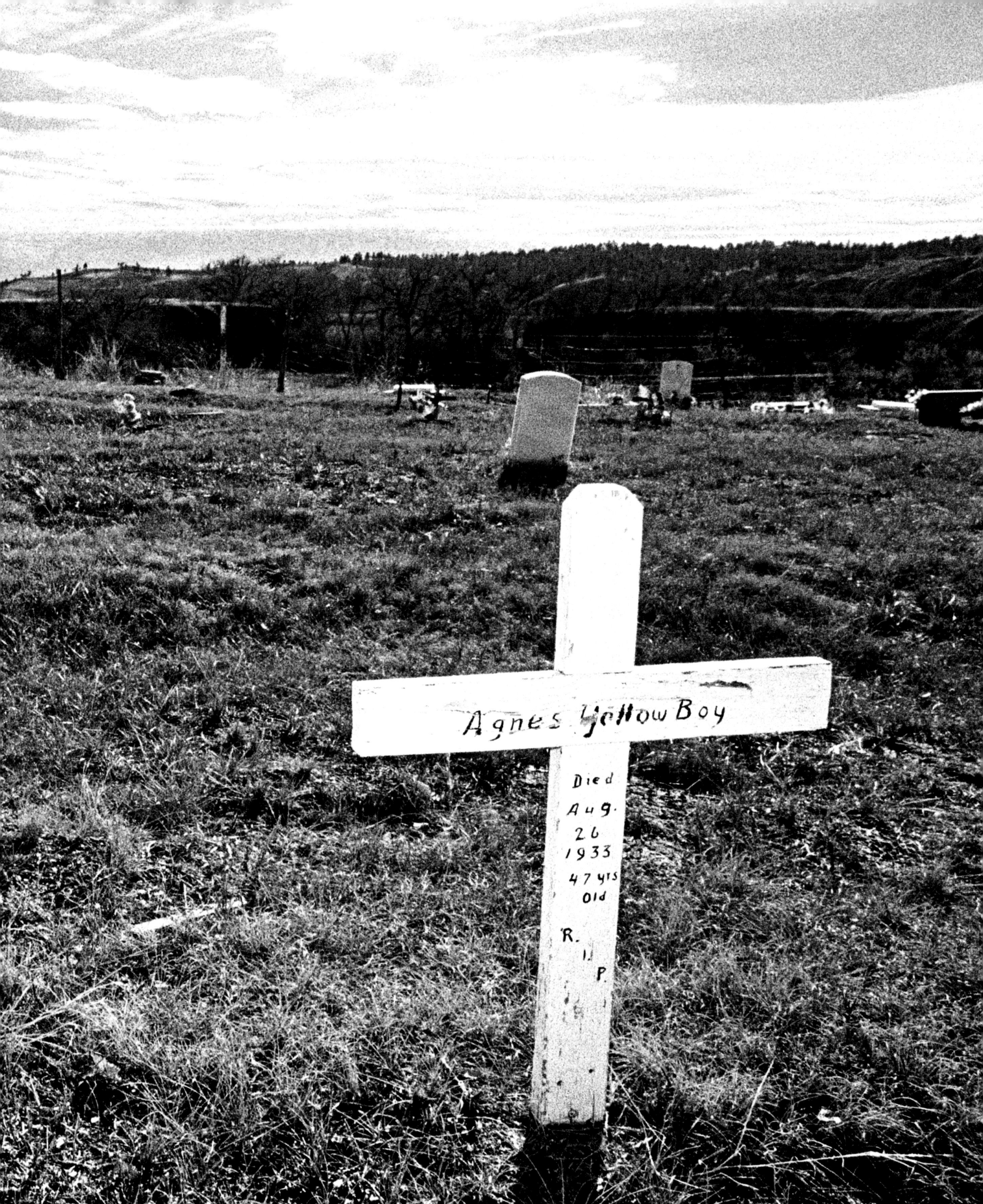
Agnes Yellow Boy
Died
Aug.
26
1933
47 yrs
old
R.
I.
P.

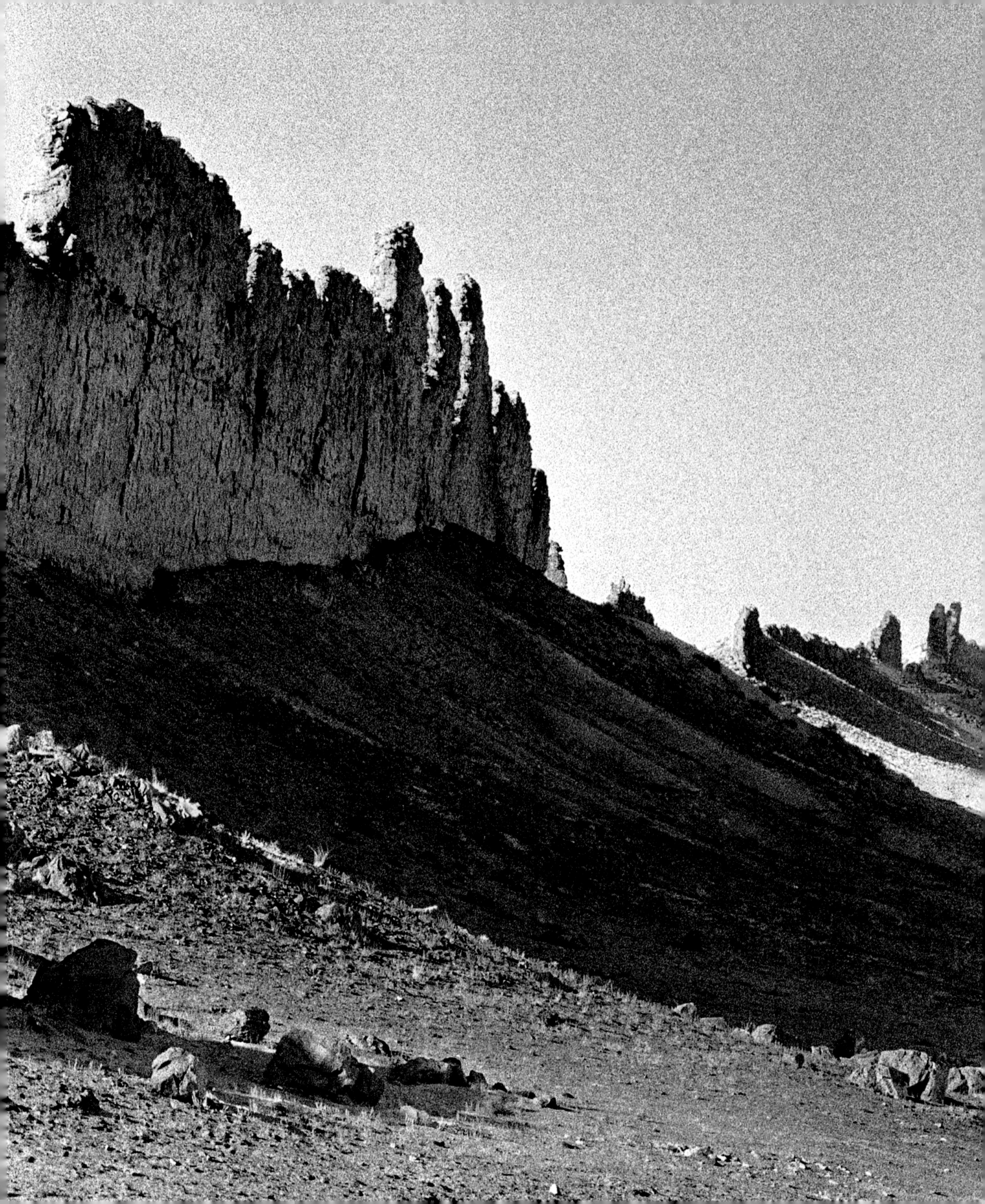

The paintings were records of air and light. Yet always and inevitably with the rising forms of the vertical necessity of life dominating the horizon. For in such a land a man must stand upright, if he would live.

—Clyfford Still, American abstract expressionist painter, 1904–1980

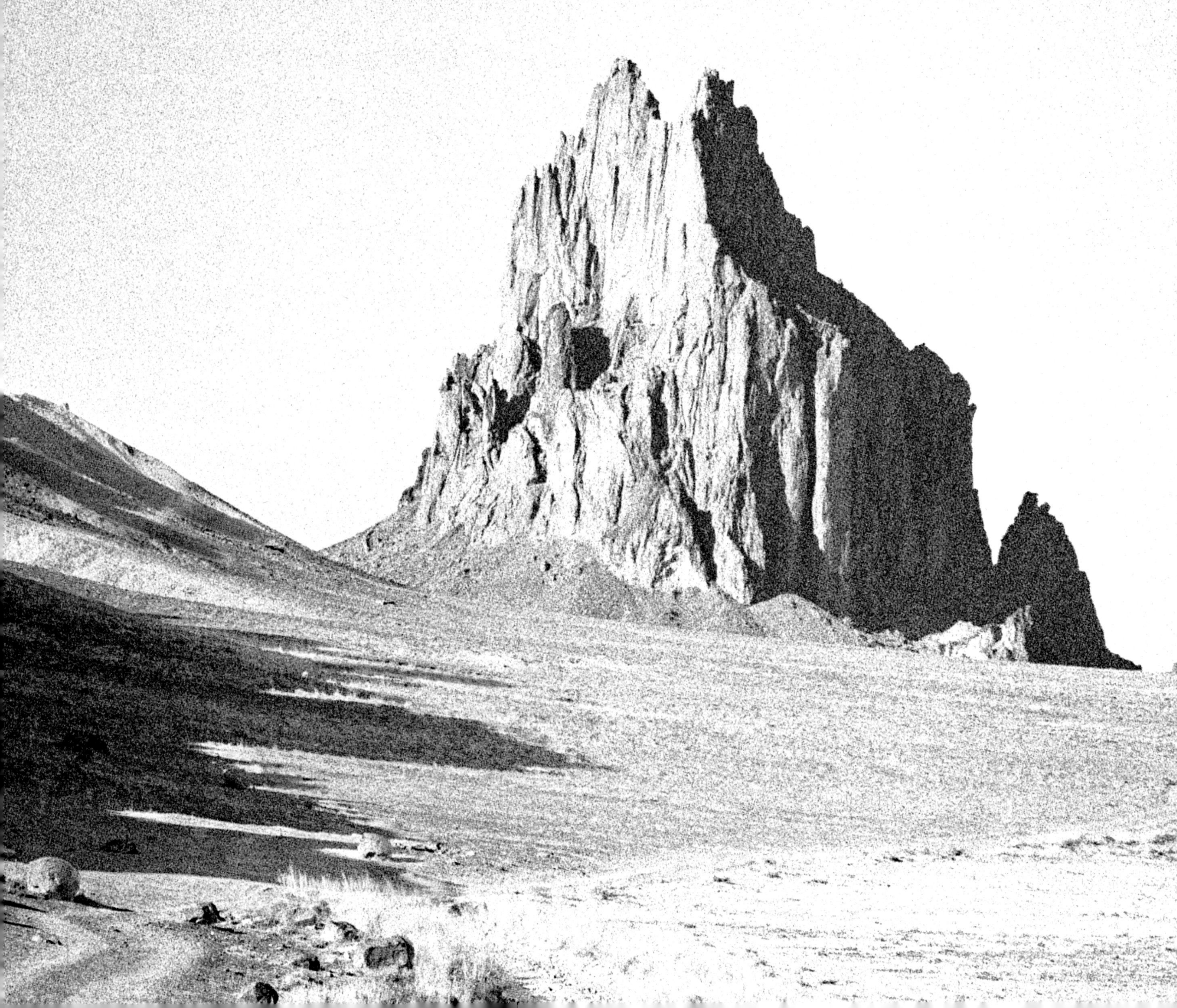

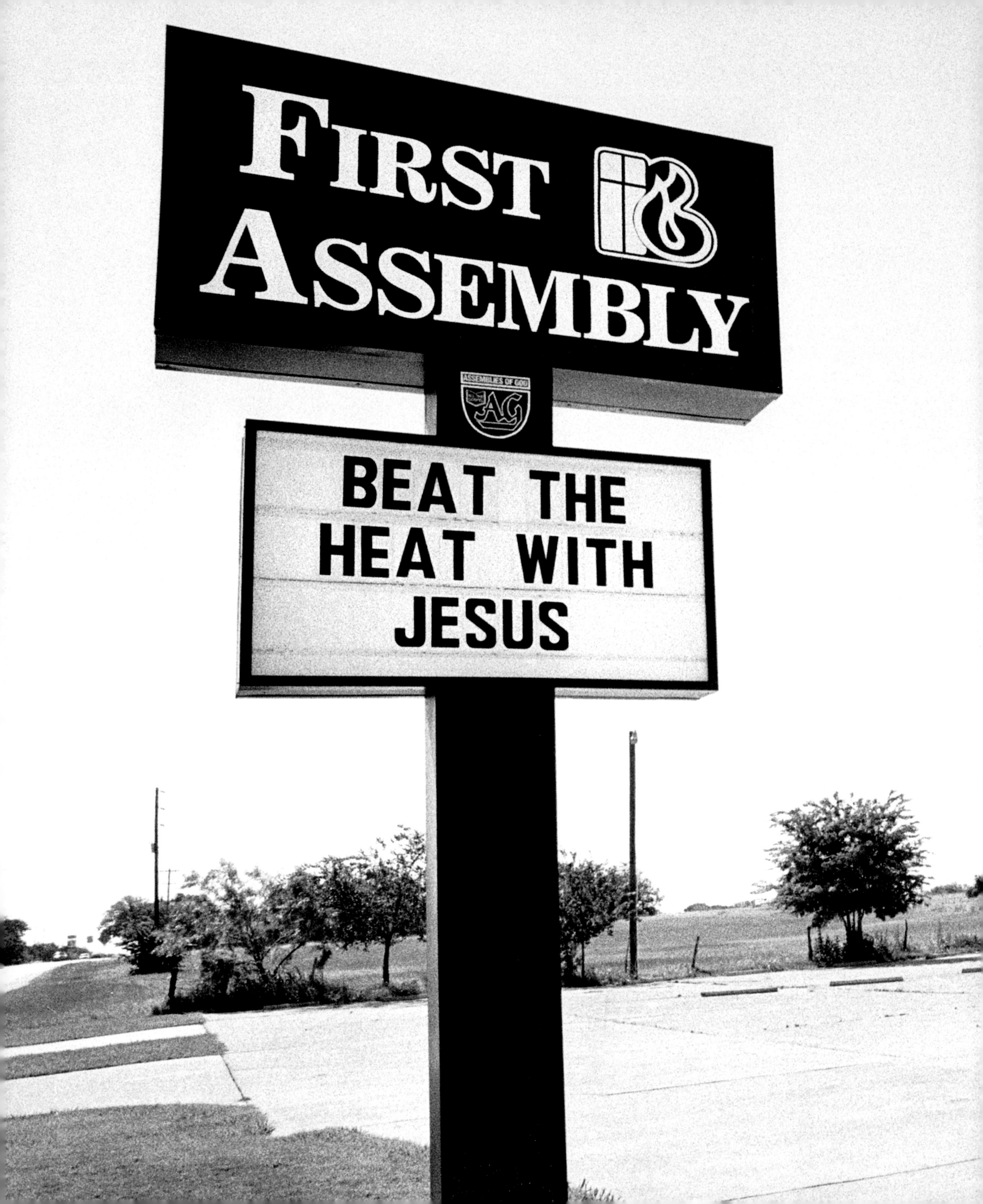

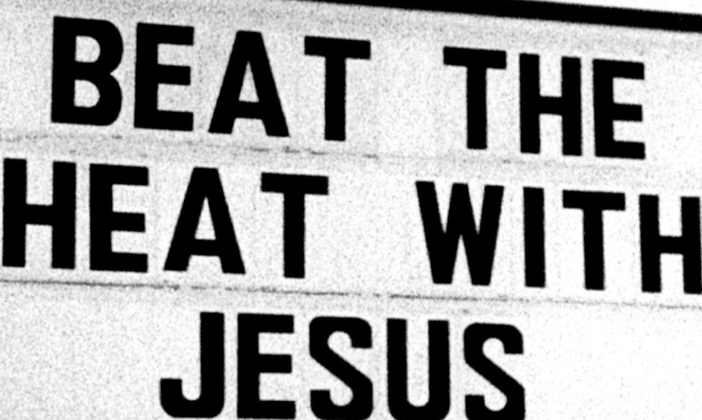
FIRST
ASSEMBLY
ASSEMBLIES OF GOD
AG
BEAT THE
HEAT WITH
JESUS

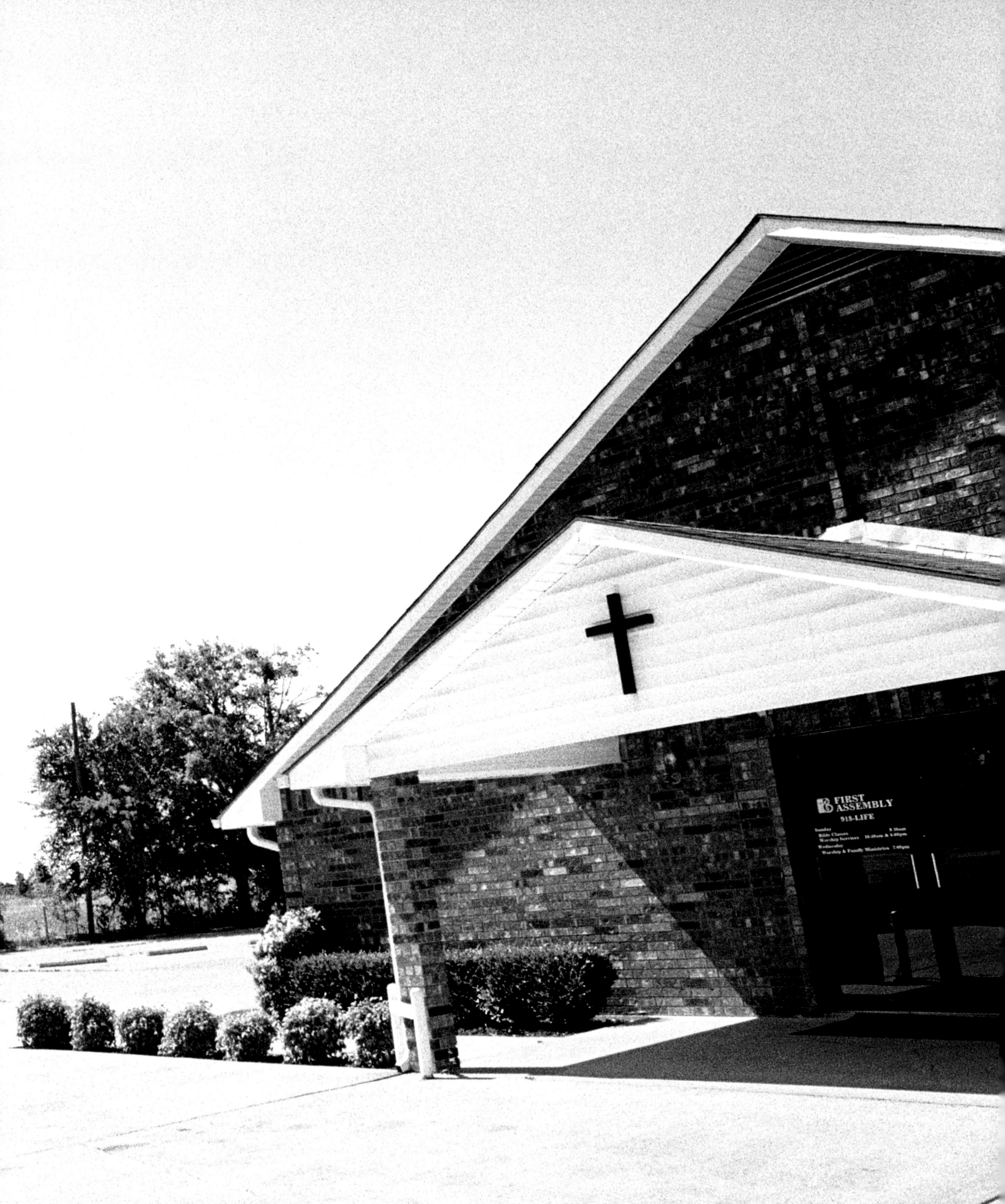
FIRST
ASSEMBLY
918-LIFE

Glory Riders

FORT WORTH, TEXAS
JUNE 9, 2002
JUNE 22, 2008

NOCONA, TEXAS
JUNE 15, 2008

The Glory Riders made a striking appearance, riding briskly in formation on white horses with white crosses on their saddles and costumes. Joy West, the group's leader, was adamant in her explanation of its mission: "We are not a riding club. We're a ministry. We've teamed up with the Lord Jesus Christ to go where He sends us so we can share His love with all." The group had been riding for glory in parades and rodeos since 1989. I first met West when she and her Glory Riders took part in a big, impressive parade celebrating the opening of the National Cowgirl Museum and Hall of Fame in Fort Worth, Texas. I then followed the group to Nocona for another parade, and caught up with them again in Fort Worth a year later.

The popularity of the Glory Riders seemed to me to be a reflection of the growth of Evangelical and Pentecostal groups. Over fifteen years, on frequent drives on the highways and byways of the West, I watched the expansion of the fundamentalist Christian frontier. The number of small places of worship seemed to triple. They often lacked steeples and stained-glass windows, but they always had a cross.

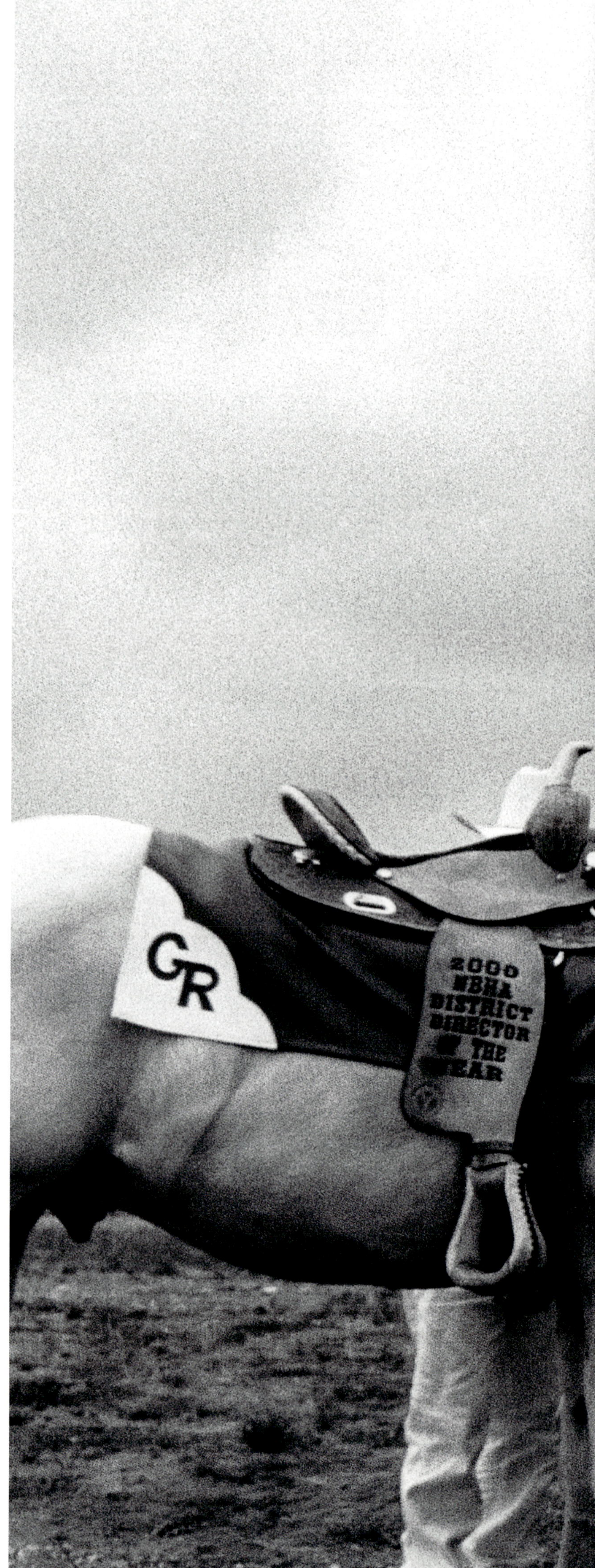

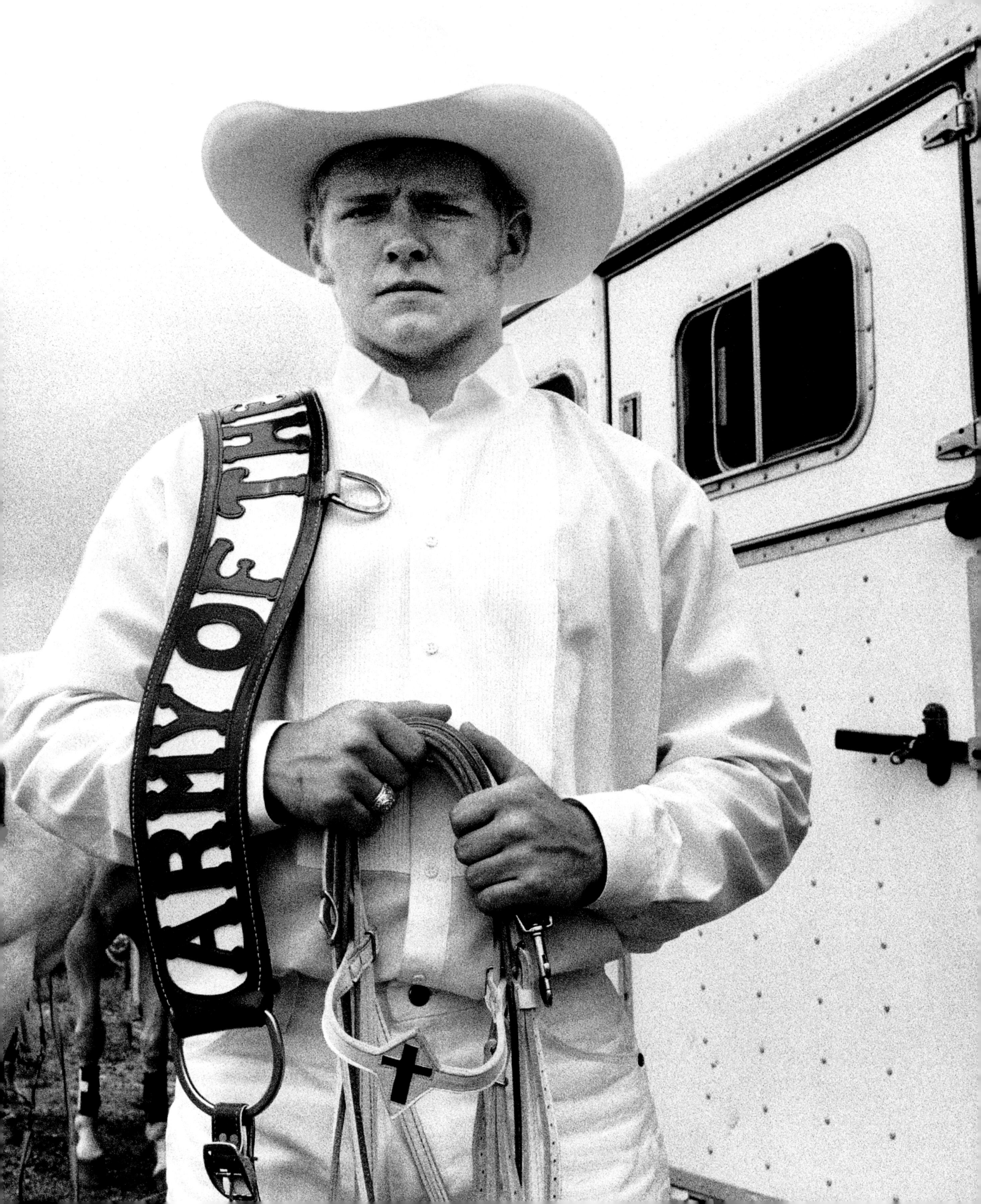
ARMY OF TH

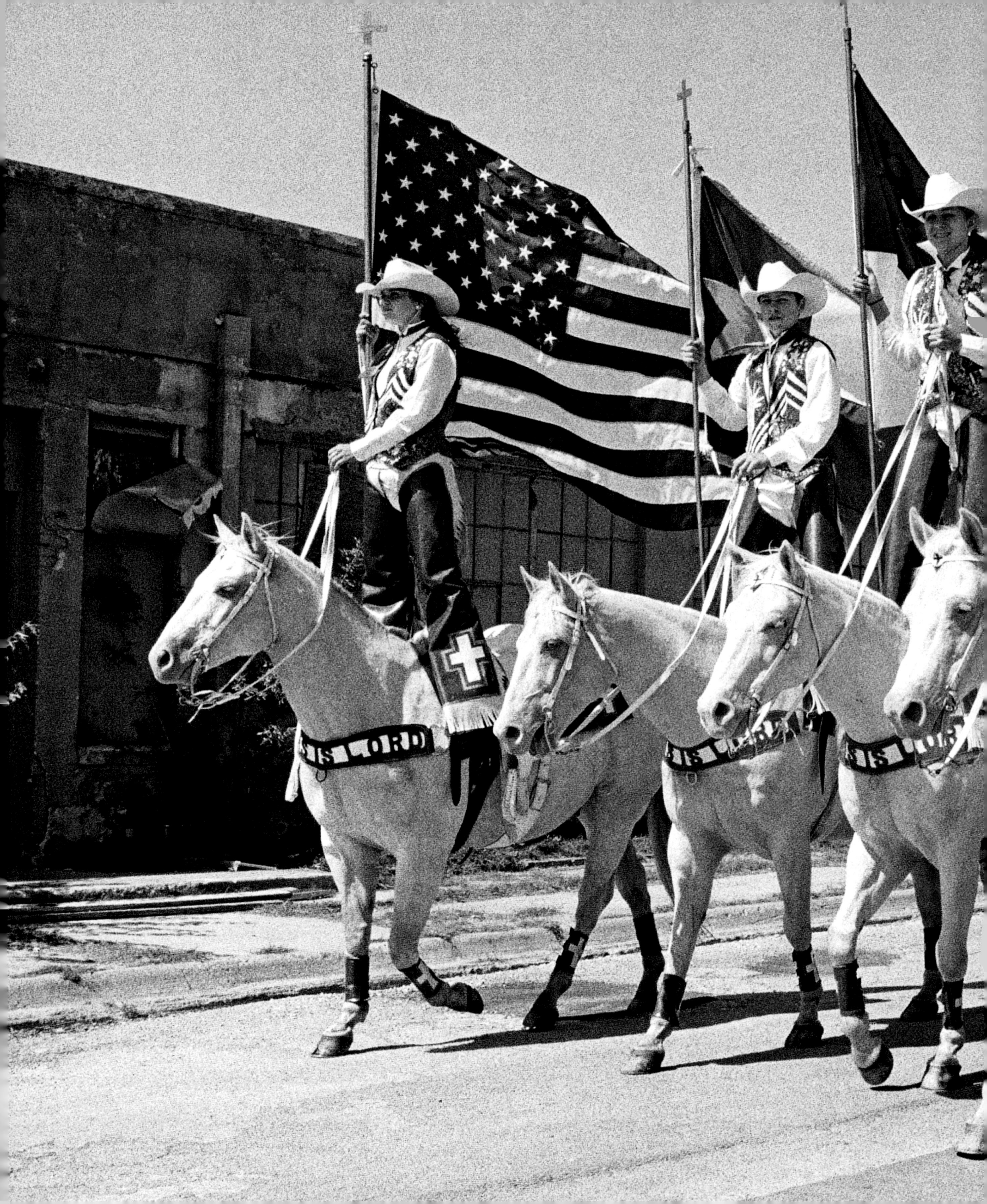
IS LORD

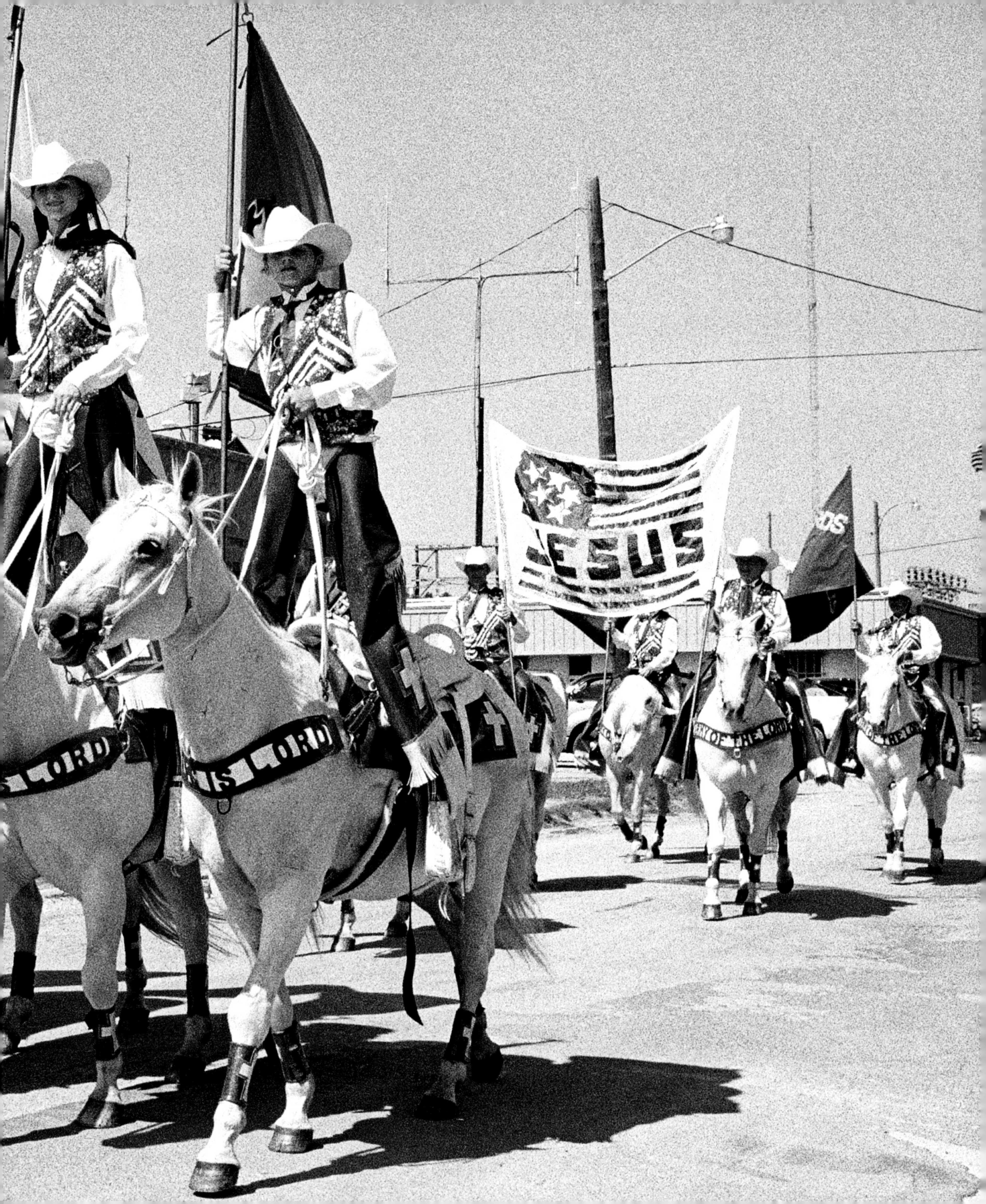
JESUS
LORD
IS LORD
OF THE LORD
THE LORD

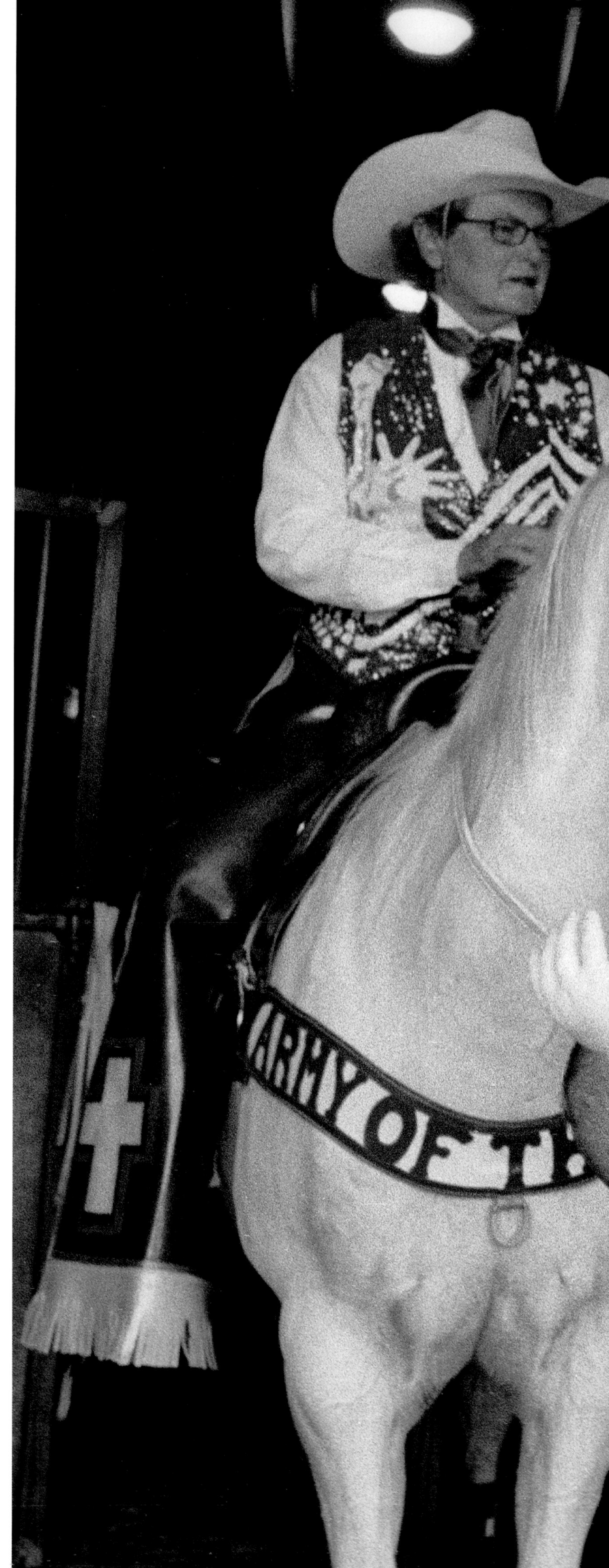
ARMY OF T

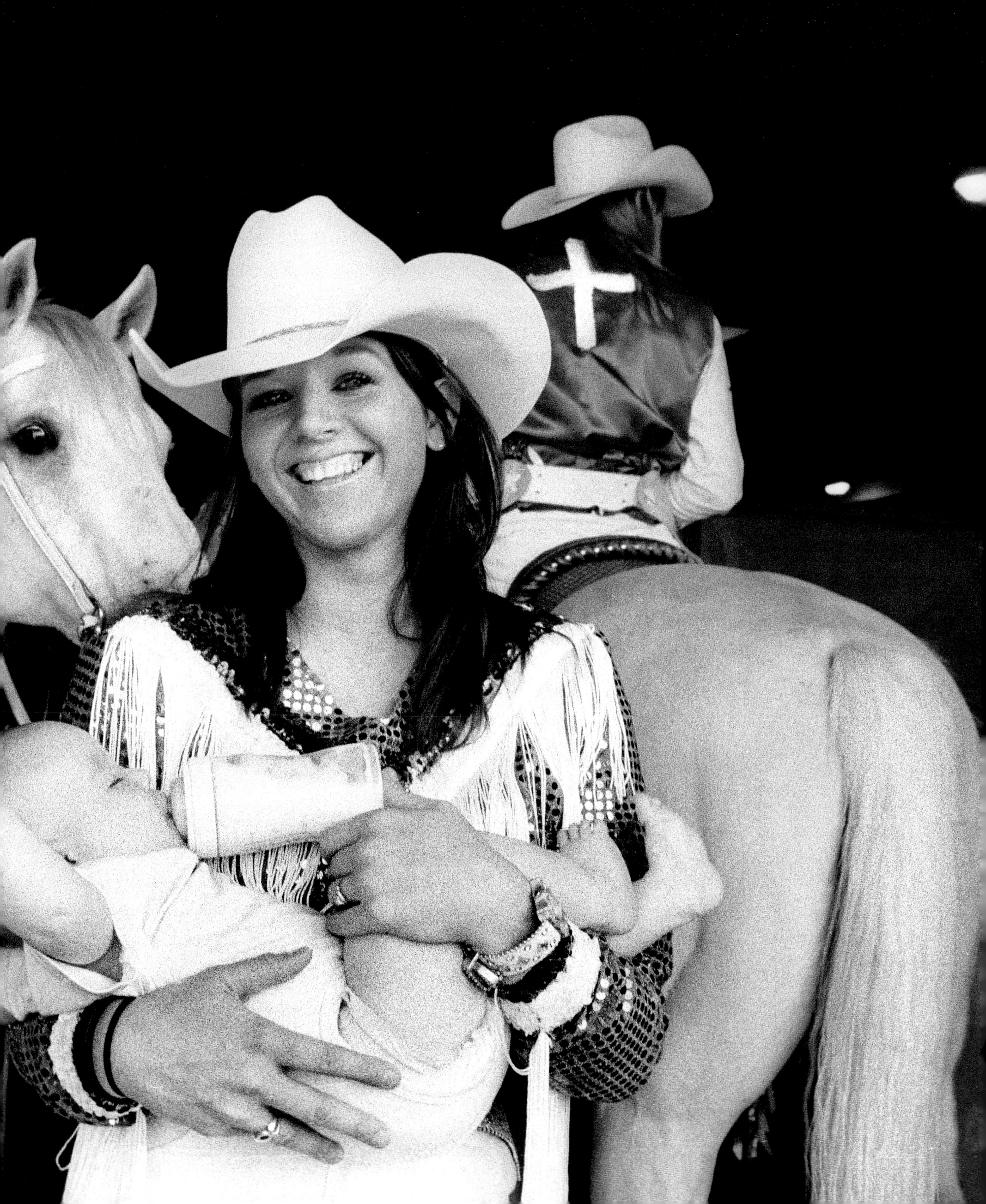

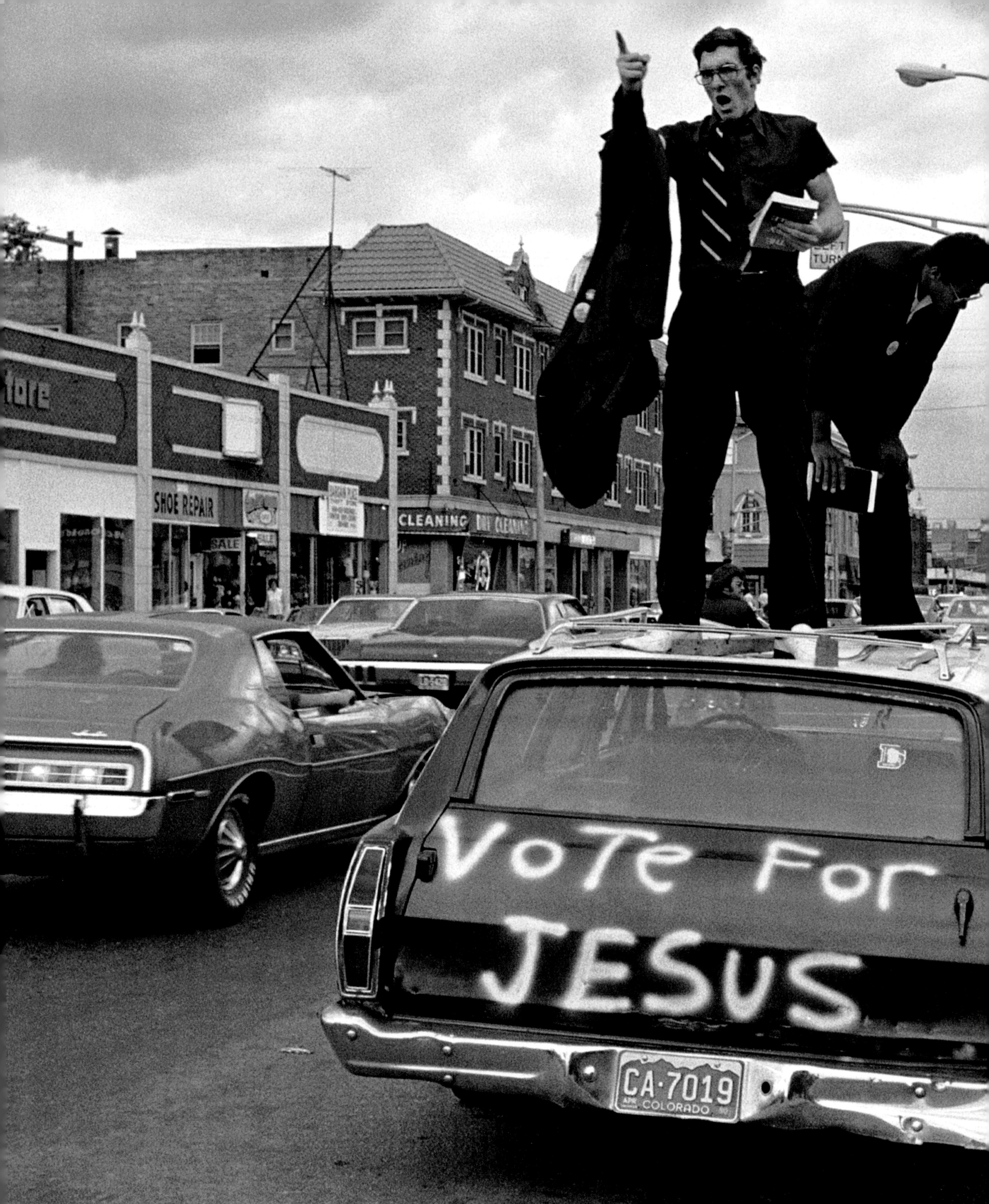
SHOE REPAIR
SALE
CLEANING
LEFT TURN
VoTe For JESUS
CA·7019
COLORADO

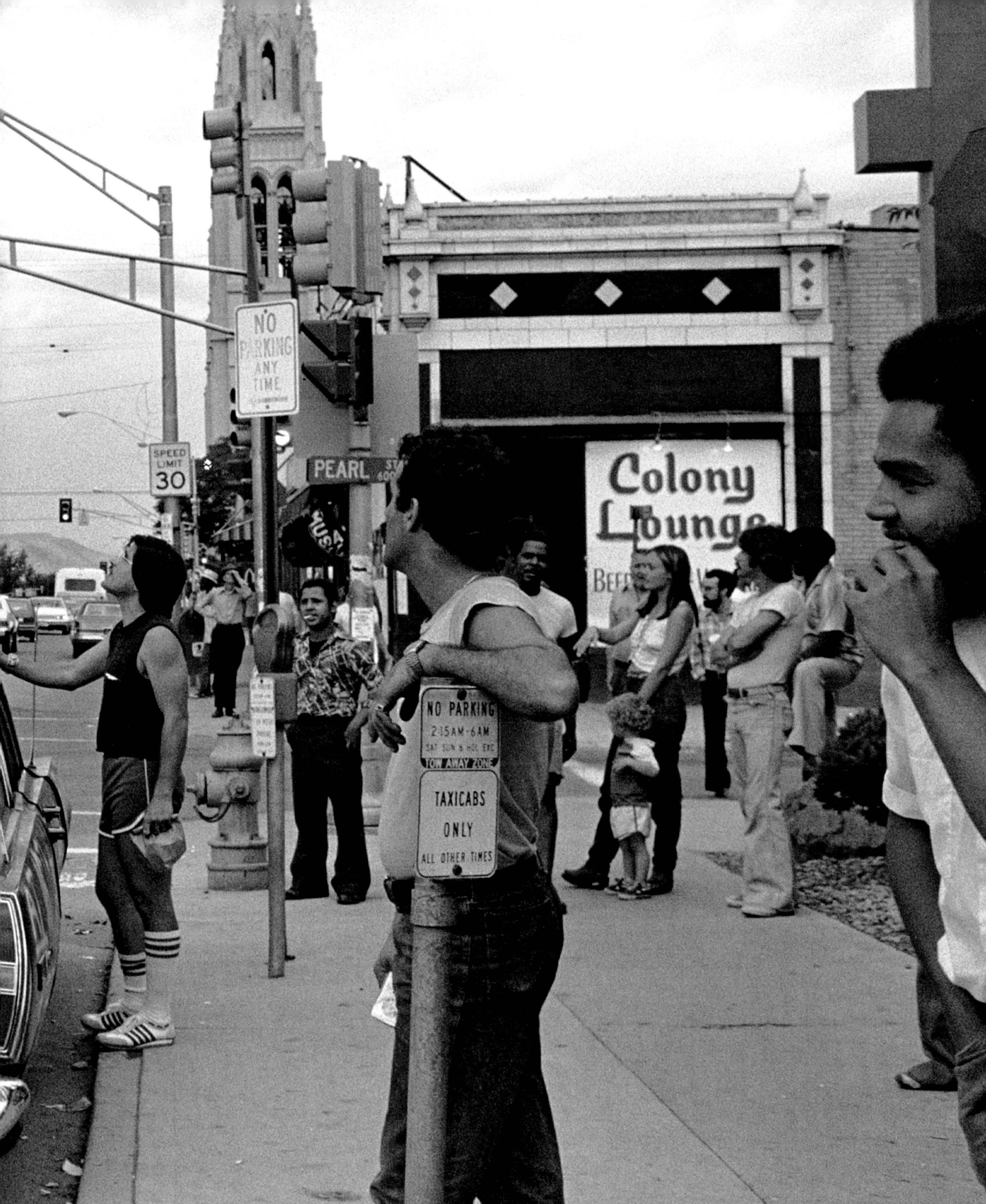
NO PARKING ANY TIME
SPEED LIMIT 30
PEARL
Colony Lounge
NO PARKING
2:15AM-6AM
SAT SUN & HOL EXC
TOW AWAY ZONE
TAXICABS ONLY
ALL OTHER TIMES

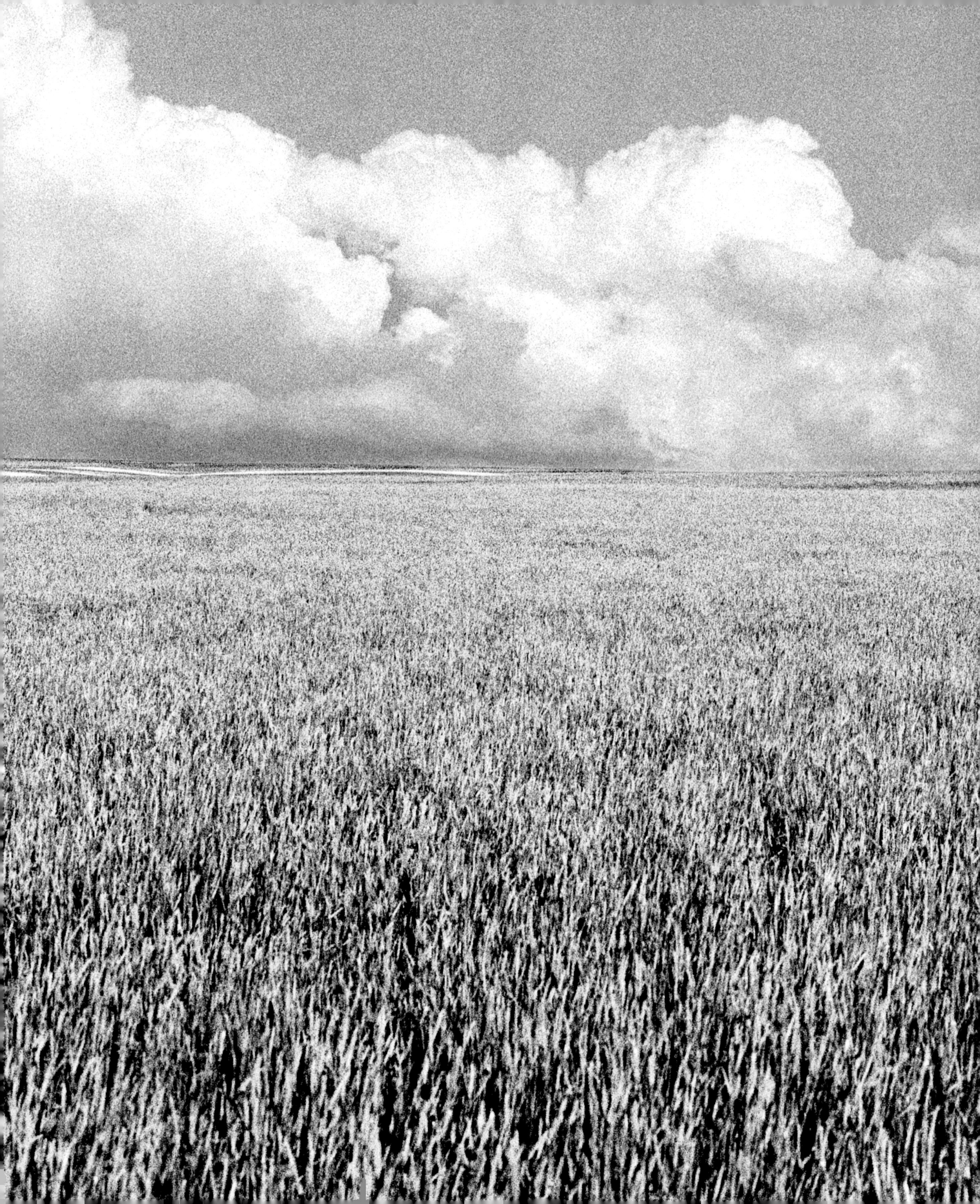

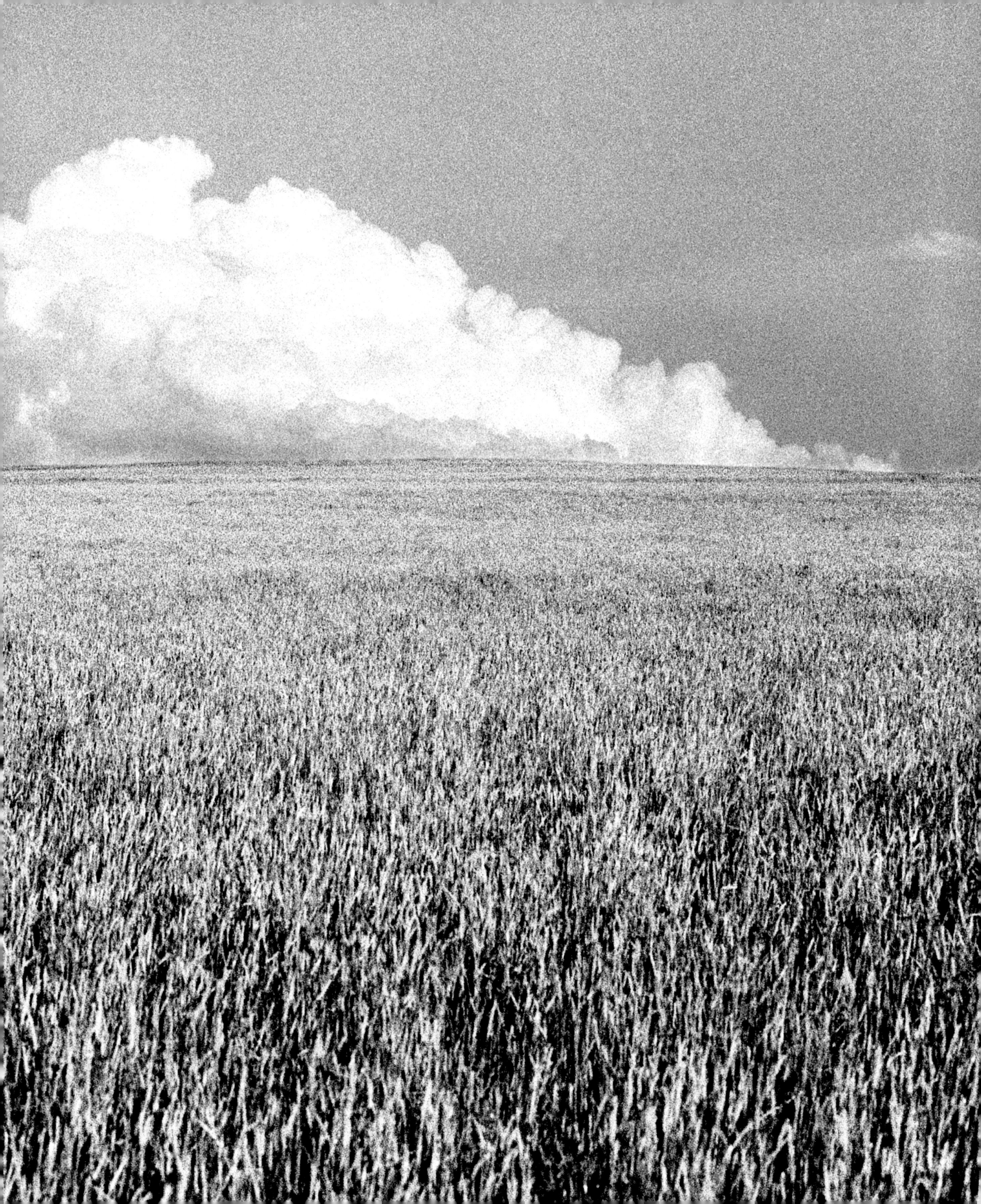

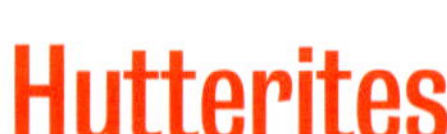

Hutterites

RYEGATE, HARLOWTON, STANFORD, AND CHESTER, MONTANA 1991–94

On the Great Plains of the northern United States, far removed from the unpredictable currents of mainstream America, lives a self-contained group of people called Hutterites. They shun the modern world whose defining values—personal freedom and financial ambition—do not define them. In an America that has largely abandoned its agrarian heritage, the Hutterites have held on to the land. They operate substantial farms and ranches and share all property and income equally. They have turned away from contemporary America more single-mindedly than even their spiritual cousins the Amish and the Mennonites. The Hutterites are less assimilated than the Amish, who own their own farms, or the Mennonites, who work for wages in the outside world. In colonies of thirty-five to a hundred or so people, the Hutterites carefully preserve their communal identity by adhering to their own traditions. They avoid worldly temptations (no televisions, no radios, no cars, no dancing), and, in this murderous century, they have remained pacifists.

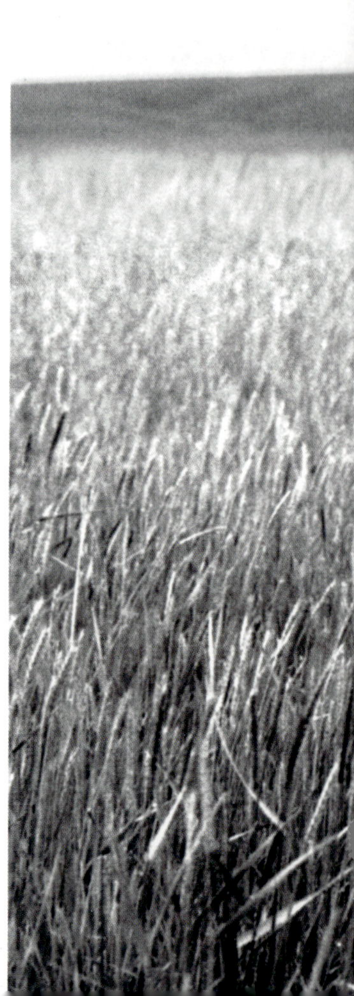

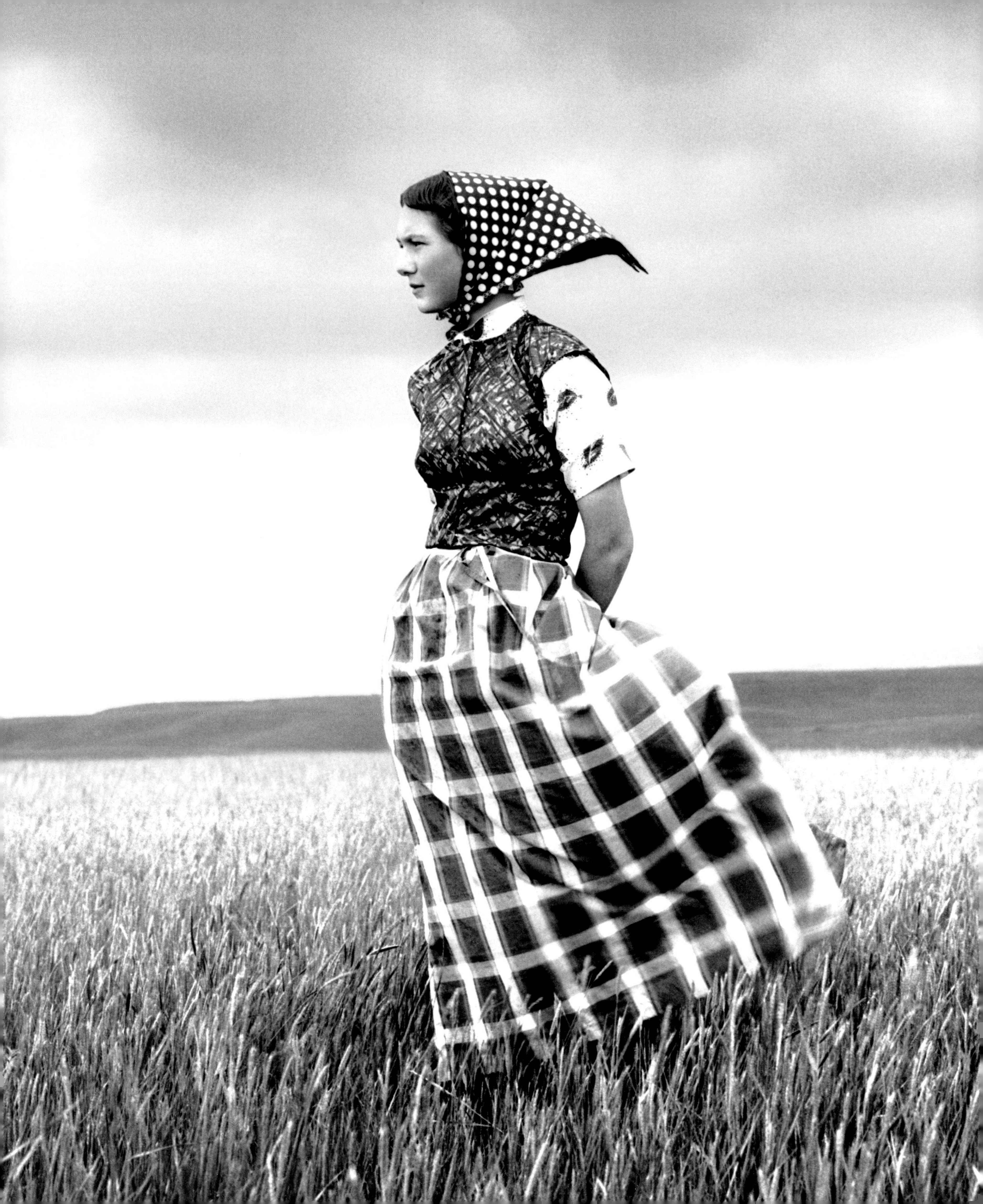

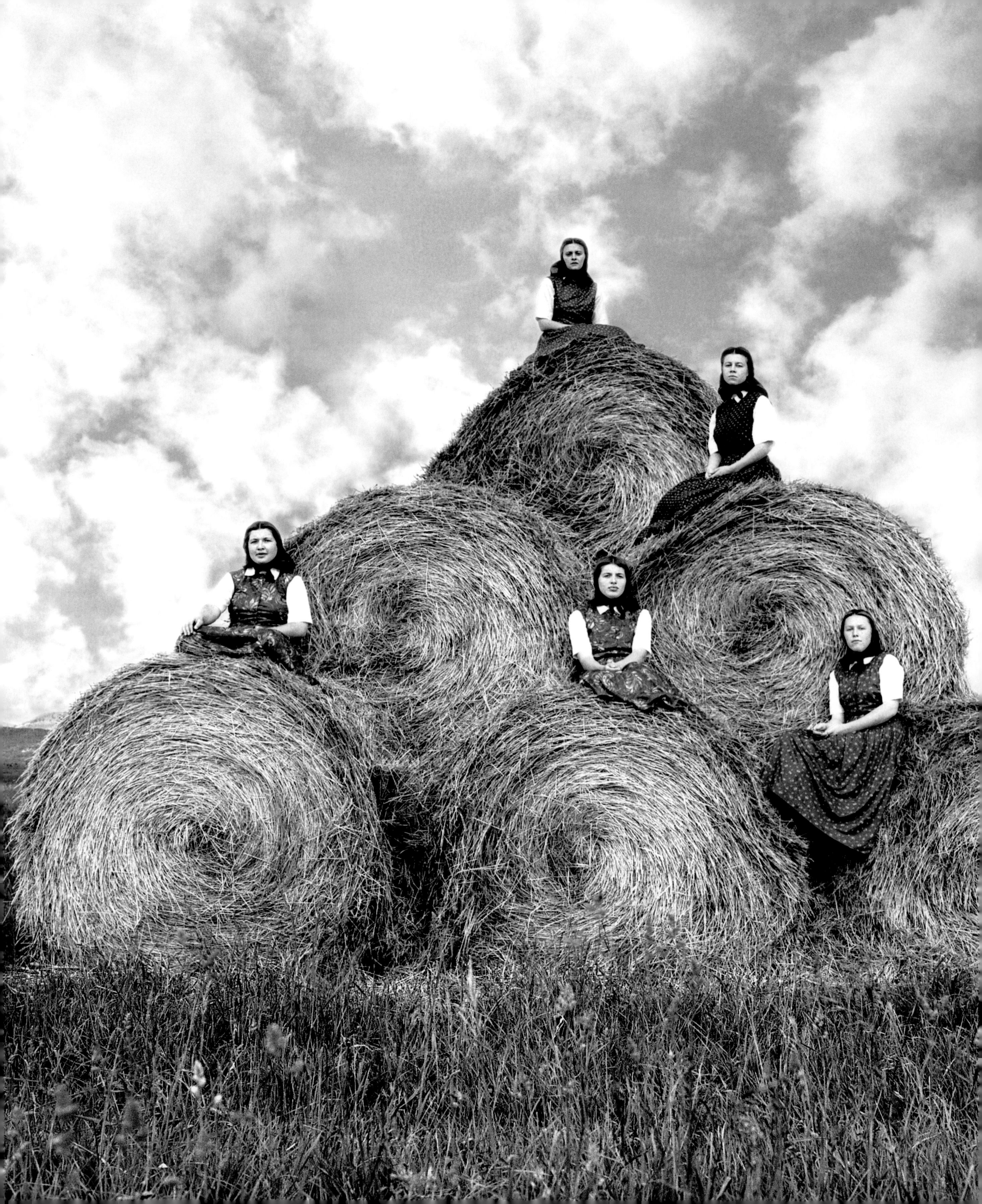

Photography is against Hutterite beliefs. To have one's picture taken is considered a worldly distraction, a direct contradiction of God's commandment that forbids vainglory. Beginning in 1985, I made several trips to colonies in Montana and did not take a single picture. The Hutterites were neither welcoming nor unwelcoming. They were watchful. They waited to see what I was about, to learn who I was. The most secure and successful colonies were the most guarded. But slowly, I began to make friends. I continued to ask permission to photograph, and the answer continued to be "no." But at last, a breakthrough came. The Reverend Sam Hofer of Surprise Creek Colony was rebuffing my request yet again—"No pictures, Laura dear, no pictures. How can I make you understand?"—when his daughter-in-law, Beckey, interrupted: "She's taking pictures, Sam, but they're only black-and-white." Through my persistence and my respect for their customs, I ultimately won their trust. They gradually allowed me in.

The Hutterites trace their beginning to 1528, when a small band of religious refugees in Moravia, now part of the Czech Republic, gathered to reject the practice of acquiring individual possessions. Communalism is the Hutterites' distinguishing principle, the primary tenet of the philosophy by which Hutterites have lived for almost five hundred years. They are also Anabaptists, as are the Amish and Mennonites, rejecting "ignorant" infant baptism in favor of "knowing" adult commitment. Like other religious minorities, the Hutterites have endured a long history of persecution, which resulted in their escape to the wide plains of the American West in the 1870s.

I worked among those colonies that held firmly to the Hutterite way and were determined to remain apart from mainstream America. The Hutterites are resisters. By distancing themselves from the materialism and secular spirit of the modern age, they have created a world of their own, an enclosed world.

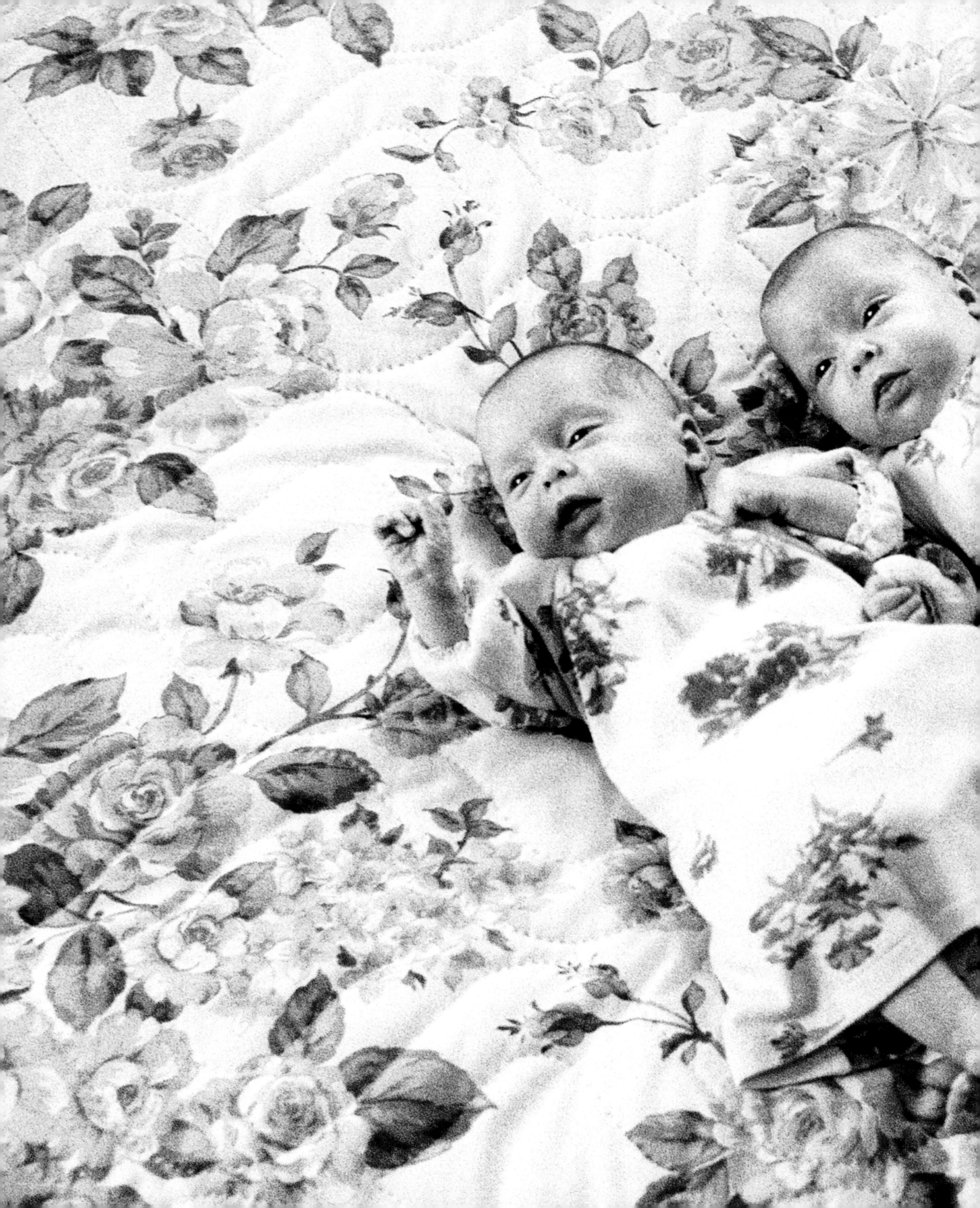

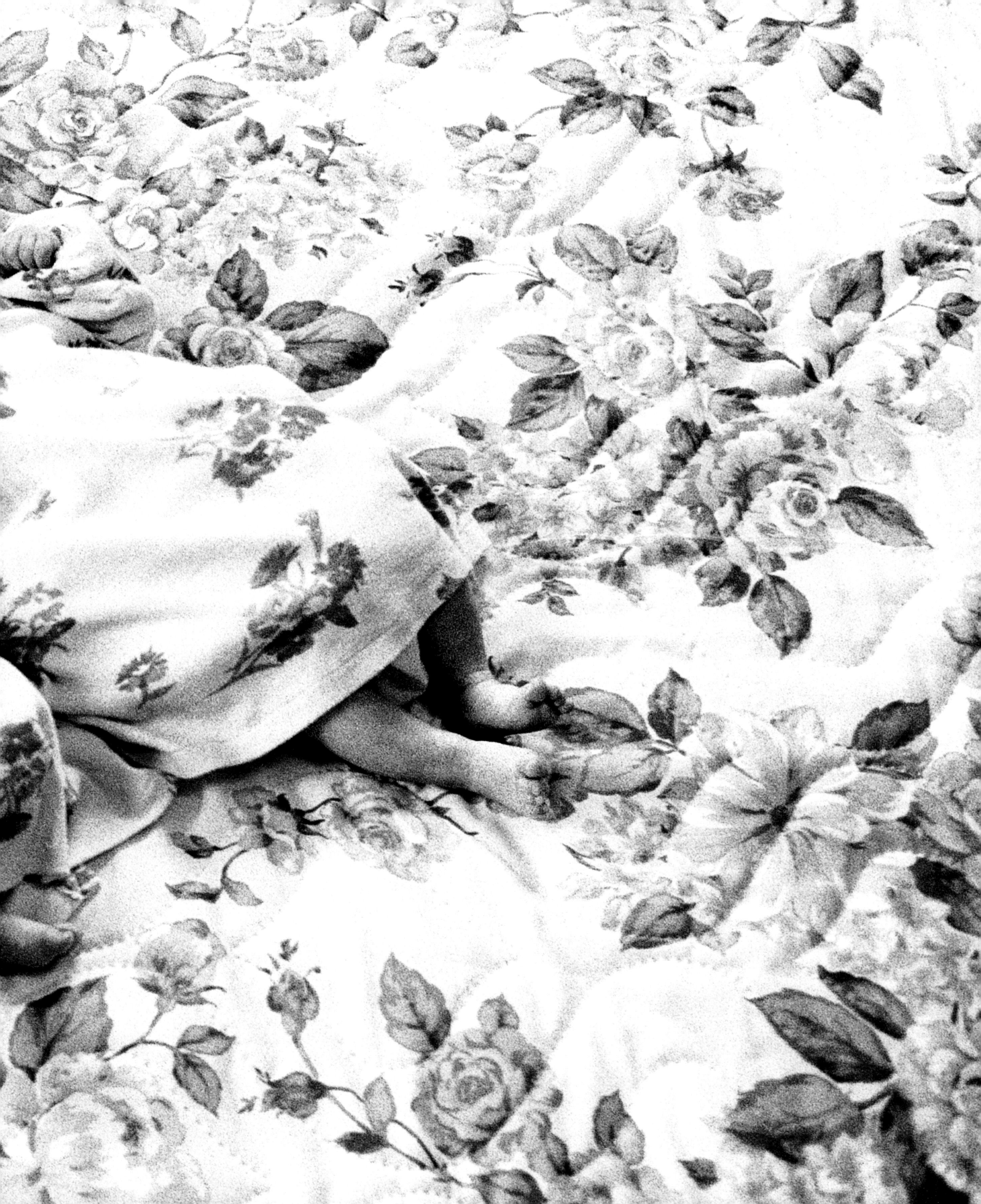

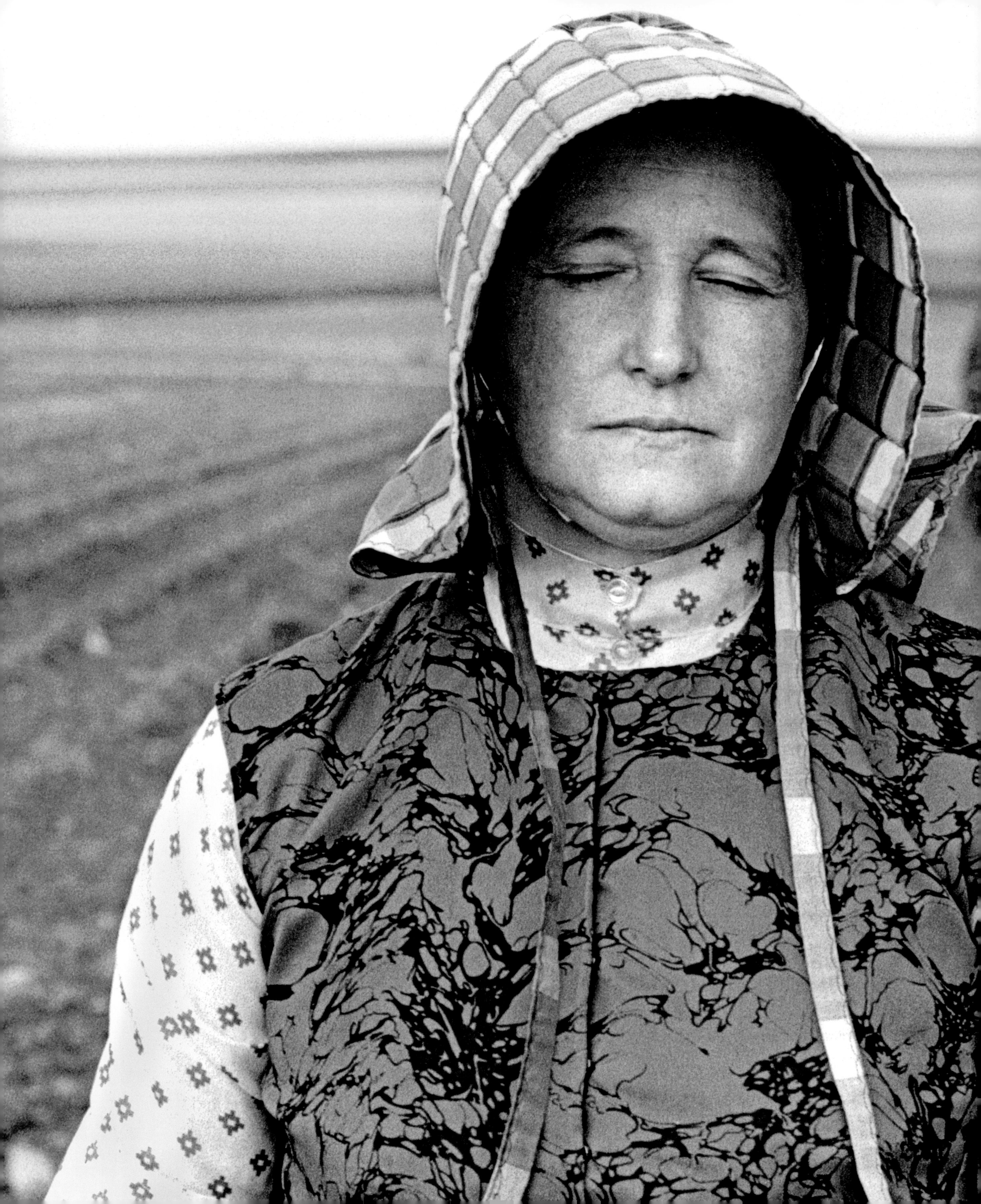

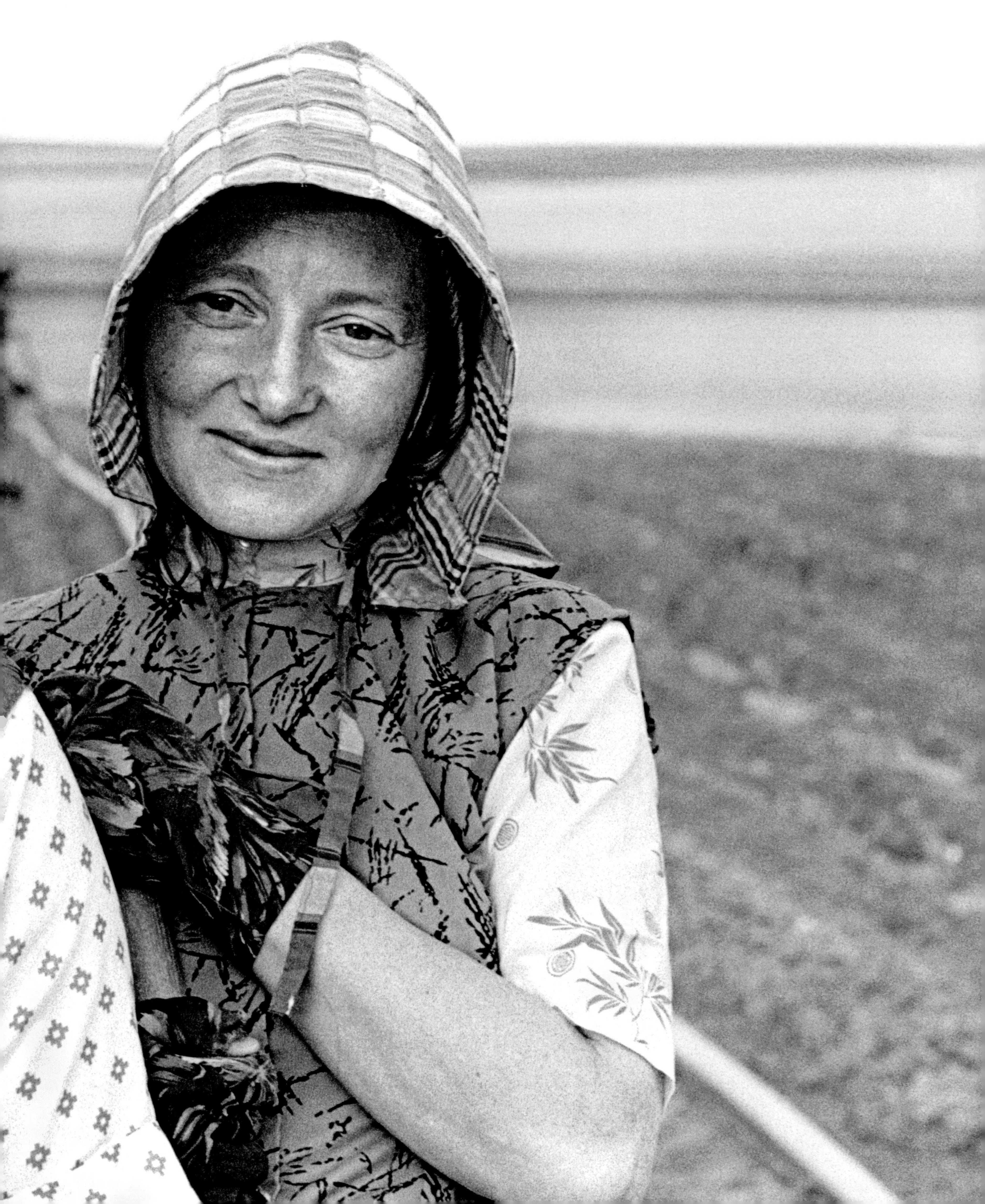

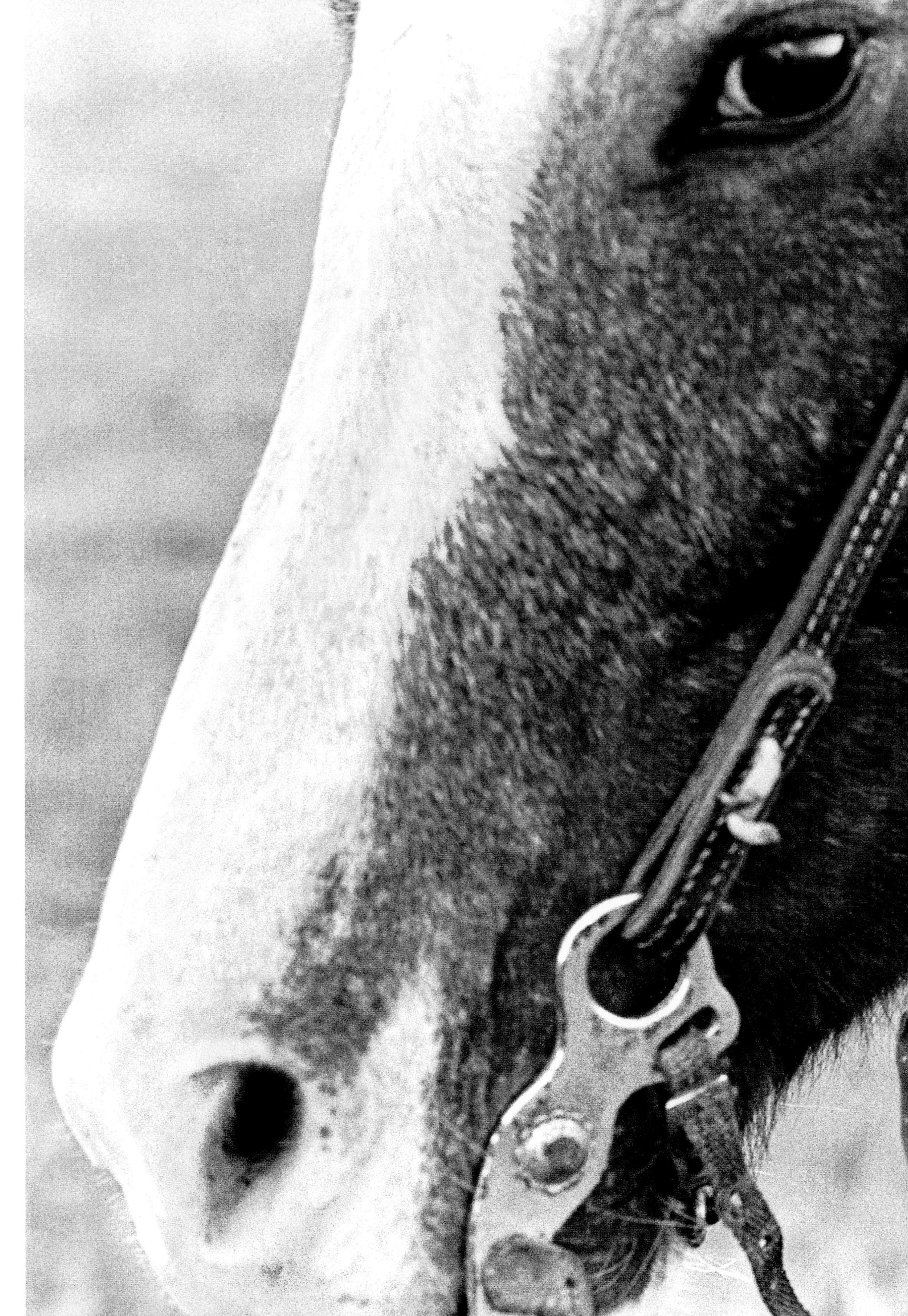

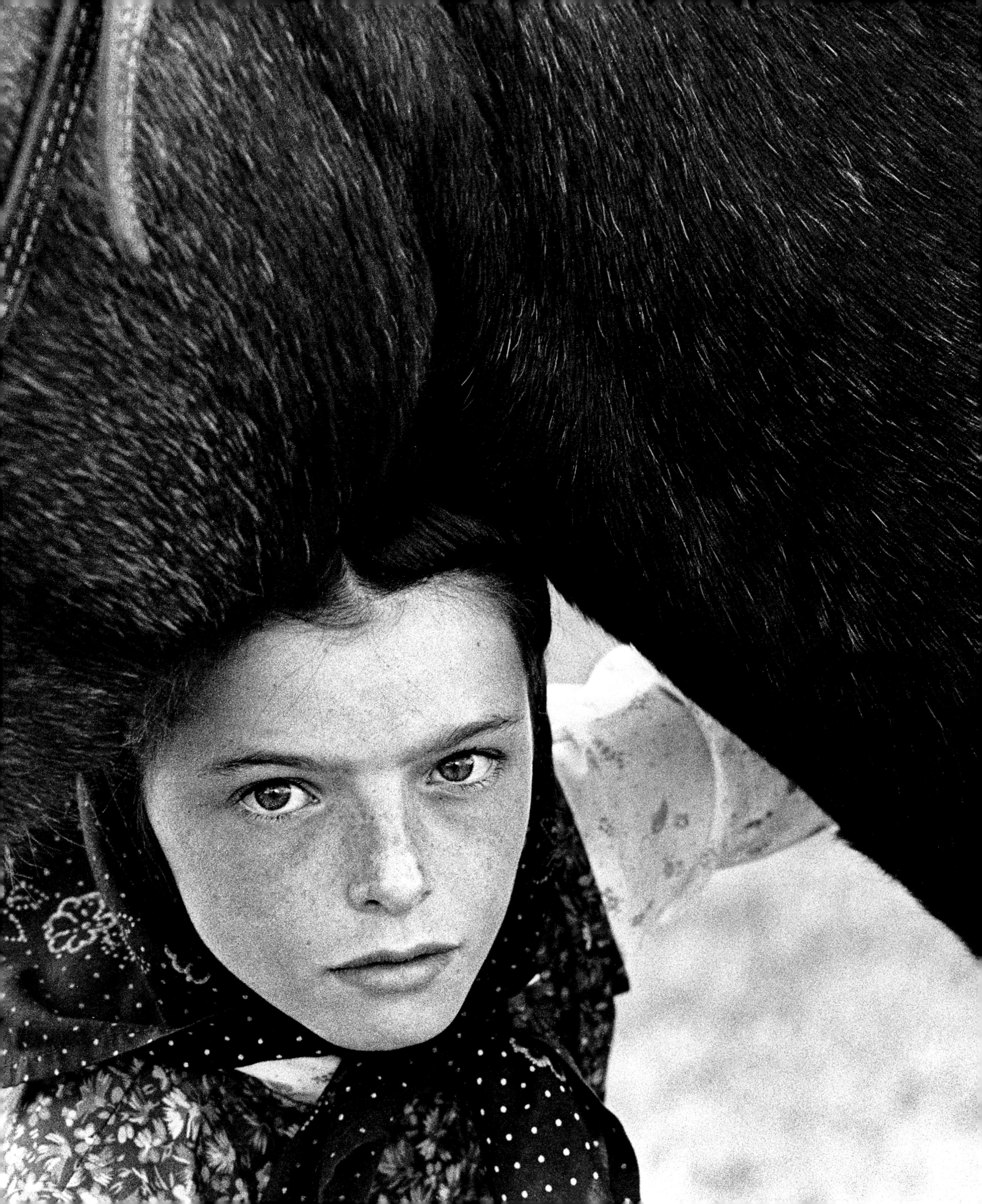

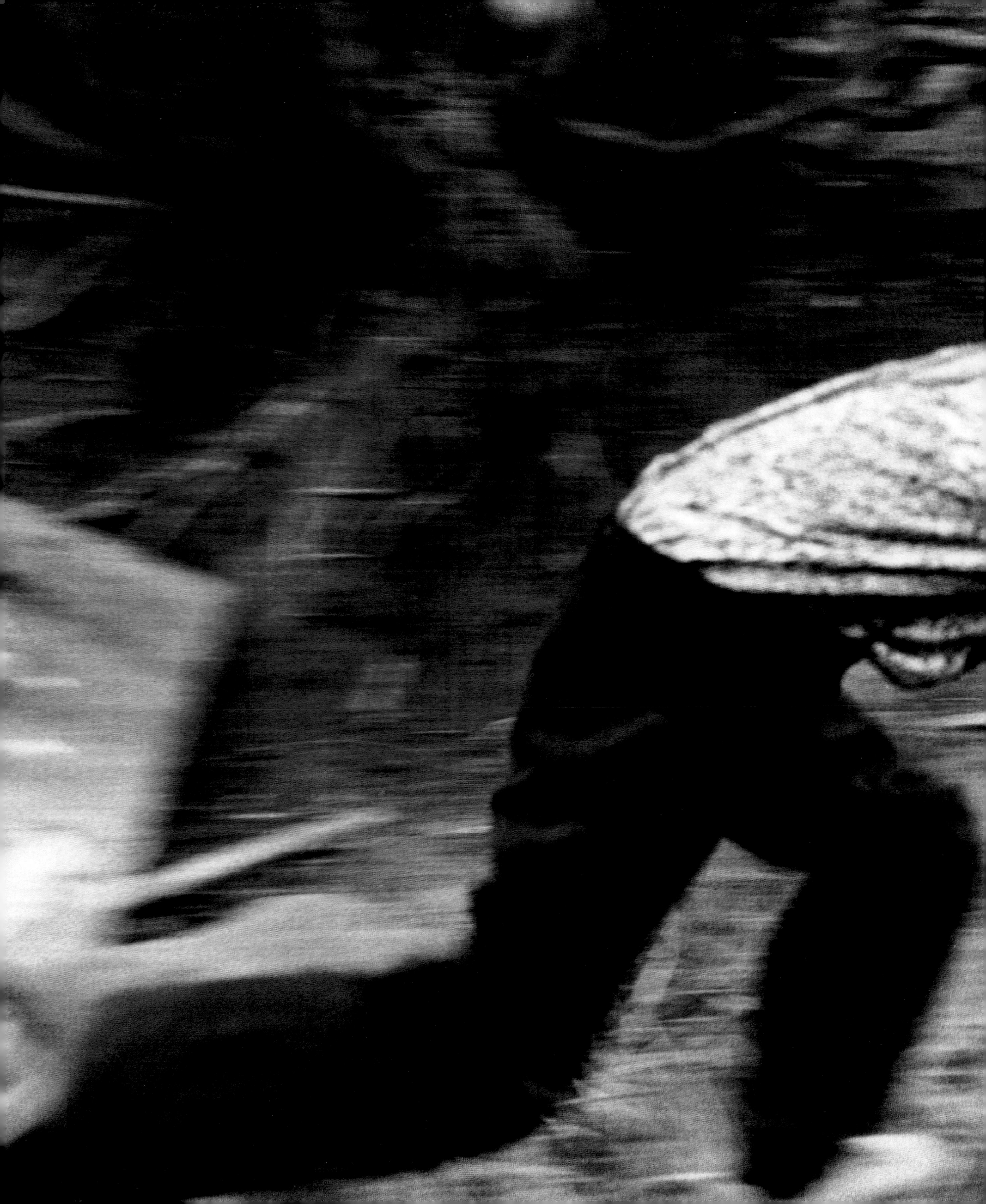

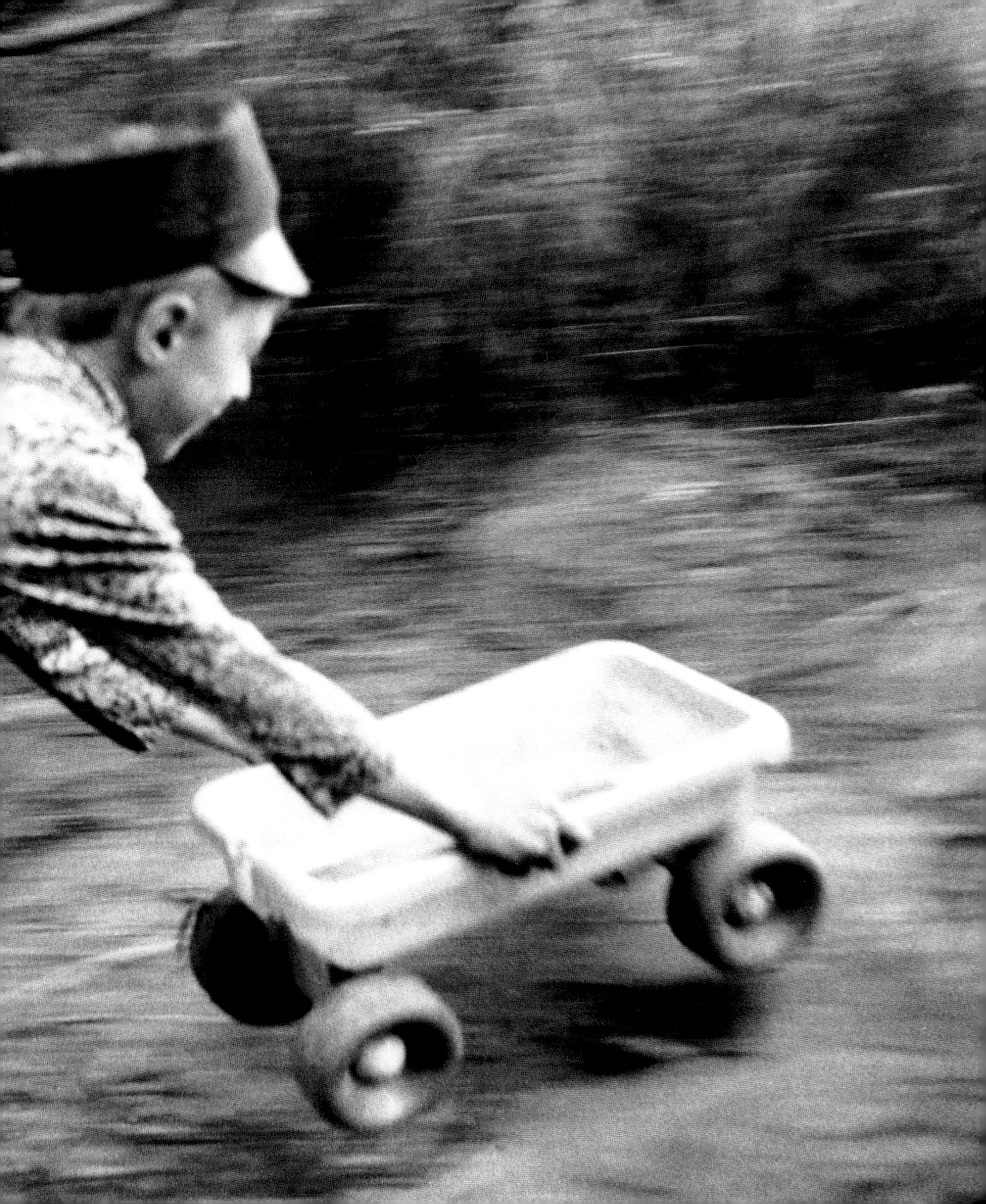

A Hutterite child is never alone: right from birth, children are held close, under the protective security of the whole community. "Our children are not raised by TV," I was told more than once. Small children are swept up in the colony's swirl of activity, with parents, brothers and sisters, aunts and uncles, and cousins and neighbors all close at hand. The children begin school at age six with state-certified teachers hired from the outside. However, their education is both limited and brief. Hutterite children complete the eighth grade but do not go on to high school. Hutterites believe that practical experiences in the fields, the machine shop, or the home are a form of continuing education. Higher education, even high school, with its emphasis on individual achievement, is considered contrary to the aims of communal life. In spite of the societal limitations and restrictions, Hutterites have surprisingly few problems with their young people. The adults are wise and flexible enough to allow their teenagers to be immature, but they do not permit them to be antisocial, to do their work poorly, or to show disrespect for authority.

After visiting various colonies in Montana over a fourteen-year period, I came away most impressed by how successfully the Hutterites have met, and continue to meet, the problems facing communities everywhere: how to provide financial security for the present and future; how to give people a sense of satisfaction in their work; how to deal with human weakness; and, most of all, how to keep their faith.

On the last day of February 1999, while I was visiting a colony in central Montana, Anna Kleinsasser, who, over time, had become my friend, told me, "With my keen conscience, I've been thinking and thinking about what you've been doing, and if it's wrong that you're taking pictures. I've come to the conclusion that maybe a soul can be saved by reading your book [*Hutterites of Montana*] and looking at the pictures—the way we dress, our modesty, the kind of life we lead. Perhaps people will stop and think. Maybe they'll be helped. That would gratify God."

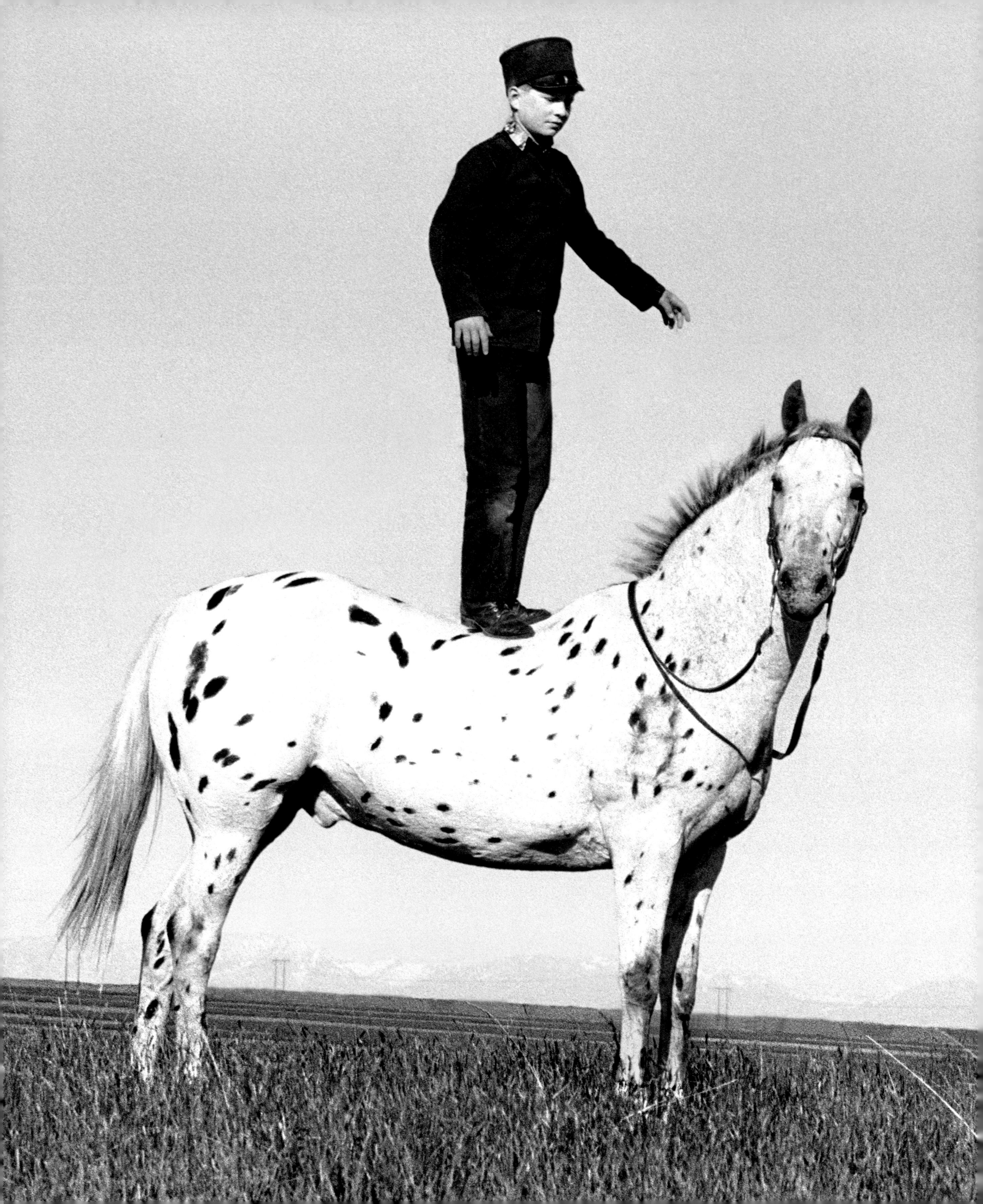

Donald Judd

MARFA, TEXAS
NOVEMBER 3–4, 1993

I was sent in November 1993 by London's *Sunday Times Magazin*e to photograph Donald Judd, whom the editor called the "minimalist maverick." I found Judd to be suspicious of me, which made him difficult to photograph, and ornery, which made me like him. I had the run of his spectacular location in Marfa on the vast grasslands of far West Texas with antelope roaming among the installations and buildings. He first came to this part of the country in the 1950s, when the Army sent him cross-country on a bus. The bus had stopped in nearby Van Horn, which was, at the time, a very small town—"like a shack thrown up around a gumball machine," Judd remembered. In Marfa, I photographed his concrete and milled-aluminum sculptures, his collections of Native American art and European furniture, his reconstituted army barracks, and remote ranch house with its beautiful, curved, twelve-foot-high stone walls. At the end of five days, we left on the same small plane, I back to Dallas, and he to see his parents in Missouri. He said he didn't feel well, that he'd picked up an amoeba while drinking from a stock tank. He was mistaken. It was cancer. Judd never returned to Marfa. Two months later, he was dead. I was the last person to photograph him.

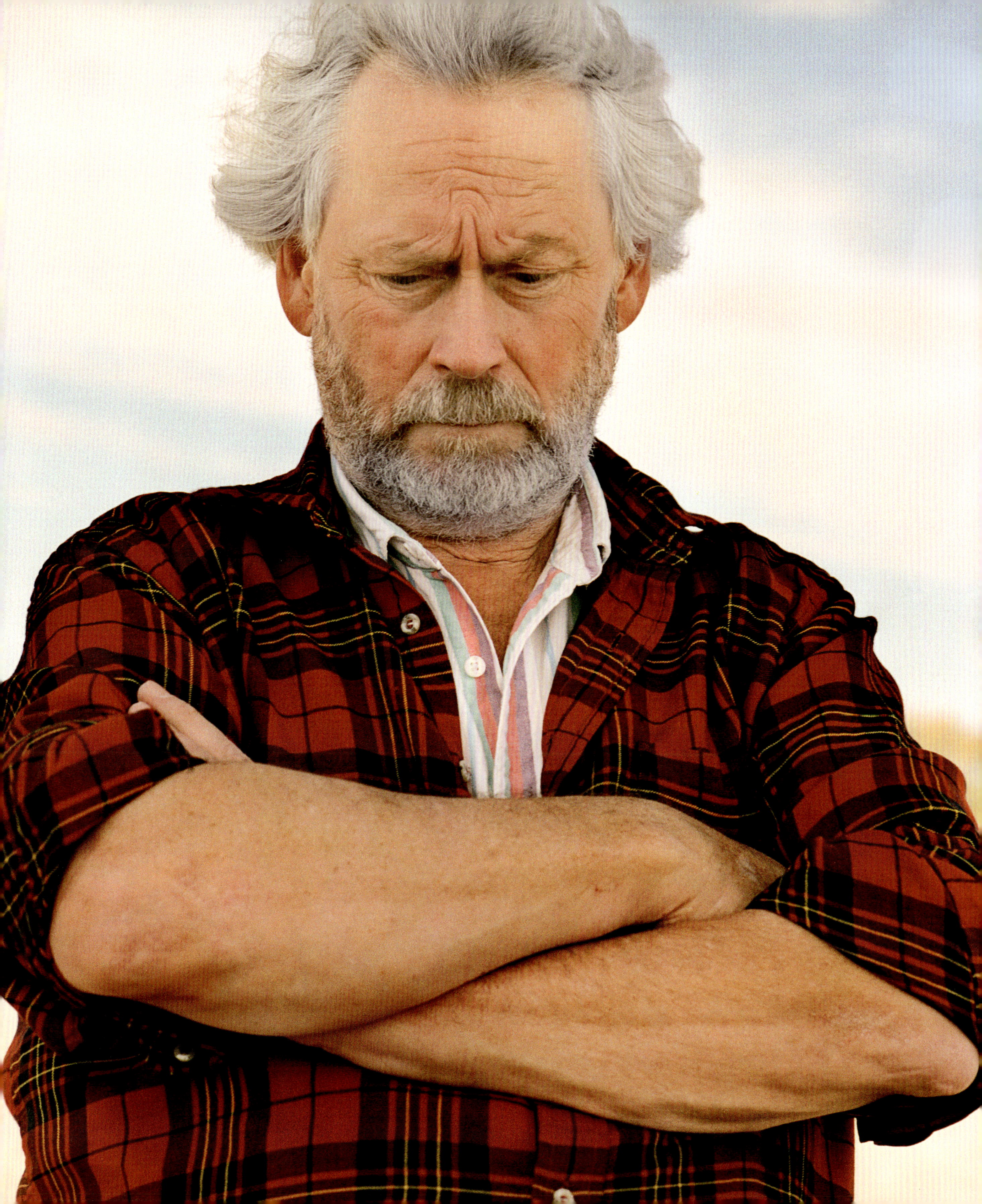

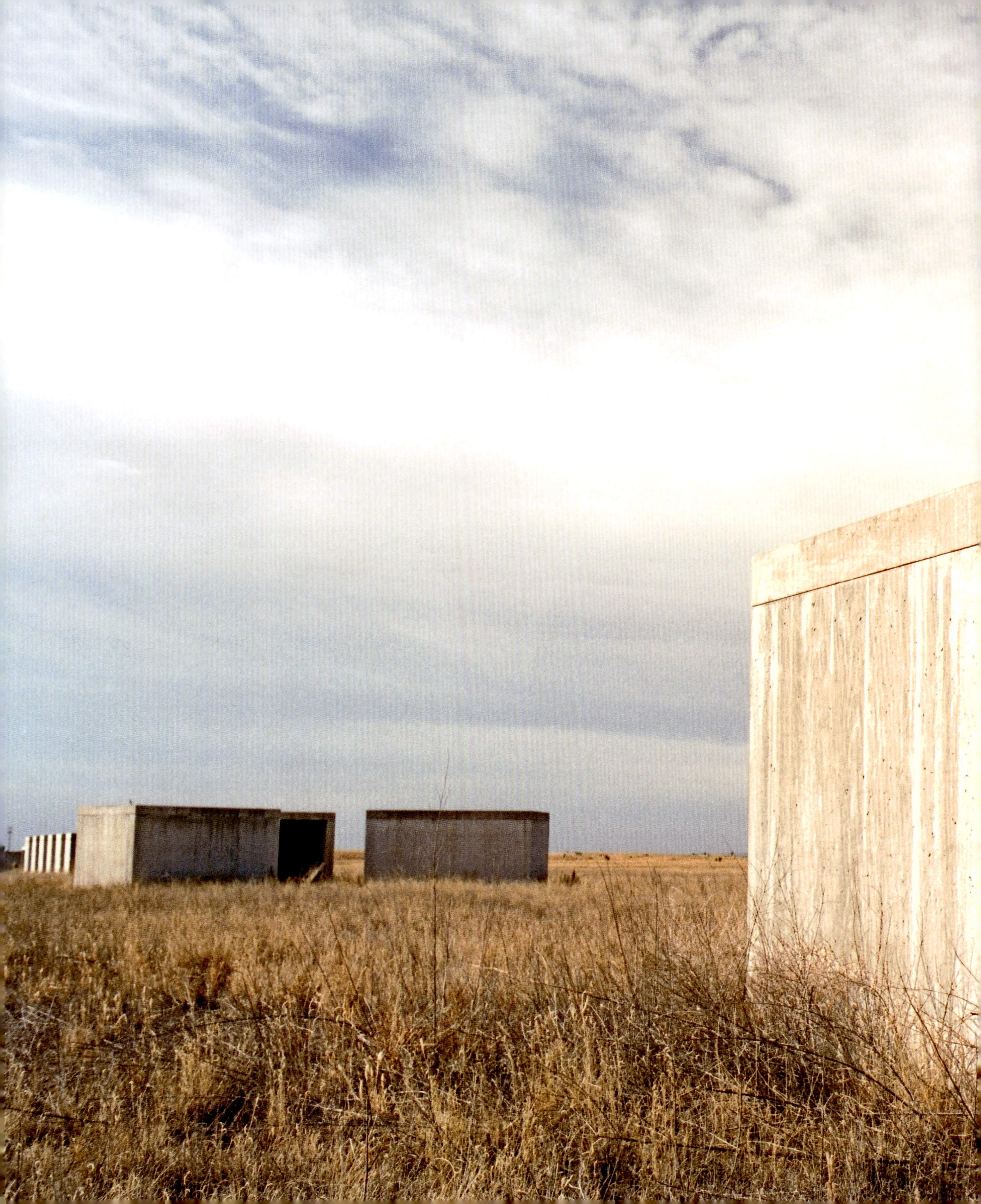

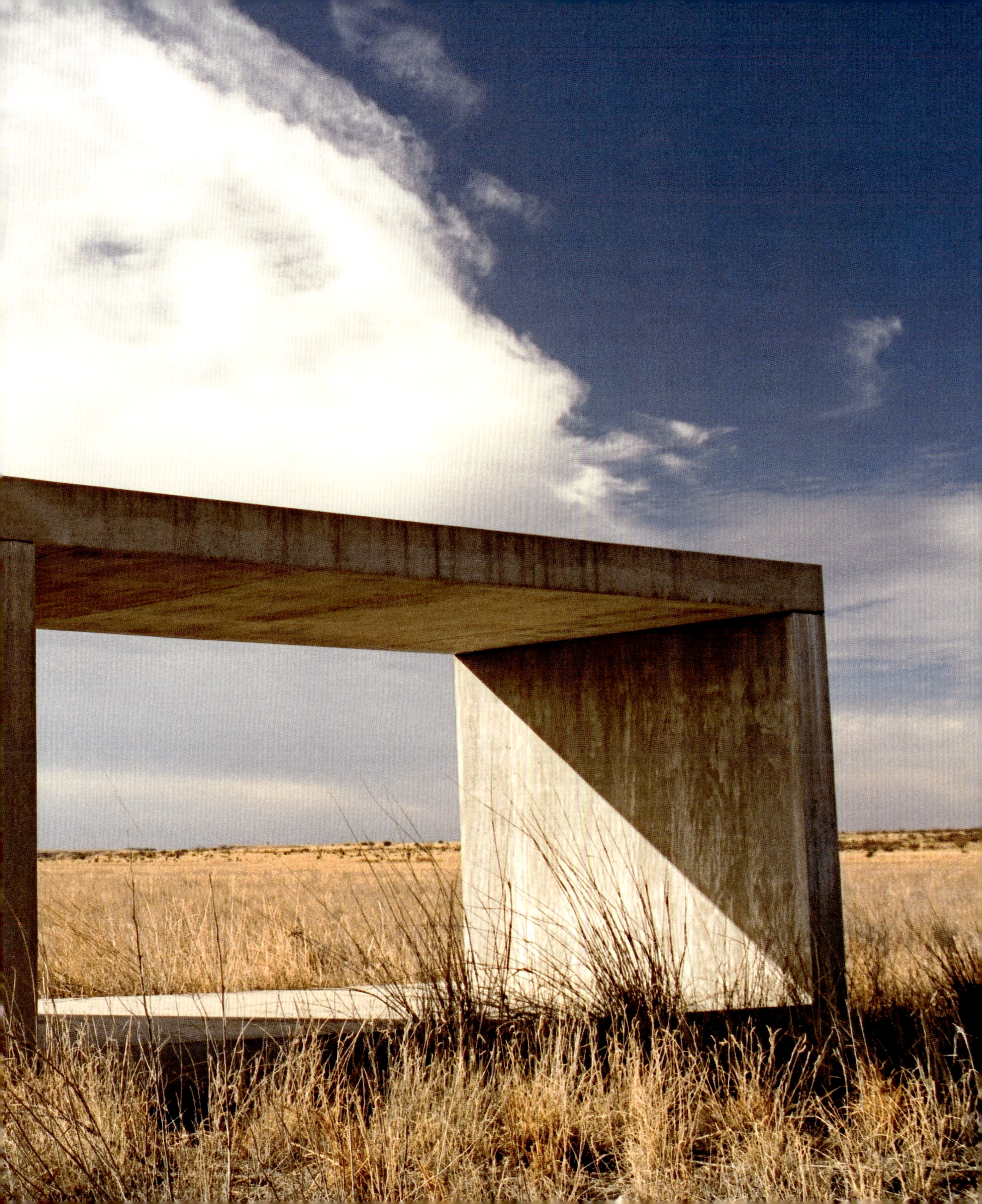

Ed Ruscha

VENICE, CALIFORNIA
JUNE 27–28, 2005

Ed Ruscha, a major American artist whose breakout work dates to 1961–62, was at the top of his game in 2005 with upcoming exhibitions in London, New York, Paris, and Venice. Over his long career, he had been photographed many times, most notably by Dennis Hopper. Ruscha had no need to be photographed by me, but had agreed after a mutual friend had spoken on my behalf. We met at his large postindustrial studio in Venice, California.

The courtyard door was opened by Harley, the mechanic, an old codger hired by Ruscha to work on several vintage cars and trucks that Ruscha owned. Each morning when Harley greeted me, he'd add a grumpy complaint about his working conditions, which I found amusing. After all, what could be more pleasant than being out in the Southern California sunshine working on beautiful, old cars? But whenever Ruscha passed by, they engaged in cheerful banter, which was how, I guess, Harley happily kept his job. The atmosphere inside the studio was serious, full of purposeful activity. There were works in progress everywhere. I photographed Ruscha as he applied a turquoise sky to one of five paintings in the series *Course of Empire,* scheduled for a show that fall at the Whitney Museum of American Art in New York. One morning, he spray-painted a series of palindromes that vividly showed his appreciation for words, while in another area of the studio, Ruscha's brother, Paul, reviewed negatives for an upcoming book to be printed in Italy. On yet another morning, Eddie, Ed Ruscha's son, helped stencil letters on a large blank canvas. All the while, Butch, a quiet, watchful black dog, stayed close to Ruscha, moving from project to project, observing the activity.

The last day I was there, my son Owen Wilson, the actor, came by to visit Ruscha and view some paintings. He took great pleasure in the clever humor of Ruscha's works, the way the words and images played against one another. As Owen was leaving, to begin work on a movie in another country, Ruscha called after him, "Hey, good luck on your celluloid light projection."

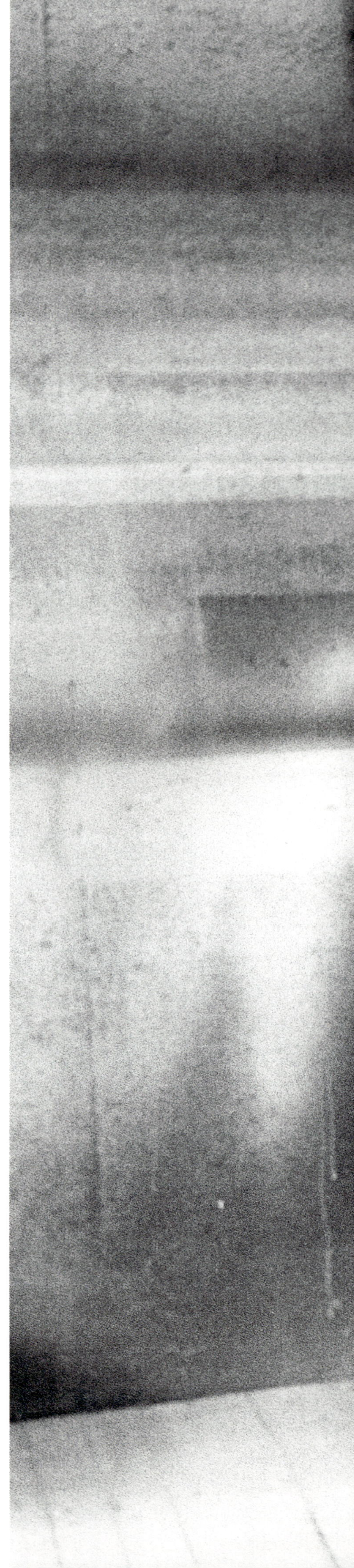

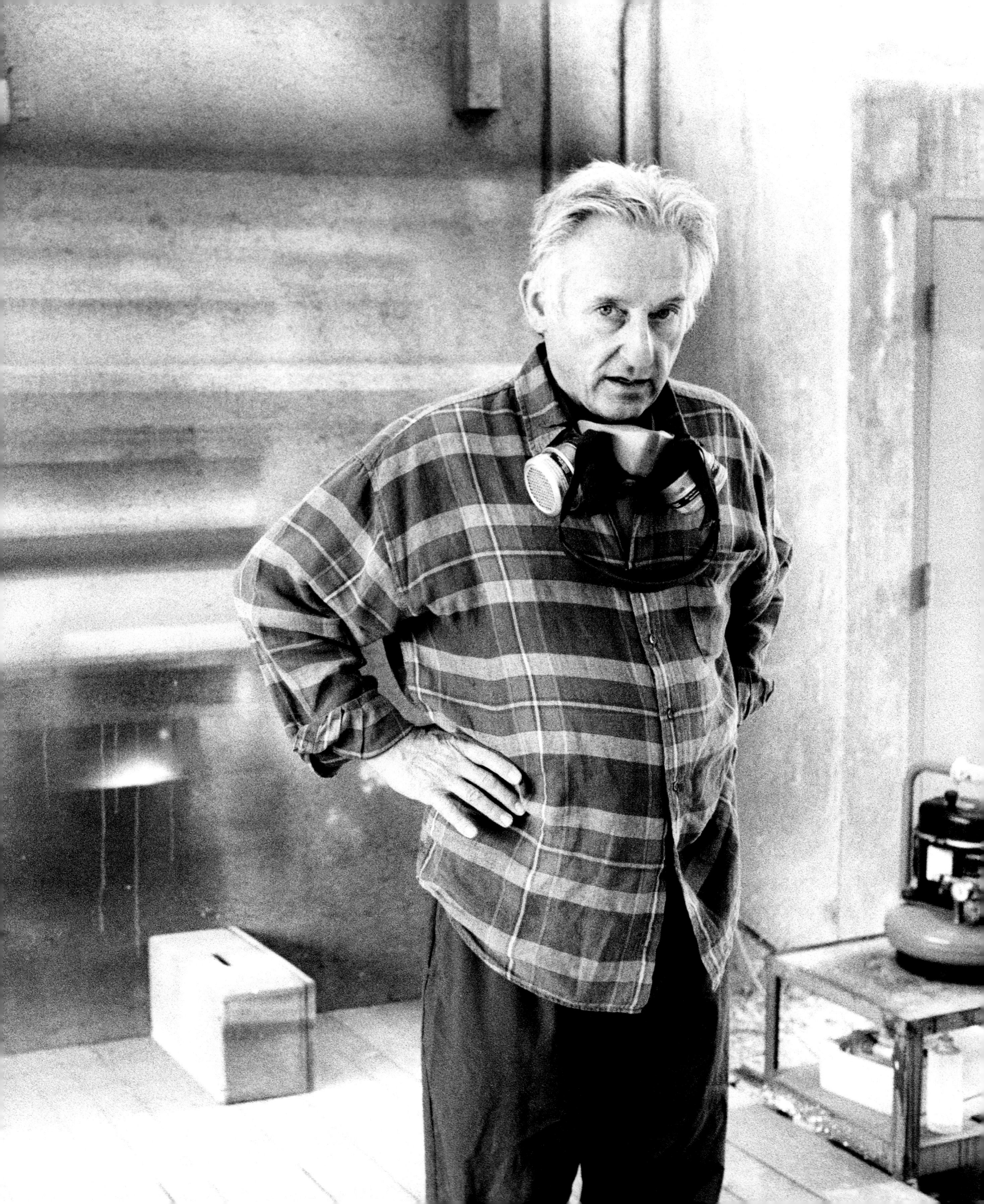

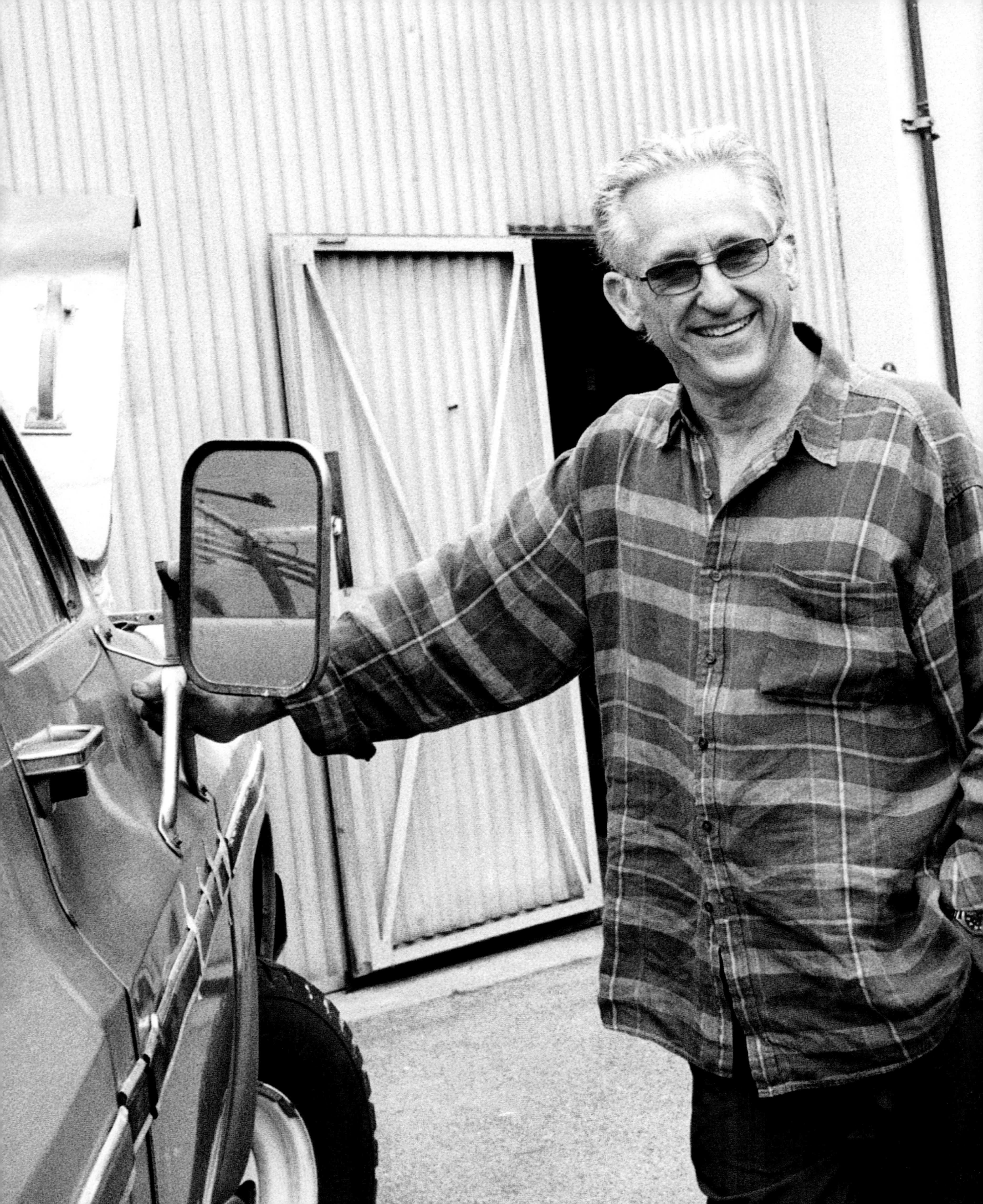

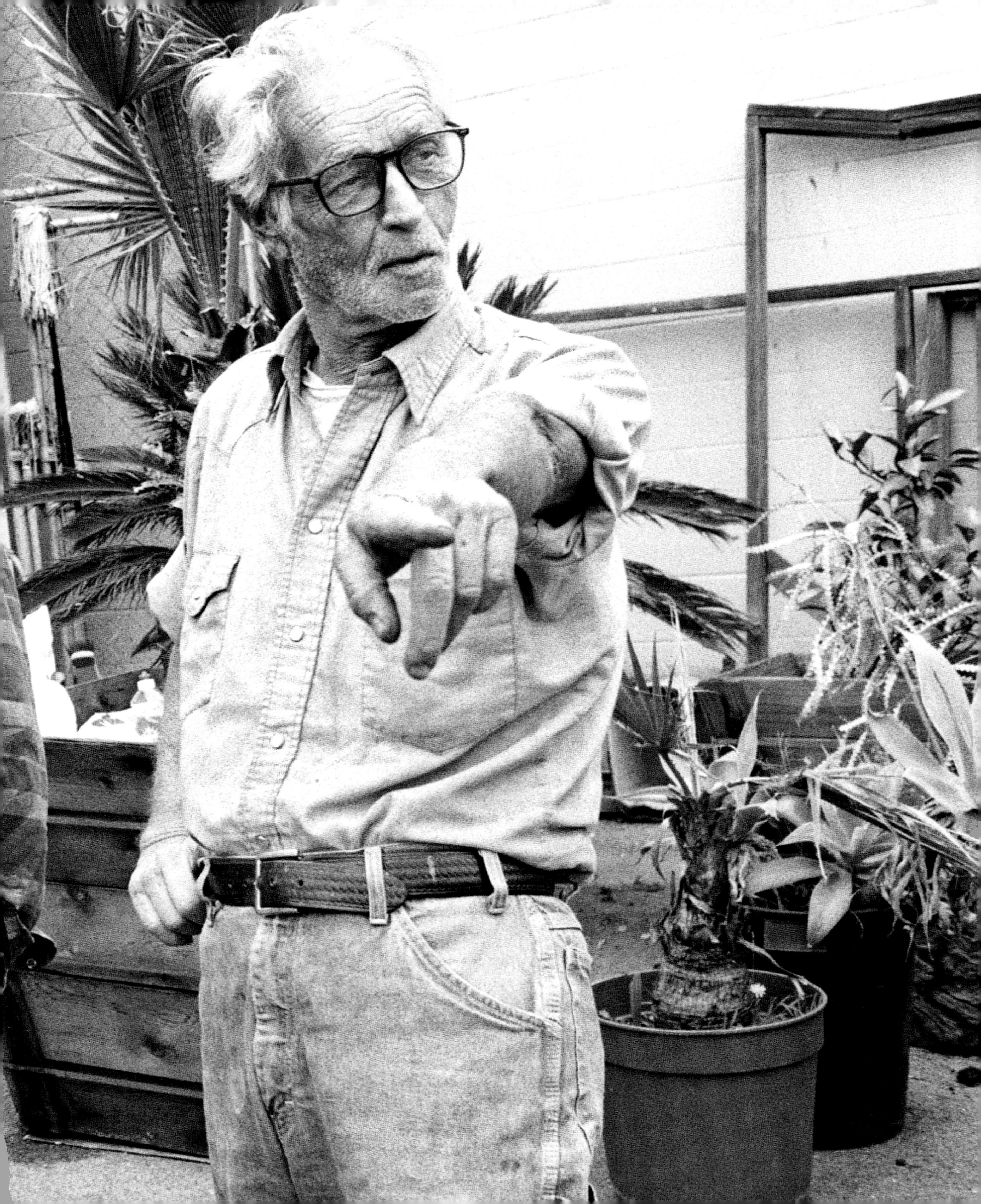

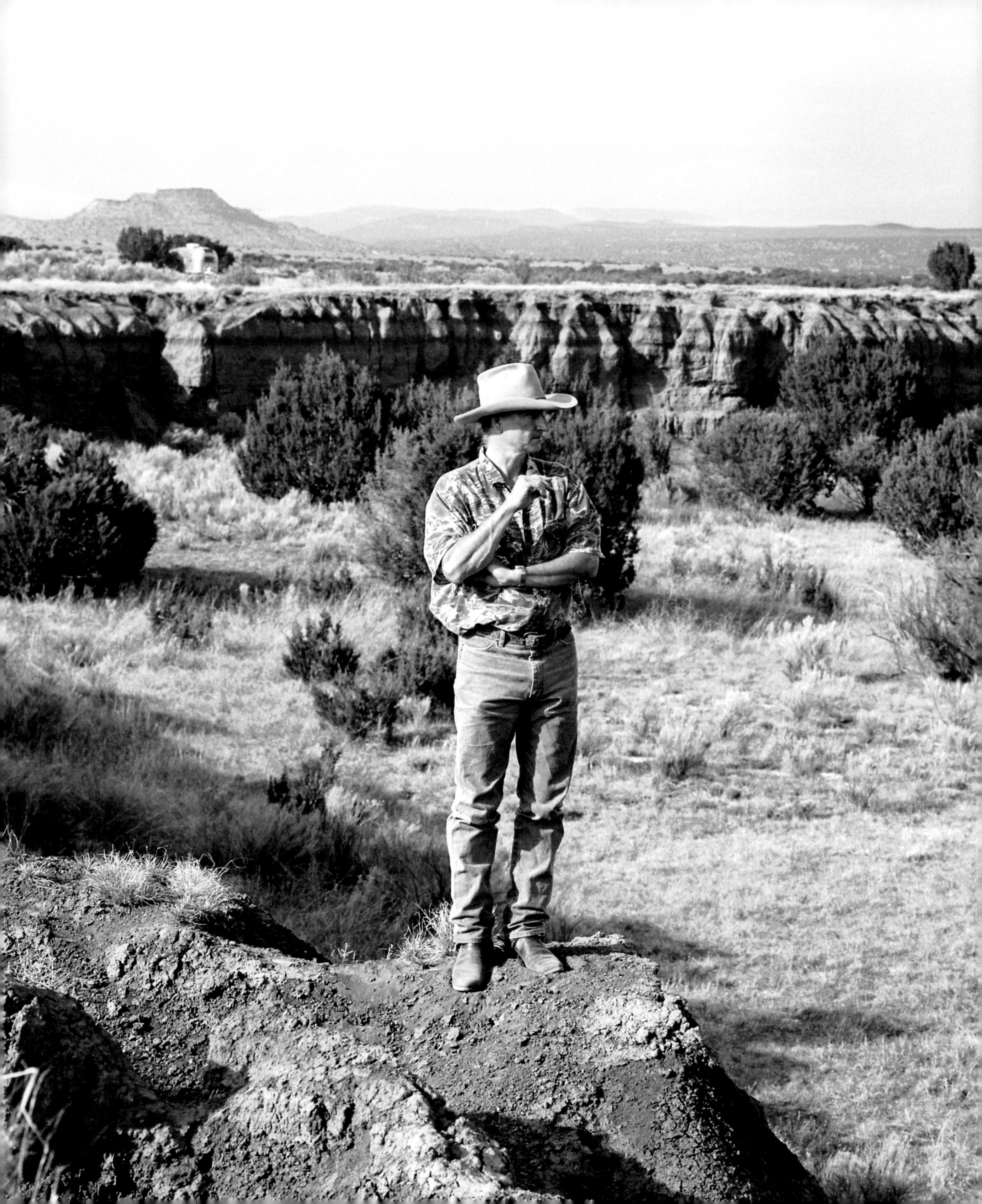

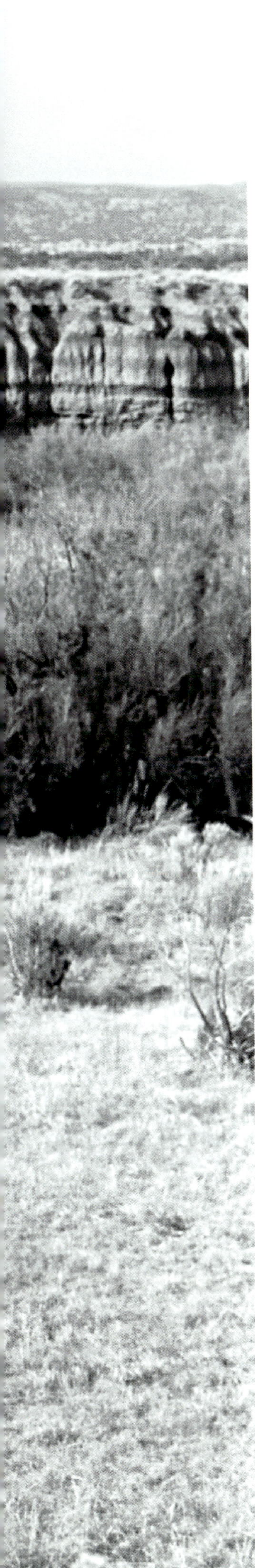

Bruce Nauman

GALISTEO, NEW MEXICO
MAY 26, 1998

One of the most influential artists of his generation has never lived in New York City. Instead, Bruce Nauman lives on a ranch called Las Madres in the mountain-ringed Galisteo Basin in northern New Mexico. Purposely distant from the art world, Nauman and his wife, the painter Susan Rothenberg, built an adobe house above a spectacular canyon where there are caves with Anasazi petroglyphs.

They each have a large studio. While I was there, gentle black dogs followed them around the property, chickens pecked among the irises in the garden, and well-bred horses stood in corrals and grazed on the rim of the canyon. It seemed to me, during my visit to Las Madres, that solitude and space provided an atmosphere in which Nauman's and Rothenberg's creativity could run free.

Richard Avedon

HARDIN, MONTANA
AUGUST 18, 1979

GALLUP, NEW MEXICO
JUNE 15, 1979

The photographer Richard Avedon came from New York City to the West in 1979, and hired me to assist him on a project that would become the most significant series of portraits in his long career. For six years, we crisscrossed the western states, going to mining camps and drilling sites, threshing bees and rodeos, rattlesnake roundups and atomic-research facilities. One June day, Avedon abruptly stopped the car in Gallup, New Mexico, and jumped out. He wanted to have his picture taken beneath a large sign that had caught his eye announcing the Rollie Mortuary. For thirty years, his camera of choice had been a Rolleiflex, commonly known as a "Rollei." "This is where I want to be buried," he said. His camera assistants held him stretched out prone beneath the sign.

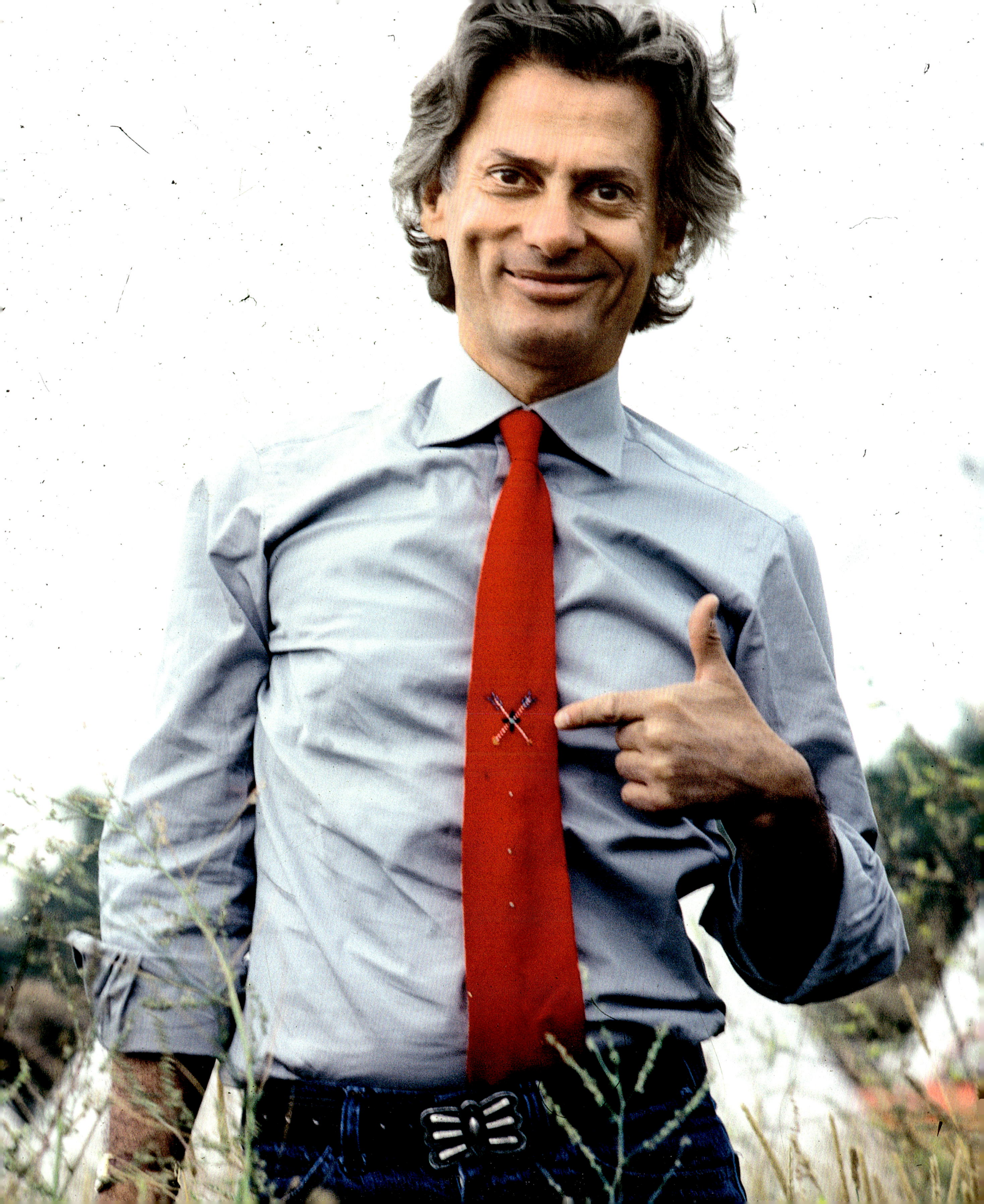

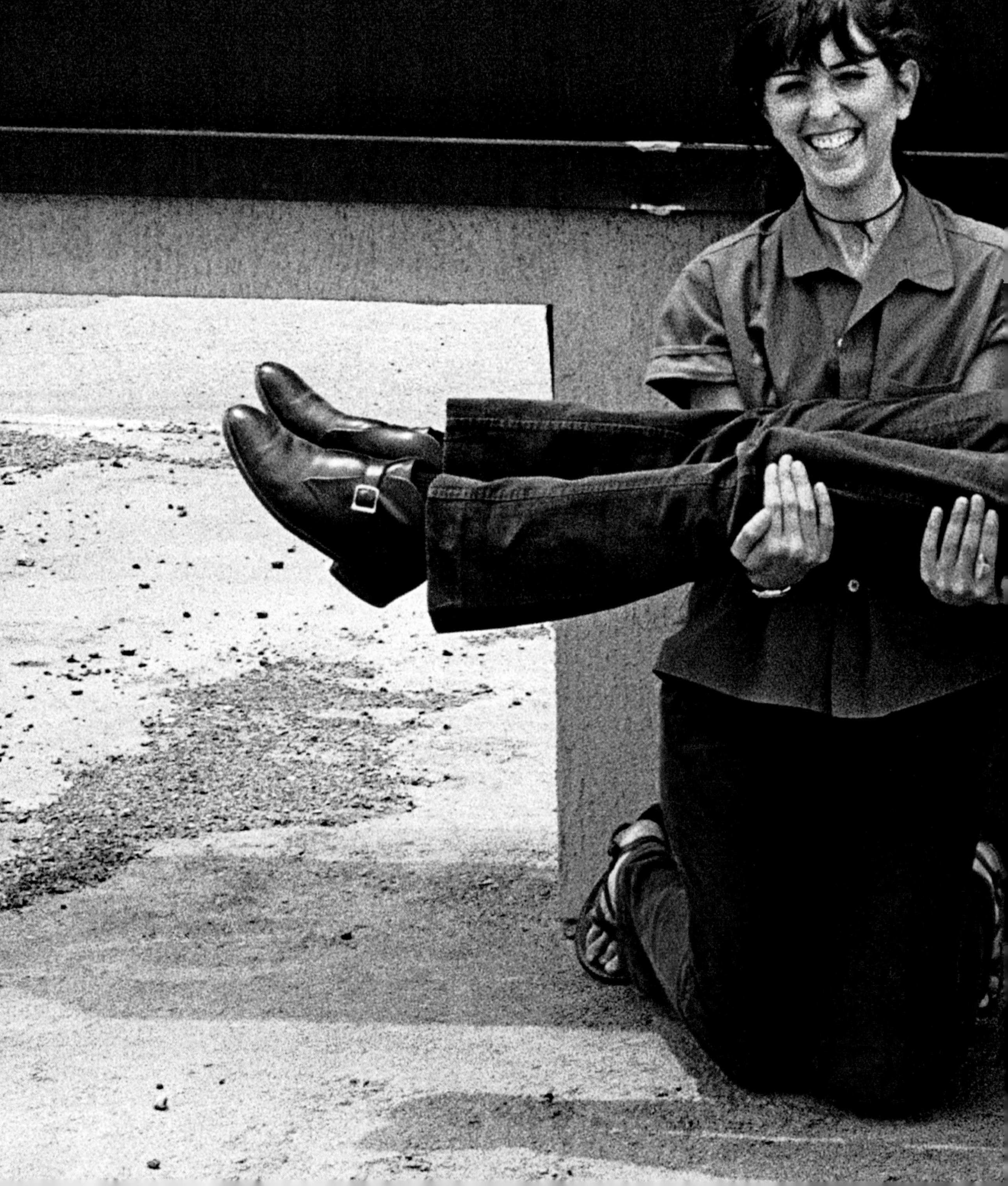
ROLLI
MORT

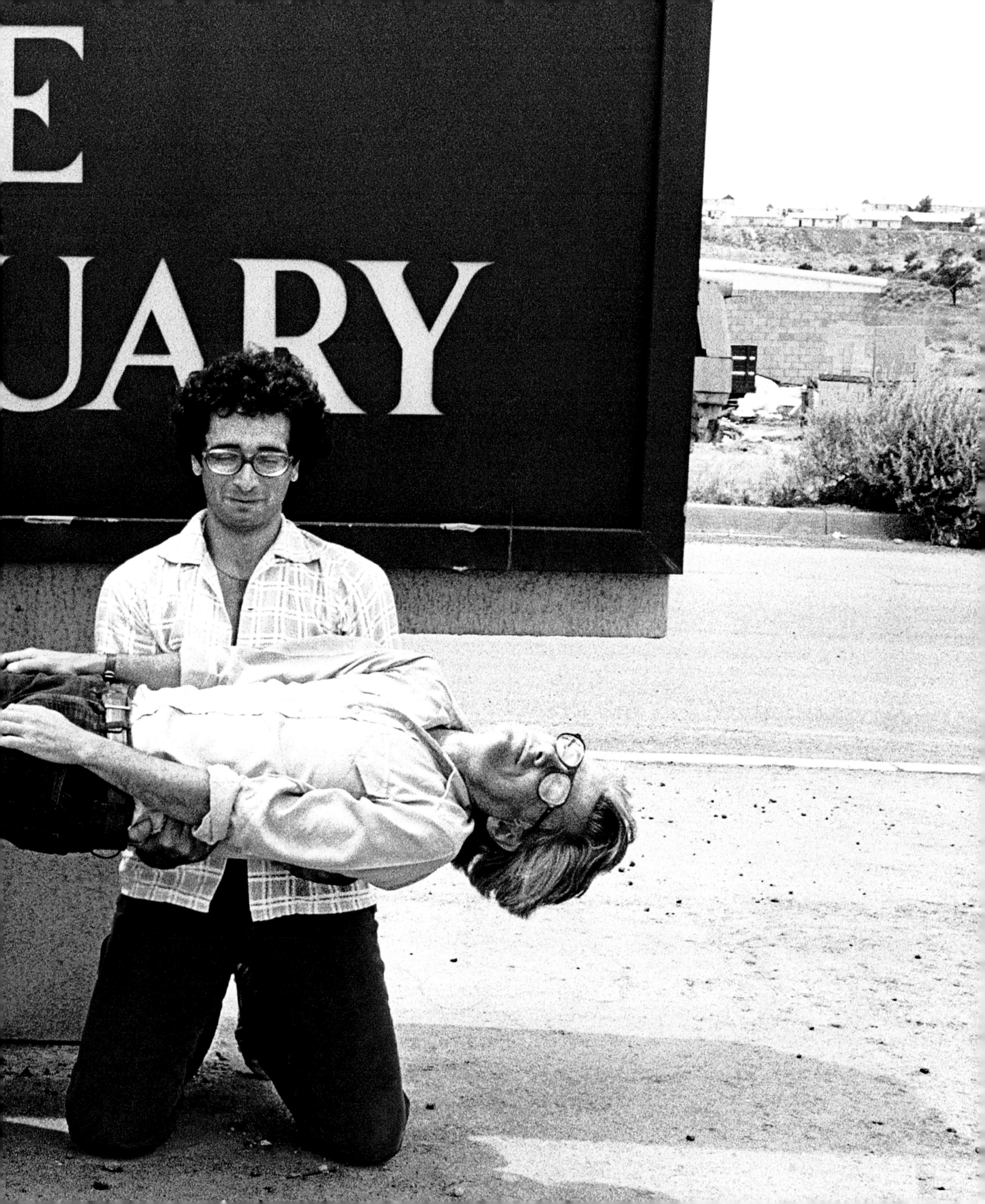

E
UARY

BROOKE ARMY MEDICAL CENTER
SAN ANTONIO, TEXAS
SEPTEMBER 24, 2004

In 2004, when Avedon was eighty-one years old, he asked me to help him once again, this time with a project for the *New Yorker*. He wanted to return to the West to round out a series of portraits he called *Democracy*. We spent two days at Fort Hood in Killeen, Texas, and then went on to San Antonio to Brooke Army Medical Center, the U.S. military's leading burn-treatment facility. We were the first photographers allowed access since the war in Iraq had begun two years earlier. Avedon saw seventeen injured soldiers before concentrating on Joe Washam, a young sergeant from Midlothian, Texas. Washam had been engulfed in flames from a chemical explosion in Baghdad. He was flown to San Antonio, where, after being in a coma for three days, he awoke to find his face and hands ravaged by third-degree burns. Avedon spoke with the soldier and learned that the clear silicone mask that he wore was specially molded to the contours of his face to prevent raised welts of scar tissue from forming.

That night, Avedon and I made plans to meet the next morning to review his layout of the story, but when I went to his room early that following day, I found him unsteady and confused. He said sadly, "I couldn't sleep. I kept seeing the burnt faces of the soldiers, even those bandaged faces I could not see." His speech was slurred. I tried to talk him into going to a hospital, but he insisted on keeping an appointment to photograph a teenage mother at 12:30 p.m.

Moments later, he lost consciousness. He had suffered a stroke. He was rushed to Methodist Hospital in San Antonio but died of a cerebral hemorrhage there five days later. Avedon's life as a photographer was far-ranging and obsessive. From the time of his first photos, in the merchant marine in World War II, to Paris in the 1950s, to civil rights in the 1960s, to Vietnam in the 1970s, right through to his last portraits for the *New Yorker*, he never stopped working. And he got his wish to die in the West, although not under the Rollie Mortuary sign.

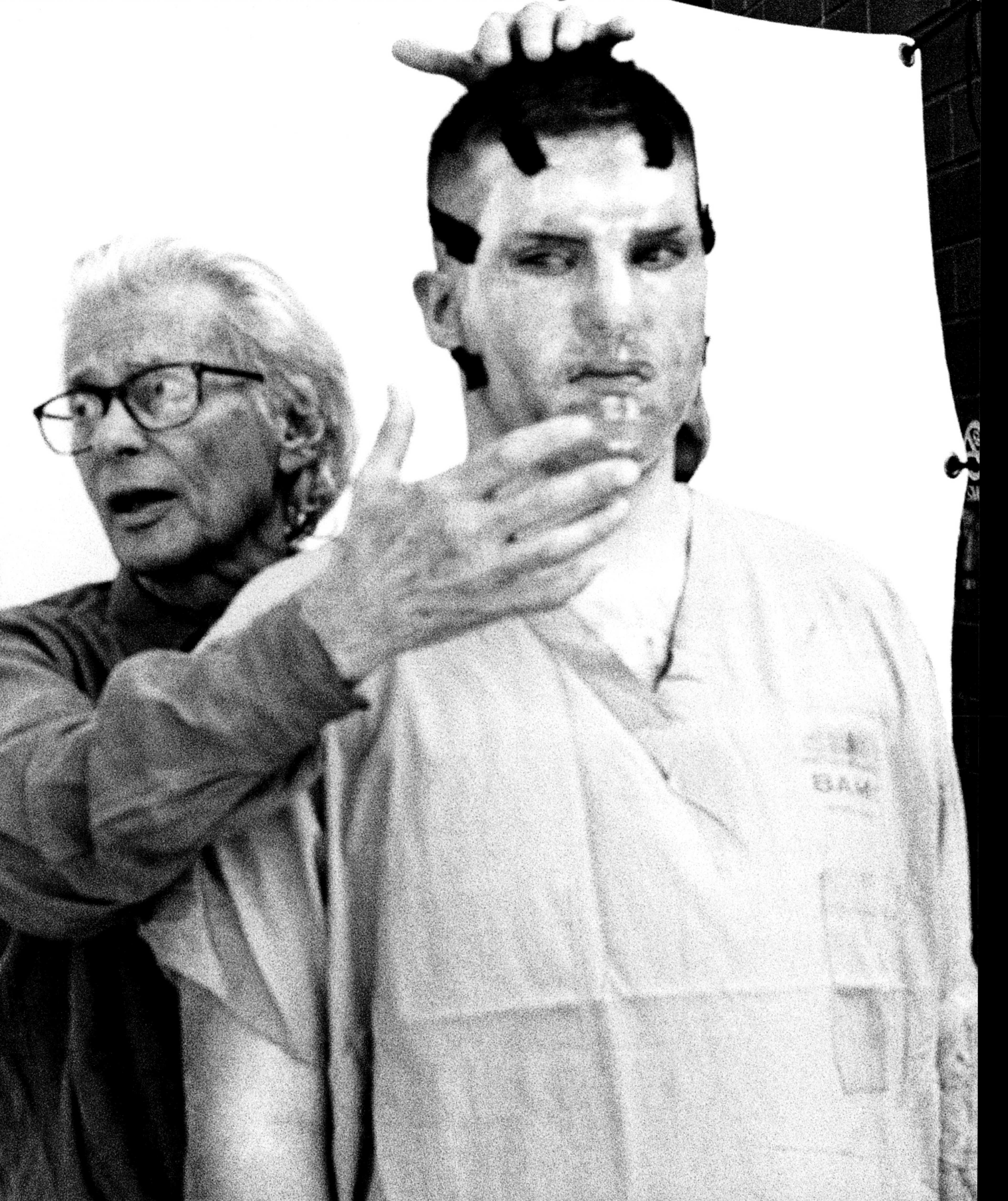
BAM

Mesquite Tree

SHACKELFORD COUNTY, TEXAS
JANUARY 9, 1988

On the plains of West Texas, coyotes have developed an acute ability to survive. With their keen vision and strong sense of smell, they are skilled and adaptable predators, feeding on deer, rodents, rabbits, snakes, and carrion. The coyote has evolved over more than a hundred thousand years. Even today, in this drought-stricken time, their population has reached an all-time high.

Coyotes have just one serious enemy: man. On rangeland all over the West, ranchers and farmers have coyotes forever in their gunsights. Once killed, they are hung up to bleed out before their hides are taken in for a bounty. On the open range, the convergence of wild and domesticated animals creates problems. In Shackelford County, Texas, a rancher showed me a cow lying dead, her half-born calf and her udder eaten away. "She must have had trouble calving, down and helpless when they attacked her," the rancher explained. "Coyotes don't kill their prey before they begin eating. They just tear open a big hole and stick their heads in. They're death on any kind of livestock."

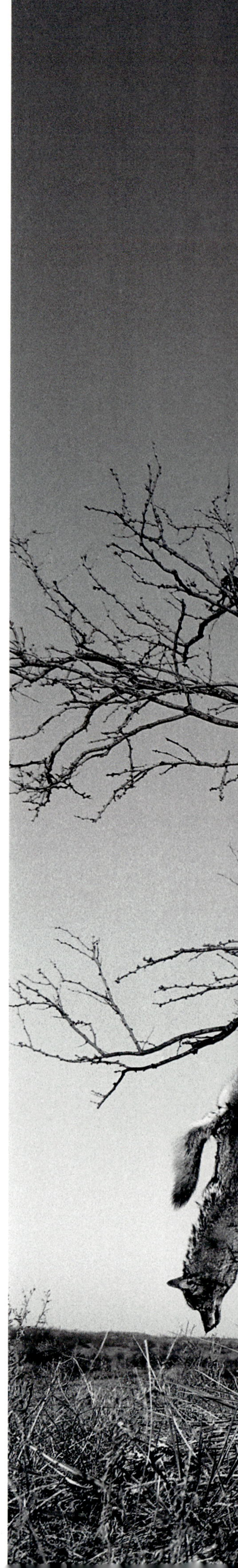

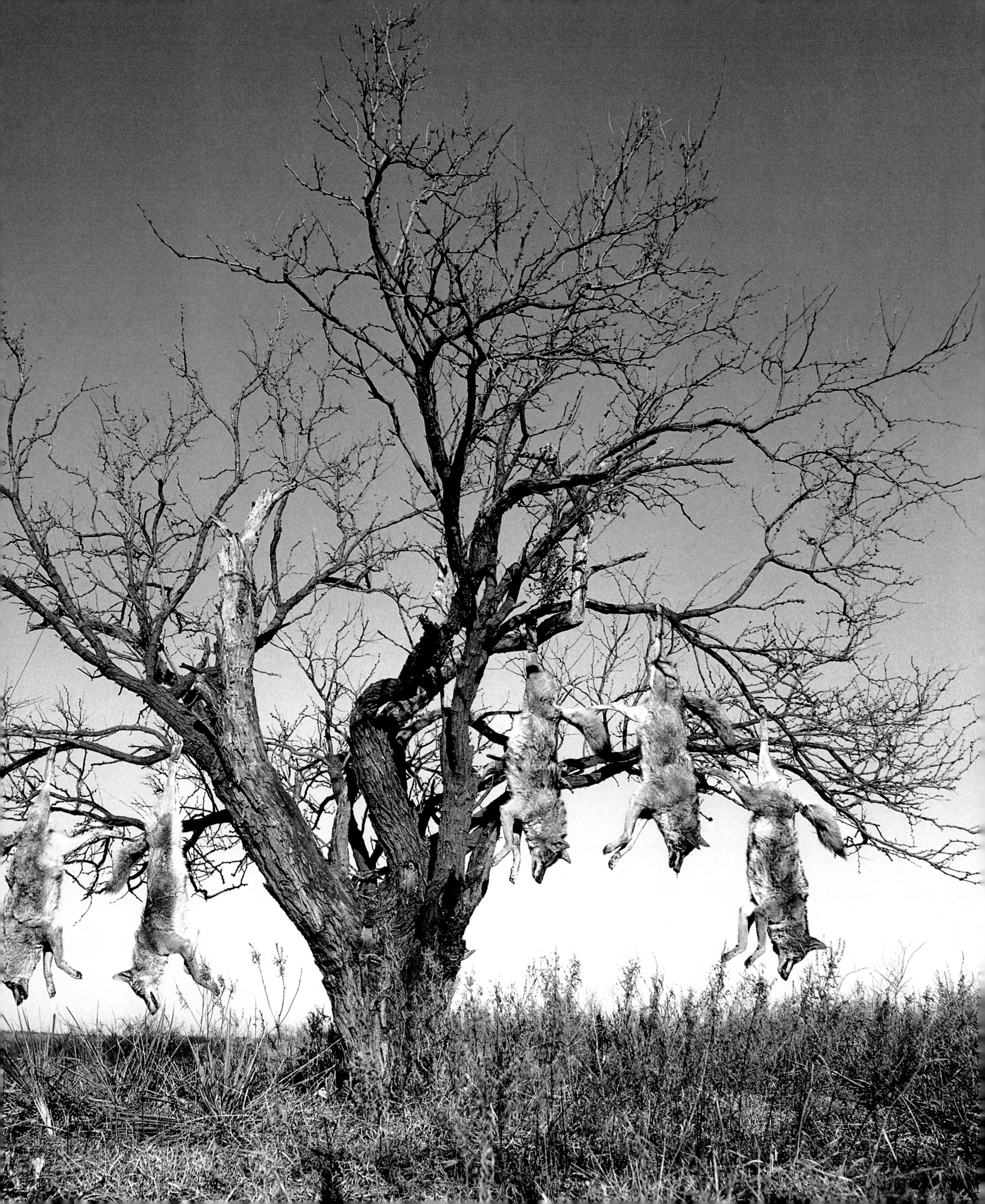

First Communion

DALLAS, TEXAS
MAY 22, 1988
MAY 16, 1993

First Communion is a solemn and important occasion for all Catholics. It is the time when children, after special classes once a week for a year, receive the sacrament meant to symbolize the body of Christ. The event is of such importance that Mexican families have an expression, *Tu quieres tirar la casa por la ventana!* ("Throw the house out the window!"), to justify break-the-bank spending. Little girls, eight or nine years old, wear elaborate, frothy white dresses signifying childhood purity with white veils and tiaras. Each child carries a candle, symbolizing the light of Jesus, a rosary to pray to Mary, and a small white Bible to learn more about God. All communicants receive the sacrament together at a special mass attended by their families, friends, and neighbors. Rosa Maria Prieto has a vivid memory of the day more than seventy years ago: "I had the measles. I was so sad I couldn't be with my class on First Communion day. A month later, all by myself, I walked down the aisle in my frilly and lacy white dress while my family and all the parishioners joined me in prayers. That was a joyful day."

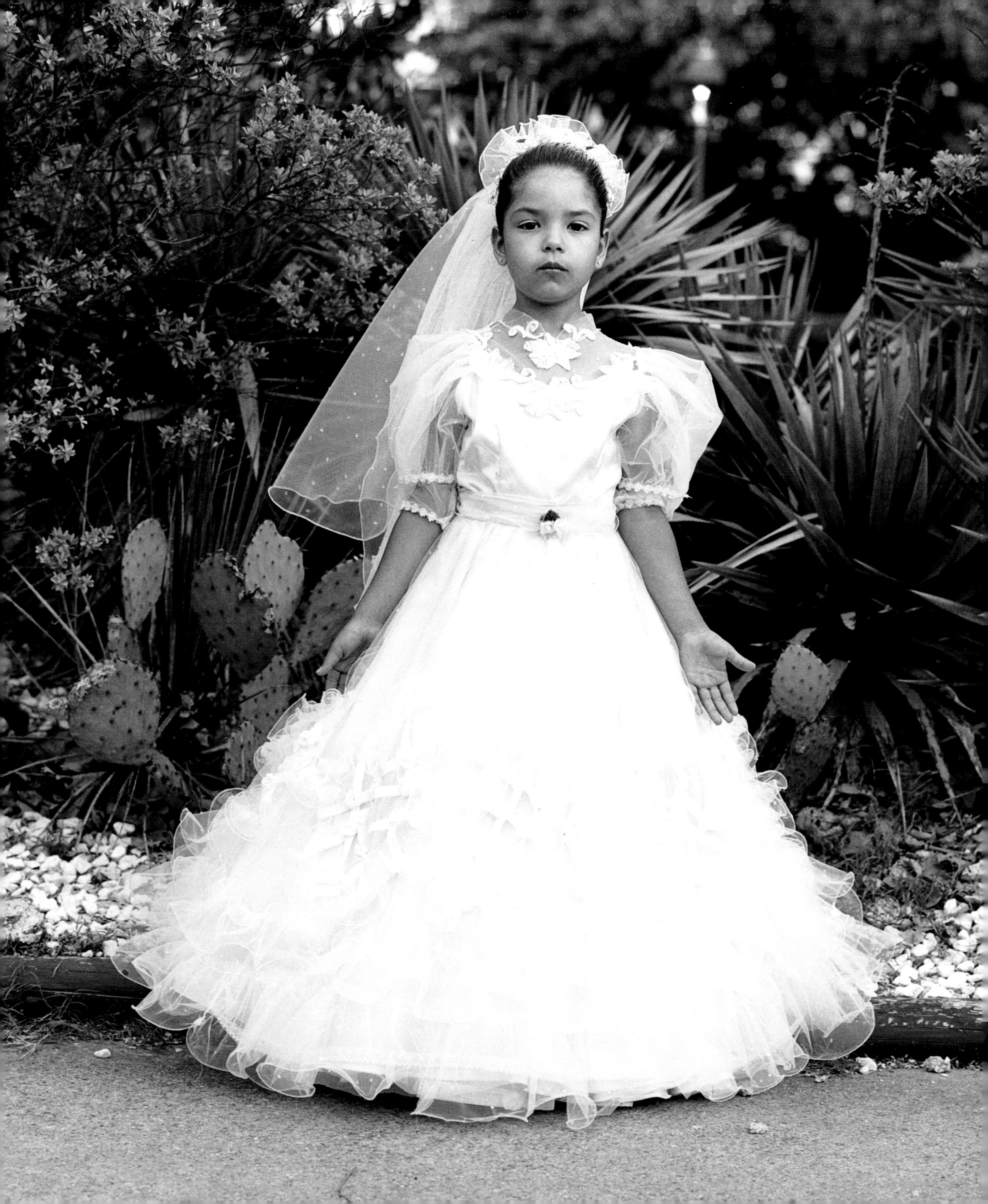

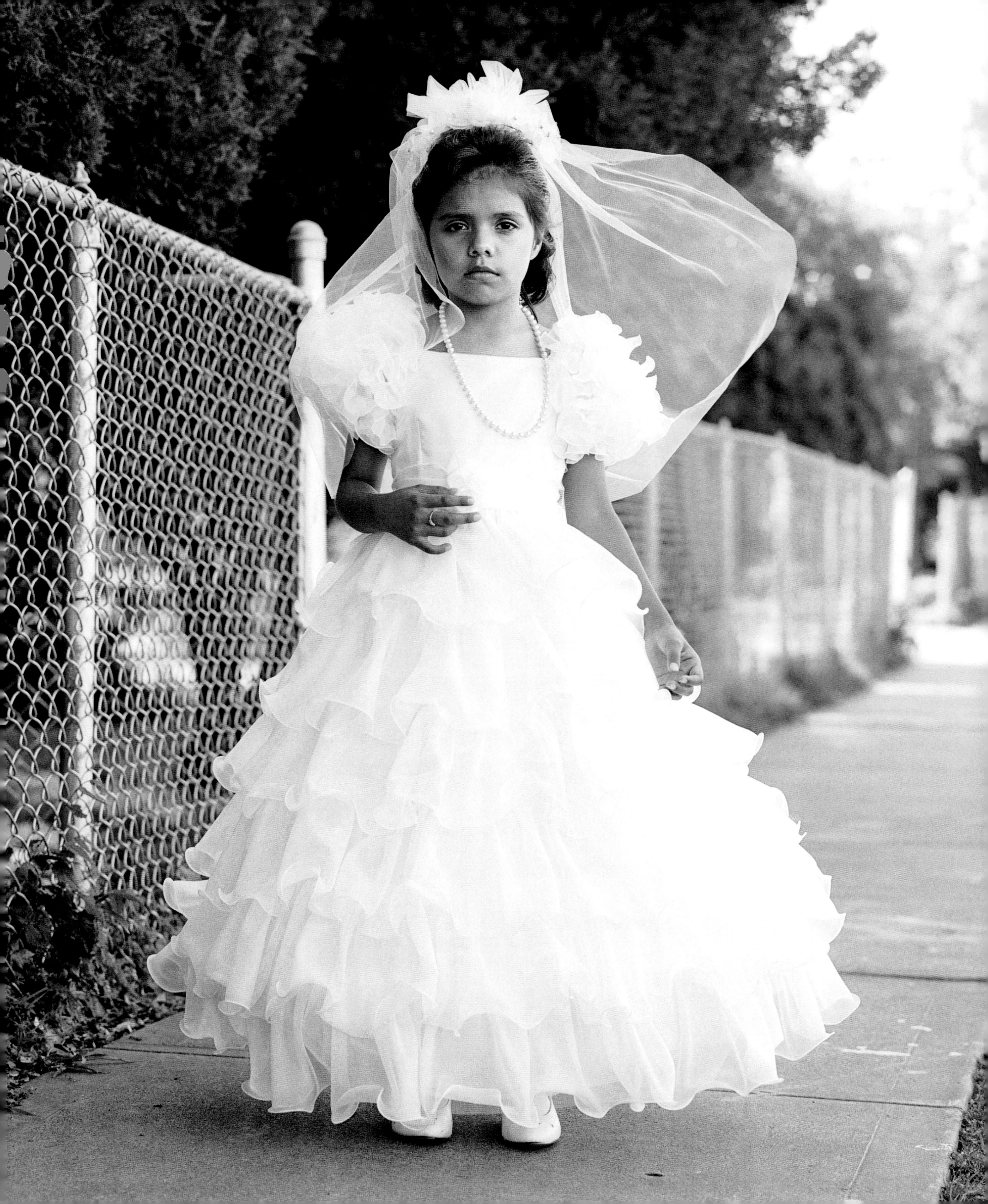

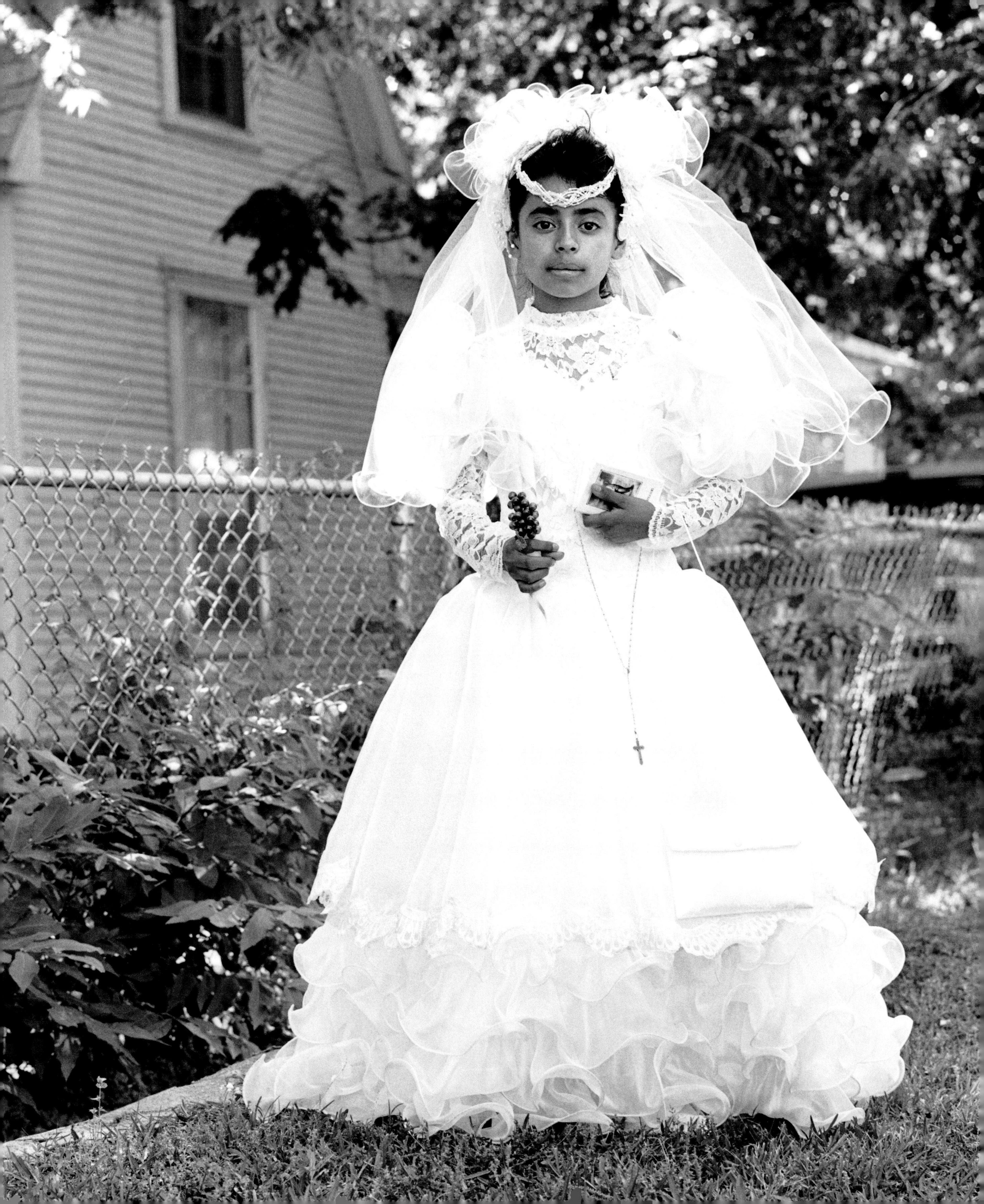

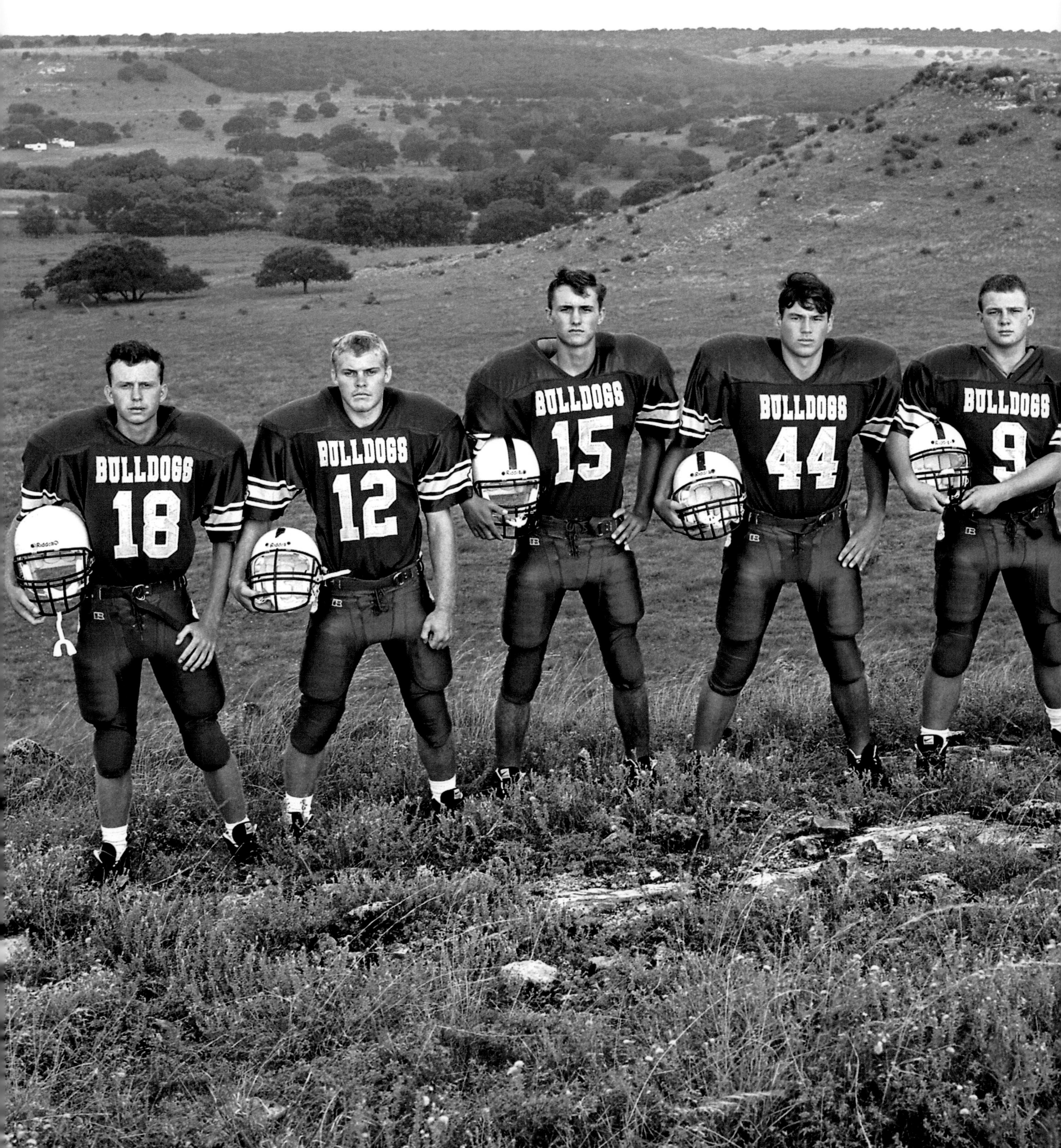
BULLDOGS
18
BULLDOGS
12
BULLDOGS
15
BULLDOGS
44
BULLDOGS
9

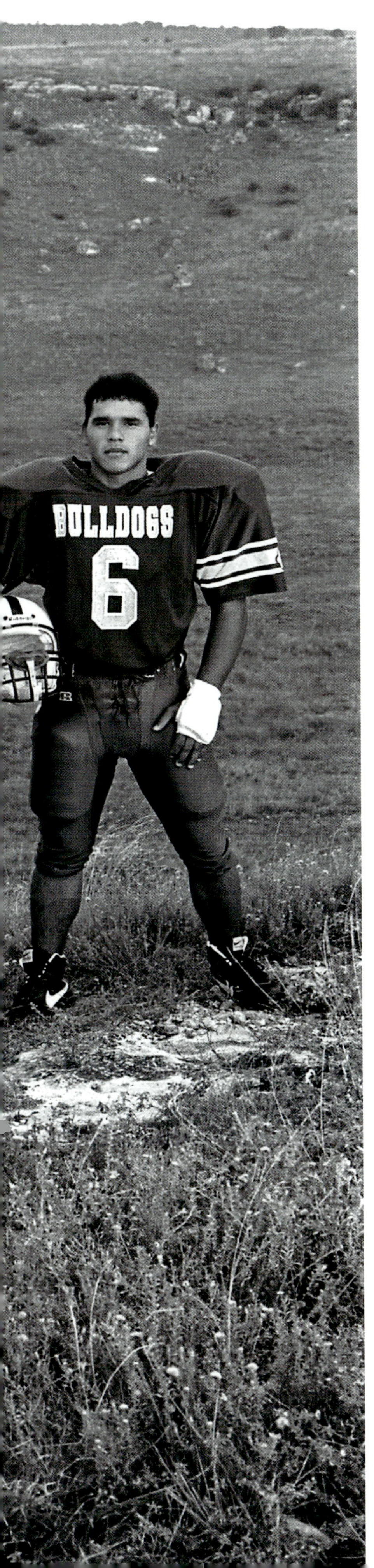

Six-Man Football

DEMOCRAT, CHEROKEE, MORAN, MULLIN, PANTHER CREEK, AND WOODSON, TEXAS 1991–2002

On the western plains, in communities too sparsely populated to field traditional eleven-man teams, many high schools in Colorado, Montana, Nebraska, and New Mexico play a more wide-open variety of the game. With fewer players, and less congestion on the field, six-man football is a speed game, full of razzle-dazzle plays and basketball-like scores. But nowhere is the game played with more enthusiasm than in Texas. On Friday nights from 1991 through the fall of 2002, I drove out to the West Texas towns of Mullin, Zephyr, Paint Rock, Spur, Panther Creek, and others.

The playing fields were crudely lit, and because I had only a simple on-camera flash, I had to get close to the action to get any pictures at all—so close that, at times, I was just a step or two away from the points of impact. These were tough country kids, hell-bent, barreling down the sidelines, hurtling into opponents. In retrospect, my style fit their version of the game. Direct and pared down, my photographs were dependent on the atmosphere and the thrill of the action. Every person in town, or so it seemed to me, turned out on these Friday nights, and in the bleachers right behind me, I could see and hear the outbursts of enthusiasm as well as the despair of parents and fans. The scale of the game, the isolation of the towns, the intensity of the crowds—everything was accessible, exposed, exaggerated. Even the scant light against the darkness was a perfect situation for me because these conditions gave my pictures immediacy.

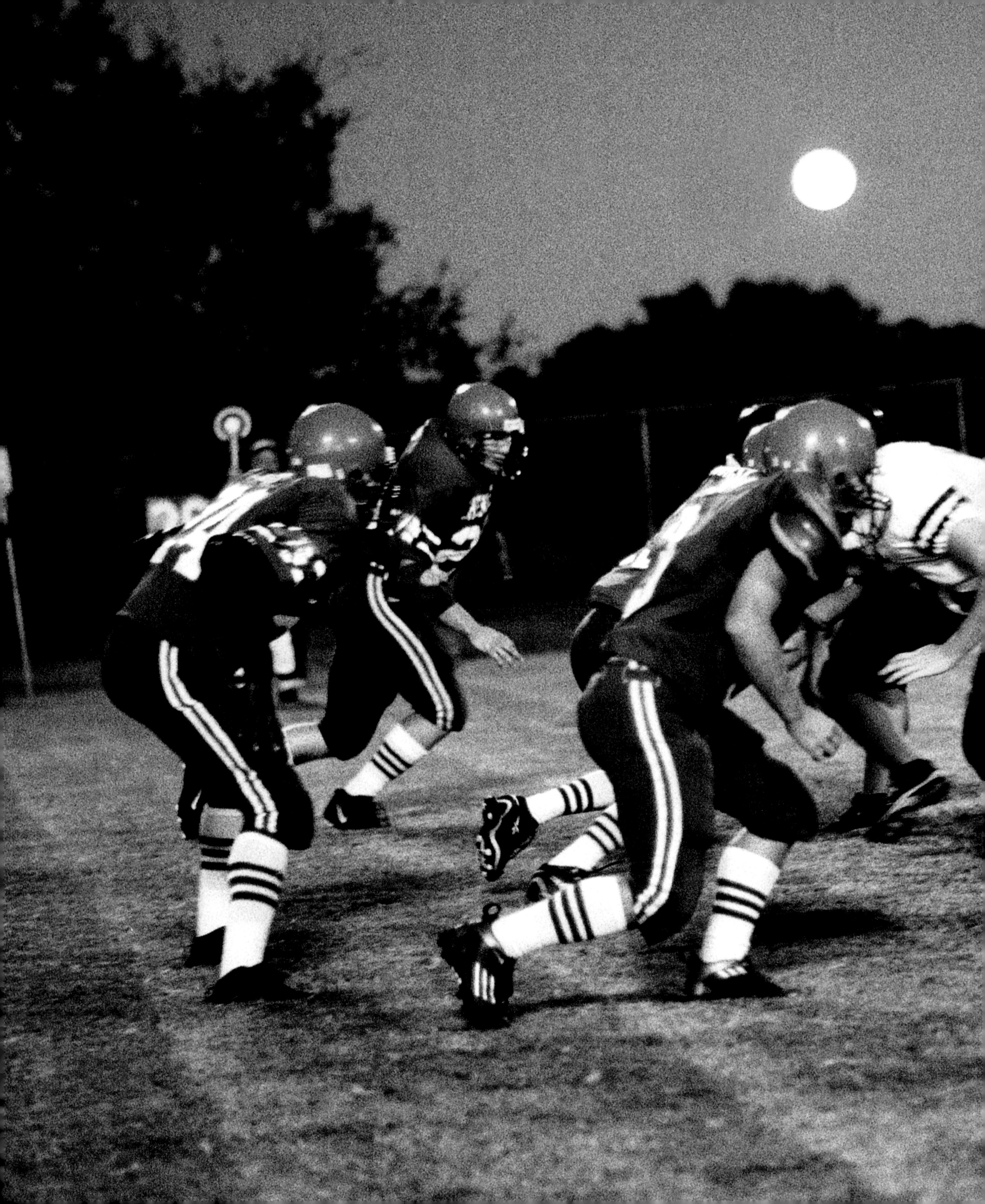

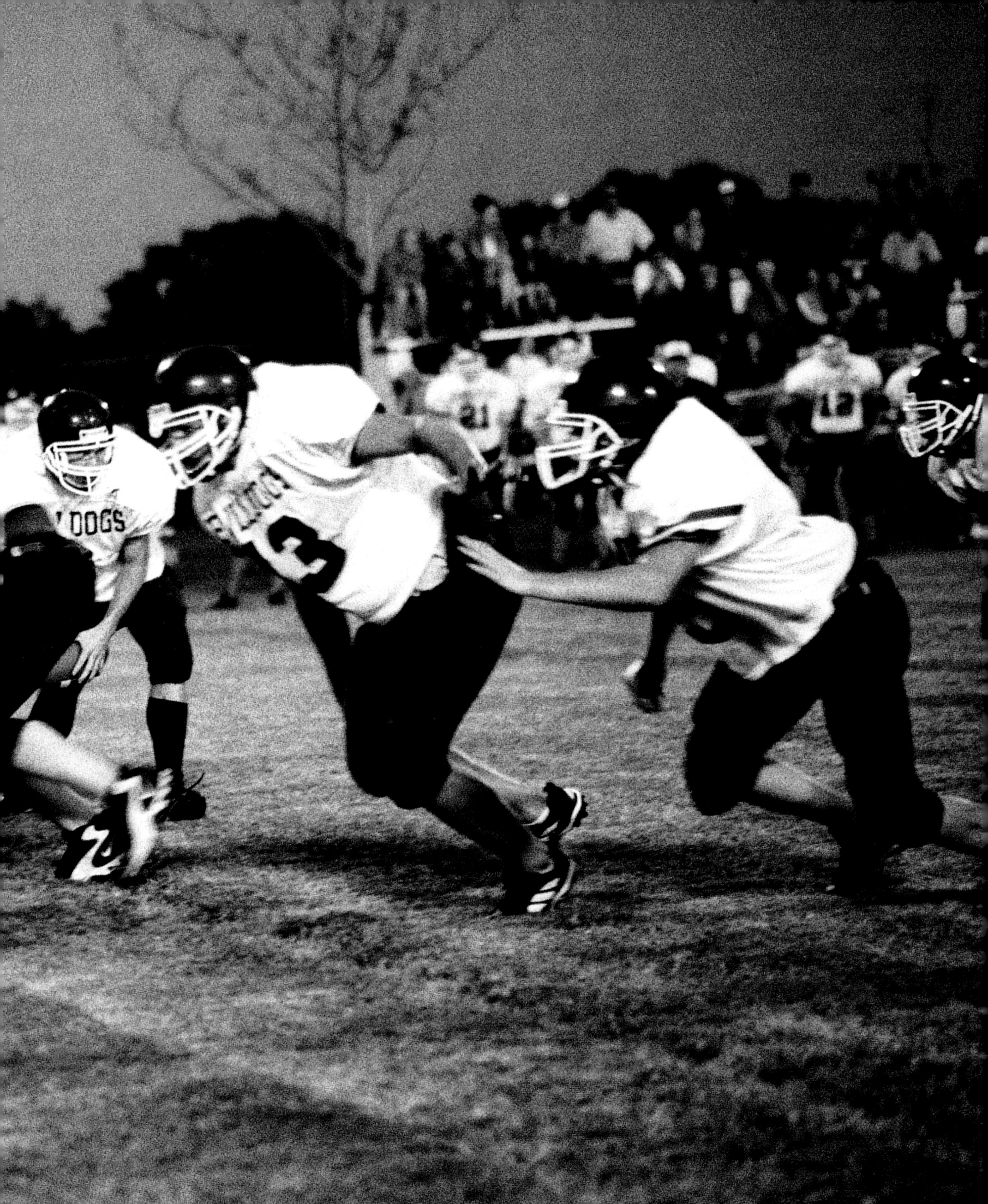
DOGS

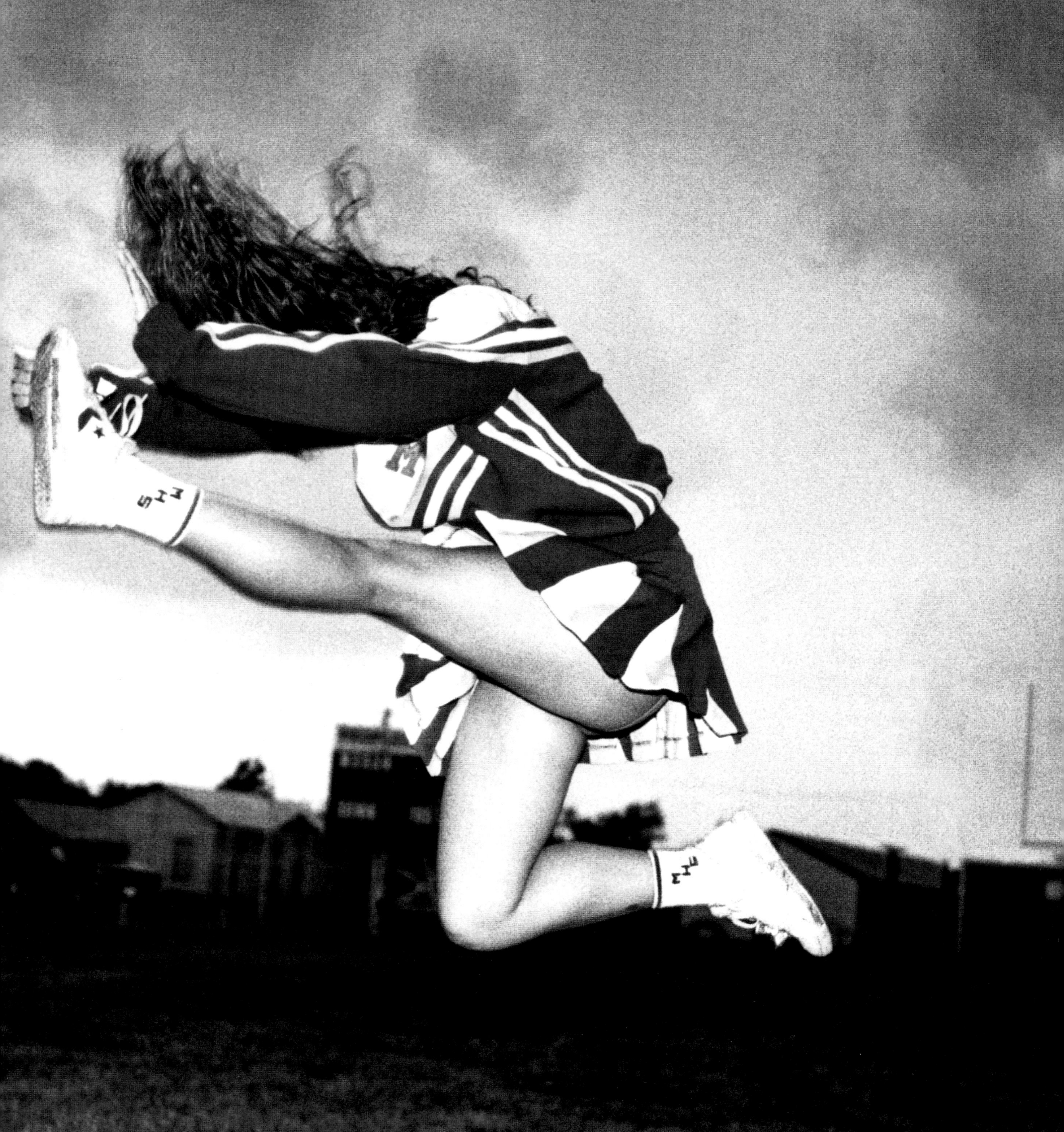
MHS

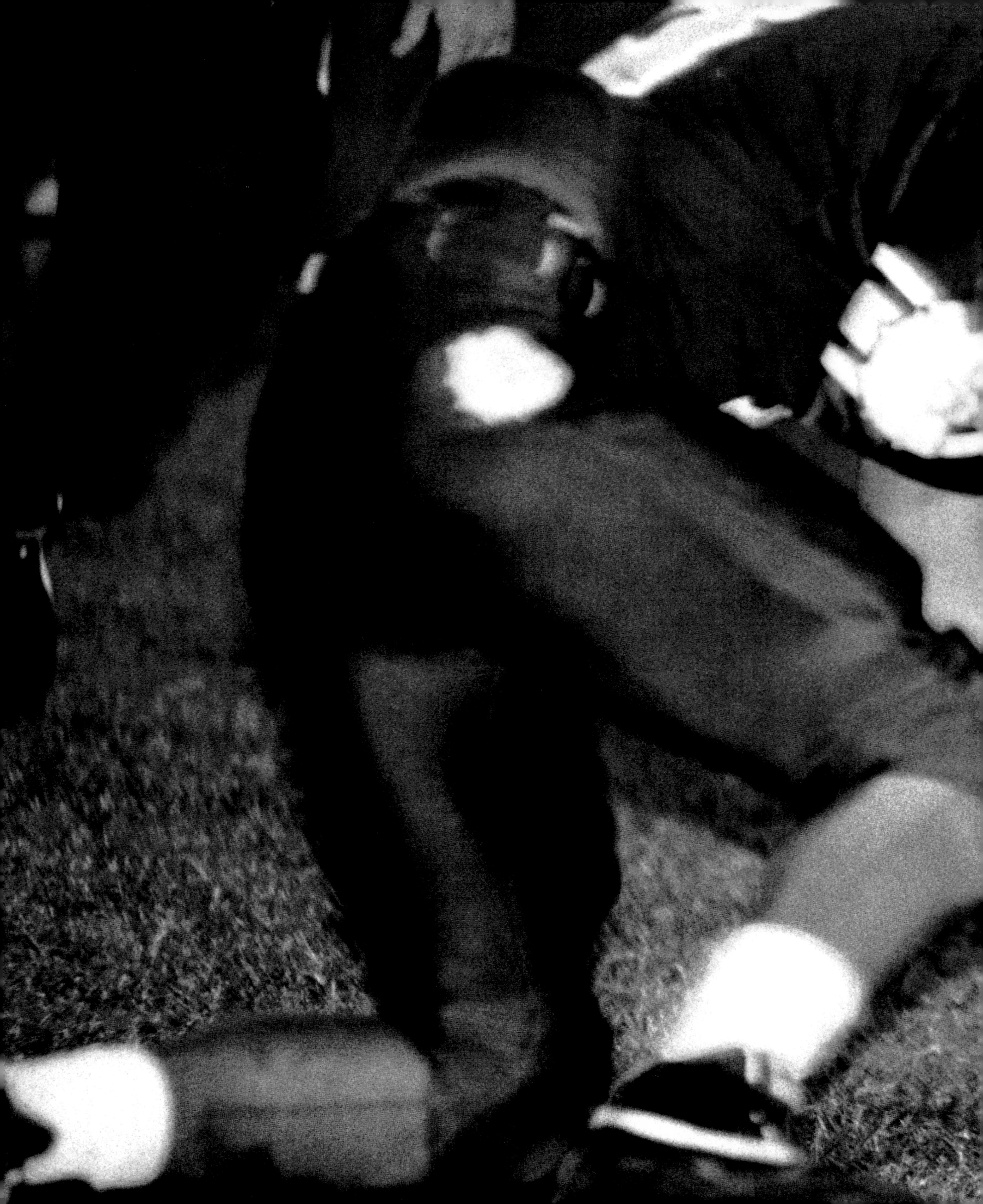

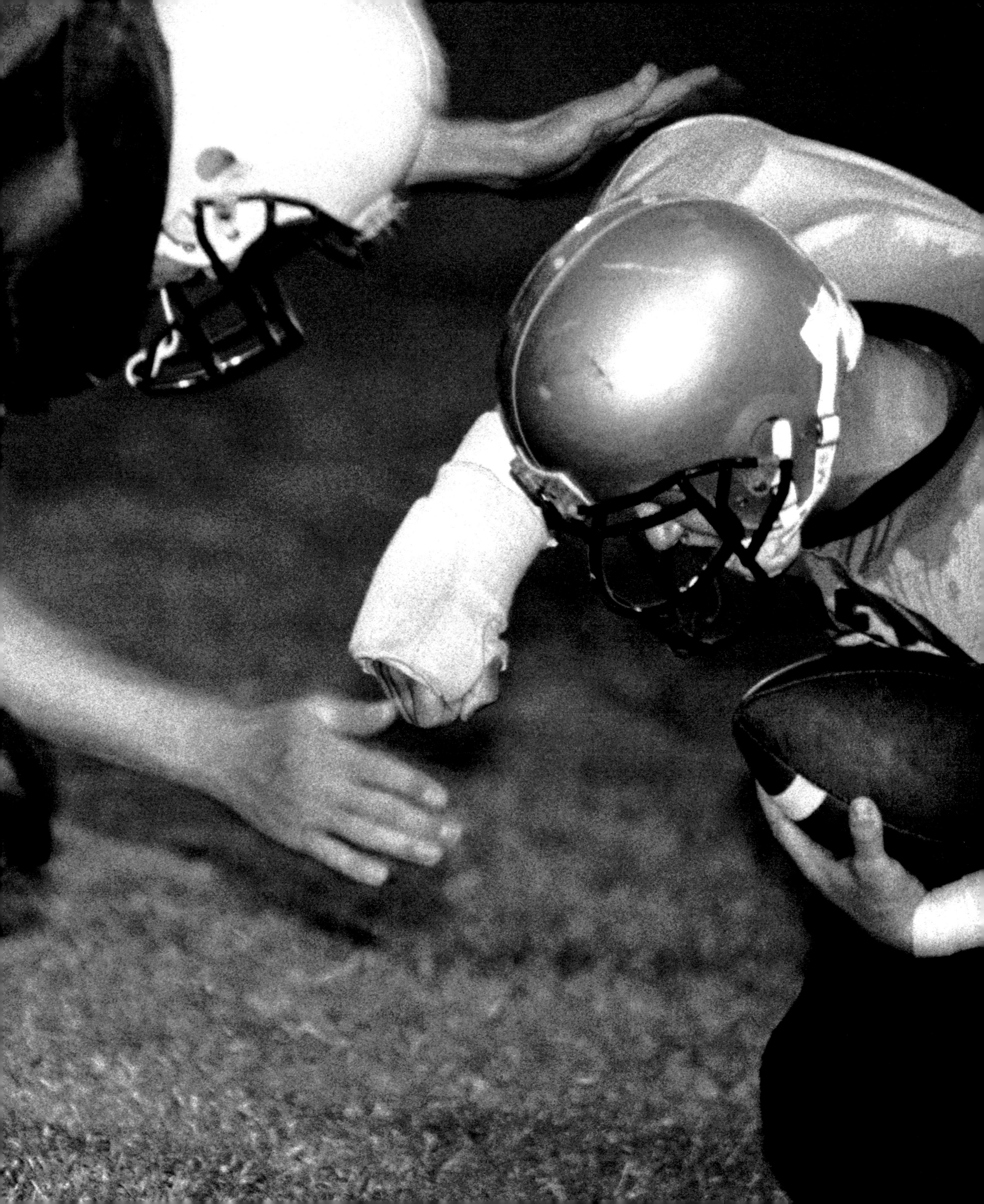

The town of Guthrie, which sits in the middle of 944 square miles of King County, had only twenty-nine boys and girls in its high school. Panther Creek High, with only sixty-nine students, seemed to float on a prairie surrounded by 550 square miles of Coleman County; and in the town of Gordon in Palo Pinto County, the coach was lucky if he had seventy kids in high school. These towns often did not have a movie theater or a restaurant, much less a shopping mall. With so few distractions, school and athletics became the focal point of the community. The parents and fans in these hardscrabble communities took responsibility for their schools, which they had to do, if the schools were to survive. In Gordon, Nelson Campbell, the most successful coach in Texas six-man football history (236-60-2) and the school principal, mowed the team's football field himself. "I did it," he said, "because I wanted them to be proud of their stadium." His son, Lyle, graduated in a class of twenty-two in 1999 and was recruited by Dartmouth College, where he played inside linebacker for four years. Remembering his hometown, Lyle told me, "My dad was coach, my grandparents and aunts and uncles and cousins came to every game. I played with three of my cousins—Jim Ed, Joe Alan, and Chris. Every fan knows every kid and every kid's family. We might have five thousand at a play-off game. We were in the play-offs seventeen out of twenty-two years."

When the leading six-man coaches talked about their winning traditions, they all spoke of their players' work ethic. "They're just ol' rawboned country boys who've worked out in the heat all their lives," said Harvey Wellman of Guthrie. Travis Wilson, a player on Mullin's winning team in 1995, said, "You know, in these smaller places, we had to get out there and work and sure 'nough sweat. I can remember, after one of my games, Papa sittin' in his truck with a gooseneck load of goats waitin' on me to leave out and go to Weatherford or San Angelo. We'd roll back in at four or five in the mornin', just long enough to get an hour's sleep, take a shower, then go to work."

Those boys who leave their rural communities for work or educational opportunities in bigger towns and cities often find it hard to put aside their memories of playing six-man football with mesquite trees beyond the end zones and maybe a horse or two fenced off from the field of play. Two brothers from West Texas, Jim Ed and Joe Alan Kofitha, off in Wisconsin for college in 1999, couldn't afford to go back to Texas for a quarterfinal game pitting their hometown of Gordon against Panther Creek, so they called their grandmother, who held the phone up to Radio Ranch KYXS 95.9 FM out of Mineral Wells for the entire game's play-by-play. They passed the phone back and forth, and at the end of the fourth quarter, amid the shouts and screams of the crowd, they heard their cousin Lyle Campbell score a clutch touchdown to put his team into the lead, fifty-four to fifty-two. The Gordon Longhorns went on to win that game and another state championship—and Wisconsin heard about it in real time.

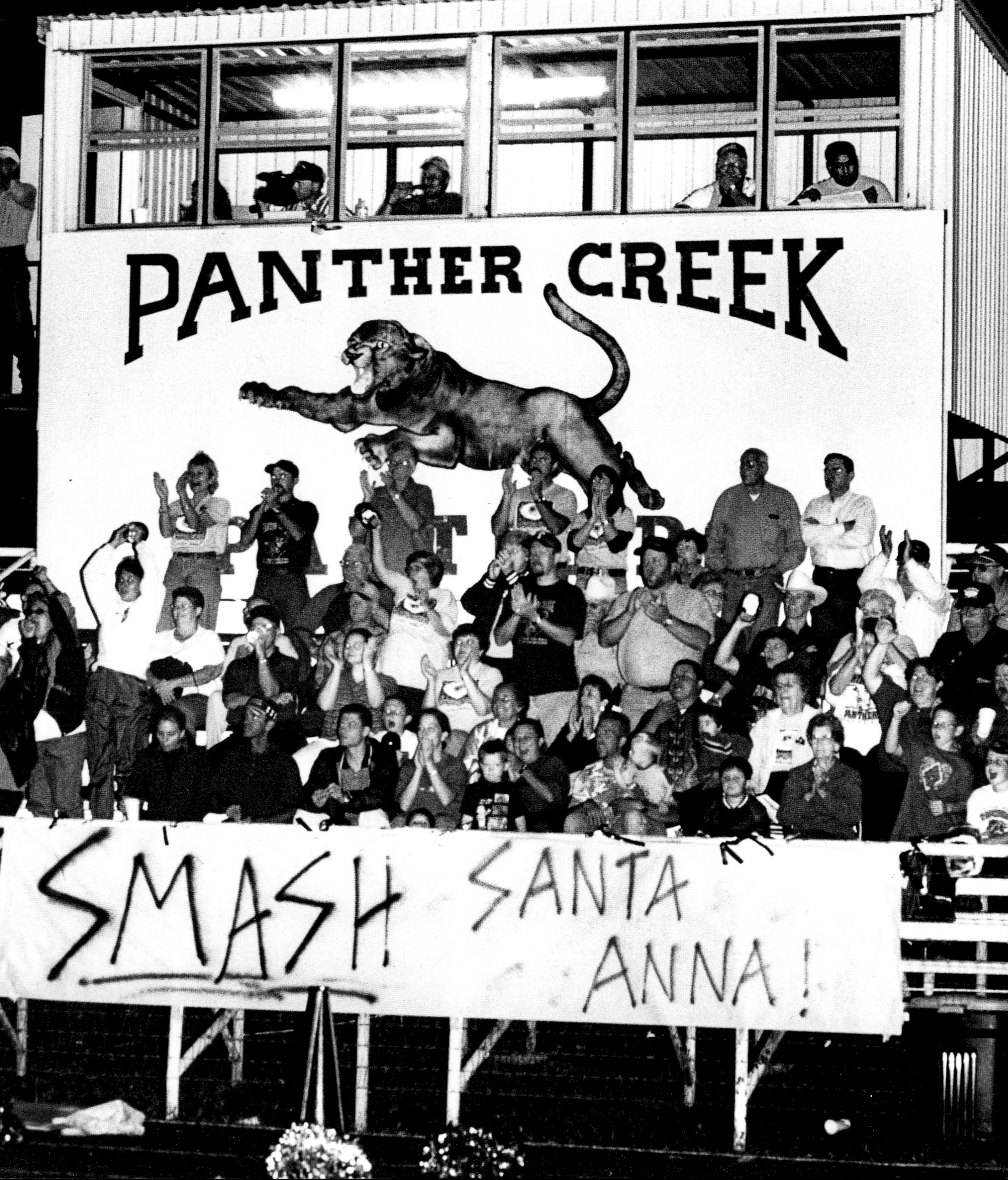
PANTHER CREEK
SMASH SANTA ANNA!

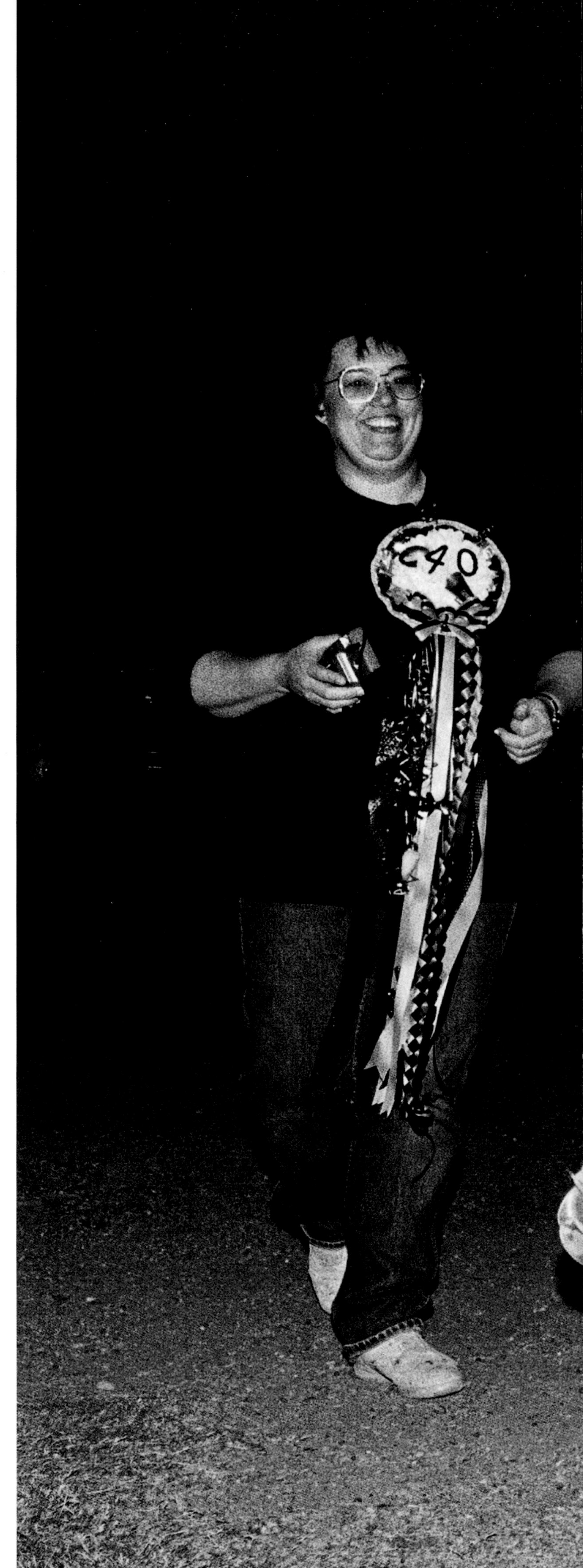
C40

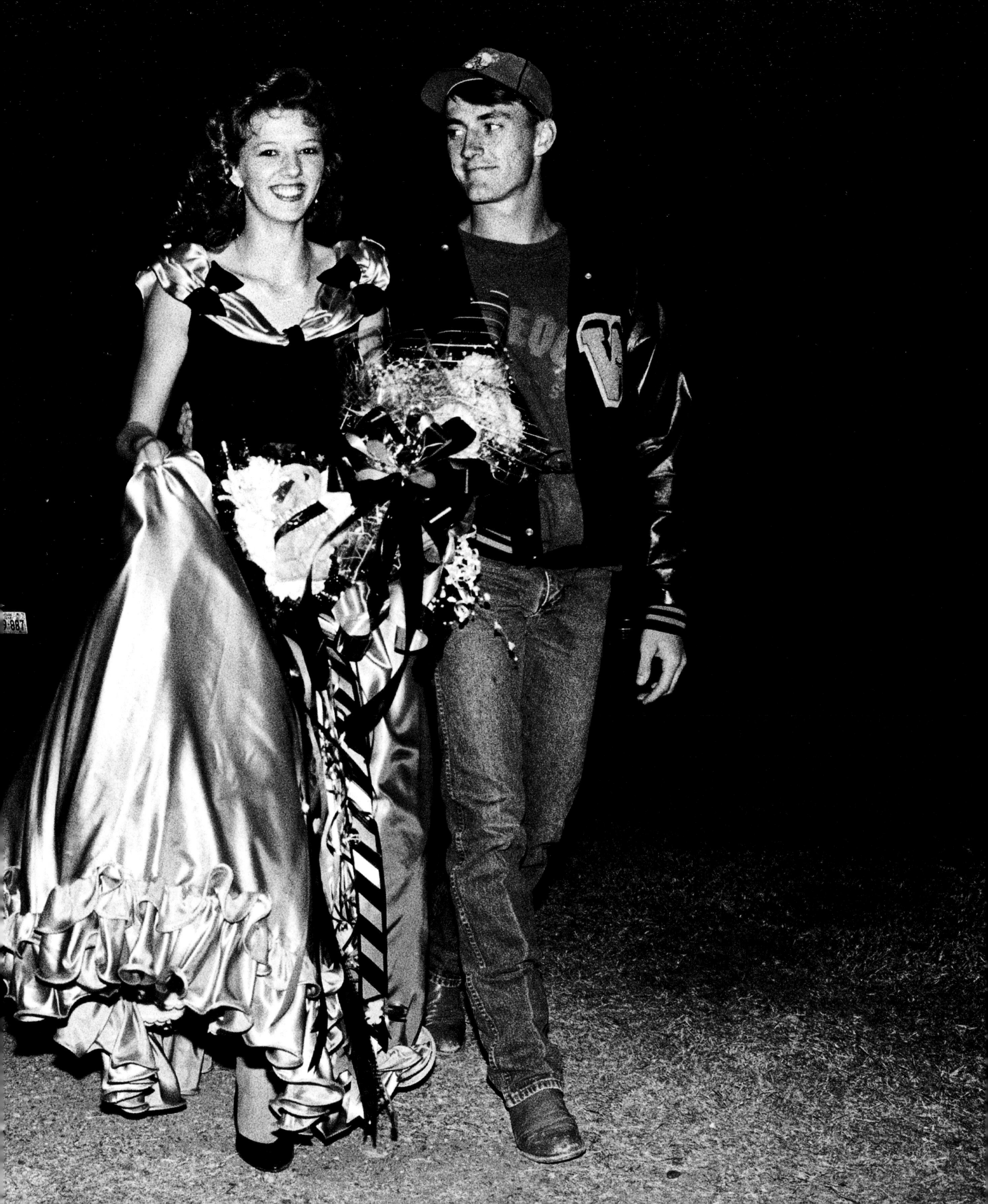

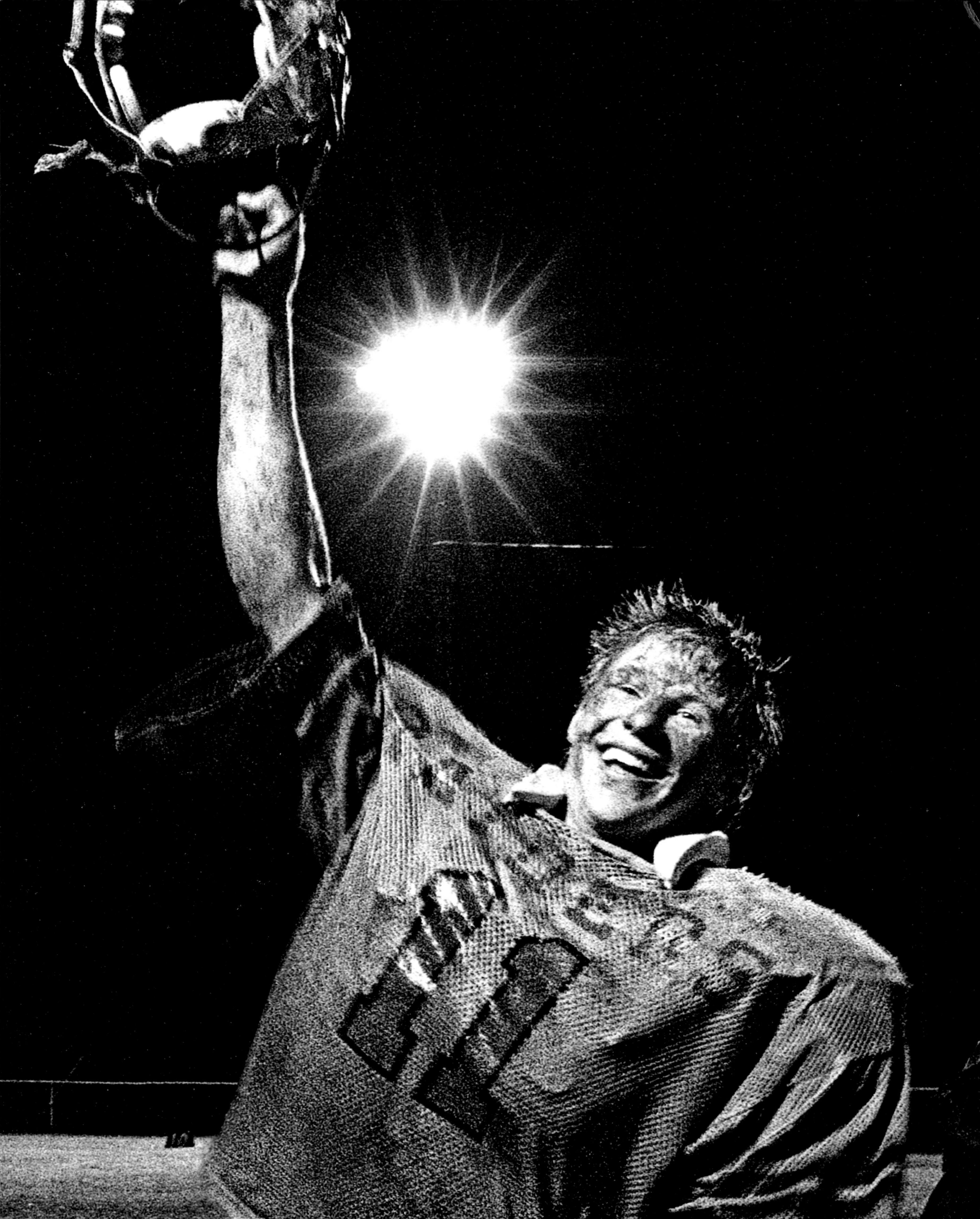

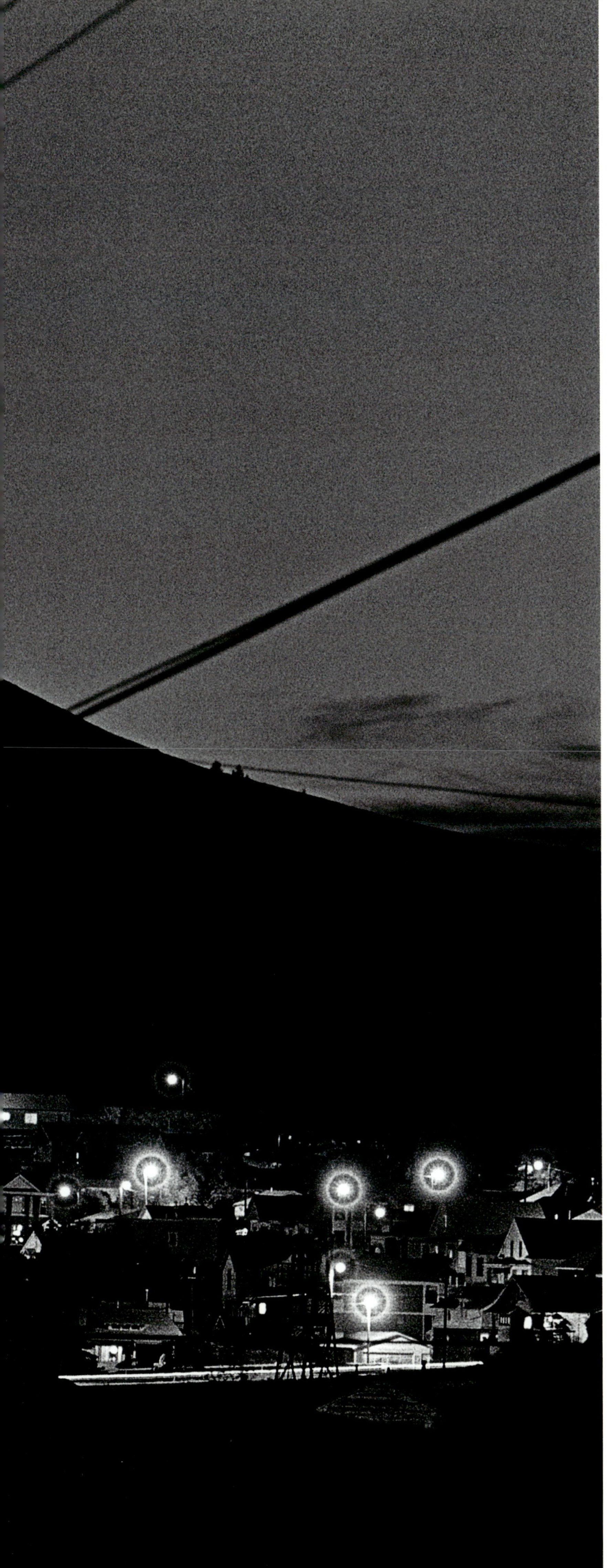

M

BUTTE, MONTANA
JUNE 30, 1981

"Don't stop in America, go straight to Butte." That's what Irish, Cornish, Italian, Finnish, and Slavic immigrants by the thousands were told in the 1870s and 1880s when looking for a new life in a new world. They became hard-rock miners in what was called "the richest hill on earth."

But that was then. By the time I arrived in Butte, the town was on the ropes, suffering from boomtown aftershock. It appeared as worn-down as it had in Robert Frank's photograph of Butte through the window of an old hotel, taken twenty-five years earlier. Three communities had been gobbled up by the expanding open hole of the Berkeley Pit, a mile long and half a mile wide. Now, all its vast reserves of copper, as well as gold and silver, were gone, depleted. The Berkeley Pit, once the world's most fertile hole in the ground, had been shut down and was now a toxic cesspool.

Still, the big neon "M" of Montana Tech glowed like a steaming hot cattle brand on the side of the now-quiet hill, a symbol of civic pride in its boomtown past. A venerable barman told me, "Why, at two in the morning, the streets were so crowded you couldn't even wiggle."

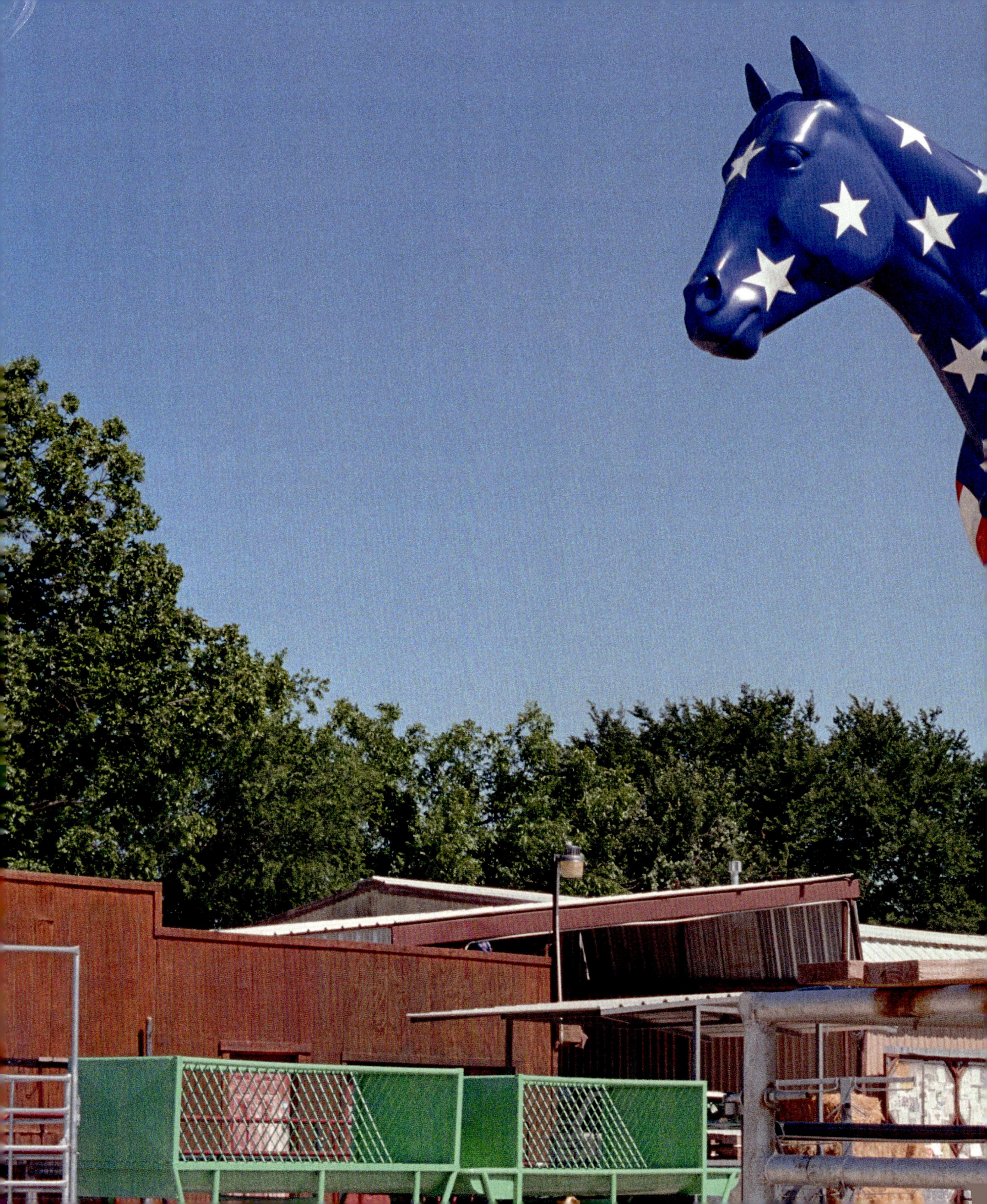

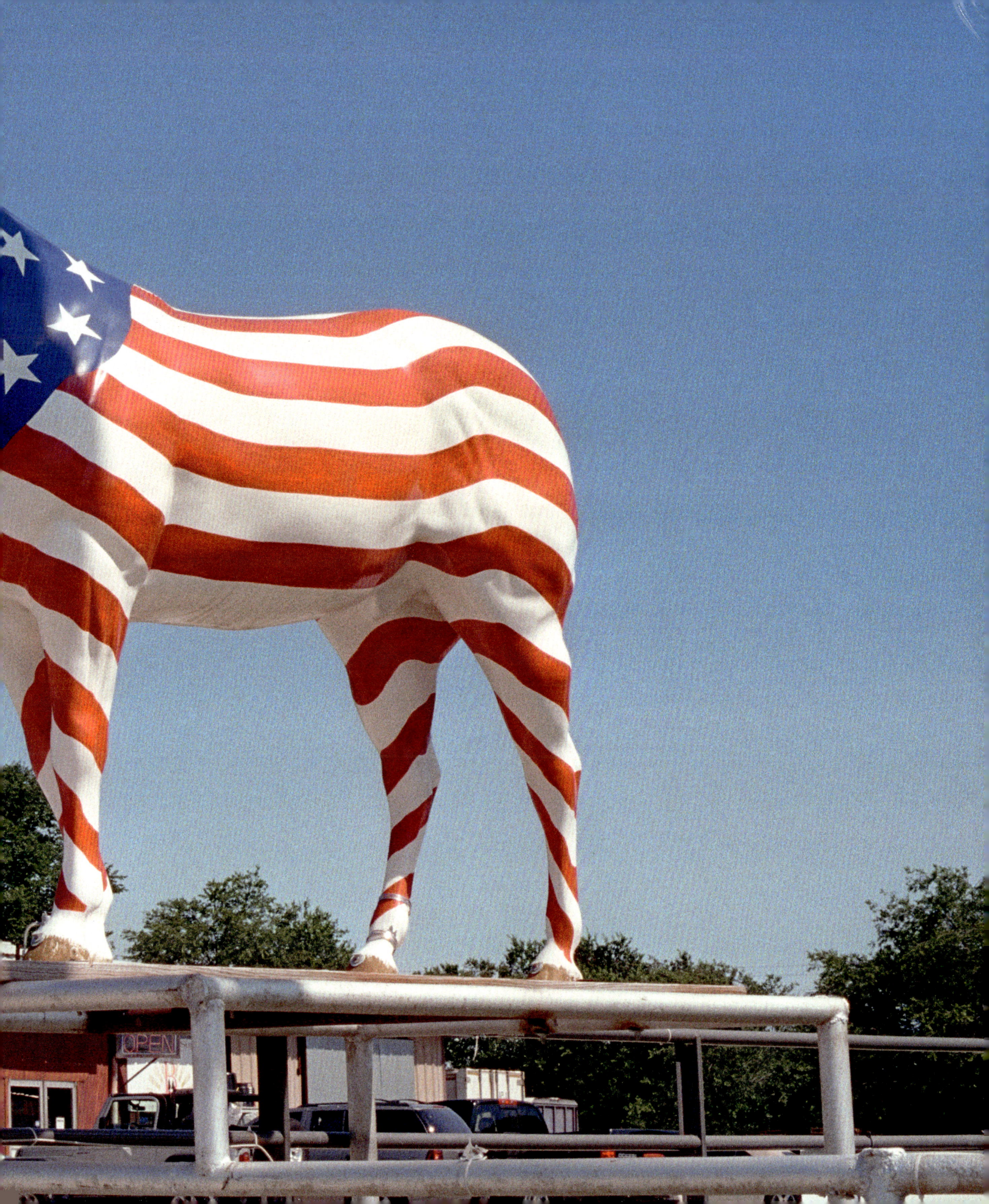
OPEN

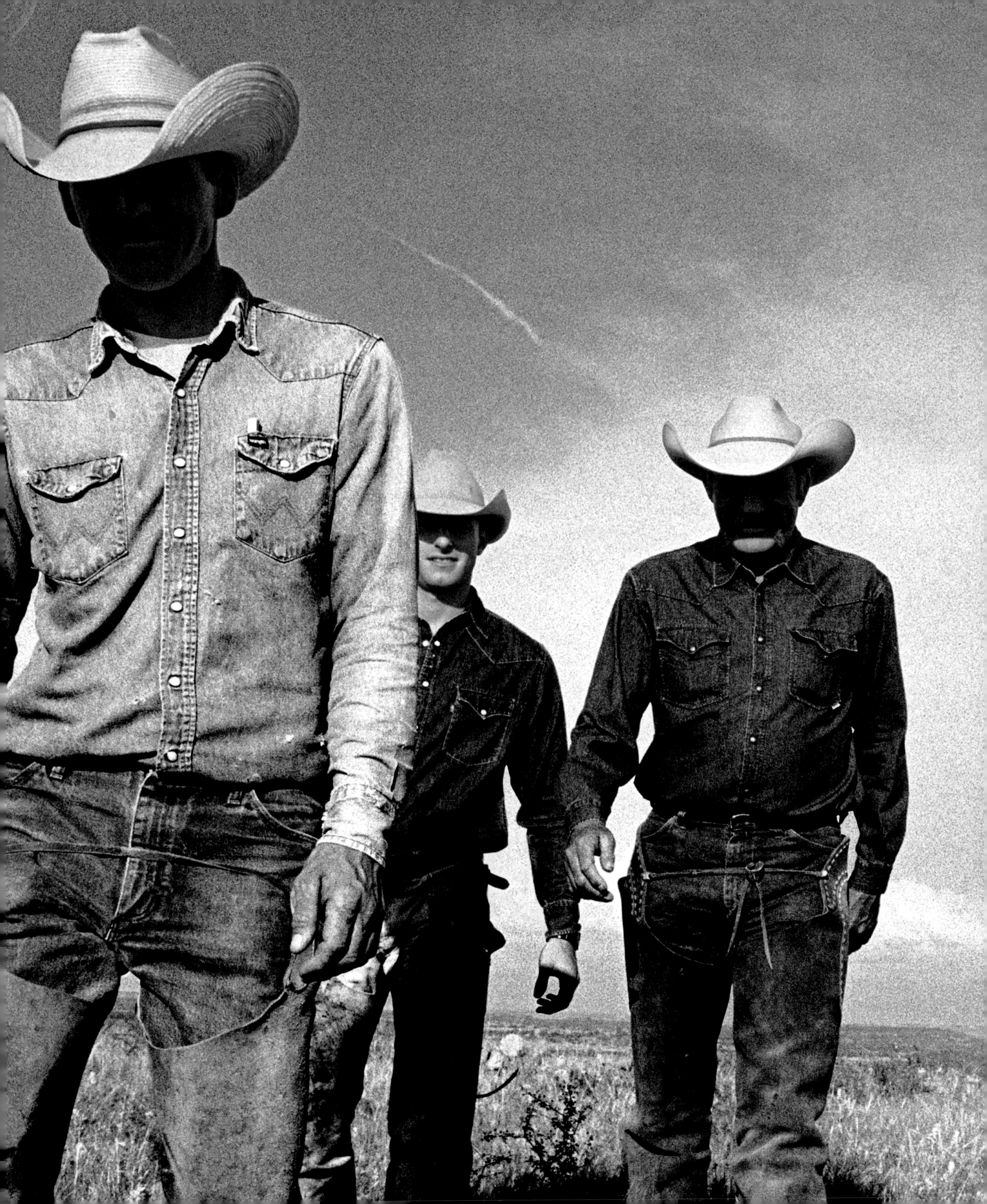

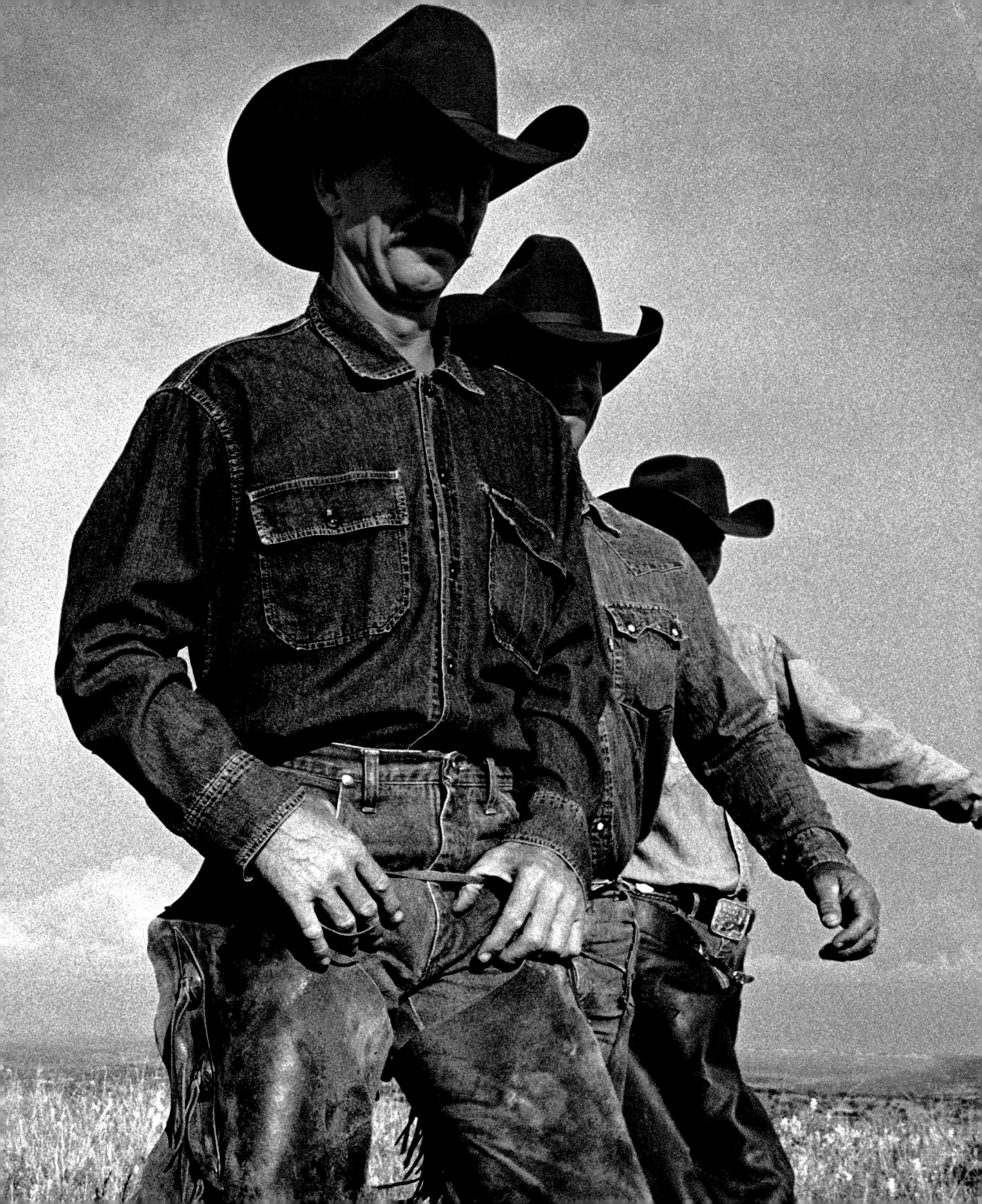

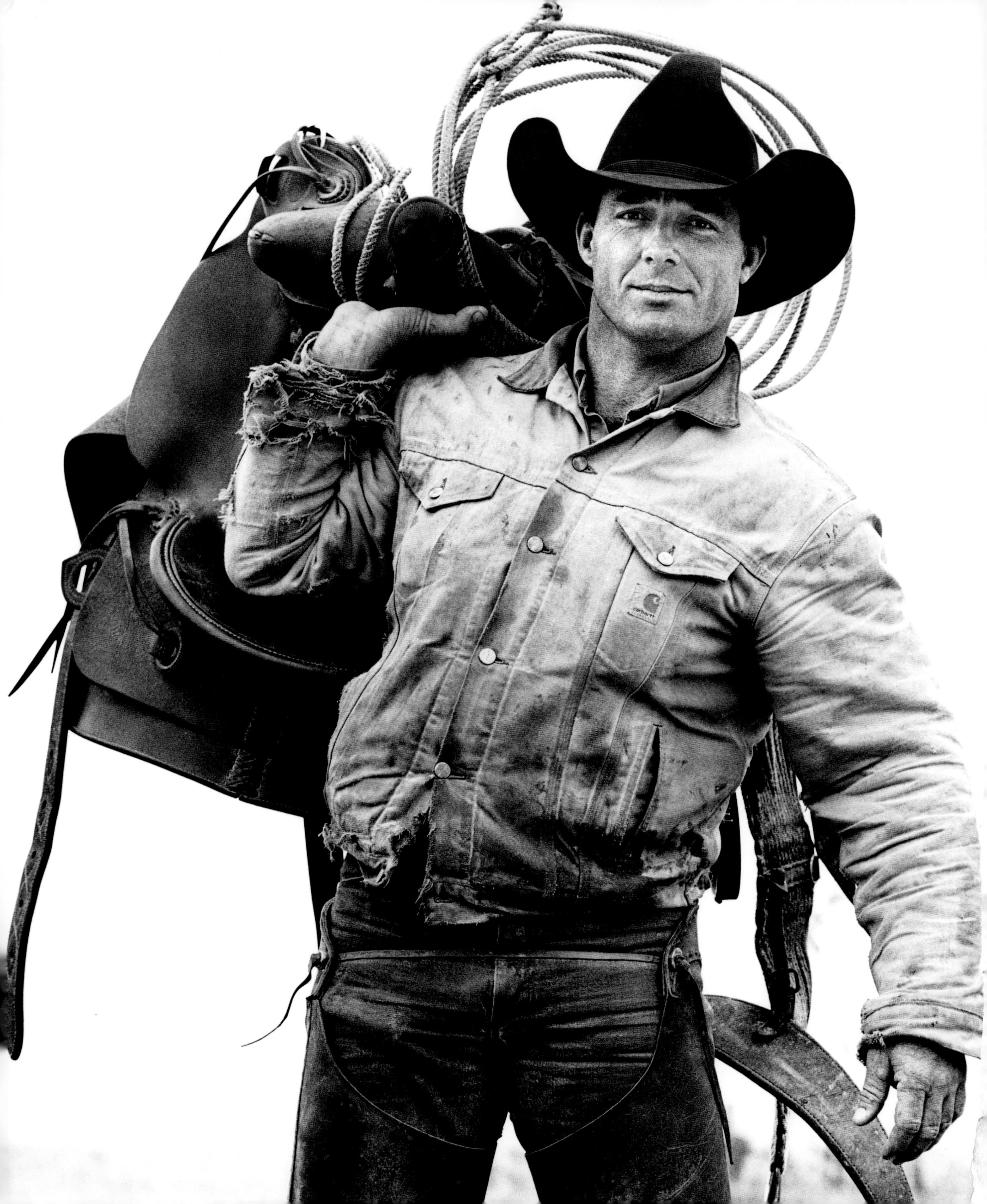
carhartt

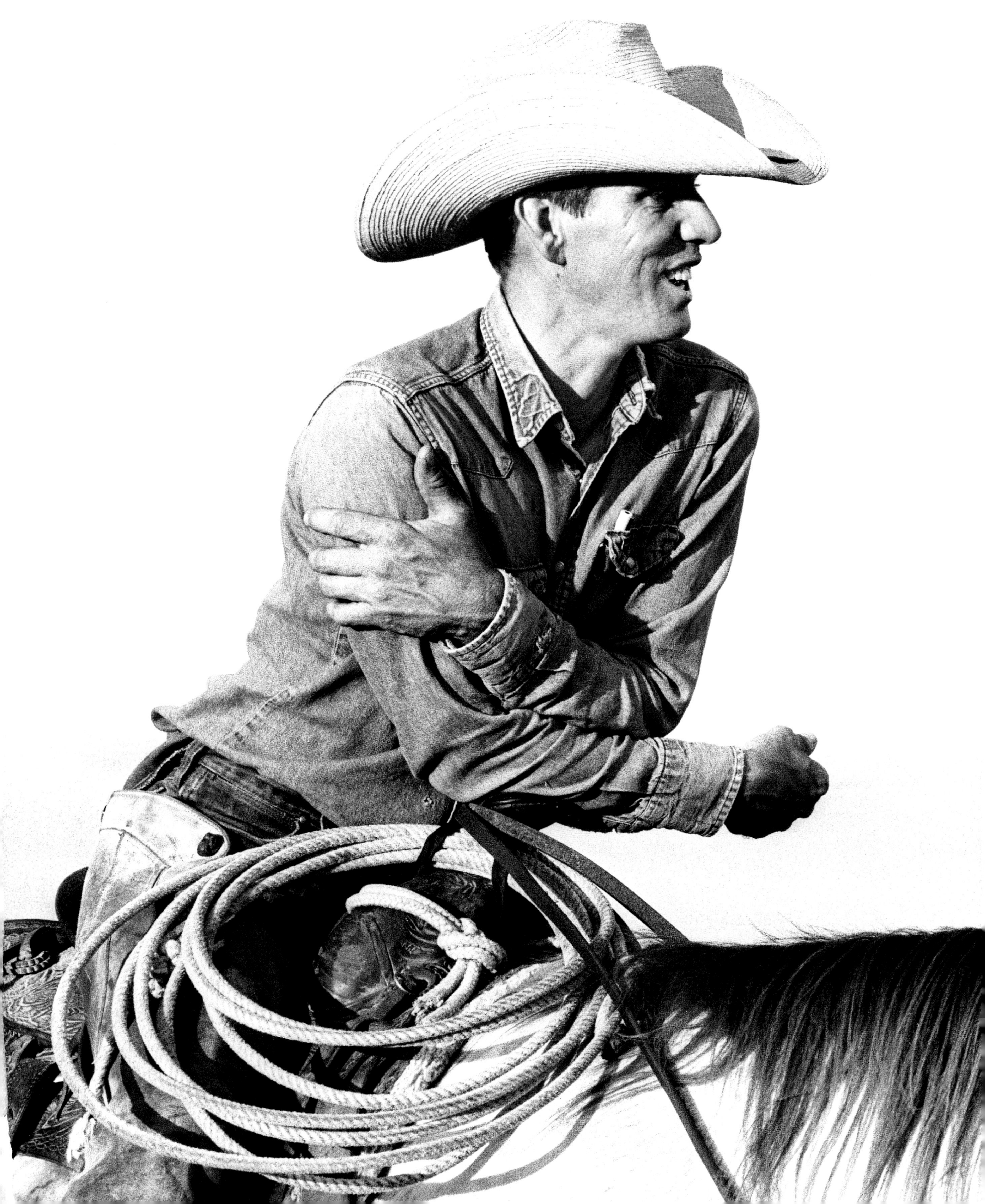

Lambshead Ranch

ALBANY, TEXAS
MARCH 11, 1987

Watt Matthews was ninety years old and still in charge. One of the last of the great Texas cattlemen, he operated Lambshead Ranch, which covered sixty-two square miles in Throckmorton and Shackelford counties. Except for four years at Princeton, Watt had spent his entire life on the ranch, and his listing in the Princeton class directory had never changed: "Rancher, Box 696, Albany, Texas." He and his ninety-eight-year-old sister, Lucile, carried within them the history of a large part of the cattle industry from the time of the Civil War. On Christmas Day, 1876, their mother, Sallie Reynolds, married their father, John Matthews. By 1883 four more Reynolds brothers had married into the Matthews family. The combined force of the two families pushed back the Comanche frontier and held the open range along the Clear Fork of the Brazos River.

When I met them, Lucile was an old lady living in a columned mansion in Fort Worth, but she frequently made the long drive out to Lambshead. She would ask her driver, J. D. Cloud, to stop in Weatherford to buy black-eyed peas. Then, in the back seat of the car, she'd sit shelling the fresh peas into a paper bag. "I don't like to come out to the ranch without something for Watt," she told me.

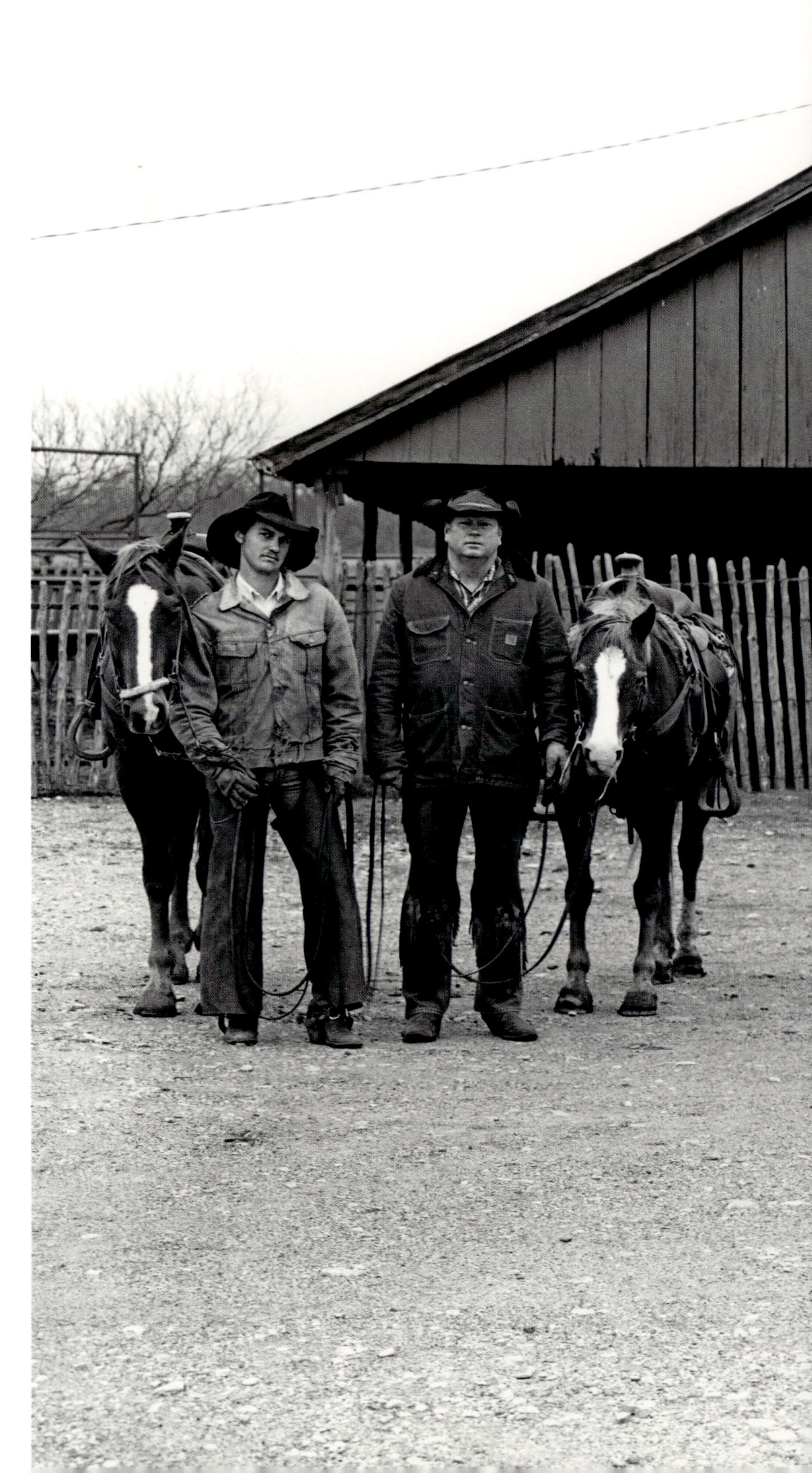

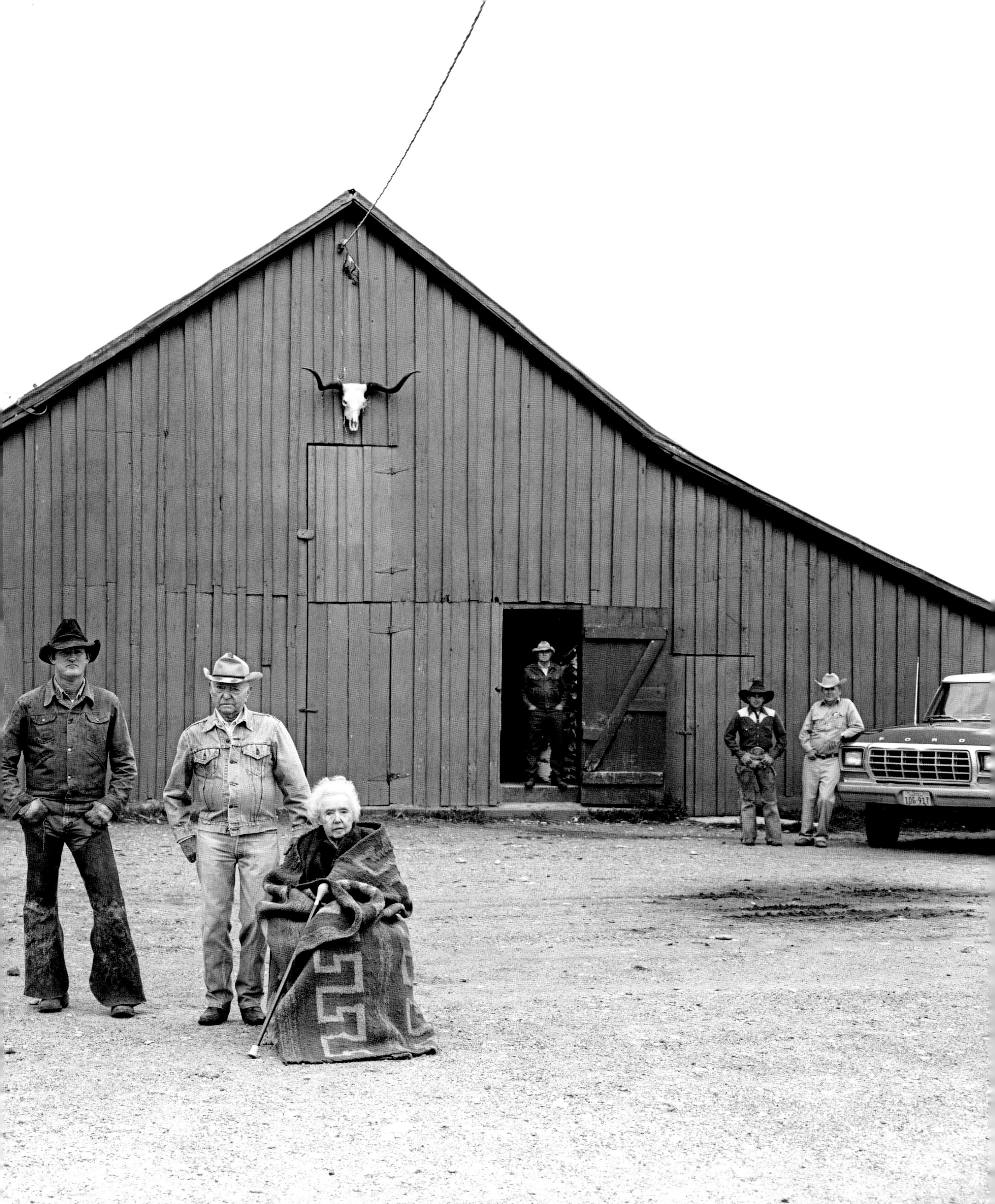
FORD
1DG-917

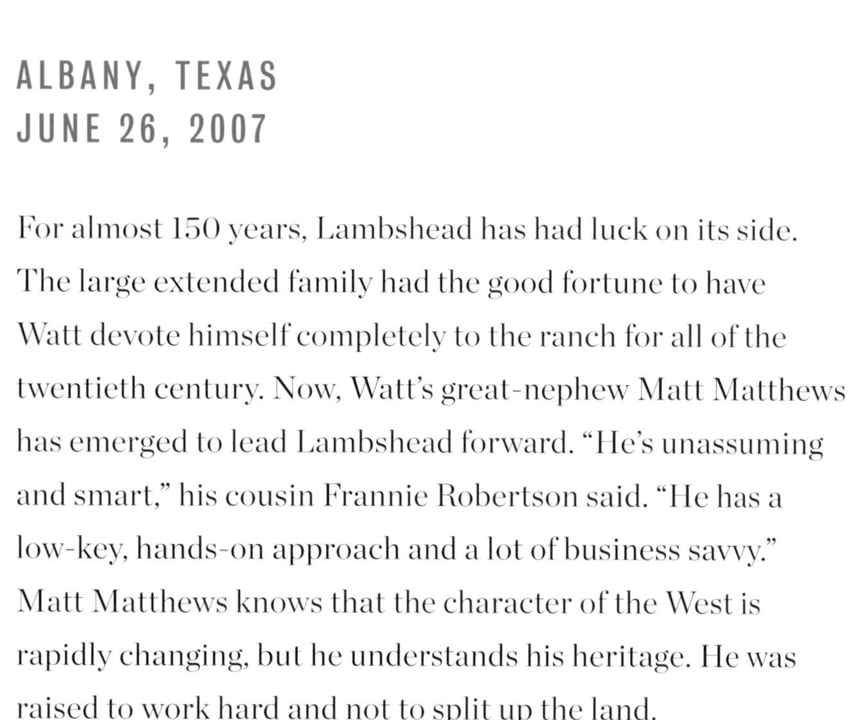

ALBANY, TEXAS
JUNE 26, 2007

For almost 150 years, Lambshead has had luck on its side. The large extended family had the good fortune to have Watt devote himself completely to the ranch for all of the twentieth century. Now, Watt's great-nephew Matt Matthews has emerged to lead Lambshead forward. "He's unassuming and smart," his cousin Frannie Robertson said. "He has a low-key, hands-on approach and a lot of business savvy." Matt Matthews knows that the character of the West is rapidly changing, but he understands his heritage. He was raised to work hard and not to split up the land.

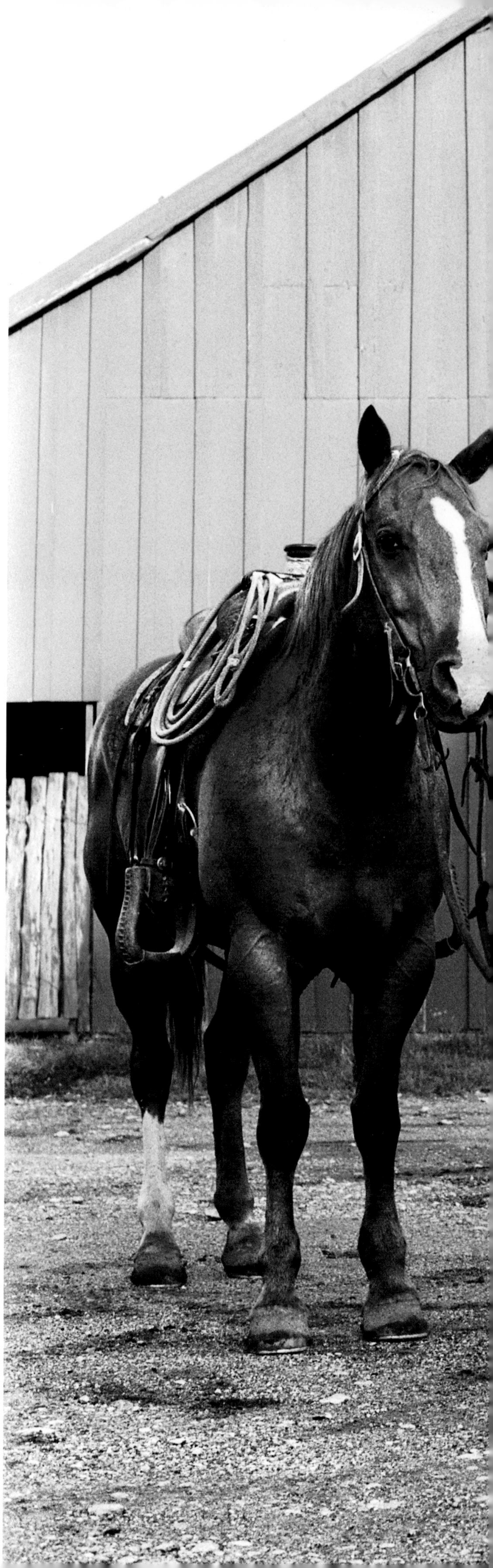

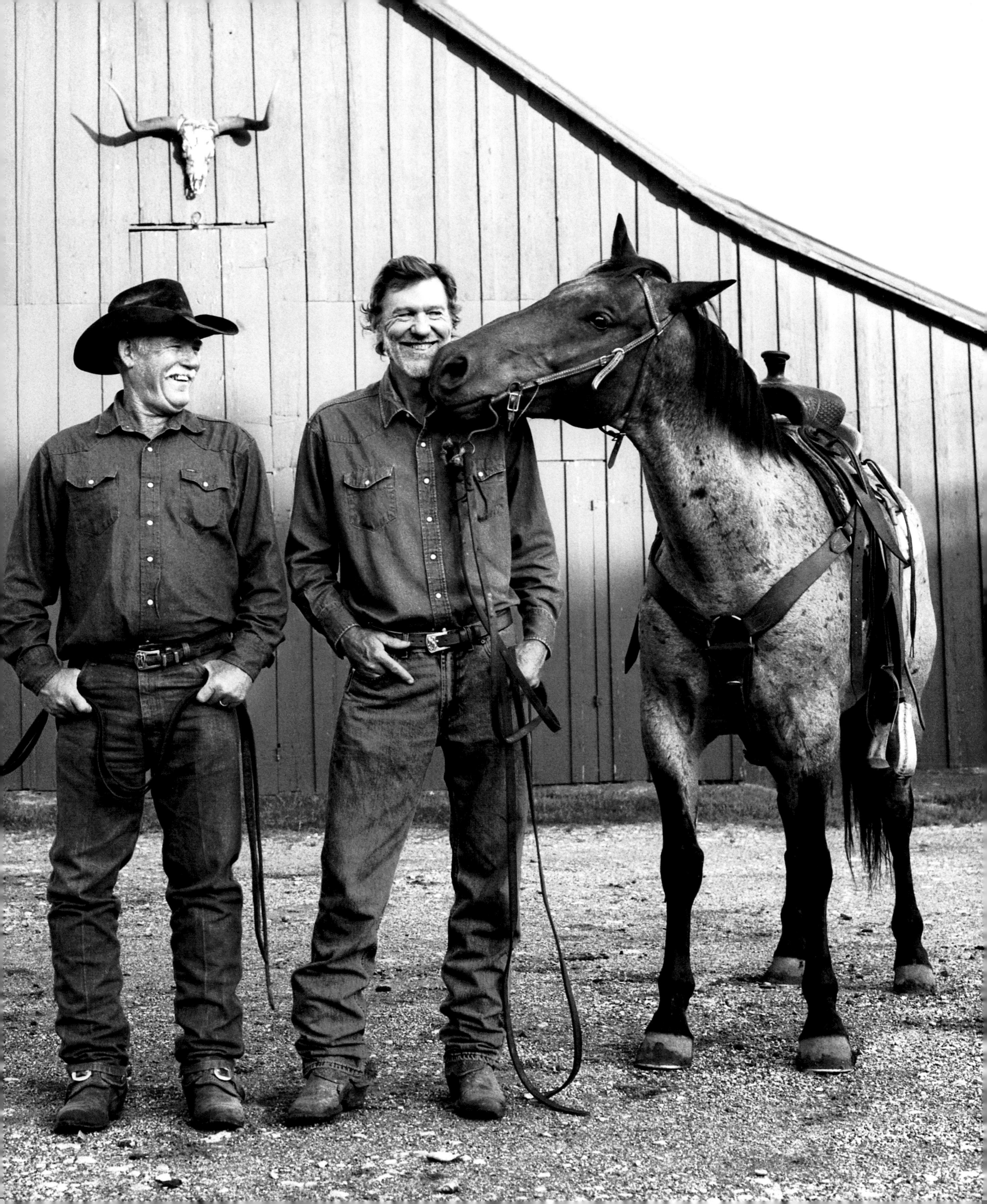

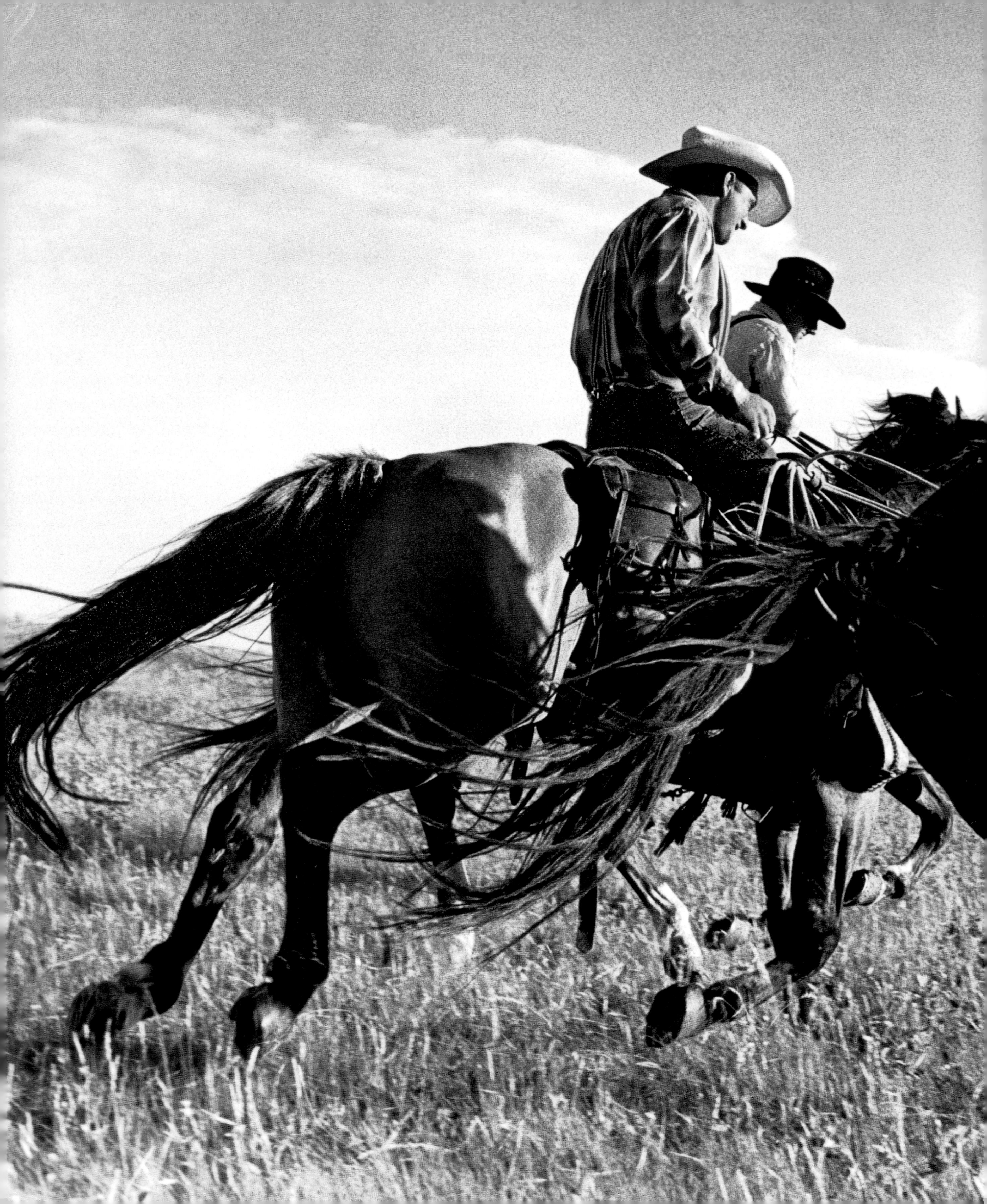

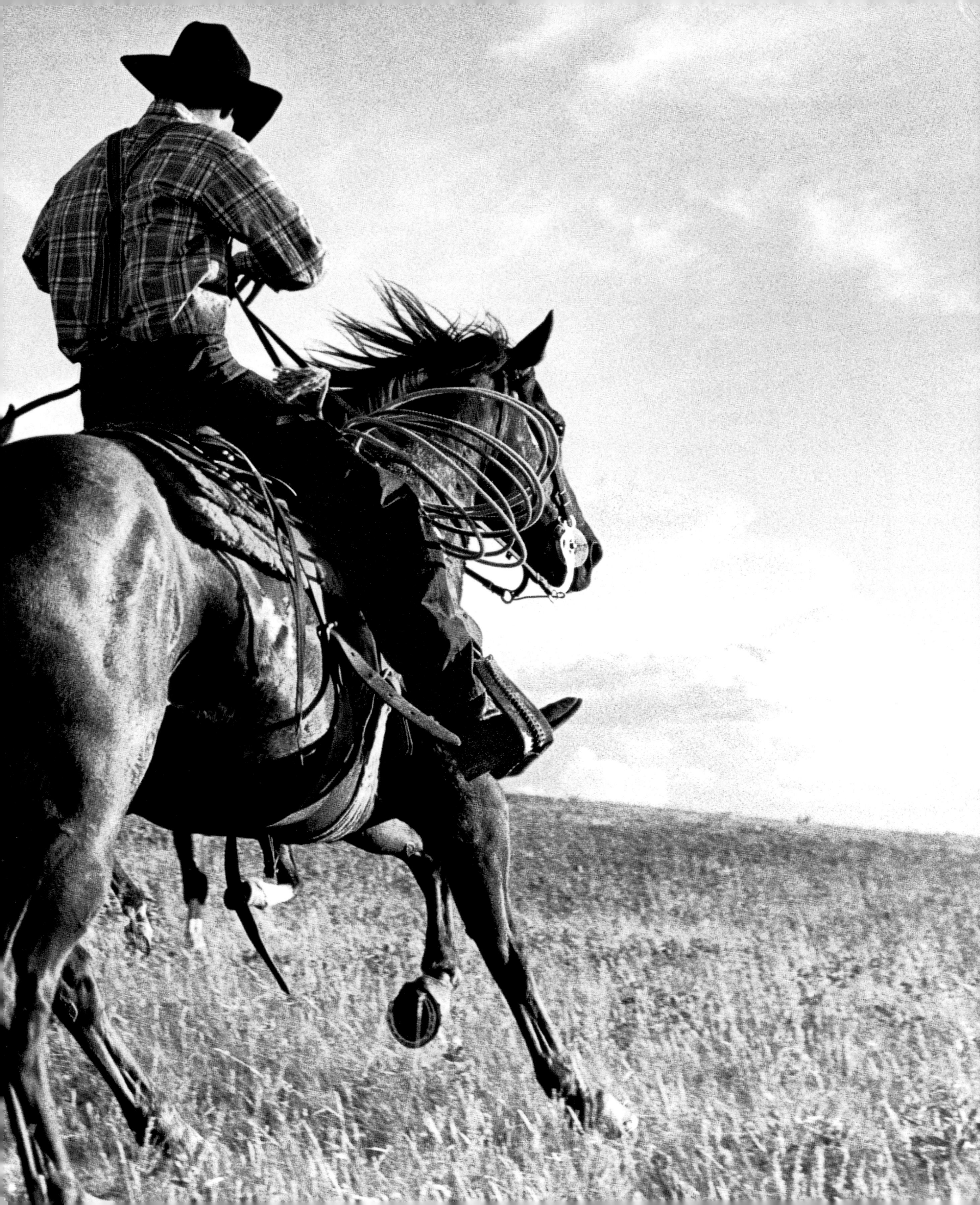

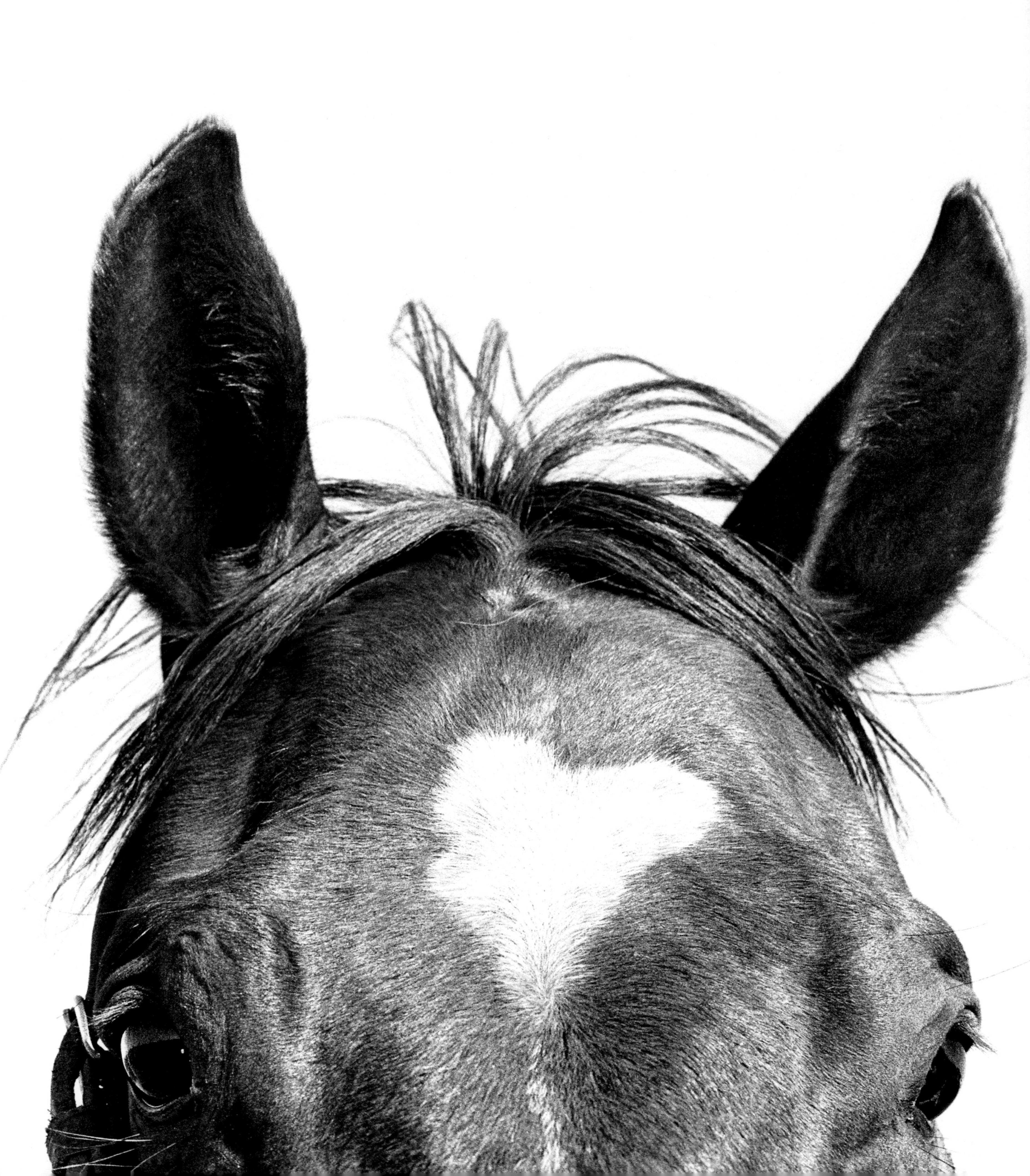

Afterword

Laura Wilson

The camera has many limitations. Abstraction is one. It seems to me that the abstract or the conceptual can be rendered more freely and convincingly by painting or writing. The power of the camera is based in reality. Its strength is in how photographers respond to what lies before them. The artist is present in the image, in his or her rendition of the real world, which in itself is so full of wonder and terror. For me, it's people that bring drama to a photograph. Every person's destiny is provisional. The face and body are expressive, and subtleties of emotion are conveyed through them. My responsibility as a photographer is to reveal these emotions, their complexities. An alert photographer's response to a person's face can take your breath away, can stop your heart.

I took these pictures in the West from 1979 to 2012. Some were taken on assignment for magazines or newspapers; others were taken on my own. I photographed what interested me. *That Day* is a recollection of those interests and concerns. I was drawn to people who live in an enclosed world—those people who live in isolated communities, whether by circumstance or accomplishment. I was curious about these groups and wanted to know more. I don't mean to say one way of life is better than another but merely to say that my wish, as Eudora Welty wrote, "would be not to point the finger in judgment but to part a curtain, that invisible shadow that falls between people, the veil of indifference to each other's presence, each other's wonder, each other's human plight."

The Photographs

2–3 / *Longhorn Bar & Grill,* Amado, Arizona, July 2, 2000.

20–21 / *Hand and Spur,* Y-6 Ranch, Valentine, Texas, June 3, 1992.

22–23 / *Cowboys on Horseback,* Y-6 Ranch, Valentine, Texas, June 4, 1992.

24–25 / *Cowboys Roping,* Y-6 Ranch, Valentine, Texas, June 5, 1992.

26 / *Bodie Means, Rancher, and Jesus Navarette,* Y-6 Ranch, Valentine, Texas, June 4, 1992.

27 / *Ramon Guillen and Alfred Gillett Means, Rancher,* Y-6 Ranch, Valentine, Texas, June 4, 1992.

28–29 / *Y-6 Ranch Women,* Y-6 Ranch, Valentine, Texas, June 4, 1992.

30–31 / *Doyle Holdridge, Texas Ranger,* The Rio Grande, Webb County, Texas, May 14, 1994.

32–33 / *Unidentified Man Crossing Rio Grande,* The International Bridge, Laredo, Texas, May 15, 1994.

34–35 / *Border Patrol Dog Inspecting Car,* Laredo, Texas, May 14, 1994.

36–37 / *Undocumented Immigrant Found by Border Patrol,* Laredo, Texas, May 14, 1994.

39 / *Tracks along the Border,* Zapata County, Texas, May 11, 1994.

40–41 / *Border Patrol Arresting Undocumented Immigrants,* Zapata County, Texas, May 11, 1994.

42–43 / *Captured,* Zapata County, Texas, May 11, 1994.

44–45 / *Pit Bull Dog,* Cotulla, Texas, May 13, 1994.

46–47 / *Men Holding Pit Bull Dogs,* Cotulla, Texas, May 13, 1994.

48–49 / *Pit Bull Dogs Fighting,* Cotulla, Texas, May 13, 1994.

50–51 / *Rattlesnake,* Zapata County, Texas, May 11, 1994.

52 / *Eduardo Longoria,* San Eduardo Ranch, Coahuila, Mexico, April 21, 1993.

54–55 / *Frederico Longoria,* Colonia Longoria, Nuevo Laredo, Mexico, April 20, 1993.

56–57 / *Debutante and Her Maids,* Laredo, Texas, February 18, 1994.

58–59 / *Debutante Dress,* Laredo, Texas, February 17, 1994.

60–61 / *Debutantes Arriving at Ball,* Laredo, Texas, February 19, 1993.

62–63 / *Debutantes on Stage,* Laredo, Texas, February 19, 1993.

64–65 / *Tom Head, Strike Fighter Pilot,* U.S. Navy, Naval Air Station, Lemoore, California, February 13, 2003.

67 / *"Walk-Around,"* Naval Air Station, Fallon, Nevada, June 15, 2004.

68–69 / *Jake Ellzey, Strike Fighter Pilot,* U.S. Navy, Naval Air Station, Fallon, Nevada, June 15, 2004.

70–71 / *Strike Fighter Pilots,* Officers' Club, Naval Air Station, Fallon, Nevada, June 16, 2004.

72–73 / *Strike Fighter Pilots,* Officers' Club, Naval Air Station, Fallon, Nevada, June 16, 2004.

74–75 / *Man Holding Fighting Cock,* Webb County, Texas, May 12, 1994.

76–77 / *Men Holding Fighting Cocks,* Webb County, Texas, May 12, 1994.

78–79 / *Fighting Cocks,* Webb County, Texas, May 12, 1994.

80–81 / *Cockfighting Spurs,* Webb County, Texas, May 12, 1994.

82–83 / *Armadillos,* Nogales, Mexico, February 13, 1992.

85 / *Tattooed Woman,* Nuevo Laredo, Mexico, April 20, 1993.

86–87 / *Street,* Nuevo Laredo, Mexico, April 20, 1993.

88–89 / *Young Woman with Child,* border camp, Arizona–Sonora border, June 30, 2000.

90–91 / *Palmilleros (grass cutters),* border camp, Arizona–Sonora border, June 30, 2000.

92–93 / *Hacienda de San Diego,* Chihuahua, Mexico, June 29, 2000.

95 / *Child with Father and Sister,* Colonia, Nuevo Laredo, Mexico, April 19, 1993.

96–97 / *Blind Woman and Child,* Colonia, Nuevo Laredo, Mexico, April 19, 1993.

98–99 / *Buffalo,* Fredericksburg, Texas, May 5, 1996.

100–101 / *Outfitter,* Bondurant, Wyoming, February 21, 1996.

102–103 / *Brother Simon, Society of Jesus,* Pine Ridge Indian Reservation, South Dakota, December 12, 1996.

104–105 / *Bill Richardson,* American Indian trader, Richardson's Trading Company, Gallup, New Mexico, January 14, 2008.

106–107 / *Stuart Hatch,* Navajo trader, Hatch Brothers Trading Post, San Juan River, Fruitland, New Mexico, November 16, 2009.

108–109 / *Mountain Lion Hunters,* Fort Davis, Texas, August 1, 1991.

110–111 / *Nathan Tindall, Sheriff, with Sam Thomas and Neal Thomas,* San Augustine County, Texas, August 4, 1993.

112–113 / *Winnemucca Bridge (Under the "W"),* Winnemucca, Nevada, September 19, 2004.

114–115 / *Sam Shepard,* Santa Fe Institute, Santa Fe, New Mexico, June 29, 2012.

116–117 / *Sam Shepard "Fly Fishing,"* Arroyo Hondo, New Mexico, June 29, 2012.

118–119 / *Jim Harrison,* Patagonia, Arizona, March 19, 2012.

121 / *Jimmie Dale Gilmore,* Bee Cave, Texas, November 9, 1995.

122–123 / *Harry Dean Stanton,* set of *The Wendell Baker Story,* Circleville, Texas, September 22, 2003.

124–129 / *Stunt Cowboy Falling off Horse,* Ventura County, California, February 20, 2007.

130–131 / *Trick Riders,* Fort Worth Stock Show and Rodeo, Fort Worth, Texas, February 1, 2001.

132–133 / *Trick Riders in Dressing Room,* Fort Worth Stock Show and Rodeo, Fort Worth, Texas, February 1, 2001.

134–135 / *Trick Rider,* Fort Worth Stock Show and Rodeo, Fort Worth, Texas, February 1, 2001.

136–137 / *Bison Bar,* Miles City, Montana, August 12, 1981.

138–139 / *Two Oglala Sioux Men,* Whiteclay, Nebraska, December 13, 1996.

140–141 / *Oglala Sioux Woman Pleading with Tribal Leader,* Whiteclay, Nebraska, December 13, 1996.

142–143 / *Oglala Sioux Family,* Pine Ridge Indian Reservation, Pine Ridge, South Dakota, December 14, 1996.

144–145 / *Cemetery,* Pine Ridge Indian Reservation, Pine Ridge, South Dakota, December 15, 1996.

146–147 / *Shiprock,* Shiprock, New Mexico, November 17, 2009.

148–149 / *"Beat the Heat with Jesus,"* First Assembly Church, Stephenville, Texas, July 31, 2001.

150–151 / *Glory Rider,* Fort Worth, Texas, June 9, 2002.

152–153 / *Glory Riders,* Nocona, Texas, June 15, 2008.

154–155 / *Glory Rider with Baby,* Fort Worth, Texas, June 22, 2008.

156–157 / *Evangelical Preacher,* Denver, Colorado, August 19, 1980.

158–159 / *Hutterite Wheat Field,* Golden Valley Colony, Ryegate, Montana, August 3, 1991.

160–161 / *Hutterite Girl in Field,* Duncan Ranch Colony, Harlowton, Montana, June 17, 1994.

162–163 / *Hutterite Girls during Hay-Making Season,* Surprise Creek Colony, Stanford, Montana, August 22, 1991.

164–165 / *Hutterite Twins,* Surprise Creek Colony, Stanford, Montana, June 6, 1991.

166–167 / *Hutterite Women Gardeners,* Riverview Colony, Chester, Montana, June 22, 1994.

168–169 / *Hutterite Girl with Her Horse, Chattahoochee,* Surprise Creek Colony, Stanford, Montana, August 15, 1992.

170–171 / *Hutterite Boy Playing in a Willow Thicket,* Duncan Ranch Colony, Harlowton, Montana, August 7, 1991.

173 / *Hutterite Boy on Appaloosa,* Golden Valley Colony, Ryegate, Montana, June 15, 1993.

175 / *Donald Judd,* Marfa, Texas, November 3, 1993.

176–177 / *Concrete Piece,* Marfa, Texas, November 4, 1993.

178–179 / *Ed Ruscha in His Studio,* Venice, California, June 27, 2005.

180–181 / *Ed Ruscha and Harley,* Venice, California, June 28, 2005.

182–183 / *Bruce Nauman,* Galisteo, New Mexico, May 26, 1998.

185 / *Richard Avedon,* Crow Fair, Hardin, Montana, August 18, 1979.

186–187 / *Richard Avedon,* Rollie Mortuary, Gallup, New Mexico, June 15, 1979.

188–189 / *Richard Avedon,* Brooke Army Medical Center, San Antonio, Texas, September 24, 2004.

190–191 / *Mesquite Tree with Coyotes,* Lambshead Ranch, Albany, Texas, January 9, 1988.

193 / *First Communion,* Dallas, Texas, May 22, 1988.

194 / *First Communion,* Dallas, Texas, May 22, 1988.

195 / *First Communion,* Dallas, Texas, May 16, 1993.

196–197 / *Mullin Bulldogs Starting Six,* Democrat, Texas, September 16, 1995.

198–199 / *Playing under a Full Moon,* Cherokee, Texas, September 27, 2002.

200–201 / *Sheila Edgar, Cheerleader,* Moran High School, Moran, Texas, November 8, 1991.

202–203 / *Closing in for a Tackle,* Mullin, Texas, September 15, 1995.

205 / *Panther Creek Fans,* Panther Creek, Texas, October 11, 2002.

206–207 / *Homecoming Queen and Her Boyfriend,* Woodson, Texas, October 30, 1992.

208–209 / *The Winner, Lueders-Avoca Raiders,* Moran, Texas, October 11, 1991.

210–211 / *M,* Butte, Montana, June 30, 1981.

212–213 / *Horse Sign,* Weatherford, Texas, May 17, 2008.

214–215 / *Cowboys Walking,* J. R. Green Cattle Company, Shackelford County, Texas, May 13, 1997.

216 / *Donny Baize, Cowboy,* J. R. Green Cattle Company, Shackelford County, Texas, March 18, 1997.

217 / *Mike McClelland, Cowboy,* J. R. Green Cattle Company, Shackelford County, Texas, May 14, 1997.

218–219 / *Watt Matthews, Rancher, and His Sister, Lucile Brittingham,* Lambshead Ranch, Albany, Texas, March 11, 1987.

220–221 / *Terry Moberley, Foreman, and Matt Matthews, Rancher,* Lambshead Ranch, Albany, Texas, June 26, 2007.

222–223 / *Hutterite Cowboys Galloping,* Surprise Creek Colony, Stanford, Montana, July 12, 1996.

224 / *Corazón,* Y-6 Ranch, Valentine, Texas, June 5, 1992.

230 / *Mike McClelland,* J. R. Green Cattle Company, Shackelford County, Texas, April 17, 1990.

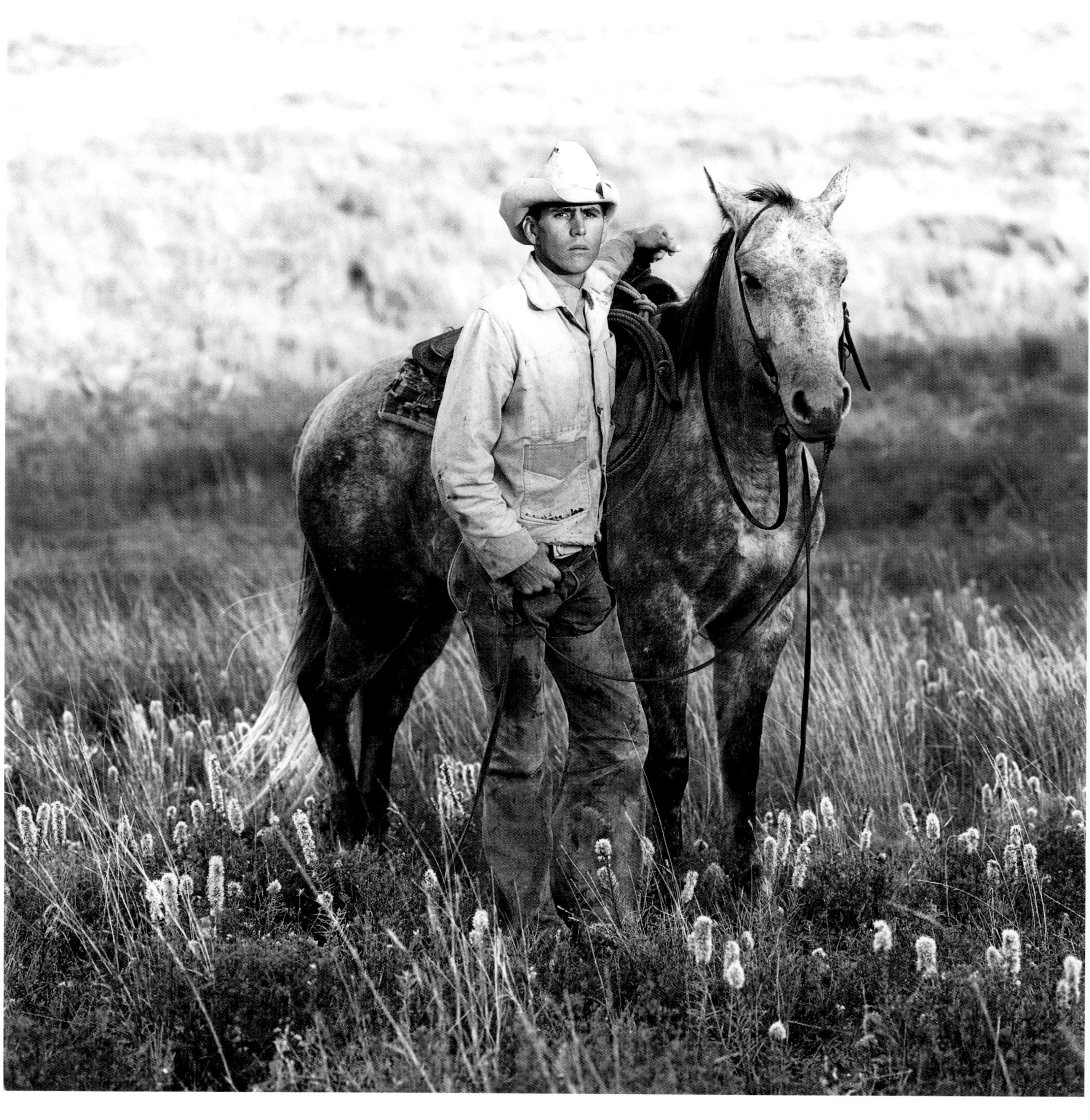

Acknowledgments

Andrew Graybill, director of Southern Methodist University's William P. Clements Center for Southwest Studies, is exceptional; he not only has great enthusiasm for promising ideas, but he has the power to green-light a project. I am deeply grateful to Andrew for his efforts on every front to bring this book to the widest possible audience.

Gregory Wakabayashi, a brilliant designer, transformed decades of various photographic projects into a unifying design with a singular vision. This book and the exhibition at the Amon Carter Museum showcase his talent.

I owe a tremendous debt of gratitude to Lilly Albritton, who runs my studio smoothly and effectively. Her judgment is unerring. On every level, she is perfection.

Gail Bruno is a highly skilled printer of digital images. Her sensitivity to photography and her desire to get things just right in spite of frequently burdensome deadlines allow these photographs to be presented in the best possible way.

Robert Messina, owner of the Color Lab, is one of the most experienced darkroom printers at work today. With his positive attitude and his ability to coax the best from each negative, regardless of its condition or the size of the final print, he has played an irreplaceable role in this project.

Heather Brand is a wonderful editor. She not only knows her grammar, but also, as a writer herself, she has a sure sense of what makes a good sentence. Her insights strengthened my essays.

I am deeply grateful to John Rohrbach, senior curator of photographs at the Amon Carter Museum. His rigorous scholarship and years of experience looking at and collecting photographs from all periods make him the best possible curator. I have flourished under his guidance.

I am also indebted to the rest of the staff at the Amon Carter Museum who have helped bring this exhibition to fruition. In particular, Margaret Conrads, deputy director of art and research, enthusiastically responded to this project, and I am grateful for her support. My thanks also go to Andrew Walker, director, for granting the imprimatur of this preeminent institution.

I would like to thank particularly my friend Mike Ritchey, who read the text and improved every aspect of each essay while offering ongoing encouragement.

Thank you to all those who supported me throughout this work—Josiah Austin, Peter Brandt, Jed Foutz, Harry Hudson, Shelley Hudson, Ross Humphrieys, Matt Lankes, Barbara Leindecker, Linda McKnight, Andrew Mitchell, Phil Ober, Mary Quiros, Tony Shafrazi, and Mike Swartz. A special thanks goes to Andrew and Owen Wilson, who inspire me to do my best.

—Laura Wilson

For their assistance and support, I thank Kelly Compton, Courtney Corwin, John Crain, Tom DiPiero, Lowell Duncan, Ruth Ann Elmore, Margie Evans, Robin Maness, Marianne Piepenburg, Sherry Smith, Rob Strauss, Bill Tsutsui, Ron Tyler, Fran Vick, and Jason Wright.

—Andrew Graybill

This book is published on the occasion of the exhibition *Laura Wilson: That Day*, presented at the Amon Carter Museum of American Art, Fort Worth, Texas, on view from September 5, 2015, through February 14, 2016.

Funding for this publication was provided by the William P. Clements Center for Southwest Studies at Southern Methodist University, Dallas, Texas.

Library of Congress Control Number: 2015938684
ISBN 978-0-300-21539-7

Published by the William P. Clements Center for Southwest Studies
smu.edu/swcenter

in association with Yale University Press, New Haven and London
yalebooks.com/art

Produced by Marquand Books, Inc., Seattle
marquand.com

Edited by Heather Brand
Proofread by Barbara Bowen
Typeset in Chronicle by Maggie Lee
Color management by iocolor, Seattle
Printed and bound in Verona, Italy, by Graphicom

Designed by Gregory Wakabayashi

CREDITS

15 / © 2015 The Richard Avedon Foundation.

16 (above left) / Lewis Hine, *A Russian Family Group at Ellis Island*, 1905. Gelatin silver print, $9\frac{5}{8} \times 7\frac{5}{8}$ inches (24.2 × 19.2 cm). Amon Carter Museum of American Art, Fort Worth, Texas, P1981.78.

16 (below left) / Library of Congress, Prints and Photographs Division, Washington, D.C.; Reproduction no. LC-DIG-fsa-8b29516.

84 / From *The Lawless Roads* by Graham Greene. © 1939 by Graham Greene.

113 / From *Motel Chronicles* by Sam Shepard. © 1982 by Sam Shepard.

124 / Jorge Luis Borges, in *The Paris Review Interviews*, vol. 1 (London: Picador, 2006), 117–18.

147 / From statement in Abram Lerner, ed., *The Hirshhorn Museum and Sculpture Garden* (New York and Washington, D.C.: Harry N. Abrams for Hirshhorn Museum and Sculpture Garden, 1974), 752.

225 / Quote from Eudora Welty, *One Time, One Place: Mississippi and the Depression, a Snapshot Album*, rev. ed. (Jackson: University Press of Mississippi, 1996), 12.